Clive Oxenden
Christina Latham-Koenig
Paul Seligson
with Lindsay Clandfield

New ENGLISH FILE

Pre-intermediate Teacher's Book

[redacted]

OXFORD
UNIVERSITY PRESS

Paul Seligson and Clive Oxenden are the original co-authors of *English File 1* (pub. 1996) and *English File 2* (pub. 1997).

OXFORD
UNIVERSITY PRESS

Great Clarendon Street, Oxford OX2 6DP

Oxford University Press is a department of the University of Oxford. It furthers the University's objective of excellence in research, scholarship, and education by publishing worldwide in

Oxford New York

Auckland Cape Town Dar es Salaam Hong Kong Karachi Kuala Lumpur Madrid Melbourne Mexico City Nairobi New Delhi Shanghai Taipei Toronto

With offices in

Argentina Austria Brazil Chile Czech Republic France Greece Guatemala Hungary Italy Japan Poland Portugal Singapore South Korea Switzerland Thailand Turkey Ukraine Vietnam

OXFORD and OXFORD ENGLISH are registered trade marks of Oxford University Press in the UK and in certain other countries

First published 2005
2009 2008 2007 2006
10 9 8 7 6 5 4 3

ISBN-13: 978 0 19 438434 6
ISBN-10: 0 19 438434 9

Printed in and bound in China

ACKNOWLEDGEMENTS

The authors would like to thank all the teachers and students round the world whose feedback has helped us to shape *New English File*.

The Publisher and Authors would like to thank the following for their invaluable feedback on the materials: Beatriz Martin, Michael O'Brien, Lester Vaughan, Wendy Armstrong, Javier Santos Asensi, Tim Banks, Brian Brennan, Susanna di Gravio, Jane Hudson, Graham Rumbelow, and Krzysztof Wierzba.

Special thanks to Beatriz Martin for her help with the Communicative photocopiable activities.

Finally, very special thanks from Clive to Maria Angeles and Lucia, and from Christina to Cristina for all their help and encouragement. Christina would also like to thank her children Joaquin, Marco, and Krysia for their constant inspiration.

Lindsay Clandfield would like to thank Sofia, Lucas, and Marcos for all their support.

The authors and publisher are grateful to those who have given permission to reproduce the following extracts and adaptations of copyright material: p.220 *Ain't got no – I got life* (from the musical *Hair*) Words and Music by Gerome Ragni, Galt MacDermot and James Rado © 1968 EMI Catalogue Partnership, EMI U Catalog Inc, EMI United Partnership Ltd, USA. Worldwide print rights controlled by Warner Bros. Publications Inc/IMP Ltd. Reproduced by permission of International Music Publications Ltd. All Rights Reserved. p.221 *Imagine* Words & Music by John Lennon © 1971 Lenono Music. All Rights Reserved. International Copyright Secured. p.222 *White flag* Words and Music by Dido Armstrong, Rollo Armstrong and Richard Nowels Jr. © 2003 Future Furniture and EMI April Music Inc, USA. (30%) EMI Music Publishing Ltd, London WC2H 0QY. (55%) Warner/Chappell Music Ltd, London W6 8BS (15%) BMG Music Publishing Ltd. Reproduced by permission of International Music Publications Ltd. All Rights Reserved. International Copyright Secured. p.223 *True blue* Words and Music by Madonna Ciccone and Stephen Bray © 1986 W B Music Corp, Bleu Disque Music Co Inc, Webo Girl Publishing Inc and Black Lion Music Inc, USA. (50%) Warner/Chappell North America, London W6 8BS. (50%) Universal/Island Music. Reproduced by permission of International Music Publications Ltd. All Rights Reserved. International Copyright Secured.

Illustrations by: Paul Daviz pp.152t, 161, 174, 175, 216; Paul Dickinson p.188, 222, 225, 226; Phil Disley pp.141, 148, 149, 164, 167, 168, 212; Martina Farrow pp.220, 223, 224, 227; Neil Gower pp.189, 210; Gary Kaye pp.140, 143, 146, 151, 159, 165, 198, 211; Nigel Paige p.170; Colin Shelbourn pp.142, 147, 152b, 169, 172, 186, 196, 209, 214; Colin Thompson pp.139 144, 153, 158, 163, 171, 191; Kath Walker pp.155, 157, 160, 162, 166, 200, 201, 205

Photographs by: Empics p.221 (EPA European Press Agency); Rex Features p.208 (Peter Brooker/Keira Knightley, Jim Smeal/Bei/Orlando Bloom)

Contents

Syllabus checklist

PRE-INTERMEDIATE TEACHER'S NEW ENGLISH

Pronunciation	Speaking	Listening	Reading
vowel sounds, the alphabet	talking about dates and times	dates and times	
third person and plural *-s*	describing a person you know well	understanding an anecdote	Who knows you better, your family or your friends?
vowel sounds	describing a painting	understanding a guide song: *Aint got no – I got life*	
pronunciation in a dictionary	giving definitions	TV game show: *What's the word?*	The Devil's Dictionary

Pronunciation	Speaking	Listening	Reading
-ed endings, irregular verbs	your last holiday	an interview about a disastrous holiday	The Holiday Magazine
/ə/	describing famous photos	Lovers at the Bastille	Famous photographs by Harry Benson and Willy Ronis
/w/ and /h/	favourite music, music quiz	song: *Imagine*	Who wrote *Imagine?*
the letter *a*	re-telling a story	Hannah and Jamie: the end of the story	Hannah and Jamie: a short story

Pronunciation	Speaking	Listening	Reading
sentence stress	talking about plans and arrangements	an interview with Rima	Airport stories
contractions (*will / won't*), /ɒ/ and /aʊ/	making positive predictions	a radio programme about positive thinking	
word stress: two-syllable words	*I'll / Shall I?* game	song: *White flag*	Promises, promises
sentence stress	interpreting dreams	psychoanalyst and patient	book extract: Understanding your dreams

Pronunciation	Speaking	Listening	Reading
vowel sounds	interviewing a partner about clothes	street interviews: *Zara* song: *True blue*	*Zara*
/h/, /j/ and /dʒ/	Has he done it yet? (information gap)		Problems with your teenage children?
sentence stress	questionnaire: Are you living faster?	vox pops: living faster	We're living faster
word stress	talking about experiences	London	The world's friendliest city

Pronunciation	Speaking	Listening	Reading
word stress	interview a partner about parties	conversations at a party	What to say (and what not to say) to people at parties
-ing	questionnaire	radio programme: learning to sing	What makes you feel good?
sentence stress	talking about language learning	journalist talking about learning Polish	How much can you learn in a month?
prepositions	telling an anecdote: most exciting sporting event	song: *We are the champions*	Your most exciting sporting moments

Pronunciation	Speaking	Listening	Reading
long and short vowels	inventing some new Murphy's Laws		Murphy's Law
stress and rhythm	questionnaire: Would you survive?	a survival expert song: *Wouldn't it be nice?*	Nature's perfect killing machine
sentence stress, *-ion* endings	Are you indecisive?		How to make decisions
/ʊ/, sentence stress	discussing advice	radio phone-in	What's the problem?
/ɪ/ and /aɪ/, sentence stress	pairwork interview	interview about a phobia	We're all afraid…
word stress	talking about a member of your family	radio programme: Sofia Coppola	biographies: Hitchcock and Tarantino
sentence stress, *used to / didn't use to*	talking about school days	listening to Melissa song: *It's all over now*	A famous rebel–but was he really?
sentence stress	passives quiz	things invented by women	surprising facts
/e/, /əʊ/, and /ʌ/	talking about weekends	radio news	The weekend
/ʌ/, /uː/, /aɪ/, and /e/, linking	What's your body age?		How old is your body?
/g/ and /dʒ/	Are you a morning or evening person?	Are you a morning or evening person? song: *I say a little prayer*	Are you allergic to mornings?
vowel and consonant sounds, sentence stress	find someone like you	completing a dialogue	Reunited
revision of vowel sounds, sentence stress	re-telling stories		Fact is always stranger than fiction.
rhyming verbs	reporting information	song: *Then he kissed me*	

Introduction

What do Pre-intermediate students need?

Pre-intermediate students are at a crucial stage in their learning. The novelty of being a beginner may have worn off, but the goal of communicating with ease and fluency can still feel a long way off. Students at this level more than ever need material that maintains their enthusiasm and builds their confidence. They need to know how much they are learning and what they can now achieve.

At the same time they need the encouragement to push themselves to use the new language that they are learning.

Grammar, Vocabulary, and Pronunciation

At any level, the tools students need to speak English with confidence are Grammar, Vocabulary, and Pronunciation (G, V, P). In *New English File Pre-intermediate* all three elements are given equal importance.

Each lesson has clearly stated grammar, vocabulary, and pronunciation aims. This keeps lessons focused and gives students concrete learning objectives and a sense of progress.

Grammar

Pre-intermediate students need

- thorough revision of Elementary structures.
- clear and memorable presentations of new structures.
- regular and motivating practice.
- student-friendly reference material.

We have tried to provide stimulating recycling of language Pre-intermediate students should already know, and contexts for new language that will engage them, using real-life stories and situations, humour, and suspense. The **Grammar Banks** give students a single, easy-to-access grammar reference section, with clear rules, example sentences, and common errors. There are then two practice exercises for each grammar point.

➲ Student's Book *p.126/7.*

The photocopiable Grammar activities in the Teacher's Book can be used for practice in class or for self-study.

➲ Teacher's Book *p.139.*

Vocabulary

Pre-intermediate students need

- to revise and reactivate previously learnt vocabulary.
- to increase their knowledge of high-frequency words and phrases.
- tasks which encourage them to use new vocabulary.
- accessible reference material.

Every lesson in *New English File Pre-intermediate* focuses on high-frequency vocabulary and common lexical areas, but keeps the load realistic. Many lessons are linked to the **Vocabulary Banks** which help present and practise the vocabulary in class and provide a clear reference bank so students can revise and test themselves in their own time. The stress in multi-syllable words is clearly marked and where we think the pronunciation of a word may be problematic, we have provided the phonemic script.

➲ Student's Book *p.144.*

Students can practise using all the vocabulary from the **Vocabulary Banks** in context with the **MultiROM** and the *New English File* student's website.

Pronunciation

Pre-intermediate students need

- a solid foundation in the sounds of English.
- systematic pronunciation development.
- to build on their awareness of rules and patterns.

With new language come fresh pronunciation challenges for Pre-intermediate learners, particularly sound–spelling relationships, silent letters, and weak forms.

Students who studied with *New English File Elementary* will already be familiar with *New English File*'s unique system of sound pictures, which give clear example words to help students to identify and produce the sounds. *New English File Pre-intermediate* continues with a pronunciation focus in every lesson, which integrates improving students' pronunciation into grammar and vocabulary practice.

➲ Student's Book *p.17.*

If you or your students have not used the *New English File* series before, the Teacher's Book provides clear guidance on how to introduce them to the sound pictures system.

➲ Teacher's Book *p.14.*

The pronunciation focus is often linked to the **Sound Bank**, a reference section which students can use to check the symbols and to see common sound–spelling patterns.

➲ Student's Book *p.156.*

Throughout the book there is also a regular focus on word and sentence stress where students are encouraged to **copy the rhythm** of English. This will help students to pronounce new language with greater confidence.

Speaking

Pre-intermediate students need

- topics that will arouse their interest.
- tasks that push them to incorporate new language.
- a sense of progress in their ability to speak.

The ultimate aim of most students is to be able to communicate in English. Every lesson in *New English File Pre-intermediate* has a speaking activity which activates grammar, vocabulary, and pronunciation. The tasks are designed to help students to feel a sense of progress and to show that the number of situations in which they can communicate effectively is growing.

➲ Student's Book *p.41.*

The Communication section of the Student's Book provides 'information gap' activities to give students a reason to communicate.

➲ Student's Book *p.108.*

Photocopiable Communicative activities can be found in the Teacher's Book. These include pairwork activities, mingles, and games.

➲ Teacher's Book *p.183.*

Listing

Pre-intermediate students need

- confidence-building, achievable tasks.
- to practise getting the gist and listening for detail.
- to make sense of connected speech.

Even high-level students often say that they find understanding spoken English one of the hardest skills to master. At pre-intermediate level students need confidence-building listening tasks which are progressively more challenging in terms of speed, length, and language difficulty, but are always achievable. They also need a variety of listening tasks which practise listening for gist and for specific details. We have chosen material we hope students will want to listen to.
➲ Student's Book *p.23*.

New English File Pre-intermediate also contains nine songs which we hope students will find enjoyable and motivating. For copyright reasons, these are cover versions.

Reading

Pre-intermediate students need

- engaging topics and stimulating texts.
- challenging tasks which help them read better.

Many students need to read in English for their work or studies, or will want to read for pleasure about their hobbies and interests. Reading is also important in helping to build vocabulary and to consolidate grammar. Students need motivating but accessible material and tasks which help them read better, e.g. guessing the meaning of words and phrases from context. In *New English File Pre-intermediate* texts have been adapted from a variety of real sources (the press, magazines, news websites) and have been chosen for their intrinsic interest.
➲ Student's Book *p.18*.

The Revise & Check sections also include a more challenging text which helps students to measure their progress.
➲ Student's Book *p.51*.

Writing

Pre-intermediate students need

- clear models.
- an awareness of register, structure, and fixed phrases.
- a focus on micro writing skills.

Worldwide, people are writing in English more than ever, largely because of the importance of e-mail and the Internet. *New English File Pre-intermediate* has one Writing lesson per File, where students study a model before doing a guided writing task themselves. These writing tasks focus on both electronic and 'traditional' text types, and review grammar and lexis from the File. There is also always a focus on a writing 'micro skill', for example, punctuation, spelling, or connectors.
➲ Student's Book *p.61*.

Practical English

Pre-intermediate students need

- to understand high-frequency phrases that they will hear.
- to know what to say in typical situations.
- to know how to overcome typical travel problems.

Students will need to use English if they travel to an English-speaking country or if they are using English as a *lingua franca*. The eight *Practical English* lessons re-visit and revise common situations (for example checking into a hotel) and introduce and practise the language for new challenges (for example, making a phone call). To help make these everyday situations come alive, there is a story line involving two main characters, Mark (American) and Allie (British), which continues from *New English File Elementary*. Don't worry if you or your students haven't used the Elementary level – there is a summary of the story so far in the first episode.
➲ Student's Book *p.12*.

The **You hear / You say** feature makes a clear distinction between what students will **hear** and need to understand, for example *With ice and lemon?*, and what they need to **say**, for example *Just ice*. The lessons also highlight other key 'Social English' phrases such as *Bless you!* and *Cheers!*

The Practical English lessons are also on the ***New English File Pre-intermediate Video*** which teachers can use with the Student's Book exercises instead of the class audio. The video will provide a change of focus and give the lessons a clear visual context. The video will make the lessons more enjoyable and help students to roleplay the situations.

Extracts from the video (the second dialogue from each lesson) are also on the MultiROM.

Revision

Pre-intermediate students need

- regular review.
- motivating reference and practice material.
- a sense of progress.

Pre-intermediate students need to feel that they are moving on, that they are increasing their knowledge, improving their skills, and expanding the number of contexts in which they can use English effectively. At the end of each File there is a Revise & Check section. **What do you remember?** revises the grammar, vocabulary, and pronunciation of each File. **What can you do?** provides a series of skills-based challenges and helps students measure their progress in terms of competence. These pages are designed to be used flexibly according to the needs of your students.
➲ Student's Book *p.14*.

The photocopiable Communicative and Grammar activities also provide many opportunities for recycling.
➲ Teacher's Book *pp.139* and *183*.

Study Link

The Study Link feature in *New English File Pre-intermediate* is designed to help you and your students use the course more effectively. It shows **what** resources are available, **where** they can be found, and **when** to use them.

The Student's Book has these Study Link references:

- from the Practical English lessons ➲ MultiROM and website.
- from the Grammar Bank ➲ MultiROM and website.
- from the Vocabulary Bank ➲ MultiROM and website.
- from the Sound Bank ➲ MultiROM and website.

These references lead students to extra activities and exercises that link in with what they have just studied.

The Workbook has these Study Link references:

➲ the Student's Book Grammar and Vocabulary Banks.

➲ the MultiROM.

➲ the student's website.

The Teacher's Book has Study Link references to remind you where there is extra material available to your students.

Student's Book Files 1–9

The Student's Book has nine Files. Each File is organized like this:

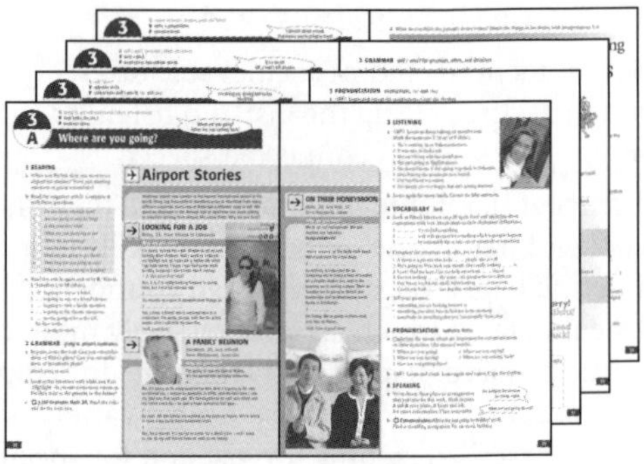

A, B, C, and D lessons Four two-page lessons which form the core material of the book. Each lesson presents and practises **Grammar** and **Vocabulary** and has a **Pronunciation** focus. There is a balance of reading and listening activities, and lots of opportunities for spoken practice. These lessons have clear references ➔ to the Grammar Bank, Vocabulary Bank, and Sound Bank at the back of the book.

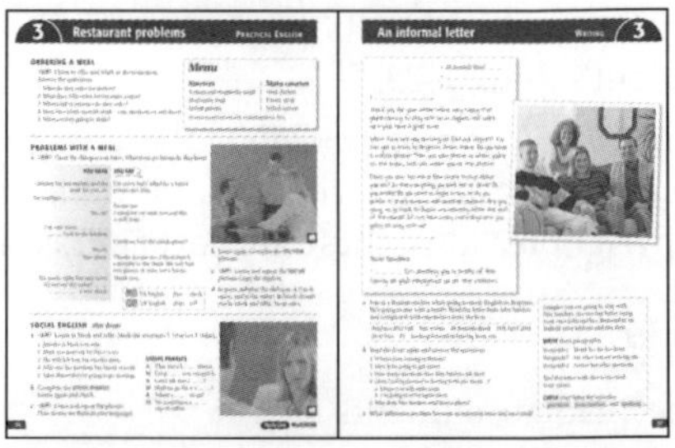

Practical English One-page lessons which teach functional 'survival' language and vocabulary (situations like making a phone call, buying medicine) and also social English (useful phrases like *What's the matter?, Never mind*). The lessons link with the *New English File Pre-intermediate Video.*

Writing One-page focuses on different text types (for example, informal letters and formal e-mails) and writing skills like punctuation and spelling.

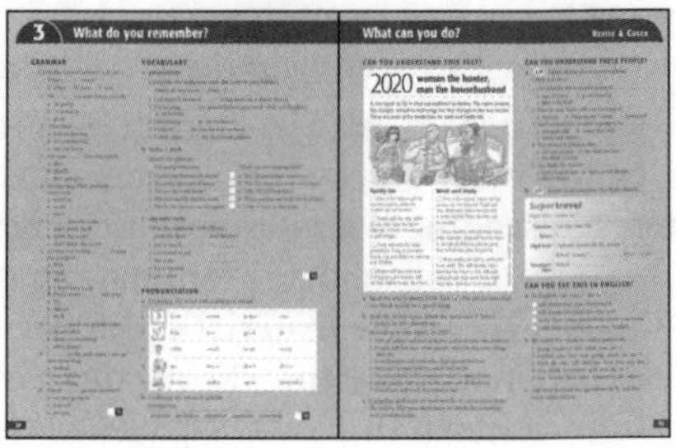

Revise & Check A two-page section – the left- and right-hand pages have different functions. The **What do you remember?** page revises the **Grammar**, **Vocabulary**, and **Pronunciation** of each File. The **What can you do?** page provides **Reading**, **Listening**, and **Speaking** 'Can you…?' challenges to show students what they can achieve.

! File 9 has two main lessons, and then four pages of revision of the whole book: a two-page **Grammar** section and a two-page **Vocabulary** and **Pronunciation** section.

The back of the book

In the back of the Student's Book you'll find these three Banks of material:

Grammar Bank *(pp.126–143)*
Two pages for each File, divided into A–D to reflect the four main lessons. The left-hand page has the grammar rules and the right-hand page has two practice exercises for each lesson. Students are referred ➔ to the Grammar Bank when they do the grammar in each main A, B, C, and D lesson.

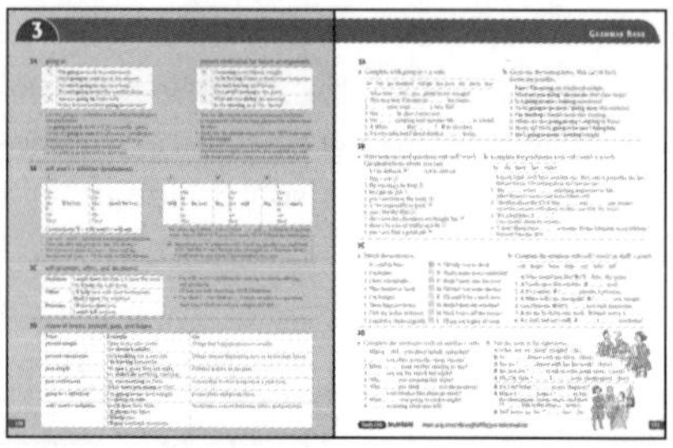

Vocabulary Bank *(pp.144–153)*
An active picture dictionary to help students learn, practise, and revise key words. Students are referred ➔ to the Vocabulary Bank from the main lessons.

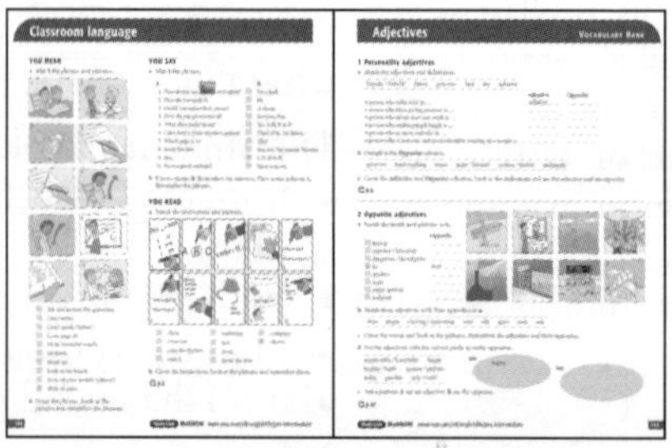

Sound Bank *(pp.156–159)* A four-page section with the *English File* sounds chart and typical spellings for all sounds. Students are referred ➔ to the Sound Bank from the main lessons.

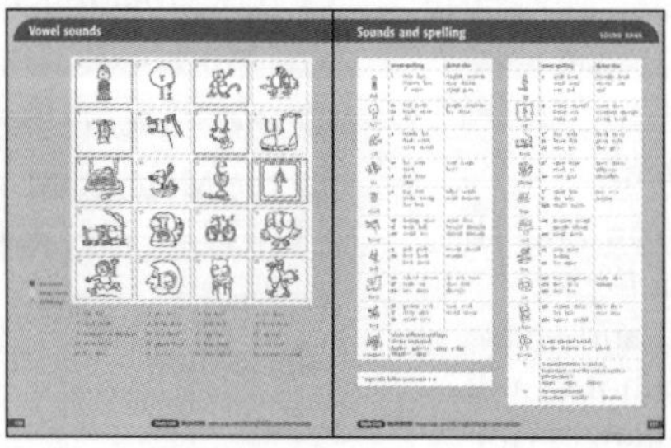

You'll also find:

- **Communication activities** *(pp.108–117)*
  Information gap activities and role plays.
- **Listening scripts** *(pp.118–125)*
  Scripts of key listenings.
- **Verb forms** *(pp.154–155)*

For students

Workbook Each A–D lesson in the Student's Book has a two-page section in the Workbook. This provides all the practice and revision students need. Each section ends with:

- **More Words to Learn**, which reminds students of new vocabulary from the lesson which is not in the Vocabulary Bank.
- **Question time**, five questions for students to answer, which show them how their communicative competence is developing. (These questions also appear on the MultiROM.)

For each File there is a **Study Skills** tip on how to learn vocabulary.

Each Practical English lesson has a one-page section in the Workbook, and includes 'Practical English reading'.

There is also a Key booklet.

MultiROM

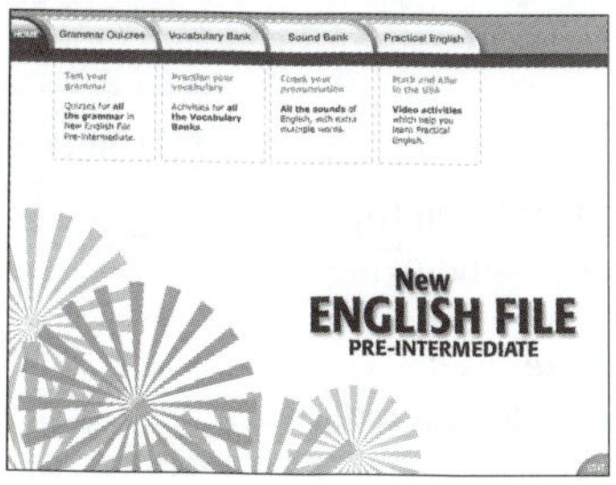

The MultiROM has two functions:

- It's a CD-ROM, containing revision of **Grammar**, **Vocabulary**, **Pronunciation**, and **Practical English** (with extracts from the Video).
- It's an audio CD for students to use in a CD player. They can listen to, repeat, and answer the questions from the **Question time** sections of the Workbook.

Student's website

www.oup.com/elt/englishfile/pre-intermediate

Extra learning resources including
- grammar activities
- vocabulary puzzles
- pronunciation games
- Practical English activities
- learning records
- weblinks
- interactive games

For teachers

Teacher's Book The Teacher's Book has detailed lesson plans for all the lessons. These include:

- an optional 'books-closed' lead-in for every lesson.
- **Extra idea** suggestions for optional extra activities.
- **Extra challenge** suggestions for ways of exploiting the Student's Book material in a more challenging way if you have a stronger class.
- **Extra support** suggestions for ways of adapting activities or exercises to make them more accessible for weaker students.

All lesson plans include keys and complete tapescripts. Extra activities are colour coded in blue so you can see where you are at a glance when you're planning and teaching your classes.

You'll also find over 80 pages of photocopiable materials in the Teacher's Book:

Photocopiable Grammar activities *see pp.139–173*

There is a photocopiable Grammar activity for each A, B, C, and D lesson. These provide extra grammar practice, and can be used either in class or for self-study.

Photocopiable Communicative activities *see pp.183–217*

There is a photocopiable Communicative activity for each A, B, C, and D lesson. These give students extra speaking practice.

Photocopiable Song activities *see pp.220–227*

New English File Pre-intermediate has a song for every File. In File 9 the song is in the Student's Book, and the other eight songs are in the Teacher's Book.

Photocopiable Quicktests and **End-of-course test** *see pp.231–240*

There are eight photocopiable one-page Quicktests which cover the Grammar, **Vocabulary**, and **Pronunciation** of each File. There is a two-page End-of-course test which also includes reading, writing, listening, and speaking.

All the photocopiable material is accompanied by clear instructions and keys.

Video This is a unique 'teaching video' that links with the Practical English lessons in the Student's Book. The video has a story line which features Allie (British) and Mark (American). Each video section can be used with the tasks in the Student's Book Practical English lessons as an alternative to using the Class cassette / audio CD. There's no extra video print material, and you don't need to find extra time to use it. It shows students language in clear contexts and will help them to role play each scene.

The speed of delivery is slightly faster than on the cassette / audio CD, as video is easier for students to understand. Extracts of the video also appear on the MultiROM.

The *New English File Pre-intermediate* package also includes:

- **Three class cassettes / audio CDs**
  These contain all the listening materials for the Student's Book.
- **Test booklets**
  These contain full-length tests for each File of *New English File Pre-intermediate.*
- **Teacher's website**
  www.oup.com/elt/teacher/englishfile/pre-intermediate
  This gives you extra teaching resources, including
  – a guide to *New English File* and the Common European Framework
  – wordlists
  – ideas for end-of-lesson coolers
  – mini web-projects
  – customizable cloze tests
  – student learning records
  – flash cards

1A Who's who?

G word order in questions
V common verb phrases, classroom language
P vowel sounds: /eɪ/, /iː/, /e/, /aɪ/, /əʊ/, /uː/, /ɑː/, the alphabet

File 1 overview

Lessons **1A–1D** mainly focus on the present. **1A** is an introductory lesson but also revises word order in questions. The present simple and continuous are revised in lessons **1B** and **1C**. Relative clauses are introduced in **1D** to give SS early exposure to paraphrasing.

Lesson plan

This first lesson has three main objectives: to help you and the SS to get to know each other, to give you a clear idea of the level of your class, and to provide some quick, efficient revision of elementary language points.

There are two activities to help you and SS learn everybody's names and to exchange personal information. The second exercise provides the context for revising an important grammar point: the order of words in questions. The vocabulary focus is classroom language phrases that SS can use in class throughout the course. The alphabet and spelling are revised and the listening activity gives you the chance to quickly revise other mini-language points like days of the week, dates, numbers etc.

Optional lead-in (books closed)

- You could do this as a more lively alternative to **1a**. Before the class choose a tape/CD of party music. You could use one of the songs from the book e.g. *True Blue* (CD 2 Track 4).
- Introduce yourself to the class. Say *Hello, I'm ...* .
- Tell SS to stand up. Divide the class into two groups, **A** and **B.** Ask both groups to make a circle, **A** inside **B.** Tell them to imagine that they're at a party. When you play the music, tell them to walk round in their circle, one clockwise and the other anticlockwise. When you stop the music, tell them to introduce themselves to the person standing opposite them. Elicit that they can say *Hello* or *Hi, I'm ...* or *My name's ...* , and should respond *Nice to meet you.*

1 INTRODUCING YOURSELF

a • Books open. Set a time limit of two minutes. Get SS to stand up and move around the class introducing themselves to as many of the other SS as they can. Tell them to try and remember the names too. Elicit that they can say *Hello* or *Hi* (more informal) and should respond *Nice to meet you.* You could join in to help you learn the SS' names.

b • Focus on the instructions. Elicit suggestions from the class for each category. Sometimes there may be more than one person for each one. If the class can't think of anybody for a particular category, SS who fit that category could remind the class of their name.

2 GETTING TO KNOW EACH OTHER

a • Focus on the photos and the questions. Elicit the verbs for the first three questions under ***Home and Family***. Put SS into pairs. Tell them to complete the other questions with the correct verbs.

• Check answers, making sure that SS understand the whole question not just the missing verb.

1 **HOME AND FAMILY** are live have
2 **JOB / STUDIES** do work like go are speak
3 **FREE TIME** listen play watch do read
4 **THE FUTURE** go do
5 **THE PAST** were study do

b 1.1

• Play the tape/CD once for SS to listen to the rhythm. Then play it again, stopping after each question for SS to repeat.

1.1 CD1 Track 2
What kind of music do you listen to?
Do you play a musical instrument?
Do you watch TV?
Do you do any sport or exercise?
What books or magazines do you read?

c • Focus on the instructions. Demonstrate the activity by getting SS to ask you a few questions first. Use full answers, giving extra information.

• Point out that in the **JOB / STUDIES** section there are two possible conversations depending on whether the person has a job or is a student.

Extra challenge

Encourage SS to ask follow up questions, e.g.
A *Do you have any brothers and sisters?*
B *I have one brother.*
A *How old is he? / What's his name? / What does he do?*

• Put SS into pairs. Give them at least five minutes to ask and answer in pairs. Monitor their conversations, as this will give you an idea of their oral level.

• Get feedback from several pairs to see what they have in common.

3 GRAMMAR word order in questions

a • Tell SS to cover the questions in 2. Focus on the instructions. Do the first one together. Give SS a minute to do the other four and check answers.

1 Where are you from?
2 Do you watch TV?
3 What kind of music do you listen to?
4 Where did you study English before?
5 What are you going to do this weekend?

b • Tell SS to go to **Grammar Bank 1A** on *p.126*. Explain that all the grammar rules and exercises are in this part of the book.

• Go through the rules with the class. Model and drill the example questions.

Grammar notes

- In questions with the auxiliaries *do, does, did* SS may leave out the auxiliary or get the word order wrong. Typical mistakes:
  You live with your parents? Why she didn't like the film?
  The memory aids ASI and QUASI may help SS here.
- In questions with *be* SS sometimes forget to invert the subject and verb. Typical mistakes:
  Ana's a student? What they're doing?
- Give SS or elicit some other examples of questions with an end preposition:
  What are you looking at?
  Who are you talking to?
  What are you looking for?

• Focus on the exercises for **1A** on *p.127*. SS do the exercises individually or in pairs. Check answers.

a 1 Are you going to go out this evening?
2 Where does your sister work?
3 What music are you listening to?
4 Does the class finish at 8.00?
5 Why didn't you write to me?
6 Do you often go to the cinema?
7 What does this word mean?
8 What time did your friends arrive?

b 1 Do you have a car?
2 Is your brother older than you?
3 How often does he write to you?
4 What time does this class start?
5 Where did you go last summer?
6 How many languages do you speak?
7 Are you going to see her this evening?
8 Who are you waiting for?

• Tell SS to go back to the main lesson on *p.5*.

4 LISTENING & SPEAKING

a 1.2

• Focus on the instructions. Give SS time to read the questions and look at the options. Play the tape/CD. Stop after each conversation and play it again, getting SS to compare answers. Monitor SS' listening ability and check how well SS remember numbers, days of the week and dates, and telling the time.

1.2 CD1 Track 3

(tapescript in Student's Book on *p.118*)

1 A When's the exam?
B Next week.
A Yeah, I know, but what day? Is it Wednesday or Thursday?
B No, it's Tuesday.

2 A The weekend goes so quickly.
B I know. I can't believe that it's Monday tomorrow.

3 A Excuse me! Do you have the right time?
B Yes, it's twenty-five to nine.
A Thanks.

4 A We're going to be late for class.
B Relax. It doesn't start until quarter past ten. It's only five past.

5 A When was she born?
B Let's see. She was born on the 23rd August 1947.
A Where?
B In Germany.

6 A Do you have any tickets left for the 5th of June?
B Let's see ... yes, we do. How many would you like?
A Two, please.
B OK, that's 27 euros please.

7 A Hello?
B Hi, it's me. I'm in your street but I can't remember the number of your house. Is it 117?
A No, it's 170.

8 A How much are those flowers?
B 50 euros.
A 50? That's not cheap.

• Check answers. Play the tape/CD again if necessary.

1 a 2 a 3 a 4 b 5 b 6 a 7 b 8 b

• Elicit the following points from SS:
– the difference in pronunciation between *Tuesday* /'tju:zdeɪ/ and *Thursday* /'θɜ:zdeɪ/ in **1**.
– the differing stress pattern between *seventeen* and *seventy* in **7**.

Extra support

Revise any or all of the following four areas if you think your SS need it.

Days of the week – get them to say the days of the week round the class. Write them on the board as they say them. Practise pronunciation.

Numbers – count to thirty round the class. Write random numbers between 20 and 1000 on the board for SS to say. Remind SS of the difference between *thirteen/thirty, fourteen/forty*, etc.

The date – get SS to practise saying the months and ordinal numbers (first, second, etc.) Then write a few dates on the board and highlight the use of *the* and *of* when we *say* the date.

Telling the time – write up times on the board (7.00, 7.15, 7.30, 7.45, etc.). Ask SS *What's the time?* Get them to say each time in two ways, e.g. *half past seven* and *seven thirty*.

b • Put SS into pairs. Get them to ask and answer the questions. Check the answers with the whole class or individual students.

Study Link SS can revise numbers, dates, and times on the *New English File Pre-intermediate* website.

5 CLASSROOM LANGUAGE

a • Focus on the cartoon and elicit the missing words in the speech bubbles (turn off, repeat).

b • Tell SS to go to **Vocabulary Bank *Classroom Language*** on *p.144*. Focus on **YOU HEAR** and explain that these are typical 'teacher instructions'.

• In pairs SS do **a**. Check answers and model and drill pronunciation.

• Focus on **b**. Get SS to cover the phrases and use the pictures to test each other for a minute.

- Focus on **YOU SAY** and elicit the answer to the first question in **a**. Get SS to do the rest in pairs. Check answers by asking one student to ask a question and another to answer it with the matching answer.

YOU HEAR
1 Work in pairs.
2 Don't speak (Italian).
3 Turn off your mobile (phone).
4 Write down the words.
5 Don't write.
6 Stand up.
7 Sit down.
8 Look at the board.
9 Go to page 33.
10 Ask and answer the questions.

YOU SAY
1 A sheep. **2** S-H-E-E-P. **3** Yes. S-H-E-E-P.
4 /ʃiːp/ **5** Very bad. **6** Here you are. **7** 84.
8 That's OK. Sit down. **9** See you. Bye.
10 You too. See you on Monday.

- Focus on **b**. Get SS to revise the expressions. From now on encourage SS to use the questions and phrases in column **A** in class.
- Focus on **YOU READ** and explain that these are typical exercise instructions. Give SS a minute to match the words and pictures in pairs. Check answers.

YOU READ
1 choose **2** circle **3** complete **4** cover the text
5 tick **6** cross **7** cross out **8** match
9 copy the rhythm **10** underline

⚠ If your SS have not used *New English File Elementary*, explain that in the **Vocabulary Bank** the stressed syllable is always underlined in multi-syllable words.

- Get SS to revise the expressions. In their pairs, ask them to cover the instructions, look at the pictures and try to remember the instructions.

Study Link SS can find more practice of these phrases on the MultiROM and on the *New English File Pre-intermediate* website.

- Tell SS to go back to the main lesson on *p.5*.

6 PRONUNCIATION vowel sounds, the alphabet

Pronunciation notes

- Emphasize the importance of being able to spell in English, particularly your name. Point out that this is especially important when speaking in English on the phone. Also point out that it is very useful to be able to recognize and write down letters correctly when people spell words to you.
- If your SS didn't use *New English File Elementary*, this will be the first time that your SS have seen the sound pictures (*train*, *tree*, etc.). Explain that the pictures will give SS a clear example of the target sound and that they will help them remember the pronunciation of the phonetic symbol. This is very important if they want to check the pronunciation of a word in the dictionary.
- Tell SS that the two dots in /iː/, /uː/, and /ɑː/ means that they are long sounds.

a • Focus on the sound pictures and elicit the words and sounds: *train* /eɪ/, *tree* /iː/, *egg* /e/, *bike* /aɪ/, *phone* /əʊ/, *boot* /uː/, *car* /ɑː/. Elicit the pronunciation of the letters after each picture, e.g. *train, A, H, K.*

b • Now focus on the letters in the box but don't elicit their pronunciation yet. In pairs, SS write them in the right place in the chart. Check answers.

train /eɪː/ AHJK	phone /əʊ/ **O**
tree /iː/ BCDE**G**PTV	boot /uː/ QUW
egg /e/ FLMNS**XZ**	car /ɑː/ **R**
bike /aɪ/ **I**Y	

- Ask SS which sounds are difficult for them. Highlight the difference between pairs and groups of letters which are often confused, e.g. a/e/i, g/j, k/q, etc.

c • Get SS to test each other by pointing at individual letters in the chart for their partner to say.

d • Slowly spell these words to SS, repeating each word twice.
jogging psychiatrist queue rhythm knee

- Check answers by getting SS to spell the words back to you. Encourage them to ask *What does it mean? How do you pronounce it?*

Extra idea

Get SS to spell their surnames and street names.

e • Put SS into pairs (or groups of three). Tell them they have to choose six words they know how to spell and pronounce, and whose meaning they are sure of.

- Pairs test another pair to see if they know the meaning and spelling of these words. Focus on the speech bubbles to show SS how the game works, and give another example if necessary. Monitor SS' lists, to check spelling and meaning before they start testing each other. Pairs get 1 point for a correct meaning and 1 point for a correct spelling. Did any pairs get 12 points?

Extra support

In a monolingual class SS can use translation to answer *What does it mean?* In a multilingual class SS will need to paraphrase, mime etc.

Extra photocopiable activities

Grammar
questions *p.139*
Communicative
Student profile *p.183* (instructions *p.174*)

HOMEWORK

Study Link **Workbook** *pp.4–5*

1B

G present simple
V family, personality adjectives
P third person and plural *-s*

Who knows you better?

Lesson plan

In this lesson the present simple (all forms) is revised in detail through a British magazine article *Who knows you better?* A family member and a friend both try to choose a suitable partner for Richard, a single man who is looking for a partner. Family words (*aunt, cousin,* etc.) and physical description adjectives (*tall, dark*) are revised from *New English File Elementary* and adjectives of personality are introduced. The lesson ends with SS describing a member of their family in detail. The pronunciation focus is the different pronunciations of the *-s* ending (third person singular verbs and regular plural nouns).

Optional lead-in (books closed)

Write up on the board:

Direct family	*Other relatives*	*Husband/wife's family*
mother	*grandmother*	*mother-in-law*

Put SS into pairs. Give them a minute to add more words to each category. Get feedback and write the words on the board.

Remind SS of the pronunciation of difficult words like *daughter*. Rub the words off the board before SS do **1a**.

1 VOCABULARY family and adjectives

a • Books open. Focus on the puzzle and the clues.
- Remind SS of the possesive (genitive) *'s*, e.g. *your brother's wife* = the wife of your brother.
- SS complete the puzzle in pairs. Check answers and model and drill pronunciation.

1 fat	3 niece	5 cousins	7 tall
2 sister-in-law	4 uncle	6 dark	8 family

- Elicit the difference between *thin* and *slim* (*slim* = thin and attractive, *thin* = less positive, can suggest too thin).

b • Elicit that *friendly* describes personality and means open and kind, and the opposite is *unfriendly*.

c • Tell SS to go to **Vocabulary Bank *Adjectives*** on *p.145* and do **Part 1 *Personality adjectives***. They can work individually or in pairs. Check answers and model and drill pronunciation.

talkative	quiet
generous	mean
lazy	hard-working
funny	serious
friendly	unfriendly
shy	extrovert

- Allow SS a few minutes to test themselves by covering the adjectives and trying to remember them from the definitions. They can then cover the definitions and try to remember them from looking at the adjectives.

Study Link SS can find more practice of these phrases on the MultiROM and on the *New English File Pre-intermediate* website.

- Tell SS to go back to the main lesson on *p.6*.

2 READING

a • Do this as an open class question and elicit SS' opinions. Tell them what you think too.

b • Tell SS that they're going to read part of a magazine article. Then give them a minute to read the introduction and answer questions 1–4 in pairs.
- Check answers. Remind SS of the *'s* as in 2 *Danny is Richard's best friend.*

1 He's a musician. He's 26. He lives in Southampton.
2 Danny is Richard's best friend.
3 They try to find him a partner/girlfriend.
4 He goes on a date with the two girls to see which one he likes best.

c • Focus on what Richard says. Go through the instructions and set a time limit, e.g. 3 minutes. Get SS to compare answers in pairs before you check.

1 T
2 F He's friendly but sometimes quite shy.
3 F He likes music but he doesn't like parties.
4 T
5 F He likes women who are good listeners.
6 T
7 T

d • Remind SS of the importance of guessing words from context when they are reading. Focus on the highlighted words. Give SS a minute to guess the meanings from context.
- Check answers and model and drill the pronunciation of *abroad* /əbrɔːd/ and *laugh* /lɑːf/. Remind SS that *too* has another meaning = *more than is good*, e.g. *too hot*.

1 in another country
2 have a good relationship
3 also
4 make a sound that shows you are happy
5 the opposite of right

- Finally ask SS if there were any other words or phrases they had problems with and explain or translate them.

3 GRAMMAR present simple

a • Focus on the instructions. Give SS a few minutes to complete the questions. Check answers.

1 does he
2 does he work
3 Does he
4 Does he do (any)
5 does he like
6 Does he talk

- Ask SS how the questions would change if they were asking you (*does* changes to *do*, *he* changes to *you*).

b • Tell SS to go to **Grammar Bank 1B** on *p.126*. Go through the chart and rules with the class. Model and drill the example sentences.

Grammar notes

Present simple

Remind SS:

– that *s/ies/es* is only added to third person singular forms.

– of the difference in pronunciation between *do* /duː/, *don't* /dəʊnt/, and *does* /dʌz/.

– the pronunciation of *goes* /gəʊz/, and *has* /hæz/.

– that the contracted forms *don't* and *doesn't* are always used in conversation.

Adverbs and expressions of frequency

- You may want to point out that *usually/normally* and *sometimes* can be used at the beginning of a present simple sentence, e.g. *Sometimes I get up late on Saturday.*
- Other common *every* expressions are *every week, every month, every year.*
- In expressions like *once a month, twice a day* remind SS that *once* and *twice* are irregular (NOT ~~one time~~, ~~two times~~). '*times*' is used with all other numbers, e.g. *ten times, thirty times (a year).*

- Focus on the exercises for **1B** on *p.127*. SS do the exercises individually or in pairs. Check answers.

a 1 Does Anna like music?
2 She has a lot of hobbies.
3 I don't get on very well with my sister.
4 My brother doesn't know me very well.
5 Do they have any children?
6 Does the film finish late?
7 He goes out twice a week.
8 We don't often talk about politics.

b 1 Do ... open
2 doesn't have
3 listen
4 doesn't talk
5 Does ... get on
6 doesn't work

- Tell SS to go back to the main lesson on *p.7*.

c • Get SS to cover the text on *p.6* or close their books. Put them into pairs. Give them a minute to write down five things they remember about Richard. Check answers then let SS look back at the text.

d • Focus on the photos of Nina and Claire. Tell SS that these are the girls Danny and Richard's mother chose for him. Ask *Who's Nina?* to elicit *His mother's choice* and *Who's Claire?* to elicit *His friend's choice*.

- Put SS into pairs, **A** and **B,** and get them to sit face to face if possible. Tell them to go to **Communication 1B *Claire and Nina*, A** on *p.108*, **B** on *p.112*.
- Go through the instructions and make sure SS are clear what they have to do. When they have both completed their charts, ask *Who do you think is Richard's type? Which girl is he going to prefer? Why?* Elicit some ideas from the class.
- Tell SS to go back to the main lesson on *p.7*.

4 LISTENING

a 1.3 / 1.4

- Tell SS they are going to listen to Richard talking about when he met Claire and Nina for the first time. Focus on the two questions. Play the tape/CD.

1.3 CD1 Track 4

(tapescript in Student's Book on *p.118*)

I was very optimistic when I went to meet Claire. My first impression was that she was very friendly and very extrovert. Physically she was my type – she was quite slim, and not very tall with long dark hair – *very* pretty. And she was very funny too. She had a great sense of humour. We laughed a lot. But the only problem was that Claire was *very* talkative. She talked all the time and I just listened. She wasn't very interested in me. At the end of the evening I knew everything about her and she knew nothing about me. Claire was the kind of woman I could have as a friend but not as a girlfriend.

1.4 CD1 Track 5

(tapescript in Student's Book on *p.118*)

When I first saw Nina I couldn't believe it. I thought 'Wow! Thanks mum'. She's very attractive – she's got short dark hair – and she's quite tall. She's Hungarian, from Budapest but her English was fantastic.
At first she was a bit shy but when we started chatting we found we had a lot of things in common – we both like music, food, and travelling. We got on really well – we didn't stop talking for the whole evening. When it was time to go I knew I really wanted to see Nina again and I asked her for her phone number. But she just smiled at me and said in her beautiful Hungarian accent, 'Richard, you're really sweet but I'm sorry, you're not my type.'

- Check answers. Play the tape/CD again if necessary.

Claire
He likes her as a friend but not as a girlfriend.
The problem is she talked a lot about herself (and not about him).

Nina
Richard likes her very much and wants to see her again. The problem is Nina doesn't think he's her type.

Extra idea

For extra suspense don't play the last two sentences of Nina's section (from 'But she just smiled ...). You could then ask SS to guess what the problem is.

b • Play the tape/CD again for SS to write down adjectives or expressions that Richard uses. Get SS to compare their answers with a partner's. Check answers.

Possible answers

Claire
friendly, extrovert, slim, not very tall, long dark hair, pretty, funny, a great sense of humour, talkative

Nina
attractive, short dark hair, tall, Hungarian, fantastic (English), shy, beautiful Hungarian accent

c • Ask *Who knows Richard better?* (his mother) and find out if SS are surprised. You may like to tell SS that the text and listening were based on a real magazine experiment. Several single people took part in the experiment and in 75% of the cases, the family member chose best.

5 PRONUNCIATION *-s*

a 1.5

- Explain that the final *-s* in the third person of the present simple and in plurals can be pronounced in three different ways.
- Focus on the sound pictures. Elicit and drill the words and sounds: *snake* /sneɪk/, *zebra* /zebrə/, and /ɪz/.

⚠ SS may have problems distinguishing between the /s/ and /z/ sounds. Tell them that the /s/ is like the sound made by a snake and the /z/ is a bee or fly.

- Play the tape/CD, pausing after each word and sound for SS to repeat.

1.5 CD1 Track 6

He works abroad.
She likes good food.
She laughs a lot.
He plays the piano.
She lives in London.
She does exercise.
She watches comedy films.
He relaxes at night.
She dresses very well.

b • Write the three phonetic symbols, /s/, /z/, and /ɪz/ on the board. Elicit the third person pronunciation of the verbs one by one and ask SS which group they belong to. Write them on the board under the correct heading.

/s/	/z/	/ɪz/
cooks	goes	chooses
stops	knows	teaches

c • Repeat as in **b** with the plural form of the nouns.

/s/	/z/	/ɪz/
books	friends	languages
parents	girls	nieces
	parties	

Extra challenge

Instead of eliciting the answers from the class for **b** and **c**, tell SS to copy the symbols from the board, and in pairs write the verbs and nouns with the correct symbol. Check answers.

d 1.6

- Play the tape/CD, pausing after each word and sound for SS to repeat.

1.6 CD1 Track 7

chooses	cooks	goes	knows	stops
teaches	books	friends	girls	
languages	nieces	parents	parties	

Pronunciation notes

- The pronunciation rules for adding an *-s* (or *-es*) to verbs (e.g. *smokes*) and nouns (e.g. *books*) are the same.
- The difference between the /s/ and /z/ sounds is very small and only occasionally causes communication problems. The most important thing is for SS to learn the /ɪz/ pronunciation.
- You may want to give SS these rules:
  – the final *s* is pronounced /ɪz/ in verbs and nouns which end in /tʃ/ (*churches*), /s/ (*dresses*), /ʃ/ (*washes*), and /dʒ/ (*bridges*).
  – the *s* is pronounced /s/ after these unvoiced sounds /k/, /p/, /f/, and /t/, e.g. *walks, stops, laughs, eats.*
  – in all other cases the final *s* is pronounced /z/, e.g. *plays, parties,* etc.

Study Link SS can find more practice on the MultiROM or on the *New English File Pre-intermediate* website.

6 SPEAKING

a • Put SS into pairs, **A** and **B.** Give SS five minutes to make a few notes about a person they know well. Monitor and help with vocabulary.

b • **A** describes his/her person and **B** listens and asks for more information. **B** should try and think if he/she knows anybody who would be a good partner for **A**'s person and say why. SS swap roles and **B** describes his/her person to **A**.

Extra photocopiable activities

Grammar
present simple *p.140*
Communicative
Who's their ideal partner? *p.184* (instructions *p.174*)

HOMEWORK

Study Link **Workbook** *pp.6–7*

G present continuous
V the body: *mouth, heart,* etc., prepositions of place: *under, next to,* etc.
P vowel sounds: /əʊ/, /aɪ/, /ɪə/, /ɑː/, /ʌ/, /e/

1C At the Moulin Rouge

Lesson plan

Famous paintings provide the context for revising the present continuous (for things happening now) and prepositions of place, and to present a new vocabulary group (the body). SS describe what is happening in a famous painting *At the Moulin Rouge* by Toulouse-Lautrec and then hear about the story behind the painting.

Optional lead-in (books closed)

Write the following pairs of words on the board:
an artist–a painter
a painting–a picture
paint (v)–draw (v)

Ask *Are they the same or different?* about each pair and give SS a few minutes to discuss in pairs.

An artist is someone who paints paintings, e.g. Van Gogh.

Painter has the same meaning but can also mean someone who paints houses, offices, etc.

A painting is only a work of art, e.g. *Mona Lisa* etc.

A picture can be a photo, an illustration, a drawing (or a painting).

To paint we use colours, paints, etc.

To draw we normally use a pencil or pen and ink.

1 VOCABULARY the body

a • Books open. Focus on the painting and ask SS if they like it or not. You could get a show of hands to see what the majority think. Elicit reasons from individuals. Tell SS what you think.

b • Focus on the words in the box. Give SS a few minutes to label the picture. SS can either write the words next to the numbers or number the words in the box. Check answers and model and drill pronunciation.

1 hair	2 ear	3 eyes
4 nose	5 mouth	6 lips
7 neck		

c • Tell SS to go to **Vocabulary Bank *The Body*** on *p.146*. Focus on **a**. Put SS into pairs and give them a few minutes to match the words and pictures. Check answers and model and drill pronunciation.

1 mouth	9 nose	17 knee(s)
2 neck	10 head	18 leg(s)
3 hand(s)	11 ear(s)	19 brain
4 stomach	12 shoulder(s)	20 teeth
5 arm(s)	13 face	21 heart
6 eye(s)	14 hair	22 toes
7 finger(s)	15 back	23 tongue
8 lip(s)	16 foot (pl. feet)	

• Focus on **b.** Give SS a few minutes to test themselves or each other.

• Get SS to look at the verbs in **c** and complete the gaps with the parts of the body that we use to do these things. Check answers.

see – eyes hear – ears smell – nose kiss – lips
bite – teeth touch – hands/fingers think – brain
feel – hands/heart/whole body kick – feet smile – mouth/lips

Extra challenge

Ask SS which verbs are irregular (*see, hear, bite, think, feel*) and elicit/teach the past simple form (*saw, heard, bit, thought, felt*).

• Give SS five minutes to test each other using the question in **d** as a model. Check answers by asking a few SS questions.

• Tell SS to go back to the main lesson on *p.8*.

d • Put SS in pairs and see which pair can write down the most words in the time limit.

Study Link SS can practise this vocabulary on the MultiROM or on the *New English File Pre-intermediate* website.

2 PRONUNCIATION vowel sounds

a • Focus on the sound pictures and elicit/teach the picture words and sounds: *phone* /əʊ/, *bike* /aɪ/, *ear* /ɪə/, *car* /ɑː/, *up* /ʌ/, *egg* /e/

Pronunciation notes

• You may want to point out that /ɪə/ is a diphthong, i.e. two sounds joined together.

b 1.7

• Put SS into pairs. Give them a few minutes to put the words in the right columns. Play the tape/CD for them to check their answers.

1.7 CD1 Track 8

phone /əʊ/	*bike* /aɪ/	*ear* /ɪə/	*car* /ɑː/	*up* /ʌ/	*egg* /e/
nose	bite	ears	arms	stomach	head
shoulders	eyes	hear	heart	touch	smell

• Play the tape/CD again stopping after each word or column for SS to repeat.

c • Tell SS to go to **Sound Bank** on *p.157*. Go through the spellings for these six sounds.

Study Link SS can find more practice on the MultiROM or on the *New English File Pre-intermediate* website.

- Tell SS to go back to the main lesson on *p.8*.

3 GRAMMAR present continuous

a • Focus on the painting on *p.9* and ask SS if they like it. Ask them what the Moulin Rouge is (a famous nightclub) and where it is (Paris). You could also ask if any SS have seen the film *Moulin Rouge*.

- Give SS a few minutes to answer the questions in pairs, either orally or in writing. Get feedback, accepting all reasonable suggestions.

Suggested answers
1 Winter clothes, hat, coats, long dresses.
2 They are talking and drinking.
3 The woman on the left is doing her hair/looking at herself in a mirror. The other woman is looking at her.
4 They are going out of the nightclub/leaving the nightclub.
5 She has fair/red hair and her face is white/blue. She has very red lips. Perhaps she's dancing, or looking at something.
6 **Don't tell SS the answer to this, but accept all suggestions. Tell SS they will find out the answer in the listening.**

b • Focus on the sentences and give SS a minute to choose the right form and discuss in pairs why the other is wrong. Check answers.

1 **are wearing** (because we are describing a picture and saying what is happening at that moment)
2 **wear** (because it's something that happens frequently)
3 **sits** (because it's something that happens frequently, a habit)
4 **is sitting** (because we are saying what is happening at the moment, now)

c • Tell SS to go to **Grammar Bank 1C** on *p.126*. Go through the chart and rules with the class. Model and drill the example sentences.

Grammar notes

- Some languages do not have (or always use) an equivalent tense to the present continuous and may use the present simple. Typical mistake: *The man in the picture wears a hat.*
- The present continuous is used to describe actions which are in progress now, at this moment (*It's raining, You're standing on my foot*). But this tense is also used to describe what is happening in a painting as if we were looking at a scene through a window.
- The future use of the present continuous (*I'm leaving tomorrow.*) is presented in **3A**.

- Focus on the exercises for **1C** on *p.127*. SS do the exercises individually or in pairs. Check answers.

a 1 Hey! You're standing on my foot!
2 They aren't playing very well today.
3 What are you studying at the moment?
4 We're thinking of you.
5 Is she wearing make-up?
6 They're making a big mistake.
7 Is your brother working in London now?
8 She isn't talking to her father at the moment.

b 1 doesn't bite.
2 are ... wearing, 's raining
3 'm not listening
4 need, don't have
5 's putting
6 Do ... cook, eat
7 are ... doing, 'm meeting

- Tell SS to go back to the main lesson on *p.8*.

4 LISTENING

a 1.8

- Tell SS that they are going to find out more about the painting on *p.9*. Go through questions 1–4. Play the tape/CD once and check answers.

1.8 CD1 Track 9

(tapescript in Student's Book on *p.118*)
OK, now the painting we are looking at now is by the French painter Toulouse-Lautrec. The painting is called *At the Moulin Rouge*. As you probably know, The Moulin Rouge is a nightclub in Paris. Maybe some of you remember the film *Moulin Rouge*? In the 19th century, the nightclub was very famous for its beautiful dancers and singers.
Toulouse-Lautrec did a lot of paintings and posters of the Moulin Rouge. He especially loved painting the dancers. And in these paintings he sometimes included his friends too.
In the middle of the picture there are five people who are sitting at a table having a drink. The woman who's wearing a hat is a dancer – her name is La Macarona – and the man sitting next to her on the left is a friend of Toulouse-Lautrec. He was a photographer.
On the right, here, there's a woman with fair hair, blue eyes, and very red lips. Her face looks very white. That's another famous dancer called Jane Avril. At the back of the picture, on the right, there are two women who are standing together. One of them is touching her hair. That's La Goulue and she was one of the most famous singers at the Moulin Rouge at that time.
Now this is very interesting. If you look carefully to the left of the two women, there are two men walking out of the nightclub. One of them is very tall and the other one is very short. The very tall man is Toulouse-Lautrec's cousin, Gabriel, and the other man is Toulouse-Lautrec himself. Toulouse-Lautrec was only 1 metre 50 centimetres tall. He had very short legs and couldn't walk very well. Some people think that this is why he loved painting the dancers of the Moulin Rouge – because they all had beautiful, long legs.

1 It was famous for its beautiful dancers and singers.
2 The dancers from the Moulin Rouge and his friends.
3 The very short man at the back, who is walking out of the nightclub.
4 Because they had beautiful long legs.

b • Now focus on the people numbered 1–6. Get SS to write in the number for Toulouse-Lautrec (4). Then play the tape/CD again for them to number the other people. Play it again if necessary. Check answers.

Toulouse-Lautrec 4
His cousin Gabriel 3
His friend, a photographer 1
Jane Avril 6
La Macarona 2
La Goulue 5

Extra support

Pause the tape/CD after each person is mentioned to give SS time to take in the information and number the person. You could also get SS to listen with the tapescript on *p.118*.

5 SPEAKING

a • Tell SS that when you are describing a picture it's important to use the right prepositions to say where things are. Focus on the prepositions and pictures and give SS a few minutes to match them. Check answers.

1 on	**2** in	**3** in front of	**4** opposite
5 behind	**6** next to	**7** between	**8** under
9 on the left		**10** on the right	
11 in the middle			

Extra support

If SS don't remember the prepositions very well, you could spend a bit more time recycling them using things in the classroom, e.g. *Where's the TV? It's* ***on*** *a shelf* ***behind*** *the table*, etc.

b • Put SS into pairs, **A** and **B** and get them to sit face to face if possible. Then tell them to go to **Communication 1C *Describe and draw*, A** on *p.108*, **B** on *p.112*.

• Go through the instructions with them and make sure SS are clear what they have to do. Stress that they just have to sketch the figures, objects, etc. according to their partner's description.

• Give SS a few minutes to look at their paintings and think about how they are going to describe them. Remind them to use the present continuous to say what the people are doing.

• When SS have finished, they can compare their drawing with their partner's painting to check they followed the instructions correctly.

• Tell SS to go back to the main lesson on *p.9*.

Extra idea

You could do this activity using postcards of paintings from an art gallery.

c • Put SS into groups of four to ask and answer the questions. You could first answer the questions yourself to give SS more listening practise and to model how they might answer. Get feedback from a few groups.

d • Do this as a whole class activity. Write the painters and names of the paintings on the board:

Dora Maar by Picasso (p.8); *At the Moulin Rouge* by Toulouse Lautrec (p.9); *Pareja Bailando* by Botero (p.108); *Concierto Campestre* by Botero (p.112).

• Put SS into pairs. Give them a few minutes to look at the paintings again and decide which one they like best, or would like to have in their house or flat. Get a show of hands for each picture to find out which is the most/least popular. Ask pairs why they chose their painting. What do they like about it?

6 SONG ♫ *Ain't got no – I got life*

1.9

• This song revises all the body vocabulary that SS have learnt.

• If you want to do this song in class, use the photocopiable activity on *p.220*.

1.9 CD1 Track 10

Ain't got no – I got life
I ain't got no home, ain't got no shoes
Ain't got no money, ain't got no class
Ain't got no skirts, ain't got no sweater
Ain't got no perfume, ain't got no beer
Ain't got no man
Ain't got no mother, ain't got no culture
Ain't got no friends, ain't got no schooling
Ain't got no love, ain't got no name
Ain't got no ticket, ain't got no token
Ain't got no god

What have I got?
Why am I alive anyway?
Yeah, what have I got
Nobody can take away?

I've got my hair, got my head
I've got my brains, got my ears
I've got my eyes, got my nose
I've got my mouth, I've got my smile
I've got my tongue, got my chin
I've got my neck, got my lips
I've got my heart, got my soul
I've got my back, I've got myself
I've got my arms, got my hands,
I've got my fingers, got my legs
I've got my feet, got my toes
I've got my liver, got my blood

I've got life, I've got my freedom
I've got life
I've got life
And I'm gonna keep it
I've got life
And nobody's gonna take it away

Extra photocopiable activities

Grammar
present simple or present continuous? *p.141*
Communicative
At an art gallery *p.185* (instructions on *p.174*)
Song
Ain't got no – I got life p.220 (instructions *p.218*)

HOMEWORK

Study Link **Workbook** *pp.8–9*

1D The Devil's Dictionary

G defining relative clauses (*a person who . . ., a thing which . . .*)
V expressions for paraphrasing: *like, for example,* etc.
P pronunciation in a dictionary

Lesson plan

In this lesson SS are introduced to simple, defining relative clauses through the context of humorous definitions and a TV game show.

The *Devil's Dictionary*, written by Ambrose Bierce in the 19th century, gave amusing and cynical definitions of common words. Bierce's dictionary has inspired numerous *Devil's Dictionary* websites on the Internet which give more up-to-date definitions. The definitions in **1e** are taken from these websites but the definition of a dentist in **1a** is from Pierce's dictionary.

SS learn how relative clauses can help them to paraphrase. They also learn some other useful phrases which will help them keep going in a conversation when they don't know the exact word for something. Finally, SS see how a dictionary can help them pronounce new words correctly.

Optional lead-in (books closed)

Play *Hangman* with the word DICTIONARY. Then do **1a**.

⚠ If you don't know how to play *Hangman*, see *New English File Elementary Teacher's Book* p.20.

1 READING

a • Books open. Focus on the dictionary definition and tell SS to work in pairs and guess what the missing word is. Tell SS not to call out the answer. Then check.

> dentist

• SS will probably realize at this point that the definition is not the kind you would get in a normal dictionary.

b • Tell SS that they are going to read to find out where the dentist definition came from. Give SS a minute to read the text and answer the question.

> From the *Devil's Dictionary*

c • Give SS two minutes to read the text again and answer the three questions. SS can compare their answers with a partner's. Check answers.

> **1** He was an American author and journalist.
> **2** A kind of doctor who looks after people's teeth.
> **3** On the Internet.

• Tell SS to underline any new words in the text and to try and guess their meaning from context. Get feedback on any vocabulary problems and deal with them. Drill the pronunciation of any difficult words.

Extra support

If SS have dictionaries with them, they could use them to check meaning and pronunciation of unknown words.

d • Demonstrate the activity by eliciting the first answer from the class (*a place where people can keep their money*). Put SS into pairs and give them two minutes to think of the remaining definitions. Check answers. Accept any suggestions that define the words well and don't worry if SS make mistakes with relative pronouns at this point.

> **Possible answers**
> **a bank** – a place where you keep your money
> **a boring person** – someone who is not interesting
> **the brain** – the organ inside your head which you use to think and feel
> **a star** – a famous person in film or music
> **a friend** – someone you know well and like
> **a secret** – something that only a few people know about and don't want others to know about

e • Put SS into pairs. Tell them to match the words in **d** to the definitions in the *Devil's Dictionary*. Check answers.

1 a star	**3** a boring person	**5** a bank
2 a secret	**4** a friend	**6** the brain

2 GRAMMAR defining relative clauses

a • Get SS to focus on the definitions in **1e** again and to look at when the words *who, which,* and *where* are used. Get feedback.

> We use **who** with people, **which** with things, and **where** with places.

b • Tell SS to go to **Grammar Bank 1D** on *p.126*. Go through the rules with the class. Model and drill the example sentences.

Grammar notes

- In conversation native speakers often use *that* instead of *who* and *which*, e.g. *A waiter is somebody that works in a restaurant.* It is better for SS to get used to using *who* and *which* in this kind of relative clause because when they later learn non-defining clauses, *that* cannot be used to replace *who* or *which.*
- The omission of relative pronouns in sentences like *This is the book I told you about* is presented in *New English File Intermediate.*

• Focus on the exercises for **1D** on *p.127*. SS do the exercises individually or in pairs. Check answers.

a 1 who 3 which 5 who
2 which 4 where 6 which

b 1 C 3 A 5 D
2 E 4 F 6 B

c 1 She's the woman who lives next door to me.
2 That's the shop where I bought my dress.
3 He's the actor who was in *Friends.*
4 They're the children who broke my window.
5 This is the restaurant where they do great pasta.
6 That's the switch which controls the central heating.
7 He's the teacher who teaches my sister.
8 That's the room where we have our meetings.

- Tell SS to go back to the main lesson on *p.10*.

c
- Give SS a few minutes to decide which three things they are going to talk about and what they are going to say.
- In pairs SS take it in turns to talk about the things they have chosen. Encourage the SS who are listening to ask follow-up questions to get more information.

3 LISTENING

a 1.10
- Focus on the question. Play the tape/CD. SS listen for the rules of the game.

1.10 CD1 Track 11

(tapescript in Student's Book on *p.118*)

P = presenter, A = Adam

P Good evening, ladies and gentlemen and welcome to *What's the word?* And our first contestant tonight is Adam. Hello Adam. Are you nervous?
A Just a bit.
P Well try and relax Adam and play *What's the word?* with us. In case you're watching the show for the first time **here's how we play the game. I have six cards with things, people, or places written on them. I'm going to give Adam definitions and he's going to try and guess the words on my six cards. But of course, I can't use any of the words on the cards in my definitions.** So, for example, if I have a card with *taxi driver*, I can't use *taxi* or *driver* in my definition. Are you ready Adam?
A Er yes.
P OK. You have two minutes to guess what's on the six cards starting NOW!

- Play the tape/CD again and get SS to compare what they understood with a partner. Then elicit the rules of the game show by asking these questions:
  1 *How many cards are there?* (six)
  2 *What's on the cards?* (people, things, or places)
  3 *Who is going to give definitions, the presenter or Adam?* (the presenter)
  4 *Who is going to guess the words?* (Adam/the contestant)
  5 *Which words can't the presenter use?* (the words on the card)
- To make the rules absolutely clear demonstrate the game to the class by drawing a card on the board and writing *taxi driver* on it. Explain that the presenter can't use *taxi* or *driver* in his definition. Elicit a possible definition, e.g. *A person who drives a car every day. He takes you to places and you pay him.*

b 1.11
- SS now listen to the rest of the show. Tell them that they have to listen to the presenter's definitions. They will not hear Adam's answers so they have to guess the six words on the card.
- Tell SS you are going to play the tape/CD twice. Explain that the first time you are going to play all the show and SS should try to write down some of the words. Tell SS not to call out the answers. Tell SS that the second time you are going to pause the tape to give SS time to write down each word.
- Play the tape/CD. Re-play any definitions that are causing a problem. Don't check answers yet.

1.11 1.12 CD1 Tracks 12+13

(tapescript in Student's Book on *p.118*)

P = presenter, A = Adam

P OK, you have two minutes to guess what's on the six cards, starting now! OK, Adam. Card number 1. It's a person. It's somebody who works in a restaurant.
A A cook.
P **No, no, it's the person who takes the food from the kitchen to the tables.**
A **Oh** (bleep)/(**a waiter**).
P **That's right**. Card number 2. It's a place. It's a place where you go when you want to buy something.
A A shop.
P **Yes, but it's a very big shop where you can buy anything.**
A **Is it** (bleep)/(**a department store**)**?**
P **Yes, well done**. OK, card number 3. It's a thing ... mmm. It's a thing which you use to talk to people.
A Your mouth?
P No, no, no. **It's a kind of machine. It's very small. And nearly everybody has one nowadays.**
A (bleep)/(**mobile phone**)?
P **That's it!** Card number 4. It's an adjective. It's the opposite of fat.
A Thin?
P **It's like thin, but it means thin and attractive.**
A (bleep)/(**slim**)?
P **Yes**! Number 5. It's an adjective again. Er ... It's how you feel when you have a lot of work.
A Worried?
P No, but it's similar to worried. It's how you feel when you have a lot of things to do but you don't have time to do them.
A **Busy?**
P **No!**
A (bleep)/(**stressed**)?
P **Yes, brilliant**. And card number six, the last one. OK. It's a verb. For example, you do this with the TV.
A Watch?
P No. It's what you do when you finish watching the TV.
A Er ... go to bed?
P **No, you do it to the TV before you go to bed.**
A **Is it** (bleep)/(**turn off**)?
P **Yes!**

c 1.12
- SS listen to short extracts from the show, (**bold** in tapescripts above) and listen to Adam's answers (in brackets above). Check answers.

1 waiter	3 mobile phone	5 stressed
2 department store	4 slim	6 turn off

4 VOCABULARY paraphrasing

a • Focus on the question and go through the possible answers **a–c** making sure SS understand them.

• Elicit answers and try to get a mini discussion going about the relative merits of each one.

> **a** is clearly the worst option.
> **b** can be useful sometimes, e.g. miming an action like *throw* or *bend*.
> **c** This is the best option.

b 1.13

• Tell SS that they are going to learn some useful expressions to help them explain words they don't know.

• In pairs, SS try to complete the ten expressions using the words in the box.

• Play the tape/CD for them to listen and check their answers.

> 1.13 CD1 Track 14
> 1 It's **somebody** who works in a restaurant.
> 2 It's the **person** who takes the food from the kitchen to the tables.
> 3 It's a **place** where you go when you want to buy something.
> 4 It's a **thing** which you use to talk.
> 5 It's a **kind** of machine.
> 6 It's the **opposite** of fat.
> 7 It's **like** thin, but it means thin and attractive.
> 8 It's **similar** to worried.
> 9 It's **how** you feel when you have a lot of things to do.
> 10 For **example**, you do this with the TV.

c • In pairs, SS write definitions for the five words. Write some of their answers on the board.

> **Possible answers**
> 1 It's somebody who visits another country on holiday.
> 2 It's a place where you can do sport.
> 3 It's a thing which you use to open or close a door.
> 4 It's how you feel when you have a problem.
> 5 You do this when somebody says something which is funny.

Extra challenge

Play *What's the word?* Get SS to sit in pairs, **A** facing the board and **B** with his/her back to the board. Then write the following six words on the board in a circle:

umbrella	*cousin*	*park*
art gallery	*nurse*	*banana*

Tell the **A**s they have one minute to try to define the words to **B** using *It's a person who, A thing which,* etc. **B** should either say the word quietly or write it down for **A** to check. The first **A** to communicate all six words to **B** is the winner.

Then they swap roles. Use these words for **B**.

policeman	*bus stop*	*doctor*
stamp	*hotel*	*newspaper*

5 SPEAKING

a • You will probably need at least 10–15 minutes for this activity. Focus on the crossword and demonstrate the activity SS are going to do in **b**. Elicit the meaning of *down* and *across*. Teach SS to say *What's 1 across?, What's 2 down?* and give them definitions of the two missing words in the crossword puzzle.

> 1 **across** definition: It's a kind of machine which you have in your house. You can watch the news or films on it (television).
> 2 **down** definition: It's a job. It's a person who designs roads and bridges (engineer).

b • Put SS into pairs, **A** and **B** and get them to sit face to face. Tell them to go to **Communication 1D *Crossword,*** **A** on *p.108*, **B** on *p.112*.

• Go through the instructions with them and make sure SS are clear what they have to do. If necessary, demonstrate with the first missing word for **A**.

⚠ If SS don't know what any of their words mean, they should put up their hand for you to go and help them.

• When SS have finished, they compare their completed crosswords to make sure they have the same answers.

• Tell SS to go back to the main lesson on *p.11*.

6 PRONUNCIATION using a dictionary

a • Focus on the dictionary extracts and on the phonetic transcription of the two words (*busy* and *guitar*). Focus on how the apostrophe (ˈ) shows which syllable is stressed.

• Elicit the pronunciation of the two words and show the correct stress by writing the words on the board with the stressed syllable underlined (<u>bu</u>sy, gui<u>tar</u>).

b • Again, focus attention on the phonetic transcription. Put SS into pairs and give them a couple of minutes to decide how the words are pronounced, using the **Sound Bank** on *p.156* to help them with phonetic symbols. Elicit answers.

Pronunciation notes

• You should make sure that SS have got a good dictionary and can use it. Having a good bi-lingual dictionary is still very important at this level although you may prefer SS to use a monolingual dictionary.

• It is worth you and SS investing time to learn the example words and symbols in the **Sound Bank**. This will help SS to work out the pronunciation of words in their dictionary.

• Encourage SS to use their dictionaries to check pronunciation of new words.

Extra photocopiable activities

Grammar
relative clauses *p.142*
Communicative
What's the word? p.186 (instructions *p.175*)

HOMEWORK

Study Link Workbook *pp.10–11*

1 Practical English at the airport

Function Answering questions at immigration
Language *I'm here for a conference,* etc.

Lesson plan

This is the first in a series of eight Practical English lessons which teach SS language to help them survive in travel and social situations. There is a story line, which is a continuation of the story in the Practical English lessons in *New English File Elementary*. However the story line in this book is completely self-standing, and so it is not a problem if your SS did not use *New English File Elementary*. These lessons feature two characters, Mark Ryder, an American who works for a music company called MTC and Allie Gray, his British counterpart. In the first part of the lesson SS meet Mark, who gives a quick summary of how he met Allie and what has happened up to now. He then explains that Allie is about to arrive in San Francisco for a conference, and the other seven episodes all take place there. As these lessons are all set in the United States, SS also learn some useful travel words in US English, e.g. *check* (bill), *parking lot* (car park), etc. These are always highlighted in an information box.

Study Link These lessons are on the *New English File Pre-intermediate* Video, which can be used instead of the Class Cassette/CD (see introduction *p.9*). The main functional section of each episode (the second section) is also on the MultiROM with additional activities.

Optional lead-in (books closed)

- Introduce this lesson by giving SS the information above (in L1 if you prefer). If your SS used *New English File Elementary*, ask them if they can remember Mark and Allie and elicit as much information about them as you can.

THE STORY SO FAR

1.14

- SS listen to Mark introducing himself and explaining how he and Allie met. Focus on the photos and elicit/explain that they are Mark and Allie, the two main characters in the story. Explain that they met in *New English File Elementary*, and that here Mark is going to introduce himself and tell them what has happened up to now.
- Focus on the questions. Play the tape/CD once the whole way through and tell SS just to listen. Then play it again, pausing if necessary to give SS time to write their answers. Get them to compare answers before checking.

1.14 CD1 Track 15

(tapescript in Student's Book on *p.118*)

MARK Hi. My name's Mark Ryder. I'm American and I live in San Francisco. I work for a music company called MTC. I'm divorced and I have a daughter.
Last month I went to England on a work trip, and I met Allie. She's British, and she works for MTC in the UK. We had a great five days. We went out for coffee. We went shopping. It was my birthday, and she bought me a present. We went out for dinner. I really liked her, and I think she liked me too.
I invited her to a conference in San Francisco, and she said yes. And now I'm at the airport. I'm waiting for her to arrive.

Extra challenge

If your SS used *New English File Elementary*, tell them to answer questions 1–5 from memory before they listen, and to guess the answer to question 6. SS work in pairs.

1 Mark is American, from California, and Allie is British.
2 They work for MTC, a music company.
3 They met when Mark came to London.
4 They went out for coffee, shopping, and dinner.
5 Yes, very well.
6 He's at the airport in San Francisco waiting for Allie to arrive.

- Elicit anything else that SS remember about what happened when Mark and Allie were in London.

Extra support

If you have time, you could get SS to listen to the tape/CD with the tapescript on *p.118* so they can see exactly what they understood. Translate/explain any new words or phrases.

AT IMMIGRATION

a 1.15

- Tell SS to cover the dialogue with their hand or a piece of paper. Focus on the picture. Ask *Who's the woman with fair hair?* (Allie) *Where is she?* (At immigration) *Does the immigration officer look friendly?*

⚠ If you think that SS won't cover their books properly, you could get them to close their books at this stage and write the first task on the board.

Extra challenge

Ask SS to predict what questions they think the immigration officer might ask Allie.

- Play the tape/CD once for SS to listen for the answer to the question. Check answers.

She's going to stay for a week.

b • Now tell SS to uncover the dialogue (or open their books). Explain that the **YOU HEAR** part is what they need to understand, and the **YOU SAY** part contains the phrases they need to be able to say.

- Give SS a minute to read through the dialogue and guess the missing words. Then play the tape/CD again, for them to complete the dialogue.
- Go through the dialogue line by line with SS and check answers. Highlight that *ma'am* is US for *madam*, and that *purpose* = *reason* but is more formal, and often used by officials.

1.15 **1.16** CD1 Tracks 16+17

IO=Immigration officer, A=Allie
IO Good evening, **ma'am**.
A Good evening. *(repeat)*
IO **Where** are you arriving from?
A From London. *(repeat)*
IO **What's** the purpose of your visit?
A Business. I'm here for a conference. *(repeat)*
IO **How** long are you staying in the US?
A A week. *(repeat)*
IO **Where** are you staying?
A In San Francisco. At the Pacific View Hotel. *(repeat)*
IO **Do** you know anybody here?
A Yes, Mark Ryder. *(repeat)*
IO **Is** he family or a friend?
A He's a colleague – and a friend. *(repeat)*
IO **Do** you have his phone number?
A Yes, his mobile is 405 655 7182. *(repeat)*
IO **Is** this your first visit to the US?
A Yes, it is. *(repeat)*
IO Enjoy your stay in San Francisco.
A Thank you. *(repeat)*

c **1.16**
- Now focus on the **YOU SAY** phrases. Tell SS they're going to hear the dialogue again. They repeat the **YOU SAY** phrases when they hear the beep. Encourage them to copy the rhythm.
- Play the tape/CD, pausing if necessary for SS to repeat the phrases.

d • Put SS into pairs, **A** and **B. A** is the Immigration Officer, **B** is Allie. Tell **B** to close his/her book and try to remember the phrases. Then **A** and **B** swap roles.

Extra support

Let SS practise the dialogue in pairs first, both with books open.

⚠ If **B** wants to use his/her own name instead of Allie that's fine, but remind **A**s to use *sir* (instead of *ma'am*) for the first line of the dialogue if they're talking to a man.

SOCIAL ENGLISH Allie arrives

a **1.17**
- Focus on the picture. Ask SS *Where is it?* (The Arrivals hall).
- Focus on the instructions and get SS to read the questions. Play the tape/CD at least twice.
- Check answers.

1 Eleven hours.
2 Because the people next to her had a baby.
3 a 7 p.m. b 3 a.m.
4 To her hotel.
5 In the parking lot/car park.

- Elicit that *parking lot* is US for *car park*, and focus on the information box.
- Ask SS if Mark and Allie are happy to see each other.

1.17 CD1 Track 18

(tapescript in Student's Book on *p.119*)
M=Mark, A=Allie
M Allie, hi!
A Hi Mark.
M You look **great**!
A You too. How are you?
M I'm fine. How was the **flight**?
A Long! Eleven hours.
M You must be really **tired**.
A Yes. I couldn't sleep at all. The people next to me had a baby with them. What's the time here? I need to change my watch.
M It's seven in the evening.
A It's three in the morning for me.
M OK, I'm going to take you right to the hotel and you can rest.
A Fine. Sorry!
M You are going to love San Francisco! I'm so **pleased** you came!
A Me too. It's great to see you **again**.
M Come on. My car's in the parking lot. Let's go.

Extra support

If there's time, you could get SS to listen again with the tapescript on *p.119* so they can see exactly what Mark and Allie said, and see how much they understood. Translate/explain any new words/phrases.

b • Focus on the **USEFUL PHRASES**. Get SS to see if they can remember any of the missing words. Play the tape/CD again and check answers.

c **1.18**
- Play the tape/CD pausing after each phrase for SS to repeat. Encourage them to copy the rhythm.
- In a monolingual class get SS to decide together what the equivalent phrase would be in their language.

1.18 CD1 Track 19

M You look great!
M How was the flight?
M You must be really tired.
M I'm so pleased you came!
A It's great to see you again.

Extra challenge

Get SS to roleplay the second conversation in pairs using the tapescript on *p.119*. Let SS read their parts first and then try to act it from memory.

HOMEWORK

Study Link **Workbook** *p.12*

1 Writing Describing yourself

Lesson plan

This is the first of eight Writing lessons, one at the end of Files 1–8. In today's world of e-mail communication, being able to write in English is an important skill for many SS. We suggest that you go through the exercises in class, but set the actual writing (the last activity) for homework.

In this first lesson SS consolidate the language they have learnt in File 1 by writing an informal e-mail about themselves.

a • Focus on the e-mail. Ask SS *Who's it to? Who's it from? Do they know each other?* and elicit that Daniel and Alessandra are probably Internet penfriends.

• Focus on the instructions. Point out that the ten mistakes are underlined. Give SS, in pairs, five minutes to decide whether each mistake is grammar, punctuation, or spelling and correct them.

Extra idea

Tell SS to mark the mistakes G, P, or Sp (= Grammar, Punctuation, Spelling).

• Check answers.

italian	P	Italian
have 19 years old	G	am 19 years old
studing	Sp	studying
foto	Sp	photo
greens	G	green
frendly	Sp	friendly
mean	G	means
dont	P	don't
becuase	Sp	because
friday	P	Friday

• Remind SS that countries, nationalities, language, days of the week, and months all begin with a capital letter in English.

b • Focus on the instructions. Set a time limit for SS to read the e-mail again. Then either get SS to cover the text and answer the questions in writing, or get them to close their books and ask the questions round the class. Check answers.

Extra idea

SS could also ask and answer orally in pairs.

1 From Argentina.
2 Because her grandmother was Italian.
3 In Mendoza.
4 Her parents and two brothers.
5 She's a student. She's studying computer science.
6 Green.
7 No, she's quite extrovert.
8 Reading and going to the cinema.
9 On Friday afternoon.

Write a similar e-mail about you

Either give SS at least fifteen minutes to write the e-mail in class, following the instructions, or set it for homework. If SS do the writing in class, get them to swap their e-mail with another student to read and check for mistakes before you collect them all in.

⚠ Tell SS to set their e-mail out in paragraphs as in the model e-mail.

Extra idea

Tell SS that there are many websites on the Internet where learners of English can find penfriends to practise their English and meet people from other countries. Encourage them to find a penfriend.

• Finally, focus on the Information box and check that SS know the meaning of these verbs in their own language.

1 REVISE & CHECK

The File finishes with two pages of revision. The first page, **What do you remember?**, revises the grammar, vocabulary, and pronunciation. These exercises can be done individually or in pairs, in class or at home, depending on the needs of your SS and the class time available. If SS do them in class, check which SS are still having problems, or any areas which need further revision. The second page, **What can you do?**, presents SS with a series of skills-based challenges. First, there is a reading text (which is of a slightly higher level than those in the File) and two listening exercises. Finally, there is a speaking activity which measures SS' ability to use the language of the File orally. We suggest that you use some or all of these activities according to the needs of your class.

GRAMMAR

1 b 2 c 3 a 4 c 5 b 6 a 7 c 8 a 9 c 10 b

VOCABULARY

a 1 How 2 mean 3 to 4 on 5 Have

b 1 niece (female family member)
2 shy (personality, not appearance)
3 generous (positive adjective)
4 fingers (normally ten, not two)
5 fair (not a part of the body)

c 1 hard-working 2 post office 3 musician 4 drink
5 pasta

PRONUNCIATION

a 1 J 2 work 3 heart 4 hear 5 give

b add<u>ress</u> uni<u>ver</u>sity <u>ex</u>trovert <u>sto</u>mach ex<u>am</u>ple

CAN YOU UNDERSTAND THIS TEXT?

a Space invaders D Small children A
Conversation makers B Nervous fliers C

b 1, 3

c 1 a 2 b 3 b 4 b 5 a

CAN YOU UNDERSTAND THESE PEOPLE?

1.19 CD1 Track 20

1
A When are you having your party?
B Well, my birthday's on the sixth. But it's a Wednesday, so I'm having my party on the ninth.
A Is that Friday?
B No, it's Saturday.

2
A Your mother looks really young. How old is she?
B Nearly 60.
A Wow, she looks more like 50.
B Well, in fact she's 59.

3
A Hello, Mr Jarvis. What's the problem?
B It's my leg – well, my knee to be precise. It's very painful. I can't move my leg at all.
A Is it the left or the right knee?
B Just the right knee, the left one's fine.
A Let's have a look.

4
A Oh John, look at that painting. It's wonderful!
B Which one?
A The one of the woman combing her hair.
B Do you really like it? I don't. I don't like the way he paints women. I prefer the one of the boy playing the guitar. The blue one.

5
A Can I help you?
B Yes, I'm look for a thing which connects my camera to the computer.
A Is it a digital camera?
B Yes.
A So you need a USB cable. Is your computer a PC?
B Yes.
A Right. Here you are. One USB cable.

a 1 b 2 a 3 b 4 a 5 c

1.20 CD1 Track 21

A Who's that?
B That's my brother, Gary. He's 19 now, but he was a lot younger there.
A Is he at university?
B No, he's travelling in the States. He's going to university next year.
A Do you get on well?
B Quite well. He's OK – but he's really lazy, which annoys me sometimes.
A Who are they?
B They're my favourite cousins. Serena lives in France – she's a journalist – and Alice is a student.
A What's she studying?
B Economics. At Sussex University.
A Are they family or friends?
B They're friends. That's Martin and that's Bill, the one with dark hair and glasses.
A Martin's tall! Is he a basketball player?
B No, in fact he hates sport! He and Bill work in a software company. I met them through work.

a 1 Alice 2 Serena 3 Bill 4 Martin 5 Gary

CAN YOU SAY THIS IN ENGLISH?

b 1 do 2 Is 3 do 4 Does 5 are

Extra photocopiable activities

Quicktest 1 *p.231*

2 A

G past simple regular and irregular verbs
V holidays
P *-ed* endings, irregular verbs

Right place, wrong time

File 2 overview

File 2 focuses on using past tenses. The past simple is revised in **2A** and the past continuous is presented in **2B**. **2C** focuses on question formation with or without auxiliaries. **2D** consolidates the two main past tenses and presents linkers: *so, because, but,* and *although.*

Lesson plan

The past simple (regular and irregular verbs) is revised in detail in this lesson through the context of holidays. SS learn new holiday vocabulary, and the pronunciation focus is on *-ed* endings and irregular verbs.

Optional lead-in (books closed)

Write MY LAST HOLIDAY on the board and tell SS they have two minutes to find out from you as much as possible about your last holiday. Elicit questions in the past simple, e.g. *Where did you go?,* etc.

1 VOCABULARY holidays

a • Books open. Focus on the instructions. Give SS a minute to write five things. They compare their list with a partner's.

• Elicit some of the verbs SS have used and write them on the board, e.g. *swim, sunbathe, go sightseeing.*

Extra idea

Tell SS to decide which activity on the board is their favourite and take a vote with a show of hands.

b • Tell SS to go to **Vocabulary Bank *Holidays*** on *p.147.* Focus on the pictures. Give SS two minutes to do **1a** in pairs. Check answers and model and drill pronunciation. Make sure SS are clear about the difference between *go out* (leave the house) and *go away* (leave your town).

a 1 go swimming/sailing	**6** go for a walk
2 go abroad	**7** go sightseeing
3 go by car, etc.	**8** go out at night
4 go to the beach	**9** go camping
5 go away for the weekend	

• Focus on **1b.** Get SS to cover the verbs and use the pictures to test themselves or a partner.

• Focus on **2a.** SS complete the phrases in pairs. Check answers. Highlight the difference between *hire* and *rent.* We normally use *rent* for a flat or something that we pay to use over a long period of time, and *hire* with something we use for a short time, e.g. *a car.*

stay in a hotel/campsite	**spend** money/time
take photos	**rent** an apartment
buy souvenirs	**walk** in the mountains/ around the town
sunbathe on the beach	**meet** friends
have a good time	**hire** a car

• Focus on **2b.** Get SS to test themselves by covering the verbs and remembering the phrases.

• Focus on **3a.** Give SS a minute to match the words and pictures. Check answers and model and drill pronunciation. Highlight that the words are all adjectives except *rain* and *snow* which are verbs or nouns, and remind SS that if we are talking about the weather now we use the present continuous, e.g. *It's raining/snowing.*

a 1 rain **2** boiling **3** foggy **4** freezing **5** windy **6** cloudy **7** snow **8** hot **9** sunny **10** cold

• Focus on **3b.** Read the example question and answer. Drill the question *What was the weather like?* Ask SS *What was the weather like yesterday?*

• Get SS to test each other in pairs by pointing at the pictures and asking and answering about the weather in the past simple.

Study Link SS can find more practice of these phrases on the MultiROM and on the *New English File Pre-intermediate* website.

• Tell SS to go back to the main lesson on *p.16.*

2 READING

a • Focus on the title of the text and ask SS why they think people might go on holiday to 'the right place' (i.e. a beautiful place) but at the wrong time. Elicit ideas, e.g. *there was bad weather, a political crisis.*

• Focus on the photos. Ask SS what they can see.

• Give SS five minutes to read the three letters and match each one with a photo. Tell them to try to guess new words from context as they read. Get SS to compare ideas and then check answers.

1 A   2 C   3 B

Extra challenge

Get SS to cover the texts and, in pairs, say why the people were in the right place but at the wrong time.

b • Focus on the task and give SS a couple of minutes to complete the sentences. Get SS to compare their answers with a partner's and then check answers.

1 Kelly	3 Tim	5 Gabriela
2 Gabriela	4 Kelly	6 Tim

c • Get SS to read the three letters again and find the five remaining words. They should write them down and underline the stressed syllable.

• Check answers and model and drill pronunciation. They should be said with strong sentence stress. Point out that as these adjectives already mean *very good* or *vey bad,* you can't use them with *very,* e.g. NOT ~~*very lovely*~~.

Very good	Very bad
lovely (letter 1)	awful (letter 2)
great (letter 1)	terrible (letter 3)
fantastic (letter 1)	
wonderful (letter 3)	

- Finally ask SS if they've ever been on holiday 'in the right place but at the wrong time'.

3 GRAMMAR past simple regular and irregular

a • Focus on the verbs and tell SS they are a mixture of regular and irregular verbs. Elicit the first one (*was/were*) and then give SS a minute to do the others in pairs. Encourage SS to do as many as they can without looking back at the text.

- Check answers and make sure SS know what they mean. Don't spend too much time on the pronunciation, as SS will be focussing on this later.

be was/were (irregular)	**sunbathe** sunbathed (regular)
want wanted (regular)	**rent** rented (regular)
go went (irregular)	**make** made (irregular)
	let let (irregular)

b • Focus on the instructions and tell SS to find and underline more positive past simple verbs in the texts. Check answers and then elicit the infinitives.

Text 2
decided – decide, booked – book, got – get, sat – sit, argued – argue

Text 3
broke up – break up, decided – decide, looked – look, saw – see, said – say, went – go, had – have, spent – spend

c • Tell SS to find and underline two negative past simple verbs. Put SS into pairs. Give them a minute to remember how to make negatives and questions. Check answers.

Possible answers

didn't want	didn't need
didn't smile	didn't tell
couldn't sleep	couldn't escape

normal verbs:
[–] = *didn't* + infinitive, e.g. *I didn't see it, I didn't want it.*
[?] = *Did* (*you* etc.) + infinitive, e.g. *Did you go...?*
***was / were*:**
[–] = *wasn't* OR *weren't*, e.g. *It wasn't cold.*
[?] = *Were* (*you* etc.)?, *Was* (*he* etc.), e.g. *Was it nice?*
***could*:**
[–] = *couldn't*, e.g. *We couldn't stay very long*, etc.
[?] = *Could* (*I*, you etc.)?, e.g. *Could you swim there?*

d • Tell SS to go to **Grammar Bank 2A** on *p.128*. Go through the charts and rules with the class. Model and drill the example sentences.

Grammar notes

You may also want to remind SS:

- that irregular forms (*went, had*, etc.) are only used in (+) sentences. In (?) and (–) the infinitive is used after *did/didn't*.
- of the word order in questions (**ASI** and **QUASI**). See **Grammar Bank 1A** on *p.126*.
- that the vast majority of verbs are regular. The irregular verbs need to be learnt, but SS already know the most common ones.

- Tell SS to go to **Irregular verbs** on *p.155* and explain that this is their reference list. Get SS to go through the list quickly in pairs, checking that they know what the verbs mean. Encourage them to highlight verbs they didn't know or had forgotten the past form of. Let SS test each other or test round the class.
- Tell SS to go to *p.129* and focus on the exercises for **2A**. SS do the exercises individually or in pairs. Check answers.

a

1 drove	**6** were	**11** went	**16** was
2 broke	**7** didn't know	**12** bought	**17** started
3 spent	**8** found	**13** wanted	**18** left
4 got	**9** stayed	**14** didn't have	
5 couldn't	**10** saw	**15** was	

b
1 Did you have a good time?
2 Who did you go with?
3 Where did you stay?
4 Why didn't you like it?
5 How much did the plane ticket cost?

- Tell SS to go back to the main lesson on *p.17*.

Extra idea

Remind SS that a very good way of learning irregular verbs is through reading stories. Show them a few Graded Readers if you can, and if you have a class library encourage them to take out a book to read at home.

4 PRONUNCIATION regular and irregular verbs

a 2.1

- Remind SS of the three different pronunciations of the *-ed* ending (see Pronunciation notes). Play the tape/CD for SS to listen and repeat.
- Elicit that you only pronounce the *e* in *-ed* endings when verbs finish in a /t/ or /d/ sound, and then the *-ed* ending is pronounced /ɪd/.

2.1 CD1 Track 22
1 We booked a holiday.
2 We walked to the hotel.
3 We sunbathed.
4 We argued all day.
5 They rented a house.
6 We decided to go to Sweden.

Pronunciation notes

- The regular past simple ending *-ed* can be pronounced in three different ways:
  1 *-ed* is pronounced /t/ after verbs ending in these unvoiced sounds (sounds made without using the voice box): /k/, /p/, /f/, /s/, /ʃ/, and /tʃ/, e.g. *looked, hoped, laughed, passed, washed, watched.*
  2 After voiced endings (sounds made using the voice box) *-ed* is pronounced /d/, e.g. *arrived, changed, showed.* This group is the largest.

3 After verbs ending in /t/ or /d/ the pronunciation of *-ed* is /ɪd/, e.g. *hated, decided.*

- The difference between 1 and 2 is very small and only occasionally causes communication problems. The most important thing is for SS to be clear about rule 3.

b • Put SS into pairs. Give them a minute to practise saying the verbs in the past. Draw three columns on the board for the sounds.

c 2.2

• Play the tape/CD for SS to hear the verbs. Then elicit which column they go in and write them on the board.

2.2 CD1 Track 23

asked	smiled
hated	stayed
needed	talked

/t/	/d/	/ɪd/
asked	smiled	hated
talked	stayed	needed

d • Focus on the verbs. Tell SS to say them out loud in pairs to find the ones with a different sound. Check answers and ask for the infinitives. Practise the pronunciation.

1 told /təʊld/ The other verbs are all /ɔː/
2 spoke /spəʊk/ The other verbs are all /ʊ/
3 said /sed/ The other verbs are all /eɪ/

5 LISTENING

a 2.3

• Focus on the photo and ask SS if they know where it is (Ibiza). Focus on the question and the three answer options. Play the tape/CD once. Check answers.

2 Because the place was very noisy.

2.3 CD1 Track 24

(tapescript in Student's Book on *p.119*)

P = Presenter host, S = Sean

P Hello and welcome to today's *Holiday Programme.* Today we've asked you to call in with your holiday horror stories – holidays where things went wrong. Our first caller today is Sean from Belfast. Hi Sean.
S Hello.
P So where was this holiday?
S Well, this didn't happen to me, it happened to my aunt and uncle, last summer.
P Where did they go?
S To Ibiza.
P A fantastic place for a holiday.
S Yes, fantastic place if you're seventeen – but they're nearly **seventy**!
P Oh ...
S And they wanted a **quiet holiday, a relaxing holiday** – you know. They like walking in the countryside, sitting on quiet beaches, things like that. They **don't go abroad very often**, but they wanted to do something different.
P So why did they choose Ibiza? It's the party island.
S Yes, it is now **but they didn't know that**. You see, they first went to Ibiza in the **late sixties**, when it was a beautiful, peaceful island with traditional cafés and restaurants, deserted beaches. And this was exactly what they wanted. So they **looked on the Internet** – my uncle loves his computer – and they booked a hotel for a week in the same part of the island where they'd been before. And they found some cheap flights. It all seemed so perfect.
P So what happened?
S You can imagine. It was a complete disaster. **Their hotel was in San Antonio, a resort that's full of bars and discos**. There was music until 5.00 in the morning, noise of car doors opening, motorbikes, and people shouting. They couldn't sleep at all. They were too tired to do anything during the day. They tried to get some sleep, but they couldn't because it was too hot. When they came home they were in a state of shock.
P Oh dear. What are their plans for this year?
S I don't know. **I think they'll probably stay at home this year ... and next year** ... and probably the year after that.
P Thank you Sean. And now ...

b • Now focus on sentences 1–9. Tell SS they are all wrong and give them a moment to read the sentences. In pairs, SS try to remember the correct information.

• Play the tape/CD again. Give SS time to compare their answers in pairs and then check answers.

2 They're nearly seventy.
3 They wanted a quiet, relaxing holiday.
4 They don't go abroad very often.
5 They didn't know it was 'The Party Island'.
6 They first went there in the 1960s.
7 They booked the holiday on the Internet.
8 The hotel was in a resort full of bars and discos.
9 They'll probably stay at home next year.

6 SPEAKING

a • Focus on the questions and elicit what words are missing (*did you* in all questions except the fifth, where SS have to change *be* to *were you*). Drill the complete questions quickly round the class.

b • Put SS into pairs, **A** and **B**. Focus on the instructions and give SS time to plan their questions. SS could talk about another holiday they remember well. Or they could talk about a holiday where they were in the right place at the wrong time.

• As speak and answer Bs questions. Monitor and correct.

c • SS swap roles.

Extra photocopiable activities

Grammar

past simple regular and irregular *p.143*

Communicative

Irregular past simple bingo *p.187* (instructions *p.175*)

HOMEWORK

Study Link **Workbook** *pp.13–14*

G past continuous
V prepositions of time and place: *at, in, on*
P /ə/

2B A moment in time

Lesson plan

In this lesson the past continuous is presented through the context of some famous photos taken by the Scottish photographer Harry Benson. The photos captured three dramatic and historic moments in time. SS then listen to the story behind another famous photo, of two lovers in Paris. The vocabulary focus is on the correct use of the prepositions *at, in,* and *on*, both for time (revision) and place. The lesson ends with SS telling each other about famous photos and finally talking about their own favourites. This lesson links to **Writing 2** *p.25* which could be done as a follow on to this lesson, or can be left until the end of the File.

Optional lead-in (books closed)

Write PHOTO on the board. Ask SS what it is short for (*photograph*) and elicit the verb we use with it (*take*). Elicit/teach the words for a person who takes photos (*photographer*) and the subject (*photography*). Write them on the board and model the pronunciation. Ask SS how the syllable stress changes and underline it on the board.

<u>pho</u>tograph	pho<u>to</u>grapher	pho<u>to</u>graphy

1 GRAMMAR past continuous

a • Books open. Focus on the three photos and tell SS to cover the text. Focus on the questions. Elicit ideas from SS but don't tell them the answers yet.

b • Focus on the introduction to the text. Tell SS to quickly read it and ask a few comprehension questions, e.g. *Who is Harry Benson?* (a photographer) *How many years did he work as a photographer?* (50 years) *Who did he take photos for?* (national newspapers and magazines)

- Now focus on the rest of the text and give SS two minutes to read it and match each paragraph with a photo. Check answers and elicit/explain the meaning of any words they don't know, e.g. *cabinet, staff, scandal, stones*, etc.
- Elicit/explain:

  In text 1 the American President was Richard Nixon. Nixon was a Republican and he was forced to resign after several men broke into the Watergate Hotel, Washington (the Democratic Party's headquarters) and tried to bug the telephones. The men had been paid by Nixon's election committee.

  The wall in text 2 was the Berlin Wall, which divided East and West Berlin. It was built in 1961 to prevent East Germans escaping from communist rule. It was knocked down in 1989.

  The group in text 3 was the Beatles.
- Highlight the use of *picture* in paragraph 1 as an alternative to *photo* or *photograph*.

1C	2A	3B

c • Put SS into pairs. Focus on the instructions. Get SS to read the three paragraphs again and to try and memorize the information.

- Then get SS to cover the text and to try to remember as much information as they can about each picture.
- Finally, try to elicit from the whole class most or all of the information in the three paragraphs.

d • Focus on the highlighted verbs in the first paragraph. Elicit/explain that *I took this picture* is the past simple and *He was saying goodbye, were standing, were feeling* are the past continuous (i.e. the past version of the present continuous). Elicit that the past simple is used to talk about a finished action, i.e. taking the photo, and that the past continuous is used to describe what was happening when the photo was taken.

Extra idea

Write on the board:

1 When my friend arrived, we had dinner.

2 When my friend arrived, we were having dinner.

Ask SS what the difference is, and elicit that in **1** we had dinner after my friend arrived, but in **2** we were *in the middle* of dinner when my friend arrived. You could draw a time line on the board to illustrate this.

e • Tell SS to go to **Grammar Bank 2B** on *p.128*. Go through the charts and rules with the class. Model and drill the example sentences.

Grammar notes

- If SS have an equivalent of this tense in their L1, then it doesn't normally cause problems. If they don't, it's important to make the use very clear (see **Extra idea** above).
- We often use the past continuous at the beginning of a story to set the scene and to say what was happening, e.g. *On April 1st I* ***was staying*** *with some friends in the country. It was a sunny day and we* ***were sunbathing*** *in the garden.*

  Very often these 'actions in progress' (past continuous) are 'interrupted' by a short, completed action (past simple), e.g. *Suddenly my mobile* ***rang***. *It* ***was*** *a woman. She* ***said*** *she* ***was*** *a journalist.*
- Highlight the similarity in form with the present continuous. It is identical except for using *was/were* instead of *am/is/are*.

- Focus on the exercises for **2B** on *p.129*. SS do the exercises individually or in pairs. Check answers.

a 1 was working	5 wasn't listening
2 were waiting	6 was driving
3 Was ... wearing	7 wasn't raining
4 were ... doing	
b 1 broke, was playing	4 didn't see, was working
2 Were ... driving, stopped	5 called, was talking
3 was snowing, left	

- Tell SS to go back to the main lesson on *p.19*.

2 READING & LISTENING

a • Focus on the photo on *p.19* and ask SS if they've ever seen it and where it is (Paris). Discuss the questions with the whole class and elicit answers/ideas. Write their ideas on the board but do not give them the answers at this stage.

b • Get SS to read the text about Willy Ronis and check their answers to **a**.
• Discuss the other two questions with the whole class then go through the text again and explain/translate any new words that are causing problems, e.g. *each other, balcony, luckily, everywhere*, etc.

c 2.4
• Now tell SS that they are going to hear Marinette and Henri, the two people in the photo as they are today, talking about their photo.
• Play the tape/CD once. Ask SS *What do they do now?* (They work in a café.), *Are they still together?* (Yes, they're married.), *Are they still in love?* (Marinette says: 'It's difficult to stay in love when you see your husband every day at home and work too.')

2.4 CD1 Track 25
(tapescript in Student's Book on *p.119*)
M = Marinette, H = Henri
M We didn't know that our picture was so famous until thirty years later. One day I was working in the café when the man from the book shop next door came in. He was holding a new book which had a photo on the cover. Suddenly I said, 'I don't believe it! That's Henri and I when we were very young!' I remember that afternoon at the Bastille very well. When the man took that photo we were arguing! Henri was standing very near me. I was saying, 'Henri, don't stand so near me, there is somebody behind us.'
H We didn't know that the photographer was taking a photo of us. We were arguing. I can't remember exactly what we were arguing about. I think I was trying to kiss Marinette and she didn't want to. Or I think maybe we were arguing about our wedding – we got married a few months after the man took the photo.
M People who know this photo always think of us as the eternal lovers, like Romeo and Juliet. But life isn't like that. It's very difficult to stay in love when you see your husband every day at home *and* you see him every day at work too. And I'm very hard-working but Henri is still a dreamer. Ah, those were the days ...

d • Focus on the true/false questions and give SS a few moments to read them before you play the tape/CD again. Get SS to compare their answers in pairs and then check answers, asking SS to explain why the F sentences are false.

1 F They didn't know it was famous until thirty years later.
2 F The man from the bookshop brought the book to the café.
3 F They were arguing.
4 F She didn't want Henri to stand near her.
5 T 6 T 7 T
8 F A few months after. 9 T
10 F She's hard-working but he's a dreamer.

Extra support

If you have time, you could get SS to listen to the tape/CD with the tapescript on *p.119* so they can see exactly what they understood. Translate/explain any new words or phrases.

3 VOCABULARY *at, in, on*

a • Focus on the sentences and tell SS to complete them in pairs without looking back at any of the texts. Check answers.

1 on 2 in, in, in 3 on, in 4 at 5 at, at

b • Tell SS to go to **Vocabulary Bank *Prepositions*** on *p.148* and do **1 *at* / *in* / *on***. Although it will only take them a minute to do the exercise, tell them to read the rules carefully.
• Check answers and go through the examples. Remind SS that we don't use an article with *at home, at work, at school.*

in, on, at

⚠ With shops and buildings, e.g. *the supermarket, the cinema* you can use *at* or *in* when you answer the question *Where were you?* With *airport* and *station* we normally use *at.*
• Focus on **b**. Get SS to close their books and test them round the class, saying a word, e.g. *home* for SS to say the preposition *at.*
• Then put SS into pairs, **A** and **B**. **A** (book open) tests **B** (book closed) for two minutes. Then they swap roles. Allow at least five minutes for SS to test each other.
• Tell SS to go back to the main lesson on *p.19.*

4 PRONUNCIATION /ə/

a 2.5
• Focus on the sound picture. Elicit the word and write *computer* on the board. Ask SS *Where's the stress?* and underline it (computer). Remind SS that the other two syllables have the /ə/ sound. Play the tape/CD and get them to repeat the word and sound a few times.

2.5 CD1 Track 26
computer /ə/

b 2.6
• Focus on the instructions. Then play the tape/CD for SS to underline the stressed syllable. Check answers.

2.6 CD1 Track 27
about exhibition photographer together
balcony October

about exhibition photographer together
balcony October

c • Now focus on the pink letters which represent the /ə/ sound. Get SS to listen and repeat the words.

Pronunciation notes

- /ə/ is the most common sound in English.
- /ə/ can be spelled by any vowel. It always occurs in unstressed syllables (never stressed ones).
- *-er* at the end of a word is always pronounced /ə/, e.g. *teacher, better*, etc.
- *-tion* is always pronounced /ʃən/.

d 2.7

- Go through the dialogue with SS. Then play the tape/CD, stopping after each sentence for SS to repeat. Get SS to practise the dialogue in pairs. Monitor to make sure the rhythm is correct.

2.7 CD1 Track 28

A Where were you at six o'clock in the evening?
B I was at work.
A What were you doing?
B I was having a meeting with the boss.

e • Focus on the questions and the times. Get SS to ask you the questions for the first two times. They then ask and answer in pairs. Monitor, helping them with the rhythm and correcting any misuse of *in, at* or *on*.

Study Link SS can find more practice of the /ə/ sound on the MultiROM or on the *New English File Pre intermediate* website.

5 SPEAKING

a • Put SS into pairs, **A** and **B**, and get them to sit face to face if possible. Tell them to go to **Communication 2B *Famous photos*, A** on *p.109*, **B** on *p.113* where they will see a famous photo and read the story about how it was taken.

- Focus on **a**. Go through the instructions. Tell **A**s to look at *The Eiffel Tower painter* and **B**s to look at *Leaving for Newfoundland* and to read the text. Encourage SS to highlight important information, e.g. names, dates, places, etc. to help them to remember. They should read their text at least twice. Give them plenty of time to do this.
- Focus on **b**. Tell **A**s to talk about their photo and, from memory, to tell **B**s as much about the picture as possible.
- Focus on **c**. SS swap roles. While they are telling each other about their photos monitor and help.
- Tell SS to go back to the main lesson on *p. 19*.

Extra support

A weak student could simply read his/her texts aloud to the other student.

b • Focus on the questions. Demonstrate the activity by getting SS to ask you the questions. Encourage them to ask follow-up questions. Then get SS to ask and answer in pairs or small groups.

- Get feedback from a few pairs/groups.

Extra idea

You could ask SS to bring one or two favourite photos to to the next class to show other SS and talk about them.

Extra photocopiable activities

Grammar
past simple or past continuous? *p.144*
Communicative
It was a cold, dark night *p.188* (instructions *p.175*)

HOMEWORK

Study Link **Workbook** *pp.15–16*

2C

G questions with and without auxiliaries
V question words, pop music
P /w/ and /h/

Fifty years of pop

Lesson plan

In this lesson SS learn to use questions without auxiliaries (*Who wrote this song?* etc.) and contrast them with questions with auxiliaries (*When did he write it?*). They first revise the meaning of the different question words in the context of a pop music quiz, and focus on the pronunciation of *Wh* (/w/ or /h/). The lesson ends with a newspaper article from the British press which claims that Yoko Ono played an important part in writing the John Lennon song *Imagine*, and the lesson ends with this song.

Optional lead-in (books closed)

Put SS into pairs and give them two minutes to brainstorm different types of music (e.g. pop, rock, classical, etc.). Get feedback and write their ideas on the board. Ask the class for an example singer/band for each music type.

1 VOCABULARY & SPEAKING

a • Books open. Focus on the questions and check SS understand *band* (= pop group). Put SS into pairs or groups to talk about their musical tastes.
• Get feedback from a few different groups.

b • Focus on the quiz. Highlight that the people in the photos are not necessarily the answers to the quiz.
• Give SS a few minutes to complete the questions with a question word from the box. Check answers.

1 When	5 What	9 Which
2 Where	6 Which	10 How many
3 How long	7 Who	11 How
4 Whose	8 Why	12 Who

• SS should have met these words before, but may not be clear about their exact meaning.
– Explain that we tend to use *Which?* when we refer to a limited number of choices, e.g. *Which do you prefer, tea or coffee?* We use *What?* when there is a wider range of possibilities, e.g. *What do you want to do this evening?*
– We normally use *How long?* to ask about a length of time, e.g. *How long did you stay? How long does it take?*

⚠ The use of *Whom* in questions is very formal.

c • Put SS into pairs and get them to answer the questions. Encourage them to discuss their reasons in English where possible. Check answers.

1 b 2 b 3 a 4 c 5 b 6 b 7 b 8 c 9 b 10 b
11 c 12 a

2 GRAMMAR questions with and without auxiliaries

a • Focus on the instructions and get SS to complete the questions in pairs. Check answers.

1 did ... sing 2 sang

b • Focus on the questions and give SS a minute to think about them. Then elicit answers from the class.

1 In question 1 the verb has the auxiliary *did* + the infinitive (of *sing*). In question 2 the verb is in the ⊞ past simple (*sang*) and there is no auxiliary *did*.
2 The subject is *Robbie Williams*.
3 The subject is *Who*.

• Ask SS which question is **QUASI** (question word, auxiliary verb, subject, infinitive) and elicit that it's question 1. Highlight that when the question word (usually *who* or *which*) is the subject, **QUASI** does not apply, because the question word and the subject are the same.

c • Tell SS to go to **Grammar Bank 2C** on *p.128*. Go through the charts and rules. Model and drill the examples.

Grammar notes

• SS will already have met questions without auxiliaries, e.g. *Who knows the answer?*, etc., but until now this type of question has not been focused on.
• Highlight that:
– the vast majority of questions in the past and present follow the **QUASI** rule.
– the only question words which can be the subject of a question, and may not need an auxiliary verb, are:
Who?, e.g. *Who wrote the song?*
Which?, e.g. *Which singer sang* My Way?
What?, e.g. *What happened?*
How many/much?, e.g. *How many students came?*
• Questions beginning with *When?*, *Why?*, *Where?*, *How long?*, etc. always need an auxiliary.

• Focus on the exercises for **2C** on *p. 129.* SS do the exercises individually or in pairs. Check answers then put SS into pairs to answer the questions in **b**.

a 1 ~~did happen~~
2 ~~means this word~~
3 ~~did come~~
4 ~~does go~~
5 ~~did win~~
6 ~~said the teacher~~

b 1	did Ayrton Senna win?	(3)
2	won	(Jimmy Carter)
3	directed	(Quentin Tarantino)
4	did Nelson Mandela become	(1994)
5	wrote	(JRR Tolkien)
6	did Sting do	(He was a teacher.)

• Tell SS to go back to the main lesson on *p.21*.

3 PRONUNCIATION /w/, /h/

a • Focus on the sound pictures and elicit the words and sounds: *witch* /w/, *house* /h/.

b • Focus on the words in the box and give SS two minutes to put them in the right column.

c 2.8

• Play the tape/CD to check answers. Then give SS time to practise saying the words in pairs.

2.8 CD1 Track 29

what when where which why
how who whose

/**w**/ what, when, where, which, why
/**h**/ how, who, whose

d • Tell SS to go to **Sound Bank** on *p.159* and look at the typical spellings for the /w/ and /h/ sounds.

Pronunciation notes

- Highlight that practically all words that begin with *h* are pronounced /h/. There are very few exceptions and the only ones SS will meet in this book are *hour* and *honest*. The only other consonant combination that is pronounced /h/ is *wh*, and again there are very few words. SS need to know *who*, *whose*, and *whole*.
- *w* (+ vowel) at the beginning of a word is always pronounced /w/. *Wh* is usually pronounced /w/ except for the exceptions above. *Wr* is pronounced /r/

Study Link SS can find more practice of English sounds on the MultiROM or on the *New English File Pre-intermediate* website.

e 2.9

• Focus on the instructions. Play the tape/CD once the whole way through and tell SS just to listen. Then play it again, pausing after each question for SS to write. Check answers.

2.9 CD1 Track 30

1 What happened to that band?
2 When did they stop playing?
3 Who wrote their songs?
4 How many records did they sell?
5 Why did they break up?
6 What's the song about?

• Play the tape/CD again for SS to copy the rhythm.

Extra challenge

Get SS to underline the stressed words before they listen again and repeat (see tapescript 2.9).

4 SPEAKING

• Put SS into pairs, **A** and **B** and get them to sit face to face if possible. Tell them to go to **Communication 2C** ***Music quiz***, **A** *p.109*, **B** *p.113*.

• Focus on the instructions in **a** and make sure SS are clear what they have to do. Monitor and make sure they form the questions correctly.

• Focus on **b**. Tell **A**s to ask their questions first. Highlight that they should give the three alternatives each time. SS swap roles. Get feedback to see who got the most right answers.

• Tell SS to go back to the main lesson on *p.21*.

Extra idea

You could end by getting SS, in pairs, to each write two pop music quiz questions of their own.

5 READING

a • Focus on the photo and ask who the people are (John Lennon and Yoko Ono). Ask SS if they know anything about them.

• Give SS three minutes to read the text and mark the sentences. Check answers.

1 T 2 T 3 F 4 F 5 T 6 F

b • Go through the instructions and make sure SS understand that they have to number the events in chronological order. Check answers.

1 C 2 A 3 B 4 D 5 G 6 H 7 E 8 F

6 SONG ♫ *Imagine* 2.10

• If you want to do this song in class use the photocopiable activity on *p.221*.

2.10 CD1 Track 31

Imagine

Imagine there's no heaven, it's easy if you try,
No hell below us, above us only sky,
Imagine all the people living for today

Imagine there's no countries, it isn't hard to do,
Nothing to kill or die for, and no religion too,
Imagine all the people living life in peace

You may say I'm a dreamer,
but I'm not the only one,
I hope some day you'll join us,
And the world will be as one

Imagine no possessions, I wonder if you can,
No need for greed or hunger, a brotherhood of man,
Imagine all the people sharing all the world

You may say I'm a dreamer,
but I'm not the only one,
I hope some day you'll join us,
And the world will live as one.

Extra photocopiable activities

Grammar
questions with and without auxiliaries *p.145*
Communicative
Make your own quiz *p.189* (instructions on *p.175*)
Song
Imagine p.221 (instructions *p.218*)

HOMEWORK

Study Link **Workbook** *pp.17–18*

G *so, because, but, although*
V verb phrases
P the letter *a*

2 D One October evening

Lesson plan

In this lesson SS revise the past simple and continuous, and past questions. They also learn to use *so, because, but,* and *although.* The context is a short story with a twist. SS also expand their knowledge of verb phrases, and work on the different pronunciations of the letter *a.* Finally SS re-tell the short story from pictures.

Optional lead-in (books closed)

Write on the board *Yellow Submarine* and ask SS what it is (a Beatles song). Then give them two minutes in pairs to see if they can think of other pop songs with a colour in the title. Elicit the songs onto the board and for each one ask who sang it.

Some examples
True Blue, Madonna, *Yellow,* Coldplay, *Lady in Red,* Chris de Burgh, *Purple Haze,* Jimi Hendrix, *Brown Sugar,* The Rolling Stones, *White Flag,* Dido, *Blue Suede Shoes,* Elvis Presley

1 READING

a 2.11

- Books open. Focus on the text and tell SS that they are going to read a story, but that first they have to put it in order. Tell them that the end of the story is on tape so the last paragraph here is not the end of the story.
- Give SS five minutes to read the paragraphs. Then put SS into pairs to discuss the order. Play the tape/CD for SS to check answers.

1 C 2 F 3 A 4 E 5 B 6 D

2.11 CD1 Track 32

Hannah met Jamie in the summer of 2004. It was Hannah's 21st birthday and she and her friends went to a club. They wanted to dance, but they didn't like the music so Hannah went to speak to the DJ. 'This music is awful,' she said. 'Could you play something else?' The DJ looked at her and said 'Don't worry, I have the perfect song for you.'

Two minutes later he said: 'The next song is by Coldplay. It's called *Yellow* and it's for a beautiful girl who's dancing over there.' Hannah knew that the song was for her because she was wearing a yellow dress. When Hannah and her friends left the club, the DJ was waiting at the door. 'Hi, I'm Jamie,' he said to Hannah. 'Can I see you again?' So Hannah gave him her phone number.

Next day Jamie phoned Hannah and invited her to dinner. He took her to a very romantic French restaurant and they talked all evening. After that Jamie and Hannah saw each other every day. Every evening when Hannah finished work they met at 5.30 in a coffee bar in the High Street. They were madly in love.

One evening in October, Hannah was at work. As usual she was going to meet Jamie at 5.30. It was dark and it was raining. She looked at her watch. It was 5.20! She was going to be late! She ran to her car and got in. At 5.25 she was driving along the High Street. She was going very fast because she was in a hurry.

Suddenly, a man ran across the road. He was wearing a dark coat so Hannah didn't see him until it was too late. Although she tried to stop, she hit the man. Hannah panicked. She didn't stop and she drove to the coffee bar as fast as she could. But when she arrived Jamie wasn't there. She phoned him, but his mobile was turned off, so she waited for ten minutes and then went home.

Two hours later a police car arrived at Hannah's house. A policewoman knocked at the door. 'Good evening, Madam,' she said. 'Are you Hannah Davis? I'd like to speak to you. Can I come in?'

b • Tell SS to read the story again in the right order and answer questions 1–12. They can answer orally in pairs, or in writing. Check answers.

Extra challenge

Get SS to answer the questions in pairs *before* they read the story again. They then re-read the story to check.

1 In the summer of 2004.
2 Because she didn't like the music.
3 Because Hannah was wearing a yellow dress.
4 Jamie was waiting at the door and asked to see Hannah again.
5 They went to a French restaurant.
6 To a coffee bar in the High Street.
7 It was dark and raining.
8 Because she was in a hurry.
9 Because he was wearing a dark coat.
10 She drove to the coffee bar and then she went home.
11 No, he wasn't.
12 A policewoman came to Hannah's house.

- Now tell SS to underline any new words or expressions in the text and try to guess their meaning from context. Explain/translate any they can't guess. Tell them they will hear the end of the story later.

2 GRAMMAR *so, because, but, although*

a • Focus on the four sentences. Tell SS not to look back at the story but to try and complete the sentences from memory. Check answers and elicit/explain the meaning of the missing words or ask SS how to say them in their L1. Model and drill the pronunciation of *so, because,* and *although.* Write them on the board and underline the stressed syllable, or write them up in phonetics (/səʊ/, /bɪˈkɒz/, and /ɔːlˈðəʊ/).

1 because 2 Although 3 but 4 so

b • Tell SS to go to **Grammar Bank 2D** on *p.128.* Go through the rules and model and drill the examples.

Grammar notes

- We usually put a comma before *so*, *although*, and *but*, e.g. *She was tired, so she went to bed.*
- SS may also ask you about *though* which is a colloquial, abbreviated form of *although*. *Though* is not usually used at the beginning of a sentence. It is probably best at this level if SS just learn *although*.

⚠ *So* has another completely different meaning which is to intensify adjectives, e.g. *He was* **so** *tired that he went to bed at 9.00.* You may want to point out this meaning too in case SS get confused.

- Now focus on the exercises for **2D** on *p. 129*. SS do the exercises individually or in pairs. Check answers.

a	**1** Although	**3** but	**5** so	**7** but
	2 because	**4** Although	**6** because	
b	**1** E, so	**4** G, but	**7** C, but	
	2 F, because	**5** H, so	**8** B, because	
	3 D, although	**6** A, because		

- Tell SS to go back to the main lesson on *p.23*.

3 VOCABULARY verb phrases

a • Focus on the two circles and the example. Tell SS that by combining a verb from **1** with a phrase from **2**, they will make verb phrases from the story.

- Put SS into pairs and give them a few minutes to match the verbs and phrases. Tell them that sometimes two verbs may be possible with a phrase. Check answers. Highlight the silent *k* in *knock*.

invite somebody to dinner	run across the road
meet in a coffee bar	be in a hurry
take somebody to a restaurant	wait for somebody
knock on the door	try to stop
play a song/CD	

b • Get SS to test themselves by covering circle **1** and remembering the verbs for each phrase.

4 PRONUNCIATION the letter *a*

a 2.12

- This exercise focuses on the five most common sounds produced by the letter *a*, and will help SS to recognize common combinations and sounds.
- Focus on the sentence from the story in the box and read it out loud. Ask SS how the two *a*s are pronounced in *Hannah* (/æ/ and /ə/) and in *Jamie* (/eɪ/).
- Focus on the sound pictures and elicit the words and sounds: *cat* /æ/, *train* /eɪ/, *horse* /ɔː/, *car* /ɑː/, *computer* /ə/. Play the tape/CD for SS to repeat.

2.12 CD1 Track 33

cat train horse car computer

b 2.13

- Now focus on the words in the box and ask SS which column the first word (*again*) should go in. Elicit that it is column 5 (*computer*).
- Put SS into pairs. Give them a few minutes to put the other words in the correct columns. Encourage SS to say the words out loud. Play the tape/CD for them to check answers.

2.13 CD1 Track 34

madly	panic	ran	romantic
later	take	play	wait
saw	talk	all	although
dance	bar	dark	fast
along	across	again	arrive

cat: ran, romantic
train: play, wait
horse: all, although
car: dark, fast
computer: again, arrive

Pronunciation notes

- *a* between consonants is often pronounced /æ/, e.g. *black, sad, fat.* But it is sometimes /ɑː/, e.g. *bath, fast, dance.*

⚠ In many regions of the UK and in US English these words are also pronounced /æ/ e.g. bath/bæθ/.

- *ar* is usually pronounced /ɑː/, e.g. *far, garden.*
- *a* + *l* or *w* is pronounced /ɔː/, e.g. *ball, awful.*
- *a* + consonant + *e* is usually pronounced /eɪ/, e.g. *same, cake* (exception: *have*).
- *ai* and *ay* are usually pronounced /eɪ/, e.g. *day, rain.*
- *a* in an unstressed syllable is usually pronounced /ə/, e.g. ***a**round, popul**a**r.*

Study Link SS can find more practice of English sounds on the MultiROM or on the *New English File Pre-intermediate* website.

5 SPEAKING

a • Re-telling a story gives SS the opportunity for some extended oral practice, and in this case to recycle the tenses and connectors they have been studying.

- Focus on the pictures and tell SS they are going to re-tell the story of Hannah and Jamie. Give them a few minutes to re-read the story on *p.22*.

b • Put SS into pairs, **A** and **B**. Get **A**s to cover the text and focus on the pictures. Tell them to tell as much of the story as they can for pictures 1, 2, and 3 while **B** looks at the story on *p.22* to prompt/correct. They then swap roles for pictures 4, 5, and 6.

6 LISTENING

a 2.14

- This listening lets SS hear what happens at the end of the story and also gives them practice in deciphering whole phrases when the individual words have been run together.

⚠ If you are doing this activity on a different day to when you did the first part of the Hannah/Jamie story, you should get SS to quickly read the story on *p.22* again (they could listen to the tape/CD at the same time). Or you could elicit the story from the class using the pictures on *p.23* as a memory aid.

- Tell SS they are now going to hear the end of the story. First focus on the information box. Remind SS that we often link words together when we speak fast, and that sometimes three words sound like one, e.g. *a lot of*, *not at all*, etc.
- Focus on the six sentences and give SS a few seconds to read them (but don't ask them to guess what the missing words are).
- Play the tape/CD once the whole way through for them to listen. Then play it again pausing after each sentence for SS to write the missing words. Give them time to compare their answers in pairs and then check answers.

2.14 CD1 Track 35

1 A policewoman **knocked at** the door.
2 Can **I come in**?
3 Well, I'm afraid I have **some bad** news for you.
4 It was a **woman in a white** car.
5 Every police officer in the town **is looking for** her.
6 Did you know your **front light** is broken?

b **2.15**

- Focus on the instructions. Explain to SS that they are going to hear the end of the story in short sections.
- Focus on question **1** and then play the tape/CD until the first pause, signalled by a few notes of music. Elicit ideas from the class, but don't tell them if they are right or wrong to help build suspense. Then play the tape/CD up to the next pause.
- Continue focussing on each question and then playing the tape/CD to the pause, getting SS to predict what's going to happen or has happened.
- When you get to the end of the story, get SS to tell you what had happened. They will probably have already guessed that Hannah ran Jamie over.

2.15 CD1 Track 36

(tapescript in Student's Book on *p.119*)
Two hours later a police car arrived at Hannah's house. A policewoman knocked at the door. 'Good evening, madam,' she said. 'Are you Hannah Davis? I'd like to speak to you. Can I come in?' The policewoman came in and sat down on the sofa.
pause
'Are you a friend of Jamie Dixon?' she said.
'Yes,' said Hannah.
'I understand you were going to meet him this evening.'
'Yes, at 5.30, at a coffee bar. But he didn't come, so I didn't see him.'
'Well, I'm afraid I have some bad news for you,' said the policewoman.
'What? What's happened?'
pause
'Jamie had an accident this evening.'
'Oh no! What kind of accident?'
'He was crossing the road and a car hit him.'
'Is he ... Is he ...OK?'
pause
'Well, he's going to be in hospital for a long time.'
'Oh no.'
'But don't worry, he's going to be OK.'
'When did this happen?'
'This evening at twenty-five past five. He was crossing the road in the High Street.'
'And the driver of the car?'
pause
'She didn't stop.'
'She?'
'Yes, it was a woman in a white car. Every police officer in the town is looking for her.'
'Can I go to the hospital to see Jamie?'
'Yes, I can take you there now.'
'I'll get my coat. OK I'm ready.'
'Is that your car, madam? The white one over there?'
pause
'Yes it is.'
'Can I have a look at it?'
'Did you know your front light is broken?'
'No, I didn't.'
'What exactly were *you* doing at 5.25 this evening, madam?'

c • Get SS to close their books and listen to the end of the story without pausing.

Extra support

If you have time, you could get SS to listen to the tape/CD with the tapescript on *p.119*.

Extra photocopiable activities

Grammar
so, because but, although p.146
Communicative
Finish the sentences *p.190* (instructions *p.176*)

HOMEWORK

Study Link **Workbook** *pp.19–20*

2 PRACTICAL ENGLISH AT THE CONFERENCE HOTEL

Revision Checking into a hotel
Function Calling reception
Language *The air conditioning isn't working, Could I have a tuna sandwich?*

Lesson plan

In this lesson SS revise the language for checking into a hotel and learn expressions for calling reception if they have a problem with their room or to order from room service. In **Social English** Mark and Allie are chatting before the conference starts, and a friend of Mark's, Brad, comes and introduces himself. He seems very interested in meeting Allie.

Study Link These lessons are on the *New English File Pre-Intermediate* Video, which can be used instead of the Class Cassette/CD (see introduction *p.9*). The main functional section of each episode (the second section) is also on the MultiROM with additional activities.

Optional lead-in (books closed)

Revise what happened in the previous episode by eliciting the story from SS, e.g. *Where was Mark in the last episode?* (At the airport) *What was he doing there?* (He was waiting for Allie), etc.

CHECKING IN

2.16

- Focus on the photo and ask *What's happening?* (The receptionist is giving Allie her room key).
- Focus on the questions. Play the tape/CD once the whole way through and tell SS just to listen. Then play it again, pausing if necessary to give SS time to write. Get them to compare their answers before checking answers.

> 1 Ms Gray 2 six nights 3 419
> 4 From seven to nine. 5 The 6th.

- Remind SS of the difference between Mrs /mɪsɪz/ (= a married woman) and Ms /mɪz/ or /məz/ (= we don't know if the woman is married or not).
- Highlight that Allie asks *Where's the* ***lift****?* (*lift* = British English), but the receptionist answers *The* ***elevators*** *are ...* (*elevator* = US English). Focus on the information box.

⚠ For the room number you can say *four nineteen* (as the receptionist does here) or *four one nine* (as Allie does later).

Extra support

If you have time, you could get SS to listen to the tape/CD with the tapescript on *p.119* so they can see exactly what they understood. Translate/explain any new words or phrases.

- Elicit the phrases Allie uses to check in, e.g *Good evening. I have a reservation. What time's breakfast?* etc.

> 2.16 CD1 Track 37
> (tapescript in Student's Book on *p.119*)
> **R = Receptionist, A = Allie**
> R Good evening, ma'am. How can I help you?
> A Good evening. I have a reservation. My name's Alison Gray. I'm here for the MTC conference.
> R Just a moment. Ah, here it is. Ms Gray. For six nights?
> A That's right.
> R OK Ms Gray. Here's your key. You're in room 419 on the fourth floor.
> A Thank you. What time's breakfast?
> R From seven to nine, in the Pavilion Restaurant on the sixth floor.
> A Thanks. Where's the lift?
> R The *elevators* are over there.
> A Thanks.
> R Do you need any help with your bags?
> A Yes, please.

CALLING RECEPTION

a 2.17

- Tell SS to cover the dialogue with their hand or a piece of paper. Focus on the picture. Ask *What's Allie doing?* (She's on the phone.) *Where is she?* (In her room.). *Who do you think she's phoning?*, etc.

⚠ If you think that SS won't cover the dialogue, you could get them to close their books at this stage and write the first task on the board.

- Focus on the questions. Play the tape/CD once. Check answers.

> She phones reception because she has a problem with the air-conditioning.
> She also phones room service because she wants a sandwich.

b • Now tell SS to uncover the dialogue (or open their books). Explain that the **YOU HEAR** part is what they need to understand, and the **YOU SAY** part contains the phrases they need to be able to say.

- Give SS a minute to read through the dialogue and guess the missing words. Then play the tape/CD again, for them to complete the dialogue.
- Go through the dialogue line by line with SS and check answers. Remind them that:
  - *I'll* = I will (they will study this in the next File)
  - *whole wheat bread* = brown bread
  - *French fries* = chips (both expressions are used nowadays, also simply *fries*)
  - *mayo* = mayonnaise.

> 2.17 2.18 CD1 Tracks 38+39
> **R = Reception, A = Allie, RS = Room service**
> R Hello, reception.
> A Hello. This is room 419. (*repeat*)
> R How can I help you?
> A I have a problem with the air-conditioning. (*repeat*) It isn't working, and it's very hot in my room. (*repeat*)

R I'm sorry, ma'am. I'll **send** someone up to look at it right now.
A Thank you. (*repeat*)

RS **Room** service. Can I help you?
A Hello. This is room 419. Can I have a tuna sandwich, please? (*repeat*)
RS Whole wheat or **white** bread?
A Whole wheat, please. (*repeat*)
RS **With** or without mayo?
A Without. (*repeat*)
RS With **french fries** or salad?
A Salad, please. (*repeat*)
RS **Anything** to drink?
A Yes, a Diet Coke. (*repeat*)
RS With **ice** and lemon?
A Just ice. (*repeat*)
RS It'll be there in five minutes, ma'am.
A Thank you. (*repeat*)

c 2.18

- Now focus on the **YOU SAY** phrases. Tell SS they're going to hear the dialogue again. They repeat the **YOU SAY** phrases when they hear the beep. Encourage them to copy the rhythm.
- Play the tape/CD, pausing if necessary for SS to repeat the phrases.

d • Put SS into pairs, **A** and **B**. **A** is the receptionist and room service, **B** is Allie. Tell **B** to close his/her book and try to remember the phrases. Then **A** and **B** swap roles.

Extra support

Let SS practise the dialogue first in pairs, both with books open.

SOCIAL ENGLISH coffee before the conference

a 2.19

- Focus on the picture. Ask SS *Where is it?* (in the hotel cafeteria) and elicit who the other man in the photo might be.
- Focus on the instructions and get SS to read the T/F sentences. Elicit that Brad in **4** is the other man in the photo. Play the tape/CD at least twice.
- Check answers and elicit why the F ones are false.

1 F (tomorrow night)	4 F (the Los Angeles office)
2 F (on Wednesday)	5 T
3 T	

2.19 CD1 Track 40

(tapescript in Student's Book on *p.119*)
M = Mark, A = Allie, B = Brad
M Here you go, Allie. A cappuccino – see, I remembered!
A **Well** done! Thanks.
M Did you **sleep** well?
A Yes, very well. How are **things**?
M They're fine.
A What are the **plans** for the week?
M Well, today we don't have any free time. But tomorrow I'm going to take you to this great little restaurant I know.
A That sounds good.
M And then on Wednesday night there's a cocktail party here at the hotel, and then a conference dinner on Thursday. Is there anything special you want to do?
A Well, I'd like to see the bay and the Golden Gate Bridge. And I'd like to go shopping if there's time.
B Hi Mark, how are you doing?
M Hi Brad. I'm fine, just fine.
B Aren't you going to introduce me?
M Oh sure. Allie, **this** is Brad Martin. Brad works in the Los Angeles office. Brad, this is Allie Gray from the London office.
A Hello.
B Hi Allie, great to meet you. Mark told me you were very nice but he didn't tell me you were so beautiful. So, is this your first time in San Francisco?
A Yes. Yes, it is.
B Has Mark shown you the sights?
A Well, not yet.
B Then maybe I can show you round. I love this city.
M Allie, it's **time** to go. Excuse us, Brad.
B Well, great to meet you, Allie. See you round.
A Yes. Nice to meet you too. Goodbye.
B Bye.

Extra support

If there's time, you could get SS to listen again with tapescript on *p.119* so they can see exactly what Mark, Allie, and Brad said, and see how much they understood. Translate/explain any new words/phrases.

- Get SS to speculate a bit about the story, and what will happen next. Ask *Do you think Allie likes Brad? How do you think Mark feels?*, etc.

b • Focus on the **USEFUL PHRASES**. Get SS to see if they can remember any of the missing words. Play the tape/CD again and check answers (see tapescript above). Remind SS that we use *This is* ... to introduce somebody, not *He is* ... or *She is* ... .

c 2.20

- Play the tape/CD pausing after each phrase for SS to repeat. Encourage them to copy the rhythm.
- In a monolingual class get SS to decide together what the equivalent phrase would be in their language.

2.20 CD1 Track 41

A = Allie, M = Mark
A Well done!
M Did you sleep well?
A How are things?
M They're fine.
A What are the plans for the week?
M Allie, this is Brad Martin.
M It's time to go.

Extra challenge

Get SS to roleplay the conversation between Mark, Allie, and Brad using the tapescript on *p.119*. Let SS read their parts first and then try to act it from memory.

HOMEWORK

Study Link Workbook *p.21*

2 Writing The story behind a photo

Lesson plan

This second writing task links to the topic in lesson 2B. The writing consolidates the use of the past simple and continuous and revises *in, at, on*. If you want to do both the preparation and the writing in class, you may want to ask SS in the previous class to bring in a favourite photo.

a • Tell SS to cover the text and look at the photo. Ask *What's the man doing? Where do you think he is?* Tell SS to quickly read the text to find out if their guesses were right. Get feedback.

• Focus on the questions. Give SS a few minutes to match them to the paragraphs. Check answers.

What was happening when you took the photo?	3
Where do you keep it? Why do you like it?	5
What's your favourite photo?	1
Who took it? When? Where?	2
Tell me more about who or what is in the photo	4

b • Focus on the instructions. Set a time limit for SS to complete the gaps. Check answers.

2 on 3 in 4 on 5 on 6 On 7 at 8 in

Extra idea

Get SS to cover the text and look at the photo and questions. In pairs they try to answer the questions from memory.

• Focus on the Information box and go through it. Ask SS where the writer of the article keeps his photo, and elicit *on the wall*. Ask SS where they keep a favourite photo to elicit answers using the different prepositions.

Write about a favourite photo

Either give SS at least fifteen minutes to write the text in class, following the instructions, or set it for homework. Ask SS to attach a copy of the photo if they can.

⚠ This task would be best done for homework when SS have had time to choose a photo. Alternatively you could ask them to choose a favourite photo before you do this lesson and get SS to bring it to class for this lesson. If SS do the writing in class, get them to swap their texts with another S's to read and check for mistakes before you collect them all in.

2 Revise & Check

For instructions on how to use these pages, see *p.27*.

GRAMMAR

1 b 2 c 3 c 4 a 5 b 6 b 7 c 8 b 9 b 10 b

VOCABULARY

a 1 take 2 go 3 stay 4 spend 5 have
b 1 at 2 on 3 in 4 on 5 at
c 1 When 2 Who 3 How many 4 What 5 Which

PRONUNCIATION

a 1 wrote 2 found 3 choose 4 when 5 argue
b in<u>cre</u>dible <u>hor</u>rible pho<u>to</u>grapher <u>su</u>ddenly al<u>though</u>

CAN YOU UNDERSTAND THIS TEXT?

a 1 F 2 T 3 T 4 F 5 DS 6 T 7 F 8 F

CAN YOU UNDERSTAND THESE PEOPLE?

2.21 CD1 Track 42

1
A Where did you go on holiday?
B Well, we booked tickets to go to Spain. But then I got a new job and we couldn't go.
A Oh, what a pity.
B Well, we went to Scotland for a weekend – that was nice. And we're going to go to Portugal for a week at Christmas.

2
A Did you have good weather in Italy?
B Well, it was good for December. It was cold but sunny.
A Did it rain?
B No, it didn't. It was dry.

3
A Where did you take this photo of Tom Cruise?
B It was in New York. I was coming into the hotel and I saw him coming down the stairs. There were a lot of journalists waiting in reception. Everybody was shouting. So I went outside and I waited until he was getting into his car.

4
A What's your favourite photo?
B This one, I think. I really like this photo because it's not the usual way you see a top model. She was waiting with the other girls for the fashion show to begin. The other girls were all talking but she was just quietly reading a book.
A It's a great photo.

5
They made what we all *thought* was their last album in 2001, and they did a world tour the same year. Everybody said that that was the end but suddenly they made another album – their last one – the next year.

a 1 b 2 c 3 c 4 b 5 b

2.22 CD1 Track 43

A Anna, tell Jane about what happened to you that time.
B Well, I was driving home from work. It was a Friday evening, about half past five. It was winter and the weather was horrible – it was pouring with rain. I live in the country and to get to my house you have to go along a road where there are a lot of trees and very little traffic. Suddenly I saw a car stopped in the middle of the road and there was a man standing there waving his arms. He wanted me to stop.
C So did you stop?
B I didn't know what to do, but in the end I stopped and got out of my car and said, 'What's the problem?' Then suddenly another man ran from behind a tree and got into my car and drove away.
C Oh no!
B And then the first man got back into his car and drove away too! So I was just left standing there in the rain with no car.
C What did you do?
B Luckily I had my mobile and I rang my friend Pete, and he came and found me.

b 1 F 2 T 3 T 4 F 5 F

CAN YOU SAY THIS IN ENGLISH?

b 1 do 2 were 3 was 4 were 5 –

Extra photocopiable activities

Quicktest 2 *p.232*

3 A

G *going to*, present continuous (future arrangements)
V *look* (*after*, *for*, etc.)
P sentence stress

Where are you going?

File 3 overview

The focus of File 3 is future tenses. In the first three lessons SS revise *going to*, learn the future use of the present continuous and the use of *will/won't* to make predictions, promises, and instant decisions. The final lesson revises present, past, and future tenses and consolidates Files 1–3.

Lesson plan

In this lesson SS revise *going to* which they learnt at Elementary level to talk about plans and predictions, and also learn a new use of the present continuous: to talk about fixed plans and arrangements. The context is a reading and listening text based on interviews with people arriving in the UK at Heathrow airport in London. Three visitors are questioned about their plans and arrangements and each has a story to tell. In **Vocabulary** SS are introduced to some common phrasal verbs (*look for, look after*, and *look forward to*). (Phrasal verbs are focused on in detail in lesson **8C**.) The pronunciation focus is on stress in questions.

Optional lead-in (books closed)

Write AIRPORT on the board. Put SS into pairs and give them two minutes to think of five things people do at an airport, e.g. *catch a plane, leave, arrive, meet somebody, check in, board, fly*, etc. Elicit answers and write some of their suggestions on the board. Then do exercise **1a.**

1 READING

a • Books open. Focus attention on the questions and elicit answers from the class.

b • Now focus on the article and the photos. Read the introduction aloud (or get a student to read it) and establish that these are interviews with passengers arriving at the airport.

• Give SS two minutes to read the whole article and match A–I with gaps 1–9. Tell SS not to write the questions in the text until they have checked the answers. Get SS to compare their answers with a partner's and then check answers.

1 C 2 H 3 A 4 F 5 G 6 B 7 I 8 D 9 E

c • Get SS to read the text again and complete sentences 2–6 with the correct initial letter.

2 R 3 J 4 M 5 J 6 R

Extra support

To check comprehension, ask some more questions on each text, e.g.

What kind of job does ***Rima*** *want? Why does she want to improve her English? Why does she want to find a job quickly?*

Why is ***Jonathan*** *going to Wales? When did he last see his dad? Why can't his father fly to Australia? Why are* ***Maki*** *and* ***Koji*** *in London? When did they get married? How long are they staying in London? Where are they staying?*, etc.

Extra challenge

Put SS into pairs, **A** and **B**. Get **A**s to re-read Rima's text and **B**s Jonathan's. Then get **A** (book open) to interview **B** (book closed) using Jonathan's questions. Then **B** interviews **A** with Rima's questions.

2 GRAMMAR *going to*, present continuous

a • In pairs, SS cover the text and together try to remember three of Rima's plans and three of Jonathan's plans. Get them to say their sentences orally and to write them down. Feedback sentences from the class and write them on the board.

Possible answers
Rima
She's going to look for a job (maybe as an au pair).
She's going to improve her English.
She's going to stay for six months or a year.
She's going to stay with a friend.
Jonathan
He's going to see his father.
He's going to go to his father's birthday party.
He's going to stay for a month.
He's going to see all his family and friends.

b • Now SS focus on using the present continuous with a future use to talk about plans and arrangements.

• Focus on the interview with Maki and Koji. Tell SS to focus on the first question *Where are you staying in London?* and the answer. Elicit from SS that they are present continuous. Then give SS a minute or so to highlight seven more examples. Check answers. Ask SS if the sentences refer to the present or the future (SS will see from the context that they refer to the future).

What are you planning to do?
Tomorrow we're doing a tour of London.
In the evening we're seeing a show.
On Tuesday we're going to Oxford and Cambridge.
On Wednesday we're flying to Edinburgh.
When are you leaving?
We're going to Paris next.

• Explain briefly that the present continuous has two main uses:

1 To talk about actions happening now (e.g. *It's raining*). SS revised this use in lesson **1C.**
2 To talk about future actions (*I'm leaving tomorrow*).

c • Tell SS to go to **Grammar Bank 3A** on *p.130*. Go through the charts and rules with the class. Model and drill the example sentences.

Grammar notes

- *Going to* is revised here with it's two main uses: plans (*I'm going to stay for six months*) and predictions (*It's going to be a big surprise for him*).
  SS already know how to use the present continuous to talk about things happening now but may find this future use (*What are you doing this evening?*) quite strange. They may find it more natural to use the present simple tense for this.
  Typical mistake: *What do you do this evening? I go to the cinema.*
- *Going to* and present continuous (future) are very similar and can often be used as alternative forms when we talk about plans and arrangements, e.g. *What are you going to do tonight/What are you doing tonight?*

⚠ *going to* but NOT the present continuous is used for predictions, e.g. *I'm sure you're* ***going to*** *find a job.* NOT ~~*I'm sure you're finding a job*~~.

- Focus on the exercises for **3A** on *p.131*. SS do the exercises individually or in pairs. Check answers, getting SS to read the full sentences.

a 1 isn't going to pass
2 Is ... going to buy
3 are going to be
4 aren't going to go, are going to stay
5 are ... going to get married
6 is going to snow

b 1 ~~do you do~~
2 ~~raining~~
3 ✓
4 ~~I meet~~
5 ✓
6 ~~being late~~
7 ✓

- Tell SS to go back to the main lesson on *p.29*.

3 LISTENING

a 3.1

- Now SS hear what happened to Rima, the girl from Lithuania who arrived in the UK at the beginning of the lesson. Focus attention on the picture. You could ask SS if they think things went well or badly for Rima.
- Focus on the task and quickly go through sentences 1–8 and make sure SS understand them.
- Play the tape/CD once and SS mark the sentences T or F. Play the tape/CD again and get SS to check their answers with a partner's. Check answers.

1 T 2 T 3 F 4 T 5 T 6 F 7 F 8 F

b • Play the tape/CD again. This time SS listen out for any extra information and correct the false sentences. Get them to compare their answers with a partner's and then check answers.

Possible extra information
1 She's working long hours as a waitress.
2 It's easy to find a job in restaurants, hotels, or cleaning.
3 She is still living with her friend. London is too expensive for her to have her own flat (she can't afford it).
4 She isn't going to English classes – she doesn't have time. But she watches TV and speaks English at work.
5 Her plans have changed because she has met someone in the restaurant (the chef).
6 She isn't leaving the restaurant next month. She's getting married.
7 Her boyfriend isn't a waiter, he's a chef.
8 Her family don't know she's getting married.

3.1 CD1 Track 44
(tapescript in Student's Book on *p.120*)
I = Interviewer, R = Rima
I So Rima, did you find a job as an au pair?
R Well, I found a job, but not looking after children. I'm working in a restaurant – an Italian restaurant. I'm a waitress. I work very long hours!
I Was it difficult to find a job?
R No. There are lots of jobs in restaurants, hotels, cleaning, things like that.
I Are you still living in your friend's flat?
R Yes, because it's very expensive here and I can't afford to rent my own flat. London is incredibly expensive!
I Your English is much better!
R Well, a bit better, but I don't go to classes, because I don't have time. As I said, I work very long hours in the restaurant. But I watch a lot of English TV, and I speak English at work.
I When are you going back to Lithuania?
R I don't know. My plans have changed a bit.
I Why?
R Well, I met someone in the restaurant. He's the chef. We're getting married next month.
I Congratulations! Is he from Lithuania too?
R No, he's Italian. From Naples. He's a fantastic cook.
I So, are you going to stay in London?
R Yes. I'm very happy here now. We both really like London – our dream is to open a restaurant together one day.
I Are your family coming to the wedding?
R No! They don't even know I'm getting married! You see, they want me to go back to Lithuania.
I Well, good luck with everything, Rima.

Extra support

If you have time, you could get SS to listen again with the tapescript on *p.120*.

4 VOCABULARY *look*

a • Here SS look back at the first interview with Rima and focus on three common verb phrases with *look*: *look for*, *look after*, and *look forward to*.

⚠ These verbs are common examples of phrasal verbs (a verb + preposition/adverb) which are focused on in detail in lesson **8C**. At this stage it is best to just teach these verbs as vocabulary items without focussing on how phrasal verbs in general work.

- Ask SS *What does* ***look at*** *mean?* and elicit the meaning/translation. Give SS a minute to find three expressions with *look* + a preposition, and match them to their definitions. Check answers.

1 look for 2 look forward to 3 look after

- Point out to SS that sometimes you can add a preposition like *for* or *after* or *up* to a verb to make a new meaning, e.g. *turn on, turn off.*

⚠ It might help to teach SS that *look forward* literally means '*look in front of you*', i.e. into the future.

b • SS now complete the sentences using the three verbs. Set a time limit and get SS to do the activity in pairs, or individually and then check in pairs.

1 after 2 forward to 3 for 4 forward to 5 for 6 after

c • Here SS make personal sentences using the three verbs. Give SS a minute to think of what they are going to say. You could demonstrate the activity to the class using your own examples.

- SS take it in turns to tell a partner their three sentences. As usual, encourage the student who is listening to ask for more information.

5 PRONUNCIATION sentence stress

a • Remind SS that in English we stress (pronounce more strongly) the words in a sentence which are the most important for communication, i.e. the information words, and say the other words more lightly.

- Focus attention on the first question and ask SS to tell you which two words are the most important for communication. (*Where* and *going*) and highlight that these are the two words you have to stress in the question (*Where are you going?*).
- Give SS a minute, in pairs, to underline the stressed words in the other questions. Do not check answers yet.

b 3.2

- Play the tape/CD once for SS to check their answers.

3.2 CD1 Track 45

1 Where are you going?
2 When are you leaving?
3 How are you getting there?
4 Where are you staying?
5 When are you coming back?

- Play the tape/CD again pausing after each question for SS to listen and repeat, copying the stress. Encourage SS to say the unstressed words as fast as they can.

6 SPEAKING

a • Demonstrate the activity by writing up on the board two or three plans or arrangements you have for the week (or weekend), e.g.:

I'm going to the dentist on Thursday.
I'm playing football on Friday.
I'm meeting some friends on Saturday night.

- Tell SS that they should think about the kind of things they would write in their diary, i.e. things they are planning to do at a fixed time or place. Focus on the first speech bubble as an example.
- Set a time limit of two minutes for SS to think of three sentences. Then focus attention on the example and the follow-up question in the speech bubbles. In pairs, SS take it in turns to tell each other their sentences. Their partner listens and asks for more information.

⚠ SS can use either the present continuous or *going to.* Both are natural here.

b • Tell SS to go to **Communication 3A** ***Where are you going on holiday?*** on *p.116.* Focus on the adverts and make sure SS understand them. Deal with any vocabulary problems.

- Now focus on the instructions in **a** and make sure SS understand what they have to do. Give SS time to choose their holiday options.
- Focus on the instructions in **b** and go through the example. Demonstrate the activity by asking a student the questions and after a couple of questions pretend that you have chosen a different option, which means that you can't go on holiday with that person. And then move on as if you were going to ask another SS.
- Make sure SS realize that they have to keep on asking other SS until they find a student who has chosen exactly the same holiday, dates, form of transport, hotel, etc. That person is then their travelling companion.
- Get SS to stand up and move around the classroom interviewing each other. Set a time limit or stop the activity either when you can see that some people have found their travelling companion or when you think it has gone on long enough. Monitor and correct any mistakes with the present continuous: form, pronunciation, and rhythm.
- Get feedback to see how many people found a travelling companion.

Extra photocopiable activities

Grammar

going to, present continuous *p.147*

Communicative

Find someone who . . . *p.191* (instructions *p.176*)

HOMEWORK

Study Link **Workbook** *pp.22–23*

3 B

G *will / won't*
V opposite verbs: *pass–fail etc.*
P contractions (*will / won't*), /ɒ/ and /əʊ/

The pessimist's phrase book

Lesson plan

In this lesson SS are introduced to the future forms *will* and *won't* for the first time. They learn a specific use of these forms, that is to make predictions in response to what somebody says to you, e.g. ***A**: England are playing Brazil.* ***B**: They'll lose.* The context for the grammar is a light-hearted pessimist's phrase book, i.e. typical pessimistic predictions. The vocabulary focus in this lesson is common opposite verbs, e.g. *pass/fail, buy/sell.* In Pronunciation SS practise the contracted forms of *will/won't* and focus on the sounds /ɒ/ and /əʊ/.

Optional lead-in (books closed)

Draw a big glass on the board which is exactly half full of water. Underneath write *The glass is half ____*. Tell SS to complete the sentence with one word but they mustn't tell anybody which word they have written.

Now elicit from the class how to finish the sentence (*full/empty*). Ask SS who have written *empty* to put up their hands. Tell them that they are pessimists (explain/translate if necessary). Now ask who wrote *full* and tell these students that they are optimists. Now do **1a**.

1 GRAMMAR *will / won't* for predictions

a • Books open. Focus on the cartoon and ask SS who is the optimist and who is the pessimist.

b • Explain that *The pessimist's phrase book* is a list of typical things that a pessimist says.

• Go through the **YOU** phrases with the class and the two examples. You may want to point out at this stage that *It'll = It will* and that *You won't = You will not* and that these are examples of the future tense. Or you could wait as this is focused on in **1e.**

• Tell SS, in pairs, to find the pessimist's other responses in the box. Do not check answers yet.

c **3.3**

• Play the tape/CD for SS to listen and check their answers.

3 They'll be late.
4 You'll break your leg.
5 It won't last.
6 He won't pay you back.
7 You won't understand a word.
8 You won't find a parking space.
9 They'll lose.
10 You'll miss it.

• Play the tape/CD again and get SS to repeat the pessimist's responses.

3.3 CD1 Track 46

1 A We're having the party in the garden.
B It'll rain.
2 A I'm doing my driving test this afternoon.
B You won't pass.
3 A We're meeting Ana and Daniel at seven o'clock.
B They'll be late.
4 A I'm having my first skiing lesson today.
B You'll break your leg.
5 A My brother has a new girlfriend.
B It won't last.
6 A I lent James some money yesterday.
B He won't pay you back.
7 A I'm going to see a film tonight in English.
B You won't understand a word.
8 A We're going to drive to the city centre.
B You won't find a parking space.
9 A My team are playing in the cup tonight.
B They'll lose.
10 A I'm catching the 7.30 train.
B You'll miss it.

d • Put SS into pairs, **A** and **B**. Tell **A**s to keep their books open, **B**s to close theirs. Tell **B**s that they are pessimists. Tell **A**s to read the **YOU** phrases and **B**s to respond with the pessimist's phrases from memory. Then SS swap roles.

e • Focus on the pessimist's responses in the phrase book and elicit answers to the two questions.

1 the future 2 *will* and *will not*

f • Tell SS to go to **Grammar Bank 3B** on *p.130.* Go through the charts and rules with the class. Model and drill the example sentences.

Grammar notes

• In *New English File Elementary* SS learnt that *going to* can be used to make predictions, e.g. *You're going to be very happy.* This use was revised in lesson **3A** (*It's going to be a surprise*).

• In this lesson SS learn that *will/won't* + infinitive can also be used to make predictions and usually both forms are possible, e.g. *I think the government will lose the election./I think the government is going to lose the election.*

However there is a small difference in usage: *will/won't* tends to be used more than *going to* to make instant, on the spot predictions in reaction to what another person says, e.g.:

***A** I'm going to see the new Tarantino film tonight.*
***B** You won't like it.*

• At this level you may prefer to simplify things by telling SS that both *going to* and *will/won't* can be used to make predictions.

• SS will learn other uses of the future (*will/won't*) in lesson **3C** (promise, offers, and decisions) and will study the use of *will/won't* in conditional sentences with *if* in lesson **6A**.

• Focus on the exercises for **3B** on *p.131.* SS do the exercises individually or in pairs. Check answers.

a	1	They won't win.
	2	Will the meeting be long?
	3	He won't get the job.
	4	Will you see him at the party?
	5	It'll be impossible to park.
	6	You won't like the film.
	7	She'll love the chocolates we bought her.
	8	There won't be a lot of traffic at 6.00.
	9	You'll be able to find a good job.
b	1	'll ... do
	2	will ... make
	3	won't last
	4	will be

- Tell SS to go back to the main lesson on *p.30*.

2 VOCABULARY opposite verbs

a • Focus on the two circles of verbs and give SS a minute to match the opposite verbs. Check answers.

pass – fail   win – lose   lose – find   lend – borrow

Extra challenge

Elicit typical objects for the verbs in the circles, e.g.:
pass/fail a driving test, an exam, etc.
win/lose a match, a competition, a prize, etc.
lose/find your keys, your glass, your wallet, etc.
lend/borrow some money, a book, a CD, etc.

b • Tell SS to go to **Vocabulary Bank *Opposite verbs*** on *p.149*.

- Give SS two minutes to do exercise **a** in pairs. Check answers.

1 win	4 miss	7 teach	10 forget
2 pass	5 find	8 turn on	11 arrive
3 send	6 buy	9 lend	12 push

- Now give SS two minutes to do **b**. Check answers.

buy – sell   **win** – lose   **lend** – borrow   **find** – lose
push – pull   **pass** – fail   **forget** – remember
turn on – turn off   **send** – get/receive   **miss** – catch
arrive – leave   **teach** – learn

- Model and drill pronunciation of all the verbs. Highlight:
  – the difference between *lend* and *borrow*, i.e. *I lend money **to** you/you borrow **from** me.*
- Focus on **c**. Get SS to cover the verbs and look at the pictures. In pairs they try to remember the verbs and their opposites.

Study Link SS can find more practice of these words on the MultiROM or on the *New English File Pre-intermediate* website.

- Tell SS to go back to the main lesson on *p.31*.

3 PRONUNCIATION contractions, /ɒ/ and /əʊ/

Pronunciation notes

- An important aspect of *will/won't* is the pronunciation of the contractions and SS get some intensive practice here. Remind SS that contractions are very common in conversation but that it is not wrong to use the full uncontracted form.
- SS often confuse the pronunciation of the contracted form of *will not* (*won't* /wəʊnt/) with the verb *want* /wɒnt/ when speaking and listening.

a 3.4

- Focus on **a** and play the tape/CD for SS to listen and repeat. Encourage them to copy the rhythm. SS often find the contracted form of *It will* (*It'll*) difficult to say.

3.4 CD1 Track 47

I'll	I'll be late	I'll be late for work.
You'll	You'll break	You'll break your leg.
She'll	She'll miss	She'll miss the train.
It'll	It'll rain	It'll rain tomorrow.
They'll	They'll lose	They'll lose the match.

b 3.5

- Focus on **b** and explain that *want* and *won't* sound quite similar. Focus on the sound pictures and elicit the words and sounds: *clock*, /ɒ/ and *phone* /əʊ/).
- Focus on the two sentences and make sure SS understand what they mean. Play the tape/CD and ask SS to listen for the difference between *want* and *won't*.
- Play the tape/CD again and get SS to repeat.

3.5 CD1 Track 48

clock /ɒ/ want
I want to pass.
phone /əʊ/ won't
I won't pass.

c 3.6

- Tell SS that they are going to hear six sentences and that they have to write them down. Explain that they all include either *want* or *won't*. Tell SS that they will hear each sentence twice.
- Pause after you play each sentence and give SS time to write down what they hear. Then elicit answers onto the board.

3.6 CD1 Track 49

1 I want to go with you.
2 They won't come tonight.
3 You won't find a job.
4 We want to learn.
5 They want to sell their house.
6 I won't win the match.

4 LISTENING

a 3.7

- Focus on the instructions and question. Make sure SS understand what a radio phone in programme is (a programme where people phone and give their opinion). Play the tape/CD and elicit ideas.

3.7 CD1 Track 50

(tapescript in Student's Book on *p.120*)

P = presenter

P Today's topic is 'positive thinking'. We all know that people who are positive enjoy life more than people who are negative and pessimistic. But scientific studies show that positive people are also healthier, get better more quickly when they are ill, and live longer. A recent study shows that people who are optimistic and think positively live, on average, nine years longer than pessimistic people who think negatively. So, let's hear what you the listeners think. Do you have any tips to help us be more positive in our lives?

b • Focus on the chart and make sure SS understand what a *tip* is (a piece of useful advice).

• Get SS, in pairs, to quickly try and guess what the missing words in the chart could be. Tell them not to write them in the chart but on a separate piece of paper. Do not check answers yet.

c **3.8**

• Play the tape/CD once for SS to check their guesses and complete the gaps. Check answers.

1 Live in the **present**, not in the **past**.
2 Think **positive** thoughts, not negative ones.
3 Don't spend a lot of time reading the **papers** or watching the **news** on TV.
4 Every week make a list of all the **good things** that happened to you.
5 Try to use **positive language** when you speak to other people.

d • Play the tape/CD again for SS to write down extra information, e.g. a reason or an example. Get them to compare their answers in pairs and then play the tape/CD again. Check answers (see tapescript).

3.8 CD1 Track 51

(tapescript in Student's Book on *p.120*)

P = presenter, C = caller

P And our first caller this evening is Andy. Hi Andy. What's your tip for being positive?

C1 Hello. Well, I think it's very important to live in the present and not in the past. Don't think about mistakes you made in the past. You can't change the past. The important thing is to think about how you will do things better in the future.

P Thank you, Andy. And now we have another caller. What's your name, please?

C2 Hi, My name's Julie. My tip is: think positive thoughts, not negative ones. We all have negative thoughts sometimes but when we start having them we need to stop and try to change them into positive ones. Like, if you have an exam tomorrow and you start thinking 'I'm sure I'll fail', then you'll fail the exam. So you need to change that negative thought to a positive thought. Just think to yourself 'I'll pass.' I do this and it usually works.

P Thank you, Julie. And our next caller is Giovanna. Hi Giovanna.

C3 Hi. My tip is don't spend a lot of time reading the papers or watching the news on TV. It's always bad news and it just makes you feel depressed. Read a book or listen to your favourite music instead.

P Thanks, Giovanna. And our next caller is Miriam. Miriam?

C4 Hi.

P Hi Miriam. What's your tip?

C4 My tip is every week make a list of all the good things that happened to you. Then keep the list with you, in your bag or in a pocket, and if you're feeling a bit sad or depressed, just take it out and read it. It'll make you feel better.

P Thanks, Miriam. And our last call is from Michael. Hi Michael. We're listening.

C5 Hi. My tip is to try to use positive language when you speak to other people. You know, if your friend has a problem, don't say 'I'm sorry' or 'Oh poor you', say something positive like, 'Don't worry! Everything will be OK.' That way you'll make the other person think more positively about their problem.

P Thank you, Michael. Well that's all we've got time for. A big thank you to all our callers. Until next week then, goodbye.

e • Do this as an open class question. You could get SS to vote for the best tip with a show of hands.

5 SPEAKING

a • Focus on the instructions and the examples. Drill the pronunciation of the phrases (*Cheer up!* etc.).

• Give SS, in pairs, three minutes to match the positive phrases with the situations and to make a positive prediction using *I'm sure* + *will*. Check answers.

Suggested answers (but others are possible)
2 Congratulations! I'm sure you'll be very happy.
3 Cheer up! I'm sure things will get better/you'll feel better soon.
4 That's great! You'll love it!/You'll have a great time.
5 Don't worry! I'll lend you some (money)/ I'll pay for you.

• Put SS into pairs. **A** reads out the sentences in **Your friend says** but in a different order. **B** closes his/her book and makes an appropriate response from memory.

b • Focus on the activity and on the six questions. Then focus on the expressions in the box (*I hope so*, etc.). Drill the pronunciation, making sure SS do not over-stress the word *so* and make sure SS are clear about the meaning. Point out that the word *so* in *I hope so*, etc. means *yes* and that *maybe* and *perhaps* mean the same.

• SS take it in turns to ask and answer each question in pairs, giving reasons for their predictions. They should then decide if they are positive thinkers. Get some feedback, e.g. ask how many people in the class think they will pass their next English exam.

Extra photocopiable activities

Grammar

will/won't (predictions) *p.148*

Communicative

The optimist's phrase book *p.192* (instructions *p.176*)

HOMEWORK

Study Link **Workbook** *pp.24–25*

3 C

G *will / won't* (promises, offers, decisions)
V verb + *back* (*come back, call back,* etc.)
P word stress: two-syllable words

I'll always love you

Lesson plan

SS continue their work on the uses of future *will*. In this lesson they learn that as well as for making predictions *will* can be used for making promises, offers, and decisions. The two contexts are a text about promises which are almost never kept (*This won't hurt.*) and cartoons illustrating common situations involving promises, offers, and decisions. The vocabulary focus is on using certain verbs with *back* (*come back, take back,* etc.) and in Pronunciation SS practise word stress in two-syllable words.

Optional lead-in (books closed)

Write the word PROMISES on the board and elicit its meaning. Teach/elicit that you can *make a promise* and then *keep* or *break a promise*.

Ask SS *What promises do people in love often make*? Try to elicit some and write them on the board, e.g. *I'll always love you/I'll never leave you/I'll marry you,* etc. Then ask SS if they think people keep or break these promises.

1 READING

a • Books open. Focus on the six promises and ask SS what they have in common. Elicit suggestions.

> They are all promises which people often break/don't keep.

b • Focus on the article ***Promises, Promises*** and read the introduction aloud to the SS. Then give SS two minutes to complete the text with the six promises in **a**. Tell them not to worry about unknown words at this point as these will be dealt with later. Get SS to compare their answers with a partner's and then check answers.

> 1 I'll come back tomorrow.
> 2 I won't tell anyone.
> 3 This won't hurt.
> 4 I'll write.
> 5 I'll pay you back tomorrow.
> 6 I'll always love you.

• Ask the class if they agree that all of these promises are often broken. Ask SS, in pairs, to decide which of the six promises is broken most often. Get feedback and find out which promise gets the most votes.

c • Focus on the instructions and give SS three or four minutes to read the text again and find the words that match definitions 1–6. Remind SS of the meaning of the abbreviations (*n* = noun, *adv* = adverb, *adj* = adjective). Get SS to compare their answers with a partner's and then check answers.

> 1 plumber 2 research 3 injection 4 journey
> 5 either 6 eternal

• Now elicit from the class which syllable is stressed in each word. Check answers, writing the words on the board with the stressed syllable underlined. Point out that *either* can be pronounced /ˈaɪðə/ or /ˈiːðə/. The first is probably more common.

⚠ In US English *research* is stressed on the first syllable. *research* /ˈriːsɜːtʃ/.

> **1** plumber **2** research **3** injection **4** journey
> **5** either **6** eternal

Extra idea

Ask SS if there are any promises they make but find very hard to keep, and elicit ideas, e.g. *I'll do the homework before next lesson.*

2 PRONUNCIATION word stress: two-syllable words

a • Focus on **a** and read the information in the box aloud to SS. Highlight that most two-syllable words in English have the stress on the first syllable, so SS only need to take note of words where the stress is on the second syllable. They should mark the stress on these words and make an effort to learn them.

• Focus on the activity and give SS, in pairs, a minute to find the five words which are stressed on the second syllable. Do not check answers yet.

b 3.9

• Play the tape/CD for SS to check their answers.

3.9 CD1 Track 52

secret	forget	exist
always	complete	dentist
borrow	e-mail	money
promise	address	doctor
builder	journey	
worry	before	

• All the other words have the stress on the first syllable.

• Play the tape/CD again for SS to practise saying the words, making sure they stress the words clearly on either the first or second syllable.

Extra support

SS could use their dictionaries to help them check the pronunciation of words in **2a**. Remind them that the stressed syllable is the one which follows the apostrophe (ˈ), e.g. *secret* /ˈsiːkrət/ and *forget* /fəˈget/.

3 GRAMMAR *will / won't* for promises, offers, and decisions

a • Focus on the cartoons and tell SS to cover sentences 1–6 in **b**. Ask SS to guess what the people are saying. SS may come up with some of the sentences or similar. Accept anything which makes sense in the context.

b • Focus on the instructions and give SS a minute or so to do the task. Get them to compare in pairs. Check answers.

A 4 I'll always **love** you.
B 2 I'll **pay** you back tomorrow.
C 5 Shall I **open** the window?
D 3 I'll **help** you!
E 1 I'll **have** the steak, please.
F 6 Yes, it's very nice. I'll **take** it.

c • Focus on the instructions and make sure SS understand *make a decision* and *offer*. Give SS, in pairs, a minute to complete the chart. Highlight that they should write the number of the sentence, not the cartoon letter. Check answers.

making a promise	2 and 4
making a decision	1 and 6
offering to do something	3 and 5

d • Tell SS to go to **Grammar Bank 3C** on *p.130*. Go through the chart and rules with the class. Model and drill the example sentences.

Grammar notes

- SS shouldn't worry about being able to distinguish between an offer, a promise, or a decision. Depending on the context *I'll help you tomorrow* could be an offer, a promise, or a decision.
- *Shall I ...?* is only used when you offer to do something, e.g. *Shall I make you a cup of coffee?* NOT *Will I make you a cup of coffee?*
  In other future contexts *Will I ...?* is used, e.g. *Will I need my passport?* NOT *Shall I need my passport?*
- In some languages the present tense is used for offers and decisions. Highlight that in English you say *I'll help you* NOT ~~*I help you*~~.

• Focus on the exercises for **3C** on *p.131*. SS do the exercises individually or in pairs. Check answers.

a 1 I 2 H 3 A 4 B 5 C 6 D 7 F
b 1 Shall I help 2 won't tell 3 'll call 4 'll pay 5 won't forget 6 Shall ... take

• Tell SS to go back to the main lesson on *p.33*.

4 VOCABULARY verb + *back*

a • Here SS learn/revise some common verbs with *back*, e.g. *come back, pay* (somebody) *back*. Focus on the question and elicit answers.

go = to move or travel from one place to another, e.g. *go to the office*
go back = to return to a place, e.g. *go back to work (after lunch)*

b • Focus on the verbs in the box and highlight that adding *back* to a verb changes the meaning. Verb + *back* = to repeat an action or to return. Demonstrate *give back* by giving something to a student and then saying *Give it back, please.*

• Give SS a couple of minutes to read the dialogues and complete them with a verb from the box. Do not check answers yet.

c 3.10
• Play the tape/CD for SS to check their answers. Get SS to act out the dialogues in pairs.

3.10 CD1 Track 53
1 A I love that shirt you gave me for my birthday. But it's a bit small.
B Don't worry. I'll **take it back** to the shop and change it.
2 A Can I speak to Bart, please?
B I'm sorry. He's not here at the moment.
A OK. I'll **call back** later.
3 A Excuse me. Could I talk to you for a moment?
B I'm really busy at the moment. Could you **come back** in five minutes?
4 A That's my pen you're using!
B No, it's not. It's mine.
A No, it's mine. **Give it back**!
5 A Can you lend me 50 euros, Nick?
B It depends. When can you **pay me back**?
A Tomorrow. I'll go to the bank first thing in the morning.

⚠ You may want to point out that the object pronoun (*it, them*, etc.) goes between the verb and *back*. Word order with these kinds of verbs + prepositions/adverbs (phrasal verbs) is dealt with in detail in lesson **8C**.

5 SPEAKING

• Tell SS to go to **Communication *I'll/Shall I? game*** on *p.117*. Put SS into groups of three or four. Focus on the game board and explain the rules of the game.
• S1 throws a coin. Heads = move 1 square, Tails = move 2 squares. When S1 lands on a square he/she has to make a sentence with *will/won't* or *Shall I?* to fill the speech bubble. SS 2, 3 (and 4) decide if the sentence is correct/appropriate. If it is, S1 stays on that square. If it is wrong/inappropriate then S1 returns to the START square. S2 then throws the coin, etc.
• SS move around the board. If a student lands on a square where another student has already been, he/she must make a different sentence. The winner is the first student to reach the **FINISH** and make a correct sentence.
• The teacher is the referee in the case of any disagreement!

Some possible sentences
1 I'll have the chicken.
2 I'll kill it./I'll get it./Shall I get it?/Shall I kill it?
3 I'll answer it./Shall I answer it?
4 I'll go to the supermarket and buy some.
5 I'll help you./Shall I help you?/I'll carry them./Shall I carry them?
6 I won't be late.
7 I'll have the green one.
8 I'll call back later.
9 I'll turn on the light/Shall I turn on the light?

• Tell SS to go back to the main lesson on *p.33*.

6 SONG ♫ *White flag*

3.11

- SS listen to a song by Dido.
- If you want to do this song in class use the photocopiable activity on *p.222*.

3.11 CD1 Track 54

White flag

I know you think that I shouldn't still love you,
Or tell you that.
But if I didn't say it, well I'd still have felt it
Where's the sense in that?

I promise I'm not trying to make your life harder
Or return to where we were.

I will go down with this ship,
And I won't put my hands up and surrender,
There will be no white flag above my door,
I'm in love and always will be.

I know I left too much mess and
Destruction to come back again,
And I caused nothing but trouble,
I understand if you can't talk to me again.
And if you live by the rules of 'it's over',
Then I'm sure that that makes sense.

I will go down, etc.

And when we meet,
Which I'm sure we will,
All that was there,
Will be there still,
I'll let it pass,
And hold my tongue,
And you will think,
That I've moved on.

I will go down, etc.

Extra photocopiable activities

Grammar

will or *going to?* *p.149*

Communicative

I'll / I won't / Shall I? *p.193* (instructions on *p.176*)

Song

White flag *p.222* (instructions *p.218*)

HOMEWORK

Study Link **Workbook** *pp.26–27*

3 D

G review of tenses: present, past, and future
V verbs + prepositions: *dream about, listen to,* etc.
P sentence stress

I was only dreaming

Lesson plan

The final lesson in File 3 provides a consolidation of not only this File but also of the first three Files of the book. The present, past, and future are revised through the context of interpreting dreams. SS read about some common symbols in dreams and listen to a psychiatrist analysing somebody's dream. Although the lesson provides a light-hearted look at dreams, the symbols and their interpretations have been taken from serious sources. SS get the chance to interpret each other's dreams in a roleplay activity. In Pronunciation SS do more work on sentence stress and rhythm. The vocabulary focus of this lesson is common verb + preposition combinations, e.g. *dream about, speak to,* etc.

Optional lead-in (books closed)

Ask SS if they dreamt last night. If they say *Yes,* elicit from three or four what they dreamt about (just the subject not the details), e.g. *I dreamt I was falling/about my exams.* Write the dreams on the board and quickly ask the class if they know what the dreams mean.

1 READING & LISTENING

a • Books open. Focus on the five statements about dreams and go through them. Deal with any vocabulary problems. Give SS a few minutes to discuss the statements and say if they think they are true or false.

• Get feedback from the class and try to find out what the majority view is on each one.

1 F You can remember dreams you had during the night when you wake up the following morning. However, if you don't tell somebody about it, or write it down, you very quickly forget it.
2 T Most experts would say that you do, although often as an onlooker rather than directly involved in the action.
3 T Repetitive dreams are very common. They are often related to something frightening that happened in childhood.
4 T Freud, Adler, and Jung are probably the most famous, and modern day psychoanalysts continue to do so.
5 T For example Abraham Lincoln dreamt that he saw a president being assassinated a few days before his own assassination.
Adapted from Collins Gem Understanding Dreams

b 3.12

• Focus on the task. Get SS to cover the dialogue with a piece of paper and look at the pictures in the top right-hand corner. Elicit that the pictures show an owl, flowers, a girl playing the violin, champagne, feet, and people at a party.

• Play the tape/CD. SS try to number the pictures 1–6 in the correct order. Get SS to compare in pairs and then check answers.

party **1** champagne **2** flowers **3**
violin player **4** owl **5** feet **6**

c • Get SS to uncover the dialogue. Play the tape/CD again for them to complete the gaps. You may need to pause the tape to give SS time to write in the missing words. Check answers.

3.12 CD1 Track 55

D = Dr Muller, PA = patient
D So, **tell** me, what did you dream about?
PA I was at a party. There were a lot of people.
D What **were** they **doing**?
PA They were **drinking**, and **talking.**
D Were **you** drinking?
PA Yes, I **was drinking** champagne.
D And then what **happened**?
PA Then, suddenly I **was** in a garden. There **were** a lot of flowers ...
D Flowers, yes … what kind of flowers?
PA I **couldn't** really see – it was dark. And I **could** hear music – somebody **was playing** the violin.
D The violin? Go on.
PA And then I **saw** an owl, a big owl in a tree ...
D How **did** you **feel**? Were you frightened?
PA No, not frightened really, no, but I **remember** I felt very cold. Especially my feet – they were freezing. And then I **woke up**.
D Your feet? Mmm, very interesting, very interesting indeed ...
PA So, what **does** it **mean**, doctor?

Extra support

Give SS a minute to read the dialogue and guess some of the missing words before they listen. Don't tell them whether their guesses are right or wrong.

d • Tell SS that they are going to interpret the man's dream. In pairs they try to match the things in his dream in the **You dream** column to interpretations 1–6 in **This means.** Do not check answers yet.

e 3.13

• Focus on the task and play the tape/CD for SS to check their answers to **d.** Elicit and check answers.

that you are at a party **2**
that you are drinking champagne **3**
about flowers **4**
that somebody is playing the violin **5**
about an owl **6**
that you have cold feet **1**

3.13 CD1 Track 56

(tapescript in Student's Book on *p.120*)

D = Dr Muller, PA = patient

PA So what does it mean, doctor?

D Well, first the party. A party is a group of people. This means that **you're going to meet a lot of people**. I think you're going to be very busy.

PA At work?

D Yes, at work ... you work in an office, I think?

PA Yes, that's right.

D I think **the party means you are going to have a lot of meetings**.

PA What about the champagne?

D Let me look at my notes again. Ah yes, you were drinking champagne. **Champagne means a celebration. It's a symbol of success**. So we have a meeting or meetings and then a celebration. **Maybe in the future you'll have a meeting with your boss, about a possible promotion**?

PA Well, it's possible. I hope so ... What about the garden and the flowers? Do they mean anything?

D Yes. Flowers are a positive symbol. So, the flowers mean that you are feeling positive about the future. So perhaps you already knew about this possible promotion?

PA No, I didn't. But it's true, I am very happy at work and I feel very positive about my future. That's not where my problems are. My problems are with my love life. Does my dream tell you anything about that?

D Mm, yes it does. You're single, aren't you?

PA Yes, well, divorced.

D Because the **violin music** tells me you want some romance in your life – **you're looking for a partner** perhaps?

PA Yes, yes, I am. In fact I met a very nice woman last month – I really like her... I think I'm in love with her. I'm meeting her tonight.

D In your dream you saw an owl in a tree?

PA Yes, an owl ... a big owl.

D **The owl represents an older person**. I think you'll need to ask this older person for help. **Maybe this 'older person' is me**? **Maybe you need my help**?

PA Well, yes, what I really want to know is does this person, this woman ... love me?

D You remember the end of your dream? You were feeling cold?

PA Yes, my feet were very cold.

D Well ... I think perhaps you already know the answer to your question.

PA You mean she doesn't love me.

D No, I don't think so. **I think you will need to find another woman. I'm sorry**.

f • Focus on pictures 1–6 again and tell SS to listen for extra details (details which aren't in *Understanding your dreams* p.35).

• Play the tape/CD, pausing after each symbol. Give SS time to compare with their partner before checking answers (see **bold** answers in tapescript above for possible answers).

Extra support

If you have time, you could get SS to listen again with the tapescript on *p.120*.

2 GRAMMAR review of tenses

a • Focus on the chart and explain that this is a summary of all the tenses SS have studied so far.

• Give SS, in pairs, a minute or so to decide where to write the example sentences, but tell them not to write them in yet. Check answers, then get SS to write the sentences in the chart.

b • Give SS time to complete the **Use** column with A–F.

Tense	Example	Use
present simple	You work in an office.	D
present continuous	I'm meeting her tonight.	C
past simple	I saw an owl.	B
past continuous	I was drinking champagne.	F
going to + infinitive	You're going to meet a lot of people.	A
will/won't + infinitive	You'll have a meeting with your boss.	E

c • Tell SS to go to **Grammar Bank 3D** on *p.130* where they will find an expanded version of the grammar chart with more examples.

• Go through the chart with the class and model and drill the example sentences.

Grammar notes

• SS should find this overview of the tenses useful but at this level you cannot expect them to be able to use all the basic tenses with real fluency.

• Focus on the exercises for **3D** on *p.131*. SS do the exercises individually or in pairs. Check answers.

a 1 Do **2** is **3** Did **4** were **5** do ... will **6** Does **7** are **8** Was
b 1 're having **2** had **3** wants **4** Shall ... buy **5** happened **6** was coming **7** stopped **8** met **9** 're going to be

• Tell SS to go back to the main lesson on *p.35*.

3 PRONUNCIATION sentence stress

a 3.14

• Focus on sentences 1–6 and tell SS that they are from the conversation about dreams. Tell SS they have to underline the stressed words.

Pronunciation notes

• Remind SS that information words are the ones which are usually stressed. These are the words which you hear more clearly when somebody speaks to you. The unstressed words are heard much less clearly or sometimes hardly at all.

⚠ Short prepositions (*up, for, in,* etc.) are not normally stressed except when they occur at the end of a sentence. Compare *Where are you from?* (*from* is stressed) and *I'm from Munich.* (*from* is unstressed).

• Negative auxiliary verbs are usually stressed, e.g. *I don't like it, I can't do it, I wasn't there.* Positive auxiliary verbs are usually NOT stressed, e.g. *I can play the guitar, I was watching TV,* etc.

- Play the tape/CD, pausing between sentences to give SS time to underline the words. Check answers.

> **3.14** CD1 Track 57
> 1 You'll have a meeting with your boss.
> 2 Somebody was playing the violin.
> 3 You're going to meet a lot of people.
> 4 How did you feel?
> 5 I'm meeting her tonight.
> 6 She doesn't love me.

- Elicit/explain that nouns, verbs, adjectives, and adverbs are usually stressed, but articles, (+) auxiliary verbs and prepositions are normally unstressed (see Pronunciation notes on *p.53*).

Extra challenge

You could do **a** as a dictation. Get SS to cover the sentences or close their books. Play the tape/CD and get SS to write down the six sentences, pausing and repeating to give SS time to write them down. Check answers. Play the sentences again for SS to underline the stressed words.

b • Play the tape/CD again for SS to repeat the sentences. Encourage SS to copy the rhythm by stressing the information words and pronouncing the other words as lightly as possible.

4 SPEAKING

- Put SS into pairs, **A** and **B**. Tell SS to go to **Communication *Dreams***, **A** on *p.110* and **B** on *p.114*.
- Focus on the instructions and make sure SS know what they have to do. Demonstrate the activity yourself if necessary.
- **A** starts by telling **B** about their dream using the pictures as a guide. **B** listens and numbers the subjects in the box in the order **A** speaks about them. **B** then interprets **A**'s dream in the order in which the things were mentioned using the notes in the box. Then they swap roles.
- Monitor and help while SS do the activity. Don't interrupt and correct (unless communication breaks down altogether), but make notes of any common errors and go through these on the board afterwards (although don't make this a post mortem – the most important thing in most speaking activities at this level is for SS to talk, without worrying about making mistakes).
- Tell SS to go back to the main lesson on *p.35*.

5 VOCABULARY verbs + prepositions

- In pairs get SS to complete the sentences and then check answers.

1 about 2 to 3 about 4 for 5 with 6 to 7 of
8 about 9 with 10 to

- Point out that:
  - *dream of* is also possible although we tend to use this for day dreaming, e.g. *I've always dreamed of having a house in the country.*
  - *think of* is usually used to ask someone's opinion about people and things, e.g. *What do you think of my shoes?*
  - *think about* = to reflect or consider an idea in your mind, e.g. *What are you thinking about? I'm thinking about the party on Saturday.*
  - *speak with* is common in US English and is heard ever more frequently in British English.
  - In US English *write* is used without a preposition, e.g. *Write me.*

Extra idea

Get SS to ask and answer the questions in pairs.

Extra photocopiable activities

Grammar
tense revision *p.150*
Communicative
Talk about it *p.194* (instructions *p.176*)

HOMEWORK

Study Link **Workbook** *pp.28–29*

3 PRACTICAL ENGLISH RESTAURANT PROBLEMS

Revision Ordering a meal
Function Complaining in a restaurant
Language *I'm sorry, but I asked for ..., I think there's a mistake ...*

Lesson plan

In this lesson SS revise the language for ordering a meal in a restaurant and learn expressions for if they have a problem. In **Social English**, Mark and Allie talk about their past relationships, and get to know each other better.

Study Link These lessons are on the *New English File Pre-intermediate* Video, which can be used instead of the Class Cassette/CD (see Introduction *p.9*). The main functional section of each episode (the second section) is also on the MultiROM with additional activities.

Optional lead-in (books closed)

Revise what happened in the previous episode by eliciting the story from SS. See if they can remember what Mark and Allie were going to do on Wednesday evening (have dinner together), and tell them this episode is in the restaurant.

ORDERING A MEAL

3.15

- Books open. Focus on the menu and go through it. Explain/translate the dishes. If necessary, remind SS what *fries* are (*chips* in UK English).
- Focus on the questions. Explain/translate *rare, medium,* and *well done* in question 4.
- Play the tape/CD once all the way through and tell SS just to listen. Then play it again, pausing if necessary to give SS time to write. Get them to compare answers with each other before checking answers.

1 Allie the tomato and mozzarella salad, Mark the mushroom soup.
2 Fried chicken.
3 Allie a baked potato, Mark (french) fries.
4 Rare.
5 Wine.

- Elicit the phrases Mark and Allie use to order, e.g *The mushroom soup for me, I'll have (the fried chicken), I'd like the steak*, etc.

3.15 CD1 Track 58

(tapescript in Student's Book on *p.121*)
W = waiter, M = Mark, A = Allie
W Are you ready to order?
M Yes, to start a tomato and mozzarella salad – is that right, Allie?
A Yes.
M And the mushroom soup for me.
W And for your main course?
A I'll have the fried chicken.
W With french fries or a baked potato?
A A baked potato, please.
W And for you, sir?
M And I'd like the steak, with french fries.
W How would you like your steak? Rare, medium, well done?
M Rare, please.
W And to drink?
M Could you bring us the wine list, please?

PROBLEMS WITH A MEAL

a 3.16

- Tell SS to cover the dialogue. Focus on the question. Play the tape/CD once for SS to identify the problems. Check answers.

The waiter brings Allie fries, not a baked potato.
Mark's steak is well done, not rare.
There's a mistake in the check/bill.

b • Give SS a minute to read through the dialogue and guess the missing words. Then play the tape/CD again for them to complete the dialogue.

3.16 3.17 CD1 Tracks 59+60

W = waiter, M = Mark, A = Allie
W Chicken for you ma'am, and the steak for you, sir.
A I'm sorry, but I asked for a baked potato, not fries. (*repeat*)
W No problem. **I'll change it.**
M Excuse me. (*repeat*)
W Yes, sir?
M I asked for my steak rare and this is well done. (*repeat*)
W I'm very sorry. **I'll send it** back to the kitchen.
M Could we have the check, please? (*repeat*)
W Yes, sir ... Your check.
M Thanks. Excuse me. I think there's a mistake in the check. (*repeat*)
We only had two glasses of wine, not a bottle. (*repeat*)
W Yes, you're right. I'm very sorry. It's not my day today! **I'll get you** a new check.
M Thank you.

- Go through the dialogue with SS and check answers. Focus on the US/UK English information box.

c 3.17

- Play the tape/CD, pausing for SS to repeat the **YOU SAY** phrases. Encourage them to copy the rhythm.

d • Put SS into pairs, **A** and **B**. **A** is the waiter, **B** is Mark/Allie. Tell **B** to close his/her book and try to remember the phrases. Then **A** and **B** swap roles.

SOCIAL ENGLISH after dinner

a 3.18

- Focus on the instructions and get SS to read the sentences. Play the tape/CD at least twice.
- Check answers. Elicit why the F ones are false.

1 F She's his daughter.
2 T
3 F They broke up because they were very young when they had Jennifer, etc.
4 F She met him at university.
5 F They're going to go for a walk and have another coffee.

3.18 CD1 Track 61

(tapescript in Student's Book on *p.121*)

W = waiter, M = Mark, A = Allie

W Your check, sir.
M Thanks.
W Thank you.
A Thank you, Mark. That was a **lovely** dinner.
M I'm **glad** you enjoyed it.
A How's your daughter?
M Jennifer? She's fine. She's with her mother in Los Angeles.
A Mark?
M Yeah.
A Can I ask you **something**? Something personal?
M Sure. What?
A How long were you married?
M Three years.
A Why did you break up?
M There were a lot of reasons. We were very young when we had Jennifer. We were both working very hard. We didn't spend much time together ... the usual story. What about you, Allie?
A Well, there was someone. I met him when I was at university. We were together for two years. We broke up.
M Why?
A I don't know. Usual story!
M Thank you. Listen, it's early – it's only nine o'clock. Shall we go for a **walk**?
A Good idea. Where **shall** we go?
M There's a place called Fisherman's Wharf, it's right on the bay. There are lots of cafés and bars. We could have **another** cup of coffee.
A Fine. Let's go.

Extra support

Get SS to listen again and answer these questions.

Where does Jennifer live? Who with?
How long were Allie and her boyfriend together?
Why did they break up?
What time is it?
Where's Fisherman's Wharf?

If there's time, SS can listen again with the tapescript (*p.121*).

b • Focus on the **USEFUL PHRASES**. Play the tape/CD again and check answers. Highlight the use of *Shall we?* to make a suggestion.

c **3.19**

• Play the tape/CD pausing after each phrase for SS to repeat. Encourage them to copy the rhythm.

3.19 CD1 Track 62

A = Allie, M = Mark

A That was a lovely dinner.
M I'm glad you enjoyed it.
A Can I ask you something?
M Shall we go for a walk?
A Where shall we go?
M We could have another cup of coffee.

HOMEWORK

Study Link **Workbook** *p.30*

3 WRITING AN INFORMAL LETTER

Lesson plan

In this third writing lesson SS practise writing an informal letter. SS use a letter as a model, but the content of their writing is based on SS own answers to questions asked in the letter. The writing consolidates the future tenses taught in File 3. The writing skills focus is on the conventions and layout of an informal letter which are contrasted with an e-mail.

a • Focus on the letter, the instructions, and the phrases in the box. Give SS, in pairs, five minutes to complete the letter with the phrases in the box. Check answers.

2 Brighton BN3 1HJ
3 14th April 2005
4 Dear Ivan
5 Looking forward to hearing from you
6 Best wishes
7 PS

Highlight that:

– the address and the date normally go in the top right corner.

– the date can also be written 14/4/2005.

– all letters begin *Dear* + the name.

– *Looking forward to hearing from you* is a very useful phrase for ending a letter or e-mail (if you hope the recipient is going to reply).

– PS (*Post scriptum* in Latin) is for anything you have forgotten or want to add to the end of a letter.

b • Focus on the instructions. Set a time limit for SS to re-read the letter. Then get SS to answer the questions in pairs. Check answers.

1 In August.
2 By plane.
3 8
4 a
5 So that he will recognize them at the station.

c • You could elicit the differences by focussing on 1–7 in **a** and asking if SS would use them in an e-mail or not and how they would change them in an e-mail. The two main differences are:

– you don't usually put your address or the date on an e-mail.

– you can start an informal e-mail *Hi* + name instead of using *Dear* + name.

Write a letter using your own information

Either give SS at least fifteen minutes to write the letter in class, following the instructions, or set it for homework.

Extra idea

Get SS to plan their answers to the letter in pairs and make notes before they write their own letter.

• If SS do the writing in class, get them to swap their letter with another S's to read and check for mistakes before you collect them all in.

3 REVISE & CHECK

For instructions on how to use these pages, see *p.27*.

GRAMMAR

1 b 2 b 3 b 4 b 5 a 6 b 7 c 8 c 9 b 10 a

VOCABULARY

a 1 about 2 after 3 forward 4 for 5 with

b 1 D 2 C 3 A 4 E 5 B

c 1 win a match 2 forget to pay 3 sell a car 4 teach Spanish 5 send a letter

PRONUNCIATION

a 1 home 2 good 3 won't 4 down 5 borrow

b pessimist prediction remember important interesting

CAN YOU UNDERSTAND THIS TEXT?

b 1 T 2 T 3 DS 4 F 5 F 6 F 7 F

CAN YOU UNDERSTAND THESE PEOPLE?

3.20 CD1 Track 63

1
A Would you like to come to the beach with us this afternoon?
B No, thanks. I don't like the beach – I can't swim. I think I'll stay at home.
A We aren't going swimming – it's too cold. We're going to play volleyball.
B Oh, OK, I'll come then.

2
A Who do you think's going to win the League this year?
B Manchester United. They've got the best team.
A But they're not playing very well. Arsenal are first at the moment, and they're playing really well. Liverpool are good too.
B I still think United will win in the end.
A Yeah, you're probably right.

3
A Are you going away for the weekend?
B Yes, we're going to the mountains. We want to go for long walks.
A I hope you have good weather.
B Me too. It rained a lot last week but on TV they said this weekend it's going to be cold but sunny and dry.

4
A Which one are you going to get?
B I can't decide. I love the red one, but the black one would be more practical.
A What about the blue one?
B No, I don't like blue. I think I'll get the red one.
A Yes, go on. Red suits you better than black.

5
A You look awful. Didn't you sleep well?
B No. I woke up in the middle of the night.
A Why?
B I had a nightmare. I dreamt I had an exam – but I hadn't studied at all.
A That doesn't surprise me!

a 1 c 2 b 3 b 4 a 5 a

3.21 CD1 Track 64

A Hello, Supertravel. How can I help you?
B I'd like some information about flights.
A Where do you want to go?
B To Rome. I want to leave on Tuesday the 6th of May and come back on Saturday the 10th.
A It'll be much cheaper if you stay the Saturday night and come back on Sunday the 11th.
B OK then, I'll go from the 6th to the 11th. I'd like to fly early in the morning if possible.
A There's a flight leaving London at 8.30 on the 6th, getting to Rome at 12.00, and then for the return flight there's one leaving at 9.00 getting to London at 12.30. Is that OK?
B Yes, that's fine. Did you say I'll get to Rome at 12.30 on the 6th of May?
A No, at 12.00. You leave at 8.30.
B And the flight back gets in at 12.30?
A That's right.
B How much does it cost?
A €195.
B OK, I'll have it.
A Can I have your name please?
B Yes, Robert Brown.
A And your credit card details.
B Yes, it's a Visa card …

b 1 Rome 2 Sunday 11th 3 12.00 4 9.00 5 Brown

CAN YOU SAY THIS IN ENGLISH?

b 1 What are you doing this weekend?
2 Are you going to study English next year?
3 Who do you think will win the next elections?
4 Do you think it will rain tomorrow?
5 How often do you remember your dreams?

Extra photocopiable activities

Quicktest 3 *p.233*

4 A From rags to riches

G present perfect (experience) + *ever, never*; present perfect or past simple?
V clothes, e.g. *coat, skirt*
P vowel sounds: /ɜː/, /əʊ/, /uː/, /aʊ/, /ɑː/, /e/

File 4 overview

In File 4 the focus is on the present perfect, and comparatives and superlatives. In **4A** SS revise/learn the present perfect with *ever/never* and contrast it with the past simple. In **4B** they carry on with the present perfect and learn to use it with *yet, just,* and *already*. In **4C** they revise comparative adjectives and learn to use comparative adverbs and *as ... as*. Finally, in **4D**, they revise superlative adjectives and adverbs, and the present perfect is recycled in the structure *It's the best ... I've ever seen*, etc.

Lesson plan

In this lesson SS revise the present perfect with *ever/never*, and contrast it with the past simple. For SS who completed *New English File Elementary* this will be revision, but for other SS this may be new, in which case you may need to spend more time on past participles and the form. The context of the lesson is clothes and fashion, with a text about the clothes chain *Zara* providing a starting point. The vocabulary focus is on clothes and related verbs, and the pronunciation focuses on the vowel sounds in common clothes words which often cause problems, e.g. *suit, shirt,* etc. The title of the lesson is an idiom used to mean when someone who was very poor, e.g. a beggar who wears rags (i.e. old, torn clothes) becomes very rich.

Optional lead-in (books closed)

Write the word CLOTHES on the board (or play hangman with it). Then ask SS how to pronounce it /kləʊðz/ and if it is singular or plural (plural). Explain that there is no singular form, and that if they want to talk about an item of clothing, they should refer to it by name, e.g. *a sweater.* Now draw a line before *clothes* on the board, e.g. ______ *clothes* and ask SS what verbs they can use with *clothes.* They should be able to produce *wear, buy, try on,* and possibly *put on* and *take off.*

1 READING & VOCABULARY

a • Books open. Focus on the questions and either answer them as an open class or get SS to answer in pairs and then get feedback.

b • Focus on the photo of the *Zara* store. Elicit/explain that it is an international chain (teach *chain*). Ask SS if they know where the chain originated (Spain) and if there are any *Zara* stores in their town (or nearest big town). Ask if SS like the *Zara* clothes. If SS don't know the *Zara* chain, tell them that they are going to find out about it in the text.

• Give SS three minutes to read the text. Then tell them to cover it and answer the questions orally in pairs. Check answers.

Extra support

Let SS find their answers in the text. Or get them to close their books and ask the questions to individual students round the class.

1 He is the person behind *Zara* / a businessman / the richest man in Spain.
2 He is a multimillionaire, but he doesn't look like one. He wears simple clothes (not a suit and tie).
3 He was a shop assistant.
4 In 1975.
5 All over the world, from New York to Moscow to Singapore.
6 It reacts to top designer fashion very quickly and cheaply, the clothes change every week, they produce 20,000 new designs a year.

• Explain/translate any vocabulary problems in the text, unless they are words related to clothes/fashion, in which case tell SS that they will be looking at them in a minute. Ask SS if there are any shops (or brands) from their country which have become international, and if they know anything about them.

• Finally you could focus on the lesson title and explain/translate *rags* (old, torn clothes).

c • Focus on the instructions. Then give SS a few minutes to underline the words in pairs.

para 1: wear, suits, tie, jeans, shirt
para 2: clothes store, pyjamas, clothes shop
para 3: designer fashions, fashionable, a new line (of clothes)
para 4: jacket, skirt

• Highlight that:
– *a suit* can be both for a man or a woman. It can be trousers and a jacket or a skirt and a jacket.
– *store* is US for *shop*, but now in the UK people use both *shop* and *store.*

d • Tell SS to go to **Vocabulary Bank *Clothes*** on *p.150.*

• Focus on **a.** SS match the clothes words and pictures in pairs. Check answers and model and drill pronunciation, especially the words where the phonetic transcription has been given.

1 top **2** shirt **3** sweater **4** dress **5** shorts
6 T-shirt **7** blouse **8** tracksuit **9** suit
10 pyjamas **11** trousers **12** jeans **13** tights
14 skirt **15** jacket **16** coat **17** belt **18** socks
19 scarf **20** tie **21** hat **22** cap **23** boots
24 shoes **25** trainers

• Highlight that plural words cannot be used with *a*, e.g. NOT ~~*a trousers*~~. If SS want to use an indefinite article, they should use *some*, e.g. *I bought some trousers/some shoes.*

Extra challenge

You could also teach *a pair of* which is often used with plural clothes words.

- Focus on **b**. Give SS a minute to test themselves/each other.
- Focus on the phrases in ***Verbs used with clothes*** **a**. In pairs SS match the phrases and pictures. Check answers. Highlight that *put on* is used with individual items of clothes, e.g. *put on your shoes, coat,* etc. but *get dressed* = put on all your clothes.

try on 1 wear 2 get dressed 3 put on 4
take off 5

- Focus on **b**. Get SS to cover the phrases and in pairs say what she is doing in each picture.

Study Link SS can find more practice of these words and phrases on the MultiROM or on the *New English File Pre-intermediate* website.

- Tell SS to go back to the main lesson on *p.40*.

2 PRONUNCIATION vowel sounds

a 4.1

- Focus on the sound pictures and elicit the words and sounds: *bird* /ɜː/, *phone* /əʊ/, *boot* /uː/, *owl* /aʊ/, *car* /ɑː/, *egg* /e/. Give SS in pairs a few minutes to put the words in the right columns. Encourage them to say the words aloud as they do this.
- Play the tape/CD for SS to check answers.

4.1 CD2 Track 2

shirt, skirt
coat, clothes
shoes, suit
blouse, trousers
pyjamas, scarf
belt, sweater

- Play the tape/CD again, pausing after each word for SS to repeat.

b • Focus on the questions. Put SS into pairs. SS ask and answer. Monitor and help, correcting the pronunciation of clothes words and teaching any other words they may want to use.

Extra idea

You could get SS to ask you the questions first.

Study Link SS can find more practice of these sounds on the MultiROM or on the *New English File Pre-intermediate* website.

3 LISTENING

4.2

- Focus on the chart. Tell SS that they're going to hear three people being asked questions 1–5. Tell them just to listen the first time to all three people, and then to write the information the second time you play the recording.
- Play the tape/CD once the whole way through. Then get SS to talk to a partner about what they understood from the first listen, and to see if they already know the answers to some of the questions.
- Play the tape/CD again. Stop after each person to give SS time to write down the answers. Get SS to compare their charts and then check answers.

	Woman 1	Woman 2	Man
1	Yes	Yes	Yes (once)
2	3 weeks ago	Last Saturday	In August
3	In London	In Paris	At Barcelona airport
4	a white jacket	a scarf	nothing (girlfriend bought shoes)
5	quite happy	Yes	

4.2 CD2 Track 3

(tapescript in Student's Book on *p.121*)

I = Interviewer, P = passer-by, W1 = woman 1, W2 = woman 2, M = man

I Excuse me sir, I'm doing a … sir? Excuse me madam, do you have a few minutes to answer …
P Sorry, I really don't have time.
I Excuse me, could I ask you a few questions about *Zara*?
W1 Yes, OK.
I Have you ever been to a *Zara* store?
W1 Yes, many times.
I And when did you last go there?
W1 About three weeks ago.
I Where was that?
W1 Here in London. In Oxford Street.
I OK, thank you. What did you buy?
W1 Er, a white jacket.
I And are you happy with it?
W1 Quite happy. I like the jacket but the colour was a mistake. It's already dirty.
I Thank you very much for your time.

2
I Hello. Do you mind if I ask you a few questions about *Zara*?
W2 How long will it take?
I Only a few minutes.
W2 Yes, all right then.
I Have you ever been to a *Zara* store?
W2 Yes.
I When did you last go there?
W2 Last Saturday.
I Where?
W2 In Paris.
I What did you buy?
W2 Just a scarf. I tried some trousers on but I didn't buy them.
I Are you happy with the scarf?
W2 Yes. I like it a lot.

3
I Have you ever been to a *Zara* store?
M Yes, once.
I When did you go there?
M In August.
I Where?
M At Barcelona airport.
I What did you buy?
M I *nearly* bought lots of things, but in the end I didn't buy anything. But my girlfriend bought some shoes.

4 GRAMMAR present perfect or past simple?

a • If there is a *Zara* store in (or near) your SS' town, get them to interview each other in pairs. If not, tell them to use another famous clothes shop.

⚠ If their partner answers *No, I haven't* to the first question, tell them to carry on asking the same question about different shops until they find one their partner has been to. Get feedback.

b • Get SS to focus on questions 1 and 2 in the chart in **a**. Tell SS to discuss the grammar questions in pairs.

1 is present perfect.
2 is past simple.
2 refers to a specific time in the past.
1 is about some time in your life.

c • Tell SS to go to **Grammar Bank 4A** on *p.132*. Go through the charts and rules. Model and drill the sentences in the charts.

• Tell SS to go to **Irregular verbs 4A** on *p.155*. Focus on the past participles and tell SS to underline and learn the ones which are different from the past simple.

Grammar notes

Present perfect simple

• For some SS the present perfect may be a new tense. They may have a similar tense in their L1 or they may not, and the use is likely to be different. It takes time for SS to learn and use this tense correctly, but this use (for past experience) is probably the simplest to understand. Lesson **4B** introduces other uses of the present perfect with *yet, already,* and *just*, and **7A** with *for* and *since*.

Present perfect or past simple?

• The contrast of general or specific experience is focused on here. The contrast is studied in more detail in lesson **7B**.

• Focus on the exercises for **4A** on *p.133*. SS do the exercises individually or in pairs. Check answers.

a 1 Have you ever bought clothes from that shop?
2 I haven't read the newspaper today.
3 We have never been to the new shopping centre.
4 Has your brother lived abroad all his life?
5 They have gone to live in South America.
6 She has never flown before.
7 He hasn't met his wife's family.
8 Have you eaten in this restaurant before?

b 1 ✗ We went to Ireland last year.
2 ✗ Have you ever been to Paris?
3 ✓ 4 ✓
5 ✗ I saw that film last week.
6 ✓ 7 ✓
8 ✗ World War II ended in 1945.

• Tell SS to go back to the main lesson on *p.41*.

5 SPEAKING

a • Focus on the instructions. Do question 1 with the whole class. Focus on the picture and elicit the missing past participle (*worn*). SS should just complete the questions with the missing participle at this stage.

1 worn 2 been 3 danced 4 worn 5 met
6 bought 7 ruined 8 had

b • Focus on the follow-up question prompts after each question in **a**. They are either one word (*Where? What?*) or have a slash (/). This indicates that they must make this question in the past simple, e.g. *When did you wear it? Did you enjoy it?*, etc.

Extra support

Elicit and drill all the follow-up questions with the class.

• Focus on the speech bubbles. Then get SS to interview you with the first three or four questions.

• Finally SS interview each other in pairs. You could get **A** to ask **B** 1–4, then **B** to ask **A** 5–8, and then swap.

6 SONG ♫ *True blue*

4.3

• This Madonna song revises the present perfect. If you want to do this song in class, use the photocopiable activity on *p.223*.

4.3 CD2 Track 4

True blue

I've had other guys, I've looked into their eyes
But I never knew love before
'til you walked through my door
I've had other lips, I've sailed a thousand ships
But no matter where I go
You're the one for me baby this I know, 'cause it's

True love, you're the one I'm dreaming of
Your heart fits me like a glove
And I'm gonna be true blue baby I love you

I've heard all the lines, I've cried oh so many times
Those teardrops they won't fall again
I'm so excited 'cause you're my best friend
So if you should ever doubt
Wonder what love is all about
Just think back and remember dear
Those words whispered in your ear, I said

True love, etc.

No more sadness, I kiss it goodbye
The sun is bursting right out of the sky
I searched the whole world for someone like you
Don't you know, don't you know that it's

True love oh baby …

Extra photocopiable activities

Grammar
present perfect or past simple? *p.151*
Communicative
Are you telling the truth? *p.195* (instructions *p.177*)
Song
True blue p.223 (instructions *p.218*)

HOMEWORK

Study Link **Workbook** *pp.31–32*

4 B

G present perfect simple + *yet, just, already*
V verb phrases: *make the bed,* etc.
P /h/, /j/, /dʒ/

Family conflicts

Lesson plan

This lesson continues work on the present perfect and SS learn to use it with *yet, just,* and *already*. The context is problems in the house, especially with teenagers, and the vocabulary focus is on verb phrases. The pronunciation focus is on consonant sounds, and the lesson finishes with a newspaper article about some parents who evicted their teenagers from the family home.

Optional lead-in (books closed)

Write the word TEENAGER on the board and ask SS what it means (young person aged between 13 and 19). Find out how many teenagers there are in your class and if you have adults with children, how many of them have teenage children.

1 VOCABULARY verb phrases

a • Books open. Focus on the title of the article. Elicit/explain that *drives them mad* = makes them angry. Then focus on the instructions and give SS a few minutes to complete the text in pairs. Check answers and deal with any vocabulary problems.

> 1 makes 2 tidies 3 leaves 4 cleaned 5 does
> 6 changes 7 take 8 does

b • Get SS to cover the text and in pairs, try to remember what the eight teenagers do. Check answers.

> 1 He never makes his bed.
> 2 He never tidies his room.
> 3 She leaves wet towels on the floor.
> 4 She walks around the house eating food without a plate.
> 5 He never does the washing up.
> 6 She changes the channel on the TV.
> 7 He never walks the dog.
> 8 She does her homework at the last minute.

c • Focus on the instructions. Go through the first two or three prompts and say if they are a problem in your house or not. SS then talk in pairs or small groups.

2 GRAMMAR present perfect + *just, yet, already*

a 4.4

• Focus on the pictures and get SS to cover the dialogues. Play the tape/CD once for SS to match the dialogues to the pictures. SS compare their answers with a partner's. Check answers.

> A 2 B 3 C 1 D 4

4.4 CD2 Track 5

1 A Have you finished yet?
B No, not yet.
A Well, hurry up! I'm going to be late for work.

2 A You've left a towel on the floor.
B Well, I haven't finished yet.
A Well, don't forget to pick it up.
B OK.

3 A When are you going to do your homework?
B I've already done it.
A Really? When?
B I did it on the bus this evening.

4 A Can you get a plate for that sandwich? I've just cleaned the floor.
B OK. Oops – sorry. Too late.

b • Get SS to read the four dialogues and guess the missing past participles. Play the tape /CD again and check answers. Elicit the infinitive of each verb.

> 1 finished 2 left 3 done 4 cleaned

c • Focus on the instructions. Give SS time to underline the words and elicit that the verb tense is present perfect. If you know your SS L1, you could elicit the translation of *just, yet,* and *already*. Otherwise elicit/explain that:
– *just* (in this context) = a very short time ago
– *already* = earlier than expected
– *yet* = until now.

⚠ *Just* has other meanings in other contexts, e.g. *only*.

d • Tell SS to go to **Grammar Bank 4B** on *p.132*. Go through the rules. Model and drill the examples.

Grammar notes

• *Yet/already* may not have an exact equivalent in SS' L1, and the meaning is not that easy to explain, as they are words which simply add emphasis. There is not much difference between *I haven't finished* and *I haven't finished yet*, but adding *yet* implies that you are going to finish.
• *Just* + present perfect. This use may be expressed in a completely different way in SS' L1.

• Focus on the exercises for **4B** on *p.133*. SS do the exercises individually or in pairs. Check answers.

> a 1 Have you made your bed yet?
> 2 She's already gone to work.
> 3 We've just had a cup of coffee.
> 4 I haven't found a job yet.
> 5 He's just sent me an e-mail.
> 6 They've already sold their house.
> b 1 I've just had breakfast.
> 2 Have you finished your homework yet?
> 3 The film has already started.
> 4 I haven't met his girlfriend yet.
> 5 They've just got married.
> 6 You're too late. He's already gone home.
> 7 Have you spoken to him yet?
> 8 I haven't read his new book yet.

• Tell SS to go back to the main lesson on *p.43*.

3 PRONUNCIATION & SPEAKING

a 4.5

- Focus on the sound pictures and elicit the words and sounds: *house* /h/, *yacht* /j/, *jazz* /dʒ/. Then play the tape/CD all the way through. Tell SS just to listen.
- Play the tape/CD again, pausing after each sentence for SS to repeat.

> 4.5 CD2 Track 6
> 1 He hasn't helped with the housework today.
> 2 Have you used your new computer yet?
> 3 Jim's just joined a judo class.

Pronunciation notes

- Remind SS that:
- *h* at the beginning of a word is almost always pronounced /h/.
- *y* at the beginning of a word is always pronounced /j/. Many words with *u* have a hidden /j/, e.g. *use, music.*
- *j* is always pronounced /dʒ/.
- *g* before *i* or *e* is also often pronounced /dʒ/, e.g. *manager, general, giraffe, German,* etc.

b
- Tell SS to go to **Communication *Has he done it yet?*** on *p.116.* Give SS one minute to look at and remember the picture. Then tell SS to go to *p.114.* Go through the instructions. They should write their nine sentences with either *yet* or *already.*
- When SS have written their sentences, put them into pairs. They read their sentences aloud to each other, to see if they have written the same. Monitor to check they are forming the present perfect correctly and are putting *yet* and *already* in the right place.
- Finally SS check with the picture to see how many of their sentences were right. Get feedback.
- Tell SS to go back to the main lesson on *p.43.*

c 4.6

- Tell SS they are going to hear some sounds of things that have just happened. Put SS into pairs and tell them first just to listen and make notes (in their L1 if they like). Play the tape/CD once.
- Play the tape/CD again, pausing after each sound effect for SS to write a sentence with *just* and the present perfect.
- Check answers. Accept all correct and possible sentences.

> 4.6 CD2 Track 7
> **Sound effects to illustrate the following sentences:**
> 1 She's just broken a plate.
> 2 They've just got married.
> 3 He's just taken a photo.
> 4 She's just seen a mouse.
> 5 The film has just finished.
> 6 The dog has just seen a cat.

Study Link SS can find more practice of English sounds on the MultiROM or on the *New English File Pre-intermediate* website

4 READING

a
- Focus on the questions, and give SS a minute to talk in pairs. Get feedback.

Extra support

Do this as an open class activity and elicit ideas.

- Now focus on the title of the article and elicit/explain the meaning of *throw out* (force someone to leave a house/building, etc. against their will).

b
- Set a time limit. Get SS to compare their order with a partner's before checking answers. You may need to explain the phrase *they went to court* at the end of B. However, try not to get involved in explaining all the words/phrases SS don't understand as this will be dealt with in **d**.
- Explain to SS that this is not the whole the story and that they will hear the ending on the tape/CD in **f**.

A 5 B 3 C 1 D 2 E 4

c
- Focus on the instructions. Get SS to compare their choice with a partner's, and then check which is the right summary (C).

d
- Now tell SS to go back through the text, paragraph by paragraph, and underline any new words or phrases. Encourage SS to guess their meaning from context before explaining.
- Tell SS to choose five new words/phrases to learn, and get them to compare their choices with a partner's.

e
- Do this as an open class activity and elicit opinions and ideas about what SS think happened at the end.

f 4.7

- Play the tape/CD once for SS to hear what happened. Play it again if necessary and get SS to compare what they have understood.

> 4.7 CD2 Track 8
> Does the story have a happy ending? Maria Serrano said, 'I think this was a lesson for our children and I think it was good for them. Things are already better. Now they respect us more and I feel happier. Of course they are welcome to come home again *if* they can show us that they have changed. I've given them a year. In any case they still come home for lunch every day!'

Extra photocopiable activities

Grammar
present perfect + *yet, just, already p.152*
Communicative
I haven't done it yet *p.196* (instructions *p.177*)

HOMEWORK

Study Link **Workbook** *pp.33–34*

G comparatives, *as … as, less … than …*
V time expressions: *spend time, waste time*, etc.
P sentence stress

4C Faster, faster!

Lesson plan

In this lesson SS revise comparative adjectives, and learn to use comparative adverbs and the structure (*not*) *as … as* to compare things. The context is a newspaper article which was based on a review of the book *Faster: the acceleration of just about everything*. It was written by an American author, James Gleick, who believes that lives are getting faster, but not necessarily better. The vocabulary focus is on expressions with *time*, e.g. *waste time*, and the pronunciation practises the /ə/ sound in unstressed syllables and words.

Optional lead-in (books closed)

Write on the board *working, eating, sleeping, relaxing*. SS in pairs say how long they spend doing these things in a typical day. Get feedback and ask SS if they have enough free time.

1 GRAMMAR comparatives, *as … as, less … than …*

a • Focus on the cartoon in the article and get SS to explain what is happening. SS will probably need help with the final picture (*The car hits him/runs him over.*).

• Now focus on the title of the article and get SS to read the introduction. Discuss the question with the class, and elicit that the article is pessimistic. Living faster does not mean living better.

b • Focus on the instructions. Give SS a few minutes to re-read the introduction and, in pairs, decide which word to cross out.

Extra challenge

Get SS to cross out the wrong word first in pairs and then re-read to check.

• Check answers.

1 ~~shorter~~ 2 ~~more~~ 3 ~~more slowly~~ 4 ~~more relaxed~~ 5 ~~longer~~

• Go through the introduction again checking that SS understand the words and expressions, e.g. *obsessed*, '*hurry sickness*' (= an 'illness' which means we are always trying to do things more quickly), etc. Tell SS that James Gleick's book refers mainly to the United States. Ask them if they think the same things are true in their country.

c • Now focus on the two sentences and get SS to complete them in pairs, or elicit the answers from the whole class. Let SS check with the text or give them the answers.

1 than 2 as, as

d • Now tell SS to go to **Grammar Bank 4C** on *p.132*. Go through the charts and rules. Model and drill the examples.

Grammar notes

• Although pre-intermediate SS have usually studied comparative adjectives before, they will probably need reminding of the rules, especially for one-syllable adjectives. Typical mistakes: *more big, more easy*, etc.

• Point out that the rules for adverbs are very similar. The only difference is that two syllable adverbs ending in *y*, e.g. *slowly* form the comparative with *more*, e.g. *more slowly* NOT ~~*slowlier*~~.

• The structure *as … as* is more common in the negative, but can also be used in the affirmative, e.g. *She's as tall as I am*. It is also very common with *much* and *many*, e.g. *I don't eat as much as you*.

You may also want to teach *the same as …*, e.g. *Your book is the same as mine*.

• Focus on the exercises for **4C** on *p.133*. SS do the exercises individually or in pairs. Check answers.

a 1 My sister is thinner than me.
2 I'm busier this week than I was last week.
3 Cambridge is further from London than Oxford.
4 I did the second exam worse than the first.
5 Chelsea played better than Arsenal.
6 The men in my office work harder than the women.
7 My new job is more boring than my old one.

b 1 Kelly isn't as tall as Cindy.
2 My case isn't as heavy as yours.
3 London isn't as big as Mexico City.
4 Tennis isn't as popular as football.
5 Adults don't learn languages as fast as children.
6 I don't work as hard as you.
7 England didn't play as well as France.

• Tell SS to go back to the main lesson on *p.44*.

2 PRONUNCIATION sentence stress

4.8

• Focus on the information box, and remind SS that the /ə/ sound is the most common sound in English.

• Now focus on the sentences. Play the tape/CD once for SS just to listen. Elicit that the pink letters are the /ə/ sound. Then play it again, pausing after each sentence for SS to repeat and copy the rhythm.

Pronunciation notes

If you encourage SS to get the stress right both in words and sentences then you should find that they will start producing the /ə/ sound quite naturally.

4.8 CD2 Track 9

1 I'm busier than a year ago.
2 Life is more stressful than in the past.
3 We work harder than before.
4 We walk and talk faster.
5 I'm not as relaxed as I was.
6 We won't live as long as our parents.

3 READING & VOCABULARY

a • SS now read the rest of the article they started in **1**, which gives some examples of how our lives are getting faster. Focus on the instructions and divide SS into pairs, **A** and **B**.

• Give SS a few minutes to each read their three paragraphs twice. Monitor and help individual SS if they are having problems with vocabulary.

b • Write the six headings from the article on the board. **A**s cover texts 1–3 and say what they can remember using the pictures and headings to help. **B**s listen with the whole text covered. Then **B**s talk about texts 4–6.

c • Get SS to read all six paragraphs, and in pairs guess the meanings of the highlighted expressions. Check answers. Model and drill *enough* and *waste*.

don't have enough time – don't have the time you need
save time – do something more quickly so that you have more time
waste time – use time badly
take a long time – last too long
spend more time – use more time
on time – punctual, not late

4 LISTENING & SPEAKING

a **4.9**

• Focus on the questionnaire (**ARE YOU LIVING FASTER?**), and go through question 1. You could answer it yourself to give SS an example.

• Tell SS they are going to hear four people answering question 1 and that they have to listen and write which thing in 1 each person is talking about.

• Play the tape/CD once. Get SS to compare before checking answers.

1 talking on the phone
2 cooking
3 sleeping
4 sitting in traffic

4.9 CD2 Track 10

(tapescript in Student's Book on *p.121*)

1 Definitely more. My daughter got married last year and she and her husband live quite far away. She rings me almost every day to tell me how everything's going, and we usually chat for hours. My phone bill is now double what it was when she was living at home.

2 I spend a lot less time than before. My youngest child has just started school, and I've gone back to work, so I never make lunch now during the week – I just have a sandwich. And in the evenings we often get take-away pizzas or Chinese food, or we heat something up in the microwave. I only really spend time in the kitchen at weekends.

3 Well, I'd say less – though I'm not sure if my parents would agree. I get so much homework now that I never go to bed before 11 or 12, but I still get up at seven in the morning. It's true I get up later at weekends, but that's only two days out of seven.

4 More, much more. Before it only used to take me fifteen minutes to get to work, and now it takes me twenty-five, or even half an hour. It's mainly because there are just more cars on the road. Sometimes I think I should use public transport, but it's quite complicated from where I live.

b **4.9**

• Focus on the instructions. Tell SS to listen for extra information. Play the tape/CD again. Check answers.

Extra support

Stop the tape/CD after each person and get SS to to answer the question. Check answers before playing the next person. If you have time, let SS listen again with the tapescript on *p.121*.

c • Tell SS to read the questionnaire all the way through and deal with any vocabulary problems.

• Put SS into pairs and get them to interview each other using the questionnaire. Monitor and make sure SS are forming the comparative correctly and using the expressions with *time*. Get feedback from a few pairs.

Extra support

Get SS to think first about their answer to question 1. They could make notes, e.g. write M (more) or L (less), (or S for the same) next to the things in question 1.

Extra photocopiable activities

Grammar
comparative adjectives and adverbs *p.153*
Communicative
Which do you prefer? Why? *p.197* (instructions *p.177*)

HOMEWORK

Study Link **Workbook** *pp.35–36*

4 D

G superlatives (+ *ever* + present perfect)
V opposite adjectives: *far*, *near*, etc.
P word stress

The world's friendliest city

Lesson plan

In this lesson SS move from comparatives to superlatives. SS who did not use *New English File Elementary* may not have studied superlatives before, in which case you will probably need to spend more time on them. The context is a light-hearted *Sunday Times* article where a journalist went to four big cities, London, Rome, Paris, and New York to find out which was the friendliest towards tourists. The present perfect is also recycled in expressions like *the most beautiful place I've ever been to*. SS learn more adjectives, and how to make opposites with prefixes. The pronunciation focuses on word stress in superlative sentences.

Optional lead-in (books closed)

Give SS a Capital city quiz. Choose six countries which are significant to your SS, and add England, France, Italy, and the United States (which are going to come up in the lesson). Ask SS *What's the capital of England?*, etc. SS can either write down the answers in pairs or teams, or you could simply do this as an open class activity.

Where appropriate, teach SS the names of the cities in English, and model and drill the pronunciation. Teach them the spelling and pronunciation of their capital city in English.

1 READING & LISTENING

a • Focus on the questions. Get SS to read the introduction and answer them in pairs. Get feedback.

Extra idea

You could also ask SS if there are any differences between people from the capital and people from their town. Or if they live in the capital, between them and people from small towns and villages.

b • Focus on the instructions and questions 1–6 (two questions for each test). Give SS three minutes to read the chart and answer the questions. Get SS to compare answers with a partner's and then check answers.

1 NY and R were both very friendly.
2 R
3 R
4 NY
5 P (more than a minute)
6 R (about eight people helped him)

Extra idea

Give SS a minute to re-read the chart. Then tell them to close their books and give them a memory test using questions 1–6. Ask more specific questions to check SS understood the details, e.g.:

Who took the photo in New York? (an office worker)
What was he doing? (eating sandwiches)
What did he say when the journalist asked him to take a photo? (Of course I'll take your picture), etc.

c 4.10

• Tell SS they are going to listen to the journalist describe what happened in London. Ask SS if anyone has been to London, and if they think it will be more or less friendly than the other three cities.
• Focus on the questions and tell them to just listen and not write the first time, and then on the second listening to answer with a couple of words, not sentences.
• Play the tape/CD once the whole way through. Then play it again, pausing after each section for SS to make notes.

Extra support

SS could write the answers in their L1.

• Check answers.

1 A man.
2 No, no, no time for that.
3 A businessman. He took one photo (but no more).
4 A key ring and a red bus in Oxford Street.
5 40 pounds
6 Yes
7 In the Tube (the London underground).
8 No.
9 Why don't you look where you're going?

4.10 CD2 Track 11

(tapescript in Student's Book on *p.121*)
First I did the photo test. I was near Charing Cross station. I stopped a man who was walking quite slowly down the road and I said, 'Excuse me, could you take my photo?' The man said: 'No, no, no time for that,' and just continued walking. Then I asked a businessman in a grey suit who was walking towards the station. He took one photo, but when I asked him to take another one he walked away quickly.
Next, it was the shopping test. I went to a tourist shop in Oxford Street and I bought a key ring and a red bus. The red bus was very expensive. The total price was forty pounds. I gave the man a hundred pounds – two fifty pound notes. He gave me sixty pounds back.
Finally it was time for the accident test. For this test I went down into the Tube (the London Underground). As I went down the stairs I fell over and sat on the floor. A man immediately stopped and looked down at me. I thought he was going to help me but he didn't – he just said 'Why don't you look where you are going?'

2 GRAMMAR superlatives (+ *ever* + present perfect)

a • Focus on the three sentences. Give SS a minute to decide on the wrong forms. Check answers.

> 1 ~~the friendlier~~ 2 ~~the more unfriendly~~
> 3 ~~gone to?~~

• Elicit/explain that:
- in 1, *the friendlier* is wrong because *friendlier* is the comparative form. *The friendliest* is the superlative form = the maximum.
- in number 2, *more unfriendly* is the comparative form and so is wrong here.
- in 3 *you've gone to* is wrong because it means that you haven't returned yet. *You've been to* = you have visited a place and returned.

b • Get SS to quickly ask and answer the questions in pairs. Get feedback.

> The answers to 1 and 2 are a matter of opinion, but the article suggests that New York was the friendliest and London was the most unfriendly.

c • Tell SS to go to **Grammar Bank 4D** on *p.132*. Go through the rules for making superlatives in the chart and the rules of use.

Grammar notes

Superlatives

- Remind SS that the rules for making superlatives are the same as for comparatives but adding *-est* instead of *-er*, or using *most* instead of *more*. Remind them to use *the* before superlatives.
- SS sometimes use comparatives where they should use superlatives. Typical mistake: *the more expensive city in Europe*, etc.
- Highlight that SS must always think if they are comparing two things (comparative), or more than two (superlative) when deciding which form to use, e.g. *The most beautiful city I've ever been to.*
- Some languages use *never* (not *ever*) in this structure. Typical mistake: *The most beautiful city I've never been to.*
- Adverbs can also be used in the superlative, e.g. *He drives the fastest.*

• Focus on the exercises for **4D** on *p.133*. SS do the exercises individually or in pairs. Check answers.

> **a** 1 the hottest 2 the worst 3 the friendliest
> 4 the most important 5 best 6 the most polluted
> 7 furthest
> **b** 1 It's the best film I've ever seen.
> 2 He's the most unfriendly person I've ever met.
> 3 It's the hardest exam he's ever done.
> 4 They're the most expensive shoes she's ever bought.
> 5 It's the longest book I've ever read.
> 6 She's the most beautiful girl I've ever seen.
> 7 It's the worst meal I've ever had.

• Tell SS to go back to the main lesson on *p.47*.

3 VOCABULARY opposite adjectives

a • Focus on the adjectives in the list and tell SS that the opposites of the adjectives were all in the text on *p.46*. Elicit the opposites, and get SS to underline the stress.

> unfriendly polite quiet interesting

• Highlight that sometimes you add a prefix to make the opposite, e.g. *friendly – unfriendly*, and sometimes it's a different word, e.g. *quiet – noisy*.

b • Tell SS to go to **Vocabulary Bank *Adjectives*** on *p.145*. Focus on **2 *Opposite adjectives***. They do the exercises in pairs or individually.

• Check answers, and model and drill pronunciation. Then get SS to test themselves/each other.

Extra challenge

After you've corrected **d**, you could point out that:
un- is the most common negative prefix.
im- is only used before some adjectives beginning with *m*, *p*.
in-, *ir-*, and *il-* are also negative prefixes, e.g. *incorrect, irregular, illegal.*

> **a**
> 1 far 2 polite 3 dangerous 4 crowded
> 5 polluted 6 noisy 7 boring 8 modern
> **b**
> boring – exciting/interesting
> crowded – empty
> dangerous – safe
> far – near
> modern – old
> noisy – quiet
> polite – rude
> polluted – clean
> **d**
> uncomfortable unhappy unhealthy untidy
> impolite impossible impatient

Study Link SS can find more practice of these phrases on the MultiROM and on the *New English File Pre-intermediate* website.

• Tell SS to go back to the main lesson on *p.47*.

c • Focus on the questions and elicit the superlatives of the adjectives. Get SS to choose a couple of questions to ask you. Then they choose five to ask their partner.

• SS ask and answer in pairs. Monitor and correct any mistakes with superlatives or the present perfect. Get feedback from different pairs.

Extra challenge

Encourage SS to ask follow-up questions, e.g. *When did you go there? Why?*, etc. Fast finishers could make and ask their own superlative questions.

4 PRONUNCIATION word stress

a • Focus on the task and give SS time, in pairs, to underline the stressed syllable. Do not check answers yet.

b 4.11

- Play the tape/CD once for SS to check. Drill the pronunciation of the adjectives.

polluted impatient comfortable interesting expensive beautiful

- Play the tape/CD again for SS to hear which other words are stressed. Check answers.
- Highlight that the prepositions *to* and *at*, which are not normally stressed, are stressed here because of their end position.

4.11 CD2 Track 12

1 It's the most polluted city I've ever been to.
2 He's the most impatient person I've ever met.
3 This is the most comfortable hotel I've ever stayed at.
4 It's the most interesting book I've ever read.
5 They're the most expensive shoes I've ever bought.
6 It's the most beautiful place I've ever seen.

c • Finally play it again and pause after each sentence for SS to copy the rhythm.

5 SPEAKING

a • Put SS into pairs, **A** and **B**. Tell SS to go to **Communication *The best and the worst*, A** on *p.110* and **B** on *p.114*.

- Go through the instructions. SS should read each sentence and then write the name of a place, person, etc. in the corresponding oval on *p.47*. Give SS time to think and write, but tell them that if they can't think of anyone or anything for one particular oval just to leave it blank.

b • Tell SS to go back to *p.47*. Focus on the speech bubbles. SS ask and answer about the things they wrote in the ovals. Tell SS that they must ask follow-up questions after their partner has told them why he/she wrote a place/name.

Extra support

You could demonstrate the activity first by completing one of **A**'s and one of **B**'s places/names. Write them on the board. Then elicit the question *Why did you write ... ?* and tell SS why. Elicit more follow-up questions to help them get the idea.

- Get feedback by asking a few SS to tell you something about their partner.

Extra photocopiable activities

Grammar
superlatives *p.154*
Communicative
The best in town *p.198* (instructions *p.177*)

HOMEWORK

Study Link **Workbook** *pp.37–38*

4 PRACTICAL ENGLISH LOST IN SAN FRANCISCO

Revision Understanding directions
Function Asking for information and directions
Language *Can you recommend a good museum?* etc.

Lesson plan

In this lesson SS revise directions, and learn more expressions for asking for information. With directions, as in *New English File Elementary*, the focus is more on understanding directions than on giving them. In the story, in Social English, Allie gets lost and asks a man for help. To her surprise it's Brad, Mark's friend.

Study Link These lessons are on the *New English File Pre-intermediate* Video, which can be used instead of the Class Cassette/CD (see introduction *p.9*). The main functional section of each episode (the second section) is also on the MultiROM with additional activities.

Optional lead-in (books closed)

Revise what happened in the previous episode by eliciting the story from the class (Mark and Allie had dinner and talked about their past).

DIRECTIONS

4.12

- Books open. Quickly revise a few simple directions, e.g. *turn right/left, go straight on,* etc. Then focus on the map and the task. Give SS time to locate Union Square, Stockton, and Sutter Street on the map.
- Play the tape/CD once the whole way through and tell SS just to listen. Ask SS *What does Allie want to do?* (go shopping) *Where does the receptionist recommend?* (Union Square – the big department stores are there).
- Play the tape/CD again, pausing if necessary to give SS time to number the directions. Get them to compare with each other before checking answers.

1 Go out of the hotel and turn left.
2 Go straight ahead, down Sutter Street.
3 Turn left at Stockton.
4 It's the third street on the left.
5 Union Square will be right in front of you.

4.12 CD2 Track 13

(tapescript in Student's Book on *p.121*)
R = Receptionist, A = Allie
R Good morning, ma'am. How can I help you?
A I want to go shopping. Where's the best place to go?
R Well, all the big department stores are around Union Square.
A Can you tell me how to get there?
R Yes, of course. Go out of the hotel and turn left. Go straight ahead, down Sutter Street. Turn left at Stockton – it's the third street on the left. Union Square will be right in front of you. You can't miss it.
A Thanks.

ASKING FOR INFORMATION

a 4.13

- Focus on the questions. Play the tape/CD once or twice. Check answers.
- Tell SS to cover the dialogue. Focus on the questions. Play the tape/CD once for SS to answer the questions. Check answers and that SS have drawn the route correctly. Elicit that SFMOMA is the blue building on the corner of 3rd Street and Howard.

Allie wants to go to the museum of modern art (SFMOMA).
She's going to walk there.

b • Now tell SS to uncover the dialogue. Give them a minute to read through the dialogue and guess the missing words. Then play the tape/CD again.

4.13 4.14 CD2 Tracks 14+15

A = Allie, R = Receptionist

A Can you recommend a good museum? (*repeat*)
R Well, SFMOMA is fantastic.
A Sorry. Where did you say? (*repeat*)
R SFMOMA. The San Francisco **Museum** of Modern Art.
A Where is it? (*repeat*)
R On **Third** Street.
A How far is it from Union Square? (*repeat*)
R Not far. It's just a **couple** of blocks.
A Can I walk from there? (*repeat*)
R Sure. It'll **take** you ten minutes.
A Can you show me on the map? (*repeat*)
R Yes, Union Square is here, and the museum is here. From Union Square you go down Geary to the **end** and turn right. That's Third Street. Go down Third and you'll see SFMOMA on the **left**.
A What time does it open? (*repeat*)
R It opens at **11.00**.
A Thanks very much. (*repeat*)
R Have a good day. I'm sure you'll **love** the museum!

- Go through the dialogue line by line and check answers. Highlight *Third Street* – many streets in the US have ordinal numbers, e.g. *Fifth Avenue*.

c 4.14

- Play the tape/CD, pausing for SS to repeat the **YOU SAY** phrases. Encourage them to copy the rhythm.

d • Put SS into pairs, **A** and **B**. **A** is the receptionist, **B** is Allie. Tell **B** to close his/her book and try to remember the phrases. Then **A** and **B** swap roles.

SOCIAL ENGLISH looking for Union Square

a 4.15

- Get SS to read the sentences and the answer options. Play the tape/CD at least twice for SS to circle the answers.
- Check answers.

1 a 2 b 3 a 4 b 5 b

4.15 CD2 Track 16

(tapescript in Student's Book on *p.121*)

A = Allie, B = Brad

A Oh, where is it? Excuse me. Can you tell me the way to Union Square?
B Hey – don't I **know** you?
A I don't **think** so.
B Allie, I'm Brad! Brad Martin from the Los Angeles office. I'm Mark's friend, remember? We met yesterday at the hotel.
A Oh yes, that's right. Brad. I'm so sorry.
B No problem. What are you **doing** here?
A I want to go shopping. I'm **looking** for Union Square. But I'm lost.
B Where's Mark?
A He's at the hotel – he had a meeting, I think.
B Listen, Allie. I'm going to take you for a cup of coffee at Del Monico's – they have the best coffee in San Francisco, and amazing cookies. And then I'll walk with you to Union Square.
A That's really **kind** of you. Are you **sure**?
B Absolutely. It's my pleasure.
A OK. Great. I'm awful with new cities. I always get lost.
B Oh, I love your British accent ...

Extra support

If there's time, you could get SS to listen again with the tapescript on *p.121* so they can see exactly what Allie and Brad said, and see how much they understood. Translate/explain any new words/phrases.

- Get SS to speculate a bit about the story, and what will happen next. Ask *What do you think Brad's intentions are? Do you think Allie is interested in Brad? Do you think she'll tell Mark she met Brad?*

b • Focus on the **USEFUL PHRASES**. Get SS to see if they can remember any of the missing words. Play the tape/CD again and check answers.

c 4.16

- Play the tape/CD pausing after each phrase for SS to repeat. Encourage them to copy the rhythm.

4.16 CD2 Track 17

B = Brad, A = Allie

B Don't I know you?
A I don't think so.
B What are you doing here?
A I'm looking for Union Square.
A That's really kind of you.
A Are you sure?

Extra challenge

Get SS to roleplay the conversation between Allie and Brad in pairs using the tapescript on *p.121*. Let SS read their parts first and then try to act it from memory.

HOMEWORK

Study Link **Workbook** *p.39*

4 WRITING DESCRIBING WHERE YOU LIVE

Lesson plan

In this lesson SS write a description of their home town, and revise adjectives from **File 4**. There is a vocabulary focus to help provide the words they will need. The writing skills focus is on correcting grammar mistakes.

a • Focus on the photos of Porto. Ask if any SS have been there.

• Focus on the text and instructions. Give SS, in pairs, a few minutes to read the text and match the questions and paragraphs. Check answers.

What's it famous for?	4
What's the weather like?	3
What's the best thing about it? Do you like living there?	5
Describe your home town.	2
Where do you live? Where is it? How big is it?	1

b • Focus on the instructions. Go through the words and check SS know *atmosphere* and *population*. Model and drill the pronunciation of the words.

• Set a time limit for SS to re-read the text and complete the gaps. Get SS to compare their choices with a partner's and then check answers.

2 population	**6** beach
3 streets	**7** tourist
4 museums	**8** river
5 weather	**9** festival
	10 atmosphere

• Give SS a few minutes, in pairs, to underline any words or phrases they don't know. Go through them explaining or translating where necessary.

c • Focus on the first mistake and its correction. Ask SS why *bigger* is wrong (it's a comparative; it should be a superlative). Get SS to continue in pairs. Check answers.

there **are** a lot of ...
it sometimes **rains** ...
which is only produced ...
lots of tourists **go**
I like **living** here ...

Write a description

Either give SS at least fifteen minutes to write the description in class, following the instructions, or set it for homework. Ask SS to attach a photo if they can.

Extra idea

In a multilingual class, you could get SS to answer questions 1–5 orally in pairs before they write. If your SS are all from the same town, they could plan the answers to 1–5 in pairs.

• If SS do the writing in class, get them to swap their descriptions with another S's to read and check for mistakes before you collect them all in.

4 REVISE & CHECK

For instructions on how to use these pages, see *p.27*.

GRAMMAR

1 b **2** a **3** c **4** b **5** b **6** b **7** a **8** c **9** a **10** b

VOCABULARY

a **1** tidy **2** pick up **3** take **4** do **5** waste
b **1** jeans **2** suit **3** try **4** off **5** trainers
c **1** polite **2** quiet **3** impossible **4** safe **5** impatient

PRONUNCIATION

a **1** coat **2** bought **3** pretty **4** earn **5** already
b pyjamas already nearly busier friendliest

CAN YOU UNDERSTAND THIS TEXT?

a **1** T **2** DS **3** F **4** DS **5** F **6** F **7** T **8** T
b **engaged** – when you have promised to marry someone
wedding – the ceremony in which people marry
wedding dress – the special dress worn by the bride
fiancé(e) – the person you are engaged to
honeymoon – the holiday you take after the wedding
marriage (n) – the relationship you have when you are man and wife

CAN YOU UNDERSTAND THESE PEOPLE?

4.17 CD2 Track 18

1
A Have you ever been to a fashion show?
B Never. Have you?
A Yeah. I went to one last year.
B Yeah. How was it?
A I went to sleep and woke up at the end.

2
A What did you buy?
B Well, I tried on a shirt but it was too big. I bought a skirt and a sweater.
A Did you get any shoes?
B No, I didn't see any I liked.

3
A Don't walk on the kitchen floor!
B Why?
A I've just washed it.
B Again?
A It was dirty again.
B It's dry now.
A No, it isn't. It's still wet.

4
A I don't go out much during the week now.
B Why not?

A Because I finish work later.
B How many hours do you work?
A When I started this job two years ago I worked eight hours a day, from nine to five. Now I work two hours more every day for the same money.
B That's the same everywhere.

5
A What's the most beautiful city you've been to?
B Well, Amsterdam is lovely. Oh, and Prague is beautiful.
A What about Venice?
B Well, of course Venice is wonderful, but I think Prague is probably my favourite.

a 1 c 2 b 3 a 4 a 5 b

4.18 CD2 Track 19

A Have you ever had to wear clothes you didn't like?
B Oh, all the time. Some of the things we have to wear are absolutely awful, but that's not a problem.
A Have you ever fallen over during a fashion show?
B Yes, once. I was wearing very high heels and I had to walk down some stairs at the end of the catwalk and I fell over.
A Did you hurt yourself?
B I broke a finger. Nothing serious.
A Do you travel a lot in your job?
B I spend my life travelling. I'm only 23 but I've already been all over the world. Europe, Asia, South America, the United States, everywhere except Africa. I haven't been there yet, but I'm doing something there next year.
A Have you been anywhere recently?
B I've just come back from Argentina. I spent a week there doing a photo shoot for a woman's magazine.
A And what's the most exciting country you've been to?
B That's difficult to answer. India probably. I'd love to go back.

b 1 T 2 F 3 T 4 F 5 T

CAN YOU SAY THIS IN ENGLISH?

b 1 What's the hottest place you've ever been to?
2 What's the worst film you've ever seen?
3 Who's the most generous person you've ever met?
4 What's the best restaurant you've ever been to?
5 What's the longest journey you've ever made?

Extra photocopiable activities

Quicktest 4 *p.234*

5 A

G uses of the infinitive (with *to*)
V verbs + infinitive: *want to, hope to,* etc.
P word stress

Are you a party animal?

File 5 overview

This File focuses on the two common verb patterns in English: verbs followed by the infinitive and those followed by the gerund (verb + *-ing* form). **5A** presents uses of the infinitive and **5B** the uses of the gerund. The two forms are contrasted briefly in **Grammar Bank 5B**. (They will be contrasted more fully in *New English File Intermediate*). In **5C** SS learn the modals *have to* and *must*. These are recycled in **5D**, where SS also learn to use verbs + prepositions to express movement, e.g. *go up, walk down,* etc.

Lesson plan

The context of this lesson is parties, which includes any kind of gathering of friends and relatives, e.g. a wedding. The focus is on how to survive at any kind of gathering when you don't know anybody – a useful life skill. There is some humorous advice on what to say (and not to say) when you meet somebody for the first time who has a particular job. In Grammar, SS learn when to use the infinitive form (*to* + verb). SS will learn some rules about the gerund (verb + *-ing*) in **5B**. In Vocabulary SS learn/revise some high frequency verbs which are followed by the infinitive form, and in Pronunciation there is more practice of word stress in words with two or three syllables.

Optional lead-in (books closed)

Write PARTY on the board in big letters. Write this question underneath: *Why do people go to parties?* and elicit SS' ideas. Encourage them to use the infinitive (*to* + verb), e.g. *to meet people, to relax, to have a good time, to drink, to make friends, to get a boyfriend/girlfriend,* etc. Write their ideas on the board.

⚠ Depending on SS' L1 they may make the typical mistake *For meet people/For to meet people.*

Continue until you have elicited five or six reasons. Then do exercise **1**.

1 SPEAKING

- Books open. Focus on the lesson title and elicit the meaning of *party animal* (someone who likes/enjoys going to parties).
- Focus on the questionnaire and quickly go through the questions. Put SS into pairs, **A** and **B**. **A** interviews **B**. Then they swap roles.
- SS decide if their partner is a 'party animal' or not. Get feedback from some pairs.

Extra challenge

Get **B** to close his/her book or cover the page so that he/she has to listen to **A**'s questions.

2 GRAMMAR uses of the infinitive (with *to*)

a • Focus on the picture and ask *What's happening? How do you think the man on the left is feeling?* Elicit that he's not very happy, perhaps because he doesn't know anybody. Ask SS if this has ever happened to them and what they do if they find themselves in this position.
• Now focus on the instructions and the text. Tell SS to read the text once but without trying to fill any of the gaps.
• Then put SS into pairs and give them three minutes to work together to complete the text with the verbs in the box. Make sure they know what all the verbs in the box mean before they start. SS are already familiar with this full infinitive form (or the infinitive with *to*) from verbs like *want* and *would like* (*to do something*). Check answers.

2 to meet **3** to ask **4** to start **5** not to dominate
6 to talk **7** to listen **8** to give **9** to talk
10 to escape **11** to get **12** to go

b • Focus on the task. Then give SS a couple of minutes to read the article again and try to remember the tips (*a tip* = good idea or piece of advice that can help you).
• Get SS to cover the text and, in pairs, they see how many of the five tips they can remember. Highlight that SS don't have to remember the exact words just the main idea.
• Finally, elicit the five tips from the whole class, and ask which one they think is the best.

c • Focus on the three examples from the text A–C and on the rules 1–3. Give SS a minute or so to study them and then to match the examples with the rules. Check answers.

1 C 2 A 3 B

⚠ If SS ask you what the other verbs in rule 1 are, tell them that they will see a fuller list when they do exercise **4 VOCABULARY**.

Extra challenge

Get SS to look at the rest of the infinitives in the article and decide if they are examples of rule 1, 2, or 3.

d • Tell SS to go to **Grammar Bank 5A** on *p.134*. Go through the rules with the class. Model and drill the example sentences.

Grammar notes

- The infinitive has two forms in English:

  1 *work* is the form which is given in a dictionary. SS have seen this used in present simple questions and negatives, e.g. *Do you work?*, *I didn't work*, and after the modal verb *can*.

  2 *to work* SS should already be familiar with the infinitive with *to* used after some verbs such as *want* and *would like*, e.g. *I'd like to work with children.*

⚠ The infinitive of purpose is only used to express a [+] reason. To express a [–] reason we use *in order not to* or *so as not to*, e.g. *We took a taxi so as not to be late* NOT ~~*We took a taxi not to be late*~~.

- Focus on exercises **5A** on *p.135*. SS do the exercises individually or in pairs. Check answers.

a 1 to meet **2** to do **3** to go **4** not to make **5** to learn **6** not to drive **7** to leave
b 1 A **2** F **3** G **4** B **5** H **6** C **7** E

Extra idea

Put SS into small groups. Get them to try to think of at least two answers to each of the questions below, using *to* + infinitive. Why do people . . .

– go to parties? *– go on holidays?*
– get married? *– learn English?*
– go to a gym?

- Tell SS to go back to the main lesson on *p.53*.

3 READING & LISTENING

a • Focus on the article and explain that this is about the right and wrong things to say to people who you meet for the first time at a party.

- Go through the article quickly with the class (you could read it aloud) but tell SS not to guess the missing words yet.
- Put SS into pairs and set them a time limit. Tell them to try and guess the missing words but not to write them in yet. They can write them on a piece of paper.

b 5.1

- Tell SS they are now going to listen to five conversations where people say the wrong thing. Play the tape/CD once, pausing after each conversation for SS to complete the phrases.
- Get SS to compare their answers with their guesses. Check answers and get feedback to find out how many SS guessed more or less correctly.

5.1 CD2 Track 20
(tapescript in Student's Book on *p.122*)

1 A Hello, you're one of Peter's friends aren't you?
B That's right. I'm Adrian.
A Hi, I'm Harry. Are you enjoying the party?
B Yes.
A So, what do you do for a living, Adrian?
B I'm a doctor.
A A doctor? Oh that's good. Listen, **I have a problem with my back. Could you have a look at it?** I've got a pain just here ...
B Sorry, can you excuse me? I've just seen Peter over there and I want to wish him a Happy Birthday.

2 A James, this is Sandra.
B Hi.
C Nice to meet you.
A Sandra's a teacher in secondary school.
B A teacher? Really? What a wonderful job. You're so lucky.
C Why lucky?
B Well, **you have really long summer holidays!**
C Yes, that's what people always say. Perhaps you would like to teach my class one day. When you teach teenagers all year, you *need* a long summer holiday.

3 A Hello. We haven't met before, have we?
B No, I don't think so.
A I'm Catherine, I'm Peter's sister.
B Oh, hi, I'm Luke. I went to school with Peter.
A Ah, Luke! You're the travel agent, aren't you?
B Yes, I am.
A Peter's told me all about you. Listen, **can you recommend a cheap holiday?** I'd like to go somewhere hot. And I want to go in August. But when I say cheap, I mean cheap. Oh and I can't fly because I'm terrified of flying …

4 A Deborah, can I introduce you to an old friend of mine, Lucy.
B Hi Lucy.
C Nice to meet you.
A Lucy's my hairdresser.
B Ah. You're just the person I want to talk to. Lucy, **what do you think of my colour?**
C Well ...
B No, come on, tell me the truth. **Is it too blonde?**
C Er ... no. I think it's fine.
B Are you sure?
A Lucy, what would you like to drink?
C Oh, a Diet Coke please.
B Do you think my hair would look better shorter?
A Deborah, Lucy's not at work now.
B Oh sorry.

5 A Hi. I'm Andrea. Nice to meet you.
B Hello. My name's Simon.
A What do you do Simon? No, don't tell me! Let me guess your job! Let me see. You look like a ... professional footballer.
B No ... I'm a psychiatrist.
A A psychiatrist! Ooh how fascinating! Simon? **Are you analysing me?**
B Er, no, I'm not. Excuse me, er, Andrea. I need to go to the bathroom.

c • Play the tape/CD again for SS to complete the conversations with an infinitive.

Extra challenge

Get SS to complete the sentences in pairs before listening to the tape/CD. They then listen to check.

- Pause the tape/CD to give SS time to write in the verbs and re-play the recording as necessary.
- Get SS to check their answers with a partner's before checking answers.

1 to wish **2** to teach **3** to go, hot **4** to talk
5 to go, bathroom

4 VOCABULARY verbs + infinitive

a • Tell SS to go to **Vocabulary Bank *Verb forms*** on *p.154*. Focus on **A** and go through the examples, helping with meaning and pronunciation.

You may want to point out that *help* can also be used with the infinitive without *to*, e.g. *I'll help you do the exercise.*

Study Link SS can find more practice of these words on the MultiROM and on the *New English File Pre-intermediate* website.

Extra idea

Give SS a minute to memorize the examples. Then, in pairs, SS cover the examples with a piece of paper and look only at the verbs. They try to remember the example sentence and then move the paper down to check if they have remembered correctly.

b • Don't go back to the main lesson. Put SS into pairs, **A** and **B**. Tell SS to go to Communication ***Guess the infinitive***, **A** on *p.110* and **B** on *p.114*.

- Here SS get some practice of the new vocabulary. Go through the instructions first for **A** and then for **B**. Use SS' L1 if necessary.
- Demonstrate the activity. Write in large letters on a piece of paper YOU NEED TO PUT ON A COAT. Then write on the board: *It's very cold. You need ____ a coat.*(+)
- Explain that there is an infinitive missing, and that the (+) sign means it's a positive infinitive. Tell them that you have the sentence on a piece of paper, and they must try to guess the infinitive you have.
- Elicit guesses, e.g. *to take, to wear, to buy* and say *Try again* until someone says *to put on*. Show SS your piece of paper with the complete sentence. Explain that the other verbs are all possible, but that they have to try to guess the verb their partner has written down. Go through the instructions to make sure SS understand.
- Give SS a couple of minutes to think about what verbs are missing from their sentences but tell them not to write the verb in.

  Emphasize that the verb must be the infinitive **with** *to*, e.g. *to work*.
- Now get SS to sit face to face if possible and tell **A** to start trying to guess the missing verbs. **B** will tell them if they are right or wrong. If they are right, they can write in the verb. When **A** has guessed all **B**'s sentences they swap roles.
- Tell SS to go back to the main lesson on *p.53*.

5 PRONUNCIATION & SPEAKING

a • Focus on the information box and give some examples, e.g.:

Two-syllable: *<u>chil</u>dren <u>luck</u>y, <u>per</u>son, <u>birth</u>day*

Three-syllable: *<u>hol</u>iday, <u>mo</u>tivate, <u>teen</u>agers*

- Highlight that this is only *usually* true and SS should focus on words that don't follow this pattern, e.g. *per<u>haps</u>, recom<u>mend</u>*. It is especially important that SS mark the stress on these words when they write them down in their vocabulary notebooks.
- Give SS two minutes to underline the stressed syllables. Do not check answers yet.

b 5.2

- Play the tape/CD for SS to check their answers.

5.2 CD2 Track 21

<u>dan</u>gerous	de<u>cide</u>	<u>dif</u>ficult	for<u>get</u>
im<u>por</u>tant	<u>in</u>teresting	<u>pos</u>sible	pre<u>tend</u>
<u>pro</u>mise	re<u>mem</u>ber		

- Play the tape/CD again for SS to listen and repeat.

c • This speaking activity reinforces the pronunciation practised in **b**. Quickly go through the questions and make sure SS understand them. Give SS time to choose five questions to ask a partner.

- Put SS into pairs. They take turns asking and answering. Monitor, making sure SS pronounce the words in bold correctly.
- Get feedback from the class.

Extra support

Get SS to choose questions to ask you first. Encourage them to ask follow-up questions for more information. You could write a few question words, e.g. *Why? When?*, etc. on the board to remind them.

Extra photocopiable activities

Grammar

the infinitive with *to p.155*

Communicative

Language school party *p.199* (instructions *p.178*)

HOMEWORK

Study Link Workbook *pp.40–41*

5 B

G verb + *-ing*
V verbs followed by *-ing*: *love, can't stand,* etc.
P *-ing*

What makes you feel good?

Lesson plan

In this lesson SS talk about things which make them feel good and through this context learn three common uses of the verb + *-ing* form (often called the gerund). The ideas in the article *What makes you feel good?* come from people in different parts of the world. The vocabulary focus is on common verbs which are followed by the gerund. In Pronunciation SS practise pronouncing the *-ing* ending correctly.

Optional lead-in (books closed)

Write on the board WHAT MAKES YOU FEEL GOOD? and elicit ideas from the class. Encourage SS to use a verb + *-ing*, e.g. *Looking at the sea, Being with my friends,* etc. Give a couple of your own examples if SS are slow to respond. When you have a good number of sentences on the board you could get SS to choose their favourite and have a vote on the most popular activity. Then do exercise **1a**.

1 READING

a • Books open. Focus on the text and illustrations. Explain the task (*mention* = say something about). Tell SS to read the text once and do the task. Give them two minutes.

• You may have to deal with a few vocabulary problems, e.g. *take off* = when a plane leaves the ground, *storm* = very bad weather with a lot of rain and strong winds, *It doesn't matter* = it isn't important, etc.

1 three (paragraphs 1, 4, 6)
2 three (paragraphs 3, 4, 5)
3 one (paragraph 10)
4 one (paragraph 5)
5 two (paragraphs 2, 7)

b • SS read the article again and tick the three things that they agree with most and cross any they don't agree with. SS compare their choices with a partner's. Get feedback from the whole class to find out which one(s) are the most popular/unpopular.

c • Give SS time to underline five words and phrases they want to remember from the text. Get some feedback on which ones they have chosen and encourage them to write them in their notebooks.

2 GRAMMAR verb + *-ing*

a • Focus on the three sentences from the text (A–C) and the rules 1–3. Give SS time to do the task. Check answers.

1 B 2 A 3 C

• Tell SS that they will see a list of verbs which are followed by the *-ing* form later in the lesson.

b • Focus on the highlighted verbs in sentences A–C and try to elicit from SS these spelling rules:

1 Add *-ing* to the infinitive form, e.g. *be – being.*
2 With mono-syllabic verbs (ending in one vowel and one consonant) you double the final consonant and add *-ing*, e.g. *sit – sitting, get – getting, swim – swimming.*
3 With verbs which end in *e*, cut the *e* and add *-ing*, e.g. *live – living, write – writing,* etc.

c • Tell SS to go to **Grammar Bank 5B** on *p.134*. Go through the rules with the class. Model and drill the example sentences.

Grammar notes

• It is very likely that in your SS' L1 an infinitive form will be used where English uses an *-ing* form.
• SS will look at other verbs followed by the gerund in exercise **4.**

⚠ In British English it is much more common to use a gerund after *like, love,* and *hate* especially when you are speaking about general likes and dislikes. However an infinitive can be used without any real difference in meaning.

Spelling rules

You may want to point out that verbs which are stressed on the last syllable also double the final consonant, e.g. *begin – beginning, prefer – preferring.*

⚠ *travel – travelling* is an exception: it is stressed on the first syllable but doubles the final consonant.

Gerund or infinitive?

• SS are asked to discriminate between the gerund and infinitive in the second exercise in the **Grammar Bank**. Before doing it you could get SS to quickly look again at the rules for both (see **Grammar Banks 5A** and **5B** *p.134*).

⚠ Remind SS that *like* is usually followed by the gerund, e.g. *I like travelling,* but *would like* is followed by the infinitive, e.g. *I would like to travel around the world.*

• Focus on the exercises for **5B** on *p.135*. SS do the exercises individually or in pairs. Check answers.

a 1 remembering 2 Teaching 3 learning 4 talking 5 being 6 Going 7 studying
b 1 Doing 2 not to go 3 to park 4 reading 5 to drive 6 doing 7 cooking, washing up

• Tell SS to go back to the main lesson on *p.54*.

d • SS write their own personal sentences and compare with a partner's. Feedback some of their ideas onto the board.

⚠ If you did the Optional lead-in you should omit this stage of the lesson.

3 PRONUNCIATION *-ing*

a 5.3

- Focus on the sound picture and elicit the word and sound: *singer*, /ŋ/. Play the tape/CD for SS to listen and repeat.

5.3			CD2 Track 22
singer /ŋ/			
thing	bring	wrong	language
sitting	watching	thanks	think

- Get SS to practise the words themselves and correct as necessary.

Study Link SS can find more practice of this sound on the MultiROM and on the *New English File Pre-intermediate* website.

b • Tell SS to go to **Sound Bank** on *p.159* and go through the typical spellings.

Pronunciation notes

- The most typical problem SS have with the /ŋ/ sound is that they sometimes add a /g/ or /k/ sound. They are also often unaware that this sound does not only occur in *-ing* but also in *nk*, e.g. *bank, think*.

c 5.4

- Focus on the information in the box and highlight that adding *-ing* to a verb does not change the pronunciation of the original verb, i.e. the sounds and stressed syllable remain the same.
- Explain the activity. SS will hear the infinitive forms of ten verbs. They have to say the *-ing* form of each verb. Get the whole class to say the *-ing* forms.

5.4				CD2 Track 23	
think	drive	study	do	go	
remember	forget	try	ski	write	fly

Extra idea

You could get SS to listen and write the *-ing* form of the verbs first as a dictation to remind them of the spelling rules. Then repeat the activity orally.

4 VOCABULARY & SPEAKING

a • Here SS learn some other common verbs which take the gerund form. Tell SS to go to **Vocabulary Bank *Verb forms*** on *p.154*. Focus on **B** and go through the examples, helping with meaning and pronunciation.

- Highlight the information in the box about *try* and *remember*.
- Highlight that *I don't mind (doing something)* = it isn't a problem for me but it isn't something I especially like doing.
- You might want to teach *can't stand (doing something)* as an alternative form to *hate*.

Study Link SS can find more practice of these words on the MultiROM and on the *New English File Pre-intermediate* website.

Extra idea

Give SS a minute to memorize the examples. Then, in pairs, SS cover the examples with a piece of paper and look only at the verbs. They try to remember the example sentence, then move the paper to check if they have remembered correctly.

- Tell SS to go back to the main lesson on *p.55*.

b • Here SS get some oral practice of the new vocabulary. Focus on the task. Highlight that SS only have to choose five things from the twelve possibilities. Give them a minute to choose their five things.

⚠ Highlight that *dream* ***of*** is used for daydreaming; *dream* ***about*** is used for dreaming while asleep.

Extra support

SS could write down their answers to help prepare them for the speaking.

c • Focus on the speech bubbles. Then demonstrate the activity by choosing a few things from the list and talking about them. Encourage the class to ask you for more information, e.g. *Why (not)?* Give SS time to choose their five things.

- In pairs, **A** tells **B** his/her five things and **B** asks for more information. When you think the **A**s are finished get them to swap roles.
- Monitor and help while SS are talking. Correct SS if they use an infinitive instead of an *-ing* form.

Extra idea

Get fast finishers to choose more topics to talk about.

5 LISTENING

a • Focus on the photo from *The Sound of Music*. Ask if SS have seen the film and what the film is about (*The Von Trapp family who all sing*).

- Get SS to ask each other the questions and get some feedback. You could get SS to ask you the questions first.

b • Tell SS they are going to listen to an interview with a director of a singing school and a student who did a course there. Explain that they will hear them talking about the things in 1–7.

- Go through sentences 1–7, reading them aloud to the class and making sure SS understand them. In pairs SS mark them true or false, writing T or F next to the sentences. Don't get feedback at this stage.

c 5.5

- Focus on the task. Play the tape/CD once. SS listen and check their answers to **b**.
- Play the tape/CD again if necessary.
- Ask if any pairs had predicted correctly.

1 T 2 T 3 F 4 F 5 F 6 T 7 F

d • Go through the six multiple choice questions. Then play the tape/CD again for SS to listen and choose the right answer. Re-play any parts of the recording as necessary. Check answers.

1 a 2 b 3 a 4 c 5 b 6 b

- Finish by asking SS if they agree with what they have heard and how singing makes them feel.

5.5 CD2 Track 24

(tapescript in Student's Book on *p.122*)

I = interviewer, M = Martin, G = Gemma

I Good evening and welcome. In today's programme we're going to talk about singing. In the studio we have Martin, the director of a singing school in London, and Gemma, a student at Martin's school. Good morning to both of you.

M/G Good morning.

I First, Martin, can you tell us, why is it a good idea for people to learn to sing?

M First, because singing makes you feel good. And secondly, because singing is very good for your health.

I Really? In what way?

M Well, when you learn to sing you need to learn to breathe correctly. That's very important. And you also learn to stand and sit correctly. As a result, people who sing are often fitter and healthier than people who don't.

I Are your courses only for professional singers?

M No, not at all. They're for everybody. You don't need to have any experience of singing. And you don't need to be able to read music.

I So how do your students learn to sing?

M They learn by listening and repeating. Singing well is really 95% listening.

I OK Gemma. Tell us about the course. How long did it last?

G Only one day. From ten in the morning to six in the evening.

M Could you already sing well before you started?

G No, not well. But I have always liked singing. But I can't read music and I never thought I sang very well.

I So what happened on the course?

G Well, first we did a lot of listening and breathing exercises, and we learnt some other interesting techniques.

I What sort of things?

G Well, for example we learnt that it is easier to sing high notes if you sing with a surprised look on your face!

I Oh really? Could you show us?

G Well, I'll try.

I For those of you at home, I can promise you that Gemma looked *very* surprised. Were you happy with your progress?

G Absolutely. At the end of the day we were singing in almost perfect harmony. It was amazing. In just one day we really were much better.

I Could you two give us a little demonstration?

M/G Oh, OK ...

Extra photocopiable activities

Grammar

infinitive or verb + *-ing? p.156*

Communicative

Find someone who... *p.200* (instructions *p.178*)

HOMEWORK

Study Link **Workbook** *pp.42–43*

5C

G *have to, don't have to, must, mustn't*
V modifiers: *a bit, really*, etc.
P sentence stress

How much can you learn in a month?

Lesson plan

The title and main context of this lesson were inspired by an article in the *Sunday Times* where an experiment was done to see how well someone could learn a foreign language in just a month. When the month was up, the person travelled to the country itself and carried out a series of tasks to see how much he or she had learnt. The grammatical focus of the lesson is modal verbs expressing obligation: *have to/don't have to* and *must*. At this level *have to* and *must* are taught as synonyms. These forms are presented through the context of class rules which could spark some interesting discussion on what are 'good rules' for a language class. The vocabulary focus is on modifiers in sentences like *It's incredibly complicated* or *My English is quite good*. In Pronunciation SS do more work on sentence stress.

Optional lead-in (books closed)

Put SS into pairs and ask them to decide what they think the two most important rules in the class are. Elicit their ideas onto the board, writing them up with *must/mustn't* or *have to* even if SS have expressed them as imperatives. Possible rules might be, e.g. *You have to do homework, You must come to class, You mustn't use mobile phones in class, You mustn't speak in (SS' L1)*, etc.

1 GRAMMAR *have to, don't have to, must, mustn't*

a • Books open. Focus on the notices and ask SS if they have seen similar ones in their school.

b • Focus on rules 1–6, and get SS to match them with the notices. Check answers.

1 C 2 F 3 E 4 D 5 A 6 B

c • Focus on the highlighted expressions and the questions. Give SS a few moments to answer the questions and then check answers. Make sure SS understand the words *obligation/obligatory, permitted* and *against the rules*.

1 You have to/You must
2 You don't have to
3 You mustn't

Extra challenge

Get SS in pairs to cover rules 1–6 and just look at the notices. Encourage them to test each other by pointing to a notice and asking *What does this mean?* Their partner responds *It means you ...* .

Extra idea

If there are any other notices (relating to rules/obligations) in your school, remind SS of them and elicit what they mean, e.g. *No smoking* – You mustn't smoke, etc.

d • Tell SS to go to **Grammar Bank 5C** on *p.134*. Go through the rules with the class. Model and drill the example sentences.

Grammar notes

Have to* and *must

- At pre-intermediate level *have to* and *must* can be treated as synonyms as a way of expressing obligation. We tend to use *have to* more often than *must* when there is an external obligation, i.e. a law or a rule, e.g. *You have to wear a seat belt in a car in the UK.*
- Watch out for the typical mistake of using *to* with *must*: e.g. *I must* ***to*** *go to the bank.*
- Highlight the impersonal use of *You* when we talk about rules and laws, e.g. *You have to drive on the left.*

Don't have to* and *mustn't

- Watch out for the typical mistake of using *don't have to* instead of *mustn't*, e.g. *You don't have to smoke in class.* (*You mustn't smoke ...*)
- In *New English File Elementary* SS learnt to use *can't* for general prohibition, e.g. *You can't park here.* In this context *mustn't* and *can't* are more or less synonymous.

• Focus on the exercises for **5C** on *p.135*. SS do the exercises individually or in pairs. Check answers.

a 1 Jane has to work very hard.
2 Do you have to wear a uniform?
3 My sister doesn't have to go to school.
4 Do I have to finish this now?
5 We don't have to get up early tomorrow.
6 Does Harry have to work tomorrow?
7 We have to hurry or we'll be late.

b 1 mustn't 2 have to 3 don't have to 4 have to 5 mustn't 6 don't have to 7 have to 8 don't have to

• Tell SS to go back to the main lesson on *p.56*.

2 PRONUNCIATION sentence stress

Pronunciation notes

- Here SS do more work on sentence stress and rhythm using the new language of the lesson. Again they are encouraged to pronounce information-carrying words more strongly and pronounce less important words more lightly. This will help them get the rhythm of English.
- Native speakers tend to pronounce *have to* as /hæf tə/. rather than /hæv tʊ:/.
- *must* can be pronounced weakly /məst/ or strongly /mʌst/ depending on whether you want to give extra emphasis to what you are saying, e.g. *You must <u>give in</u> your <u>homework</u> before <u>Friday</u>.* (= weak stress). *You <u>must</u> come to class on time* (= strong stress).

a 5.6

- Focus on the activity and tell SS that they are going to hear six sentences which they have to try and write down. All of the sentences contain a form of *have to* or *must*.
- Play the tape/CD, pausing after each sentence to give SS time to write down the sentences.
- Play the tape/CD again for SS to check their answers. Check answers, writing the correct sentences onto the board.

5.6 CD2 Track 25

1 I have to wear a uniform at my school.
2 We mustn't be late.
3 Do we have to do an exam?
4 He doesn't have to work at weekends.
5 You must do your homework.
6 My sister has to travel a lot.

b • Play the tape/CD again and get SS to repeat, trying to copy the rhythm. Give more practice as necessary. Elicit that the first *t* is silent in *mustn't* and remind SS that the *have* in *have to* is not contracted.

c • Focus on the instructions and give SS, in pairs, a couple of minutes to complete their sentences.

⚠ For simplicity in this exercise only *have to* (and not *must*) is used to express (+) obligation.

- Check answers. Encourage SS to say their sentences with correct stress and rhythm.

3 READING & LISTENING

a • Focus on the question and elicit some opinions from the class. Try to get a short discussion going if SS seem to be interested in the question.

b • Focus on the photo and tell SS that they are going to read about a British journalist who tried to learn Polish. Focus on the lesson title, and ask SS how much they think she learnt in a month. See what they think and then tell them they are going to find out.

- Focus on the instructions and give SS a few minutes to read the article once. Then get them to cover the article and answer the questions. Get SS to compare their answers with a partner's and then check answers. Elicit/explain the meaning of any unknown words in the text.

Extra support

Let SS find the words in the text rather than doing it from memory.

1 French and Spanish
2 Because her great-grandmother was Polish and she has relatives in Poland.
3 At a language school in Birmingham (UK).
4 grammar and pronunciation
5 In Kraków.
6 get a taxi, order a drink in a bar, ask for directions and follow them, phone and ask to speak to someone, ask somebody the time
7 She mustn't use a dictionary or a phrasebook, or speak English, or mime or use her hands.

c 5.7

- Focus on tests 1–5 in the article and ask SS the two questions. Get some feedback from the whole class.
- Then play the tape/CD of Anna doing the tests in Kraków. SS just listen to hear which test was the easiest and which was the most difficult. Feedback answers.

The easiest test for Anna was probably getting a taxi. The most difficult was asking for directions.

5.7 CD2 Track 26

(tapescript in Student's Book on *p.122*)

I arrived at Kraków airport with Kasia, my guide. Test number one. I had to get a taxi to the hotel. I said to the taxi driver, in Polish, 'To the Holiday Inn Hotel, please,' – *Proszę, do hotelu Holiday Inn*. No problem. The driver understood me. But then he started talking to me in perfect English. I felt a bit stupid.

We got to the hotel, checked in, and then we went to the hotel bar for test number two. A waitress came up to us and I said '*Proszę piwo*,' that is, a beer please. Then the waitress said something in Polish and I understood her! She said: 'A big or small beer?' 'Big,' I said. I was so happy that I could understand her. I really enjoyed that beer.

Next we went out into the street for test three, asking for directions. I decided to ask for directions to a chemist, because I knew the word for chemist, *apteka*. I stopped a woman who looked friendly and I said, in Polish: 'Excuse me please, is there a chemist's near here?' No problem. But then she started talking really fast and pointing. I tried to listen for left or right or anything I could understand but no, I couldn't understand anything. I was sure that Kasia was going to give me zero for this test!

I was feeling less confident now. We went back to the hotel for test four: making a phone call. Kasia gave me a phone number and told me to ask to speak to her friend. His name was Adam. I dialled the number. A woman answered the phone. 'Is Adam there?', I said hopefully. '*Adama nie ma*,' she said. I understood that! Adam's not in. I wanted to say 'When will he be back?' but I could only say 'When home?' *Kiedy domu*? And I didn't understand her answer. So I said thank you and goodbye very politely. Kasia smiled, so I thought, well, not bad.

Finally, test five: asking the time. I *knew* this test was going to be very hard. Numbers in Polish are incredibly difficult and I've always found telling the time is impossible. But I had a brilliant idea. I stopped a man in the street and said: 'Excuse me, what's the time?' I couldn't understand the answer but I just said: 'Sorry, can I see your watch please?' He showed it to me. Twenty past seven. Perfect!

How well did I do in the tests? Well, Kasia gave me 5 out of 10 for language and 8 for imagination. So can you learn a language in a month? Not Polish, definitely!

d • Focus on the task and quickly go through sentences 1–9 before playing the tape/CD. Play the tape/CD again, pausing the tape to give SS time to mark T or F. Re-play all or part of the recording as necessary. Check answers.

1 F His English was perfect.
2 T
3 F She ordered a big beer.
4 F She asked for directions to a chemist's.
5 T
6 T
7 F She knew it was hard/difficult.
8 F She did because she asked the man to show her his watch.
9 F Kasia gave her five out of ten for her Polish (and eight for imagination).

Extra support

If you have time, you could get SS to listen to the tape/CD a final time with the tapescript on *p.122* so they can see exactly what they understood/didn't understand. Translate/explain any new words or phrases.

4 SPEAKING

a • Focus on the two questions and elicit answers from the whole class.

b • Here SS do a short speaking activity based on their experience in using English. Quickly run through the questions before SS start.

• Put SS into pairs and get them to ask and answer the questions. Either **A** can ask **B** all the questions and then they swap roles or they can take turns to ask and answer. Encourage them to use *What about you?* after they have answered.

• Get some feedback from the class about their experiences.

5 VOCABULARY modifiers

a • In this activity SS revise/learn some useful modifiers. Focus on the two examples in the box and elicit the meaning of the highlighted words (*incredibly* = very, very, *a bit* = a little).

• Focus on the chart. Make sure SS understand that they have to complete it with the words in the box in order of difficulty. Elicit the first one (*incredibly*) from the whole class. Give SS a minute or so to complete the chart with the rest of the words. Check answers.

Polish is	incredibly really very quite a bit not very	difficult

• Highlight that:
– *incredibly* /ɪnˈkredəbliː/ has the stress on the second syllable.
– *really* is a little stronger than *very*. Compare *She's very well* and *She's really well.*
– *quite* means an intermediate amount – neither a lot nor a little.

b • Give SS time to complete the sentences so that they are true for them and then get them to compare their answers with a partner's. Get feedback.

Extra photocopiable activities

Grammar
have to, don't have to, mustn't p.157
Communicative
UK rules, OK? *p.201* (instructions *p.178*)

HOMEWORK

Study Link **Workbook** *pp.44–45*

5 D

G expressing movement: *go over*, etc.
V prepositions of movement: *into, through*, etc., sport: *team player*, etc.
P prepositions: *along, towards*, etc.

The name of the game

Lesson plan

The context of this lesson is sport. The grammar of the previous lesson (modals expressing obligation) is consolidated through an activity where SS guess some well known sports by reading the rules. At the same time a new grammar point is introduced: the use of a verb + preposition to express movement. There are two vocabulary focuses: prepositions of movement and words related to sport. Pronunciation focuses on using correct word stress in prepositions like *towards* and *through*.

Optional lead-in (books closed)

Give SS, in pairs, two minutes to think of English words for sports. Tell them that they must try to write down at least ten. Choose a pair and get them to read out their list. Correct pronunciation if necessary. Then ask if other SS have any different ones. Don't write them on the board yet.

1 VOCABULARY & SPEAKING sport, prepositions of movement

a • Books open. Focus on the photos and the three columns. Tell SS that *play, go,* and *do* are the three verbs that we use with sports, and that the photos show 12 different sports.

• Give SS, in pairs, a minute to write the sports in the photos in the right column. Do not check answers yet.

⚠ Tell SS to copy the chart into their notebooks so they can add more sports.

b 5.8

• Copy the chart onto the board. Play the tape/CD for SS to listen and check answers.

• Write the sports into the chart on the board, asking SS to spell the difficult words and correcting pronunciation. Many of the words may exist in a very similar form in SS' L1 but with a different pronunciation.

5.8 CD2 Track 27

play	go	do
golf	skiing	judo
football	swimming	aerobics
tennis	cycling	
rugby		
basketball		
volleyball		
baseball		

• When the chart is complete elicit these general rules:
 – Use *play* with sports with a ball.
 – Use *go* with sports that end in *-ing*.
 – Use *do* with martial arts and activities that you do in a gym.

• Highlight also that with the word *sport* you can use *do* or *play*.

Extra idea

Elicit more sports for each column, or if you did the lead-in, add other sports SS came up with to the columns.

Other examples:

play	go	do
handball	sailing	gymnastics
hockey	riding	karate
badminton	climbing	athletics

c • Focus on the activity and make sure SS understand all the vocabulary. Get SS to explain/demonstrate the meaning of the **bold** words.

• Give SS, in pairs, two or three minutes to answer the questions. Check answers.

Team sports:
baseball (9 players)
basketball (5 players)
football (11 players)
rugby union (15 players)
volleyball (6 players)

You *hit* the ball in baseball, tennis, and volleyball.
You *throw* the ball in baseball, basketball, rugby.
You *kick* the ball in football and rugby.
You *shoot* in basketball and football.

d • In the same pairs SS ask each other the questions. Demonstrate the activity by getting the class to ask you the questions first.

e • Focus on the pictures and the activity. Give SS time to complete the sentence with the five prepositions.

The ball went **over** the wall, **along** the street, **down** the steps, **across** the road, and **into** the river.

f • Tell SS to go to **Vocabulary Bank *Prepositions Part 2*** on *p.148*. In pairs SS complete **a**. Check answers and model and drill pronunciation.

1 down	5 out of	9 towards
2 across	6 through	10 round
3 over	7 past	11 along
4 into	8 under	12 up

• Focus on **b**. Get SS to cover the prepositions in **a** and look at the pictures. From memory they take turns to tell their partner where the dog went.

Study Link SS can find more practice of these words on the MultiROM and on the *New English File Pre-intermediate* website.

- Tell SS to go back to the main lesson on *p.58*.

2 GRAMMAR expressing movement

a
- Focus on the activity and explain that SS have to match rules 1–5 with a sport from **1a**.
- Give SS in pairs or individually two or three minutes to complete the task. Help with vocabulary as SS will probably need it. Insist that they ask you using *What does ... mean?*

b 5.9
- Play the tape/CD for SS to listen and check their answers.

5.9 CD2 Track 28

Sound effects of the five sports:

1 golf 2 tennis 3 cycling 4 football
5 rugby

c
- Focus on the highlighted words in the rules and elicit the answer from the whole class.

You use a verb and a preposition of movement.

d
- Tell SS to go to **Grammar Bank 5D** on *p.134*. Go through the rules with the class. Model and drill the example sentences.

Grammar notes

- In English, movement is expressed by adding a preposition of movement to a verb, e.g. *walk up the steps, climb over the wall.* In your SS' L1 this may be expressed in a different way, e.g. by just using a single verb.

- Focus on the exercises for **5D** on *p.135*. SS do the exercises individually or in pairs. Check answers.

a 1 to, into 2 past 3 along 4 over 5 towards
6 over, into 7 round
b 1 out 2 in 3 out of 4 into

- Tell SS to go back to the main lesson on *p. 59*.

Extra challenge

With a class which is very keen on sport, you could get SS to practise more sports rules. Put SS in groups of four. **A, B, C, D. A** thinks of a sport he/she knows well. The others have to guess it by asking a maximum of ten *yes/no* questions, e.g. *Is it a team sport? Do you play it inside? Do you have to throw the ball?*, etc. When they have guessed, **B** thinks of a sport, etc.

3 PRONUNCIATION prepositions

Pronunciation notes

- This exercise focuses on getting SS to pronounce several prepositions correctly which are often mispronounced. At the same time SS are reminded of the usefulness of being able to recognize phonetic symbols and use them to pronounce new words correctly.

a
- Focus on the activity and give SS time to match the words and phonetics, and to decide how the words are pronounced. Remind them that they can use the sound charts on *pp.156* and *158* to help them remember the phonetic symbols.
- Check answers, asking SS to pronounce the words using the phonetics to help them. Do not correct them yet.

1 into 2 along 3 round 4 towards 5 across
6 through 7 over

b 5.10
- Play the tape/CD for SS to check their answers. Give SS time to underline the stressed syllables and then tell them to practise saying the prepositions a few times.

5.10 CD2 Track 29

1 <u>in</u>to 2 a<u>long</u> 3 round 4 to<u>wards</u>
5 a<u>cross</u> 6 through 7 <u>o</u>ver

c
- Put SS into pairs, **A** and **B**. Tell them to go to **Communication *Cross country*** on *p.117*. If possible, get SS to sit opposite each other.
- Focus on the instructions. Make sure SS know what a cross country race is (*a race where the runners run across the countryside*) and understand what they have to do.
- Give SS time to draw their route on the map headed **My race**. Monitor to make sure they draw a suitable route including all the things on the map (trees, hill, lake, etc).
- SS take it in turns to describe their route to their partner who draws the route on the map headed **My partner's race**. SS shouldn't look at each other's maps. Monitor and help as SS do the task.
- When the majority of pairs have finished, get SS to compare routes to see if they drew them correctly.
- Tell SS to go back to the main lesson on *p.59*.

4 READING & SPEAKING

a
- Focus on the photos and ask some questions to generate interest, e.g. *Which teams are they? What match is it?* (Manchester United and Bayern Munich. The 1999 Champion's League Final.)
- Focus on the two questions and elicit answers from the class.

A normal football match lasts 90 minutes. It depends – time is added for time lost because of injuries, etc.

b • Focus on the article and on the words in the box. Ask SS how many of the words they know. Elicit/teach the meaning of new words. Get SS to underline the stress in *referee*.
• Give SS five minutes to read the article and complete it with the words from the box. Get them to compare their article with a partner's before checking answers.

1 match **2** stadium **3** fans **4** team **5** players **6** scored **7** goal **8** referee **9** champions **10** pitch

c • Set SS another time limit to read the text again and number the events A–F in the order they happened. Get SS to compare their order with a partner's before you check answers.

1 D 2 B 3 C 4 F 5 A 6 E

• Deal with any other vocabulary problems, and ask SS to choose five words or phrases they want to learn from the text and get them to write them in their notebook.

d • Focus on the task. Give SS several minutes to think about the most exciting sporting event they have ever seen and to prepare their answers to the questions. Help them with any vocabulary they may need, especially to answer question 5.

Extra idea

Do the activity yourself, and get SS to interview you first.

e • Put SS into pairs. SS take turns to ask a partner about the sporting event. Monitor and help while SS are doing the activity. Get feedback from a few pairs of students.

5 SONG ♫ *We are the champions*

5.11

• Here SS listen to a song, originally recorded by Queen, which is often heard at sporting events.
• If you want to do this song in class use the photocopiable activity on *p.224*.

5.11 CD2 Track 30

We are the champions

I've paid my dues
Time after time
I've done my sentence
But committed no crime
And bad mistakes
I've made a few
I've had my share of sand kicked in my face
But I've come through
And we mean to go on and on and on and on

We are the champions, my friends
And we'll keep on fighting till the end
We are the champions
We are the champions
No time for losers
'Cause we are the champions of the world

I've taken my bows
And my curtain calls
You brought me fame and fortune and everything that goes with it
I thank you all
But it's been no bed of roses
No pleasure cruise
I consider it a challenge before the whole human race
And I ain't gonna lose
And we mean to go on and on and on and on

We are the champions ...

Extra photocopiable activities

Grammar
verbs and prepositions *p.158*
Communicative
Prepositions race *p.202* (instructions *p.178*)
Song
We are the champions p.224 (instructions *p.219*)

HOMEWORK

Study Link **Workbook** *pp.46–47*

5 PRACTICAL ENGLISH AT A DEPARTMENT STORE

Revision Buying clothes
Function Taking something back
Language *Excuse me, I bought this ... but ...*

Lesson plan

In this lesson SS revise buying clothes, and learn expressions for taking things back to a shop. In **Social English**, it is the evening on the same day Allie got lost in **Practical English 4**. Allie, Mark, and Brad all meet at a cocktail party at the hotel, and Mark is irritated to find that Brad and Allie know each other better than he thought.

Study Link These lessons are on the *New English File Pre-intermediate* Video, which can be used instead of the Class Cassette/CD (see introduction *p.9*). The main functional section of each episode (the second section) is also on the MultiROM with additional activities.

Optional lead-in (books closed)

Revise what happened in the previous episode by eliciting the story from the class. (Allie tried to find a museum but got lost. She met Brad, by chance, who took her for a cup of coffee and showed her the way to the museum).

BUYING CLOTHES

5.12

- Focus on the questions. Play the tape/CD once the whole way through and tell SS just to listen. Then play it again, pausing if necessary to give SS time to answer the questions. Get them to compare their answers with each other before checking answers.

1 A black sweater.
2 Medium.
3 No.
4 39.99
5 By credit card (MasterCard).

- Ask what the problem is about the price and elicit that although the sweater is marked 39.99, in California you have to pay 8.5% extra sales tax.

5.12 CD2 Track 31
(tapescript in Student's Book on *p.123*)
SA = shop assistant, A = Allie
SA Can I help you?
A Yes, I really like this sweater. Do you have it in a medium?
SA Let's see ... we have it in red in a medium.
A No, I want it in black.
SA Just a minute, I'll go and check. Here you are. A black medium. Do you want to try it on?
A No, thanks. I'm sure it'll be fine. How much is it?
SA 43.38.
A It says 39.99.
SA Yes, but that doesn't include sales tax – that's 8.5% extra.
A Oh, OK. Do you take MasterCard?
SA Yes, of course.

TAKING SOMETHING BACK

a 5.13
- Tell SS to cover the dialogue. Focus on the questions. Play the tape/CD once for SS to answer the questions. Check answers.

The sweater is too big. She asks for her money back.

b • Now tell SS to uncover the dialogue. Give them a minute to read through the dialogue and guess the missing words. Then play the tape/CD again.

5.13 5.14 CD2 Tracks 32+33
SA = shop assistant, A = Allie
SA Can I help you?
A Yes, I bought this sweater about half an hour ago. (*repeat*)
SA Yes, I remember. Is there a **problem**?
A Yes, I've decided it's too big for me. (*repeat*)
SA What **size** is it?
A Medium. (*repeat*)
SA So you need a **small**. I don't see one here.
A Do you have any more? (*repeat*)
SA I'll go and check. Just a **minute**.
I'm sorry but we don't have **another** one in black.
A Oh dear. (*repeat*)
SA We can order one for you. It'll only take a few **days**.
A No, I'm leaving on Saturday. (*repeat*)
SA Would you like to exchange it for **something** else?
A Not really. Could I have a refund? (*repeat*)
SA No problem. Do you **have** the receipt?
A Yes, here you are. (*repeat*)

- Go through the dialogue line by line and check answers. Highlight *too big* = bigger than what you want/need (this use of *too* is studied in more detail in **8B**). Also highlight the pronunciation of *receipt* /rɪˈsiːt/.

c 5.14
- Play the tape/CD, pausing for SS to repeat the **YOU SAY** phrases. Encourage them to copy the rhythm.

d • Put SS into pairs, **A** and **B**. **A** is the shop assistant, **B** is Allie. Tell **B** to close his/her book and try to remember the phrases. Then **A** and **B** swap roles.

SOCIAL ENGLISH the conference cocktail party

a 5.15
- Focus on the instructions and the photo. Ask *Where do you think they are?* and elicit that they're on the roof terrace of the hotel at the conference cocktail party.

⚠ Tell SS that this is the same evening, i.e. Allie met Brad in the street, went shopping, and visited the Museum of Modern Art that morning.

- Play the tape/CD at least twice. Let SS compare their sentences with a partner's and then check answers.

1 Allie, Mark
2 Brad, Mark, Allie
3 Mark, Brad, Allie
4 Mark, Allie
5 Mark

5.15 CD2 Track 34

(tapescript in Student's Book on *p.123*)

M = Mark, A = Allie, B = Brad

M Allie! You look great, as usual. How was your morning?

A Really good. First I went shopping, and then I went to the Museum of Modern Art.

M What did you **think** of it?

A It was wonderful. But I didn't have enough time to see it all. Never **mind**.

M Maybe next time.

A What a **lovely** evening!

B Hi, Allie. How was the shopping?

A Great, thanks.

B Hi Mark. And did you like the museum? I hope you didn't get lost again!

M Hey, I didn't know you two were friends already.

A We met this morning. I got **lost**. I was trying to find Union Square – and suddenly Brad appeared.

B So I took her to my favourite coffee shop.

M Allie, what would you like to **drink**?

A I'd like a cocktail please. A margarita.

B What a good **idea**. I'll have one too. Mark, could you get us a couple of margaritas?

M Oh, so now I'm the waiter, am I?

B So tell me about the museum, Allie. What was your favourite painting?

- Get SS to speculate a bit about the story, and what will happen next. Ask *Do you think Allie prefers Brad to Mark? Do you think Mark is being reasonable? What do you think is going to happen* etc.

b • Focus on the **USEFUL PHRASES**. Get SS to see if they can remember any of the missing words. Play the tape/CD again and check answers.

c 5.16

- Play the tape/CD pausing for SS to repeat each phrase. Encourage them to copy the rhythm.

5.16 CD2 Track 35

M = Mark, A = Allie

M What did you think of it?

A Never mind.

A What a lovely evening!

A I got lost.

M What would you like to drink?

B What a good idea.

HOMEWORK

Study Link Workbook *p.48*

5 WRITING A FORMAL E-MAIL

Lesson plan

In this fifth writing lesson SS practise writing a formal e-mail. The writing skills focus is on the conventions of a formal e-mail which are contrasted with an informal one.

a • Focus on the e-mail and the instructions. Give SS, in pairs, a few minutes to read it and tick the questions that Adriano wants answered.

- Check answers.

How much do the courses cost?
When do the courses start and finish?
Where can I stay?

- Elicit the expressions in the e-mail which he uses to get the information he wants, e.g. *Could you please send me information about dates and prices? I would also like some information about accommodation.*

b • Focus on the instructions and the highlighted expressions. Do the first one with the class, and elicit that an informal e-mail would normally begin *Hi* (or *Dear*) + the person's name. Get SS to continue in pairs. Check answers.

Extra support

You could let SS compare this e-mail with the informal e-mail on *p. 13*.

Formal e-mail	Informal e-mail
Dear Sir/Madam	Hi/Dear…
I am writing	I'm writing
I would like	I'd like
I look forward to hearing from you	Looking forward to hearing from you/Write soon
Yours faithfully	Best wishes

- Highlight that:
  - in formal e-mails (and letters) we do not normally use contractions, e.g. *I am writing*. In informal e-mails (and letters) it is normal to use contractions, e.g. *I'm writing*.
  - if you are writing a formal (or business) e-mail and you don't know the name of the person that you are writing to, you should begin *Dear* Sir/Madam. If you *do* know the name, you should begin *Dear* + title + name, e.g *Mr Brown*, and finish *Yours sincerely*.

c • Focus on the advertisements and instructions. Give SS two minutes, in pairs, to brainstorm possible questions for both advertisements, e.g *Is the accommodation with families? Does the price include the flights? How many people are there in each group?* Get feedback and write the questions on the board.

Write a formal e-mail asking for information

Either give SS at least fifteen minutes to write the e-mail in class, following the instructions, or set it for homework. If SS do the writing in class, get them to swap their e-mails with another S's to read and check for mistakes before you collect them all in.

5 REVISE & CHECK

For instructions on how to use these pages, see *p.27*.

GRAMMAR

1 b 2 a 3 c 4 a 5 c 6 b 7 b 8 c 9 a 10 c

VOCABULARY

a 1 mind 2 forget 3 dream of 4 need 5 decide 6 learn 7 hate 8 hope 9 Try 10 start
b 1 into 2 over 3 to 4 round 5 through
c 1 play 2 went 3 does 4 goes 5 doing

PRONUNCIATION

a 1 mind 2 promise 3 have 4 throw 5 mustn't
b <u>pro</u>mise de<u>cide</u> for<u>get</u> en<u>joy</u> <u>prac</u>tise

CAN YOU UNDERSTAND THIS TEXT?

a 3
b 1 T 2 DS 3 T 4 F 5 T 6 T 7 DS

CAN YOU UNDERSTAND THESE PEOPLE?

5.17 CD2 Track 36

1
A Hi, is that Anna?
B Yes, hi Rob.
A Hi there. Look, there's a party on Saturday. Would you like to come?
B Well, I'm not sure. I don't really like parties. Whose party is it?
A Linda's. It's her birthday. There'll be lots of people you know. I'm sure you'll have a good time.
B Well, I'll think about it and I'll tell you tomorrow.

2
A What did you do at the weekend, Martin?
B I went to a concert. The Philharmonia at the City Hall.
A What was it?
B Beethoven's Ninth Symphony.
A Was it good?
B Well, not bad. The orchestra were fantastic, but the singers weren't very good.
A Oh, that's a pity.

3
A OK, now please can you go to page 24? Come in. Oh, hello Maria. You're a bit late.
B Sorry, I miss the bus.
A Oh, you missed the bus. You missed the bus on Monday too. And last week. OK, well come on and sit down.

4
A Are you good at languages?
B Well, quite – I can speak good French, and I can read Italian well, though I can't speak it very well.
A What about German?
B I can understand it a bit, but I can't really speak it.
A Well, I think that's brilliant. I can only speak a bit of Spanish and that's it.

5
… at Highbury Stadium. And Ljundberg passes the ball to Henry, and he's running towards the goal and he's going to shoot and … ah the ball's just gone over the bar – just a metre or so too high …

a 1 c 2 b 3 c 4 a 5 b

5.18 CD2 Track 37

A Hello. How can I help you?
B I'd like some information about the sports centre. My daughter wants to learn to play a team sport.
A How old is she?
B She's 12.
A Well, she could learn volleyball, football, basketball.
B I think she'd like basketball. She's quite tall for her age.
A Well, there are two groups. One trains on Tuesdays and one on Thursdays.
B I think Thursdays would be best for her. She finishes school early on Thursdays. What time is the class?
A From 6.00 to 7.30. Is that OK for her?
B Yes, that's fine.
A Can I have her name, please?
B Yes, her name's Susan Stevens.
A Can you spell the surname?
B Yes, S-T-E-V-E-N-S.
A Right, I'll put her down for the Thursday group then.
B How much do the classes cost?
A You don't have to pay, they're free.
B Oh, great! Well, she'll be there on Thursday at 6.00 then. Bye.
A Bye.

b 1 basketball 2 Thursday 3 6.00 4 7.30 5 Susan Stevens 6 free

CAN YOU SAY THIS IN ENGLISH?

Accept any answer which makes sense.
b 1 *to go*
2 e.g. *to dance*
3 e.g. *reading*
4 e.g. *wear a uniform*
5 e.g. *to learn*

Extra photocopiable activities

Quicktest 5 *p.235*

6A

G *if* + present, *will* + infinitive (first conditional)
V confusing verbs: *carry, wear, win, earn* etc.
P long and short vowels: /ɪ/, /iː/, /ɒ/, /ɔː/, /ʊ/, /uː/

If something bad can happen, it will

File 6 overview

The focus in File 6 is on conditional tenses and modals with a future meaning. In **6A** and **6B** SS learn the first and second conditionals. Learning the two conditionals one after the other should help SS contrast and assimilate the difference between them. In **6C** the modal verbs *may* and *might* carry on the theme of possibility, and finally in **6D** the presentation of *should* in the context of advice allows both conditionals and modals to be recycled.

Lesson plan

This lesson presents the first conditional through the humorous context of 'Murphy's Law', which states that if something bad can happen, it will happen. The presentation is an easily memorized chain story. SS then read a text with some common examples of Murphy's Law and finally invent their own rules of life. The vocabulary focus is on verbs which are often confused, like *know/meet* and *borrow/lend*. In Pronunciation there is work on long and short vowels.

Optional lead-in (books closed)

Write the following words and phrases on the board inside circles:

read *listen to music* *talk to the person next to you*
sleep *work*

Ask SS *Which of these do you do when you are travelling (by bus, train,* etc.*)?* Tell them to talk to a partner and say why they do the things. Get feedback, and ask them if there's anything else they do when they are travelling. Then do **1a**.

1 GRAMMAR *if* + present, *will* + infinitive

a • Books open. Focus on picture 1 and the beginning of the story. Give SS a minute to read it. Elicit possible answers to the question, e.g. *because he wants to read it, because he doesn't like lending things,* etc.

b • Focus on the other pictures and tell SS that they show what the man's answer is. Focus on the first picture and sentence 1 (*If I lend you my newspaper ...*). Tell SS that this is the beginning of the conversation. Then tell SS, in pairs, to number the other sentences 2–9, using the pictures to help them.

c 6.1

• Tell SS they're going to hear the Italian man giving his explanation. SS listen and check their order. Play the tape/CD once. Check answers.

> **6.1** CD2 Track 38
> If I lend you my newspaper, we'll start talking.
> If we start talking, we'll become friends.
> If we become friends, I'll invite you to my house in Venice.
> If I invite you to my house, you'll meet my beautiful daughter, Nicoletta.
> If you meet Nicoletta, you'll fall in love with her.
> If you fall in love with her, you'll run away together.
> If you run away, I'll find you.
> If I find you, I'll kill you.
> So that's why I won't lend you my newspaper.

• Tell SS to focus on the pictures and cover the sentences. Play the tape/CD again, pausing after each *if* clause to elicit the continuation of the sentence.
• Now drill the story with the whole class, eliciting it line by line. Finally put SS into pairs, **A** and **B**. **A** covers the sentences and retells the story using the pictures. **B** prompts and corrects. Then they swap roles.

d • Now focus on the tenses and elicit that the verb after *if* is in the present simple and the other verb is in the future (*will/won't* + infinitive). Explain that sentences with *if* are often called conditional sentences, and that this structure (a sentence with *if* + present + future) is often called the first conditional.

e • Tell SS to go to **Grammar Bank 6A** on *p. 136*. Go through the rules and model and drill the example sentences.

Grammar notes

• Since first conditional sentences refer to future possibilities, some SS may try to use the future after *if*. Typical mistake: *If he'll phone, I'll tell him.*
• The present simple and future *will* are also used after *when, as soon as,* and *until,* e.g. *I'll tell him when he arrives. As soon as you get here, we'll have lunch.* This use is taught in *New English File Intermediate.* However you may want to point this out in this lesson.

• Focus on the exercises for **6A** on *p.137*. SS do them individually or in pairs. Check answers.

> **a** 1 D 2 E 3 F 4 G 5 A 6 B
> **b** 1 start, will come
> 2 'll be, don't tell
> 3 don't write, won't remember
> 4 Will . . . call, get
> 5 ask, 'll help
> 6 won't pass, don't study

• Tell SS to go back to the main lesson on *p.64*.

2 VOCABULARY confusing verbs

a • Focus on the sentences and give SS a few minutes, in pairs, to decide which verb is right in each sentence and why. Check answers and ask SS why. Ask SS how to say these verbs in L1 to highlight the difference.

> 1 meet (= you will see and speak to her for the first time)
> 2 know (= you have met and spoken to him before)
> 3 borrow (= you give me your newspaper)
> 4 lend (= I give you my newspaper)

b • Tell SS to go to **Vocabulary Bank *Verbs*** on *p.149* and do **2 Confusing verbs.** In pairs SS match the verbs and pictures. Check answers, and model and drill pronunciation as necessary, e.g. *earn* /ɜːn/.

1 win/earn	5 watch/look at
2 hope/wait	6 know/meet
3 look/look like	7 make/do
4 wear/carry	

⚠ Some of these verbs are often confused because in your SS' L1, one verb may be used for both meanings. For this reason it's better for SS to learn these verbs in a phrase, e.g. *know someone well, meet someone for the first time,* etc. rather than just learning a translation.

- Get SS to cover the words and phrases and look at the pictures. SS test themselves or each other.

Study Link SS can find more practice of these words on the MultiROM and on the *New English File Pre-intermediate* website.

- Tell SS to go back to the main lesson on *p.64.*

3 READING

a • SS get further practise of the first conditional in this reading text about Murphy's Law. Focus on the first question. SS will probably try to express that the queue they were in before will move faster. Then tell SS that this is an example of what we call Murphy's Law and ask if they have heard of this law before.

b • Give SS a few minutes to read the introduction and answer the question. Check answers.

> Murphy was an American aeroplane engineer. His law is 'if something bad can happen, it will happen'.

c • Give SS time to read the rest of the article. Tell SS to cover the continuations in exercise **d** and in pairs guess how they think the laws might end. Elicit ideas.

Extra support

Do **c** as a whole-class activity, not in pairs.

d • Tell SS to uncover **d**. SS work in the same pairs and match the sentence halves with A–H. Check answers. Explain/translate *spill* (= accidentally let a liquid fall).

> 1 B 2 G 3 A 4 H 5 C 6 F 7 E 8 D

e • In pairs SS try to remember the laws using the first half of the sentences as prompts. Elicit some more laws from SS, but don't spend too long as SS will be making their own laws in exercise **5**.

4 PRONUNCIATION long and short vowels

a 6.2

- Focus on the sound chart and elicit the three pairs of sounds: /ɪ/, /iː/, /ɒ/, /ɔː/, /ʊ/, /uː/. Remind SS that the two dots after the phonetic symbol means that the sound is long.

> **6.2** CD2 Track 39
> /ɪ/ /iː/ /ɒ/ /ɔː/ /ʊ/ /uː/

b • Now focus on the words in the box. Do the first two with SS, and then get them to continue in pairs.

c 6.3

- Play the tape/CD once for SS to check their answers. Then play it again pausing after each word or group of words for SS to listen and repeat.

> **6.3** CD2 Track 40
> if, will, win
> leave, meet, we'll
> borrow, stop, wash
> law, story, talk
> look, push, took
> beautiful, move, queue

d • Tell SS to go to **Sound Bank** on *p.157* and focus on the typical spellings for these sounds.

Study Link SS can find more practice on the MultiROM or on the *New English File Pre-intermediate* website.

- Tell SS to go back to the main lesson on *p.65.*

5 SPEAKING

- Focus on the prompts for SS to make new 'Murphy's laws'. Highlight that there is not one right answer, but that there will be a vote for the best 'laws'.
- Put SS into groups of four (or pairs if you have a small class). Then tell them that they have to choose six 'laws' to complete. Remind them of the original law: *if something bad can happen it will happen.*
- While SS complete their laws, monitor and help with vocabulary and spelling. Fast finishers can complete the other three laws.
- Get feedback and write the 'laws' on the board. Accept all logical endings. There maybe several variations for each sentence. Take a vote on the 'best' laws, i.e. the most typical.

> **Possible endings**
> they won't like you.
> you'll need it later.
> you'll see a parking space very near.
> he/she'll wake up early.
> there'll be a lot of traffic.
> it will be delayed.
> your boss will arrive early.
> a lot of people will ring you.
> it will be 'pull'.

Extra photocopiable activities

Grammar
first conditional *p.159*
Communicative
Guess my sentence *p.203* (instructions *p.179*)

HOMEWORK

Study Link **Workbook** *pp.49–50*

6B Never smile at a crocodile

G *if* + past, *would* + infinitive (second conditional)
V animals: *lion, tiger, goat,* etc.
P stress and rhythm

Lesson plan

In this lesson SS look at the second conditional. The context, a survival quiz where SS choose the best way to survive, helps to show SS that the second conditional is often used in hypothetical situations. In Vocabulary, SS learn the names of animals, and the grammar and vocabulary are both recycled in the Speaking activity. The lesson ends with an article about crocodile attacks in Australia.

Optional lead-in (books closed)

Write on the board:

LULB ROCILDECO ARBE

Tell SS to re-arrange the letters to form the names of three animals. Check answers and get SS to spell the words. Model the pronunciation and underline the stress in *crocodile.*

bull crocodile bear

1 SPEAKING & LISTENING

a • Books open. Focus on the photos and elicit the three animals. Now focus on the quiz and the instructions. Go through the answer options for each question and check SS understand *climb, lie, ground, shout,* etc. Give SS a few minutes to read the questions and choose their answers.

• Get SS to compare their choices with a partner's. Encourage them to try to say why they have chosen each option.

b 6.4

• Tell SS they are going to listen to a survival expert who will tell them which is the best option for each situation. The first time they listen they should just focus on which is the right option.

• Play the tape/CD once. Check answers and find out how many SS would survive in each situation.

1 c 2 b 3 b

6.4 CD2 Track 41

(tapescript in Student's Book on *p.123*)

I = Interviewer, M = Michael

I OK, Michael, can you tell us what to do in these three situations? First, what about the crocodile attack?

M Well, once a crocodile has seen you it will attack you, so doing nothing is not really an option. And a crocodile attacks so quickly that people never have time to swim to safety. The crocodile will try to get you in its mouth and take you under the water. Your only hope is to try to hit it in the eye or on the nose. If you did this and you were very lucky, the crocodile would open its mouth and give you time to escape. But I have to say that it's very difficult, although not impossible, to survive a crocodile attack.

I What about the bear attack?

M When a bear attacks someone, their natural reaction is always to try to run away or to climb up a tree. But these are both bad ideas. Bears can run much faster than we can and they're also much better and faster at climbing trees. The best thing to do in this situation would be to pretend to be dead. A bear usually stops attacking when it thinks that its enemy is dead and so, if you were lucky, it would lose interest in you and go away.

I And finally, the bull attack?

M Well, if you were in the middle of a field, forget about running. Bulls can run incredibly fast. And don't shout or wave your arms because bulls react to movement, and this will just make the bull come in your direction. The best thing to do is to try not to move, and just stay where you are, and then at the last moment to throw something, a hat or your shirt, away from you. If you were lucky, the bull would change direction to follow the hat or shirt and you'd be able to escape. By the way, it doesn't matter what colour the shirt is. It isn't true that bulls like red. They don't see colour, they only see movement.

c • Focus on the instructions and play the tape/CD again. When SS have compared, check answers.

1 **a** is wrong because crocodiles attack very quickly so you don't have time to swim.
b is wrong because as soon as a crocodile sees you, it will attack.
2 **a** is wrong because bears can climb better than we can.
c is wrong because bears can run faster than we can.
3 **a** is wrong because bulls can run incredibly fast.
c is wrong because noise or a sudden movement will attract the bull and make it come towards you.

Extra idea

Stop the tape/CD after each situation. Check answers and elicit more details by asking, e.g. *Where exactly should you hit a crocodile?* (in the eye or on the nose).

Extra support

If you have time, you could get SS to listen again with the tapescript on *p.123* so they can see exactly how much they understood. Translate/explain any new words or phrases.

2 GRAMMAR *if* + past, *would* + infinitive

a • Focus on question 1 in *Would you survive?*. Get SS to discuss questions 1–3 in pairs, or go through them with the whole class. Check answers.

1 b 2 past simple 3 *would/wouldn't* + infinitive

b • Tell SS to go to **Grammar Bank 6B** on *p.136*. Go through the rules and model and drill the example sentences.

Grammar notes

- SS may find it strange to be using past tenses in the *If* half of these conditional sentences and it needs emphasizing that they do not refer to the past but rather to a hypothetical situation.
- SS have seen and used *would/wouldn't* + infinitive before with the verb *like*, so should not have problems with the form of *would*.
- Highlight that we often use the expression *If I were you, I'd* ... to give advice.

- Focus on the exercises for **6B** on *p.137*. SS do them individually or in pairs. Check answers.

a 1 G 2 A 3 E 4 B 5 F 6 D
b 1 would buy, had
2 knew, would phone
3 would learn, worked
4 stayed, would be able to/could
5 would see, lived
6 would go, were

- Tell SS to go back to the main lesson on *p.66*.

3 PRONUNCIATION stress and rhythm

Pronunciation notes

- SS may have problems pronouncing *would* and *wouldn't* correctly. Some SS pronounce the /w/ as /g/ or pronounce the *l* which should be silent.

a 6.5

- Focus on the sentence halves. Play the tape/CD, getting SS to listen and repeat each half separately first, and then the whole sentence.
- Give SS a few minutes to practise saying the sentences.

6.5 CD2 Track 42
1 If I saw a crocodile, I'd climb a tree.
2 What would you do if you saw a snake?
3 We could have a dog if we had a garden.
4 If a bear attacked me, I wouldn't move.
5 If I were you, I'd go on a safari.

b • Tell SS to close their books. Read the first half of each sentence, and elicit the second half, encouraging SS to get the rhythm right.
- Then get SS to open their books, cover the right-hand column, and remember the sentences.

4 VOCABULARY animals

a • Focus on the questions. SS either interview each other in pairs, or answer the questions together. Monitor and help SS with any animal words they want to use but don't know. Get feedback.

b • Tell SS to go to **Vocabulary Bank *Animals*** on *p.151*. Focus on **a**. In pairs, SS match the words and pictures. Check answers and model and drill the pronunciation.

a 1 dolphin	**9** mosquito	**17** elephant	**25** kangaroo
2 cow	**10** eagle	**18** wasp	**26** bee
3 mouse	**11** horse	**19** whale	**27** tiger
4 sheep	**12** crocodile	**20** giraffe	**28** swan
5 lion	**13** camel	**21** fly	**29** bull
6 gorilla	**14** bear	**22** pig	**30** rabbit
7 chicken	**15** spider	**23** shark	
8 goat	**16** butterfly	**24** duck	

- Focus on **b**. Give SS a few minutes to test themselves or each other.
- Tell SS to go back to the main lesson on *p.67*.

c 6.6

- This listening consists only of sound effects and its aim is to recycle the animal vocabulary in a fun and amusing way. Play the tape/CD pausing after each sound for SS to say or write the name of the animal.

6.6 CD2 Track 43
1 chicken
2 horse
3 cow
4 duck
5 elephant
6 lion
7 bull
8 mosquito
9 sheep
10 shark
11 mouse
12 whale

Extra idea

You could make this a team game where you divide the class into two or more teams and play the tape/CD twice for them to decide which animals they are and write them down. The team with the most right answers wins.

5 SPEAKING

- Go through the questions and make sure SS understand them all. Then ask five different students to choose a question to ask you. Answer, giving as much detail as you think SS will understand.
- Put SS into pairs, and tell them to choose the five questions they want to ask a partner.
- SS then ask and answer in pairs. Encourage them to ask for more information (*Why?*, etc.). Fast finishers can choose more questions.
- Monitor and help SS, correcting any misuse of tenses in the second conditional.

6 READING

a • Do this as an open class question and elicit that you have to try to hit the crocodile in the face.

b • Tell SS they're going to read an article about Australian crocodiles (the most dangerous in the world) and some real cases where someone survived an attack and others didn't. Focus on the nine sentences and ask SS whether they think 1, 2, and 3 are true or false. Then tell them to read the article and mark all ten sentences T, F, or DS. Set a time limit of three minutes.

• Check answers, and get SS to correct the false ones.

1 T
2 DS
3 F (they can also attack people on land)
4 F (there were warning signs)
5 DS
6 F (they were washing their bikes)
7 T
8 F (the boy was attacked, not his aunt)
9 T

c • Get SS to cover the text and ask them if they can remember what the first number (7) refers to. Elicit that crocodiles can grow up to 7 metres long. Then tell them to continue in pairs.

Extra support

Get SS to first find and highlight the numbers in the text. Then they cover the text and remember what the numbers refer to.

d • SS quickly check the numbers with the text. Check answers.

7: Australian crocodiles can grow up to 7 metres long.
1000: The biggest ones can weigh 1000 kilos.
40: Crocodiles have 40 muscles to close their mouths.
17: They can run on land at 17k/h.
24: The German tourist was 24 years old.
22: The two Australian boys stayed in a tree for 22 hours.
19: Norman Pascoe was 19.

7 SONG ♫ *Wouldn't it be nice*

6.7

• If you want to do this song in class, use the photocopiable activity on *p.225*.

6.7 CD2 Track 44

Wouldn't it be nice

Wouldn't it be nice if we were older
Then we wouldn't have to wait so long
And wouldn't it be nice to live together
In the kind of world where we belong

You know it's going to make it that much better
When we can say goodnight and stay together

Wouldn't it be nice if we could wake up
In the morning when the day is new
And after having spent the day together
Hold each other close the whole night through
Happy times together we've been spending
I wish that every kiss was never-ending
Wouldn't it be nice
Maybe if we think and wish and hope and pray it might come true
Baby then there wouldn't be a single thing we couldn't do
We could be married
And then we'd be happy
Wouldn't it be nice

You know it seems the more we talk about it
It only makes it worse to live without it
But let's talk about it
Wouldn't it be nice

Extra photocopiable activities

Grammar
second conditional *p.160*
Communicative
I think you'd . . . *p.204* (instructions *p.179*)
Song
Wouldn't it be nice p.225 (instructions *p.219*)

HOMEWORK

Study Link **Workbook** *pp.51–52*

6 C

G *may / might* (possibility)
V word building: noun formation: *decide – decision*
P sentence stress, *-ion* endings

Decisions, decisions

Lesson plan

This lesson presents the modal verbs *may* and *might* through the context of a person who is very indecisive and can't make up her mind. SS also do a questionnaire to see if they are indecisive, and read an article about how to make decisions. The pronunciation focus is sentence rhythm, and the lesson ends with a vocabulary focus on word building.

Optional lead-in (books closed)

Write DECIDE on the board. Ask SS what part of speech it is (verb, noun, etc.) and elicit that it's a verb. Then ask *What's the noun from decide?* and elicit that it's *decision.* Then elicit/teach the adjective *decisive* and it's opposite *indecisive.* Tell SS to go to **1a**.

1 SPEAKING

a • Focus on the definitions and the words in the box. Give SS a few moments to complete the definitions. Then say the words out loud a couple of times for them to listen and underline the stressed syllable. Check answers.

1 de<u>cide</u> 2 de<u>ci</u>sion 3 de<u>ci</u>sive 4 inde<u>ci</u>sive

b • Focus on the questionnaire. Go through the questions and explain/teach *change your mind* (= take a decision and then change it).

Extra challenge

You could also teach SS the idiom *make up your mind* as an alternative *to decide, make a decision.*

• In pairs SS interview each other using the questionnaire. Monitor and encourage SS to ask for/give more information, and to illustrate their answers with examples.

Extra idea

You could get SS to interview you first. Give as many examples as you can.

• Get feedback, and find out (with a show of hands) if the majority of the class is indecisive.

2 GRAMMAR *may / might*

a 6.8

• Focus on the pictures and explain that the two women are friends. Mel is the one with brown hair and Roz is the one with blonde hair.

• Focus on the instructions. Tell SS to cover the dialogue (or close their books). Play the tape/CD once and check answers.

Roz is indecisive about: going to the party, what clothes to wear, and how to get there.

6.8 CD2 Track 45

R = Roz, M = Mel

R Hi Mel. It's me ... Roz.
M Hi Roz.
R Listen Mel. It's about the party tonight.
M You're going, aren't you?
R I don't know. I'm not sure. <u>I might **go**</u> ... but <u>I might not</u>. I can't decide.
M Oh come on. You'll love it. And <u>you might **meet**</u> somebody new.
R OK. I'll go then.
M Good. So what are you going to wear?
R That's the other problem. I'm not sure what to wear. <u>I might **wear**</u> my new black trousers. Or perhaps the red dress – what do you think?
M If I were you, I'd wear the red dress.
R But the red dress <u>may **be**</u> too small for me now .....
M Well, wear the black trousers then.
R OK. I'll wear the black trousers.
M How are you getting there?
R <u>I might **go**</u> with John ... or Ruth ... or <u>I may **walk**</u> there ... I'm not sure yet.
M OK. I'll see you there. Bye.
R Bye.
M Hello?
R Mel? It's me again. Roz. Listen. I've changed my mind. Sorry. I'm not going to go to the party.

b • Tell SS that the missing words are all verbs. Play the tape/CD, pausing if necessary. Check answers (see **bold** verbs in tapescript).

c • Focus on the instructions. Elicit that the first example is *I might go*, and get SS to underline the rest. Check answers (see tapescript 6.8). Elicit that we use *may* and *might* (+ infinitive) to talk about a possibility.

d • Tell SS to go to **Grammar Bank 6C** on *p.136.* Go through the rules and model and drill the example sentences.

Grammar notes

• *May* and *might* are synonyms. *May* is probably more frequent in written English than *might* and *might* is more frequent in spoken English than *may.*
• *May* and *might* are introduced here more for recognition than production as they are examples of 'late assimilation' language. At this level SS are more likely to express the same idea in another way, e.g by using *It's possible or possibly.*

• Focus on the exercises for **6C** on *p.137.* SS do them individually or in pairs. Check answers.

a 1 H 2 G 3 A 4 C 5 B 6 E 7 F

b 1 might (or may) be ill
2 might be in a meeting
3 might not like it
4 might not have time
5 might win
6 might be cold

- Tell SS to go back to the main lesson on *p.69*.

3 PRONUNCIATION & SPEAKING

a 6.9

- Focus on the instructions. SS should look at the underlined phrases in the dialogue on *p.68* when they listen and repeat. Play the tape/CD once the whole way through and then play it again, pausing after each phrase for SS to repeat.
- Elicit that *may* and *might* are stressed.

6.9 CD2 Track 46

1 I might go … but I might not.
2 You might meet somebody new.
3 I might wear my new black trousers.
4 The red dress may be too small for me now.
5 I might go with John.
6 I may walk there.

b
- Put SS into pairs. Tell them to go to **Communication *Decisions, decisions*, A** on *p.110* and **B** on *p.115*. Go through the instructions and make sure SS understand what they have to do.
- Demonstrate the activity. Take the role of the indecisive person. Get **B** to ask his/her first question (*What's the next film you're going to see?*), and answer with lots of alternatives, e.g. *I don't know yet, I might see ..., or I may...* . Be theatrical, and then ask SS to help you make a decision. Elicit *If I were you, I'd ...* and encourage them to give reasons.
- SS then ask and answer in pairs. Monitor and help, encouraging SS to use and stress *may/might*.
- Tell SS to go back to the main lesson on *p.69*.

4 READING

a
- Focus on the instructions and make sure SS cover the text (or get them to close their books). Stress that they should try to predict just one tip.
- Get feedback and write each pairs' tip on the board (with their initials).

b
- Now focus on the article and get SS to skim read to see if their tips (or something similar) are there. Tick any ones on the board that appear in the article.
- Focus on the verbs in the box, and give SS a few minutes to re-read the text and complete it. Get SS to compare their answers with a partner's and then check answers.

1 Take 2 Make 3 compare 4 ask 5 confuse
6 Use 7 feel 8 wait 9 have 10 make

Possible tips
Don't be afraid to change your mind. Your first instinct may not be right. Toss a coin and accept your 'fate', etc

c
- Finally get SS, in pairs, to decide which tip is the best. Get feedback and find out which tip is considered the best by the whole class.
- In the same pairs, SS try to think of one more tip to add to the list. Get feedback and write their tips on the board.

5 VOCABULARY noun formation

a
- Focus on the chart, and highlight the *-ion* ending and the spelling changes. Then elicit the next noun (*information*) and get SS to continue in pairs.

b 6.10
- Tell SS to listen the first time to see if they have the right word. Play the tape/CD. Check answers.

6.10 CD2 Track 47

confuse	confusion
decide	decision
imagine	imagination
inform	information
elect	election
invite	invitation
organize	organization
educate	education
translate	translation
communicate	communication

- Play the tape/CD again for SS to underline the stress.
- Focus on the questions, and elicit that *-sion* and *-tion* are pronounced /ʃən/ or /ʒən/ (*imagination* and *decision*) and that the stress is always on the syllable before this ending.

c
- Give SS a few minutes to complete the sentences. Check answers, making sure they are stressing the words correctly.

1 decision	4 election
2 information	5 organization
3 invitation	6 communication

d
- Get SS to ask you the first question. Answer, and elicit more follow up questions.
- SS then ask and answer in pairs. Monitor and help, encouraging them to ask for and give more information.

Extra photocopiable activities

Grammar
may or *might p.161*
Communicative
It might rain *p.205* (instructions *p.179*)

HOMEWORK

Study Link **Workbook** *pp.53–54*

6 D

G *should / shouldn't*
V *get*: *get angry*, *get lost*, etc.
P /ʊ/, sentence stress

What should I do?

Lesson plan

This lesson presents *should/shouldn't* for giving advice. The context is a radio programme where people phone in with problems, and then listeners are asked to e-mail their advice. There is a focus on the pronunciation of *-ould* (as in *should*, *could* etc.) and on sentence rhythm. SS practise giving advice both orally and in written notes. The lesson ends with a focus on the uses of *get*, which are recycled in a questionnaire.

Optional lead-in (books closed)

Ask SS *If you had a problem, who would you ask for advice?* and elicit ideas, e.g *my family, friends* etc. Elicit also the idea of contacting a radio programme or a magazine/Internet problem page. Find out from the class what they think of these more impersonal options and how many people in the class would think of using them instead of asking a family member or friend. Now do **1a**.

⚠ *advice* is uncountable in English – it can't be used in the plural. *My family usually give me good advice* NOT ~~*good advices*~~.

1 LISTENING & READING

a • Books open. Focus on the three questions and give SS a minute to read the extract. Check answers with the whole class.

1 It's an advice programme.
2 To explain a problem they have and ask for help/advice.
3 SS' own answer.

Extra challenge

Ask SS how often the programme is on, to elicit *every day*, and teach the word *daily*. Then ask if it is only for certain kinds of problems (no, for all kinds), and teach *whatever* (= it doesn't matter what your problem is).

b 6.11

• Focus on the instructions and the words in the box. Make sure SS understand *jealousy* (= the noun of *jealous*, i.e. feeling angry/upset because you think your partner is interested in somebody else).
• Play the tape/CD once. Let SS discuss in pairs what each problem is about and write it in. Check answers.

Barbara's problem is about money.
Kevin's problem is about jealousy.
Catherine's problem is about clothes.

6.11 CD2 Track 48

(tapescript in Student's Book on *p.123*)
P = presenter, B = Barbara, K = Kevin, C = Catherine

P Welcome to this morning's edition of *What's the problem*? Today we're talking about friends, so if you have a problem with one of your friends, call us now. And if you're listening to the programme and you think you can help with any of the problems, then just send an e-mail to our website. Our e-mail address is what.problem@radiotalk.com. Our first caller today is Barbara. Hello Barbara.
B Hello.
P What's the problem?
B Well, I have a problem with a friend called Jonathan (that's not his real name). Well, Jonathan often goes out with me and my friends. The problem is that he's really mean.
P Mean?
B Yes. He never pays for anything. When we have a drink he always says he doesn't have any money or that he's forgotten his money. So in the end one of us always pays for him. At first we thought 'Poor Jonathan, he doesn't have much money.' But it's not true. His parents work, and he works on Saturdays in a shop – so he must have some money. Do you think we should say something to him?
P Thanks, Barbara. I'm sure you'll soon get some e-mails with good advice. OK, our next caller is Kevin from Birmingham. Hello Kevin.
K Hi.
P What's the problem?
K Yes. My problem is with my best friend. Well, the thing is, he's always flirting with my girlfriend.
P Your best friend flirts with your girlfriend?
K Yes, when the three of us are together he always says things to my girlfriend like, 'Wow! You look fantastic today' or 'I love your dress, Suzanna', things like that. And when we're at parties he often asks her to dance.
P Do you think he's in love with your girlfriend?
K I don't know ... but I'm really angry about it. What can I do?
P Well, let's see if one of our listeners can help, Kevin. And our last caller is Catherine. OK Catherine, over to you. What's the problem?
C Hello. I'm at university and I live on the university campus. I live in a flat and I share a room with this girl. She's really nice, I get on very well with her ... but there's one big problem.
P What's that?
C She always borrows things from me without telling me.
P What does she borrow?
C Well, first it was CDs and books, but now she's started taking my clothes as well, sweaters, jackets, and things. Yesterday she took a white sweater of mine and she didn't tell me. So when I wanted to wear it this afternoon it was dirty. I don't want to lose her as a friend but what should I do?
P Thank you, Catherine. So, if you can help Barbara, Kevin, or Catherine, e-mail us at ...

c • Focus on the instructions. Tell SS that the important thing is to be clear about the basic problem. Play the tape/CD again and pause after each caller to give SS time to talk to a partner. If necessary, play the tape a third time. Check answers.

1 She has a friend who's very mean. When he goes out with her and her friends he never pays, but he's not poor.
2 His best friend flirts with his girlfriend.
3 Her flatmate always borrows her things without telling her, CDs, books, clothes, etc.

Extra challenge

Ask more comprehension questions for each problem, e.g. (for 1) *What's her friend's name? Is that his real name? What does he say when they go out for a drink?* etc.

Extra support

Let SS listen again with the tapescript on *p.123*. Deal with any problematic vocabulary.

d • Now focus on the e-mails and the instructions. Give SS two minutes to read and match the e-mails to the problems. Let SS compare answers with a partner's and then check answers.

1 Kevin **2** Catherine **3** Kevin **4** Barbara **5** Catherine **6** Barbara

e • Go through the e-mails and explain/translate any vocabulary that is causing problems, e.g *lock, get the message, sensitive*, etc. Now tell SS to read them again and decide whose advice they think is best and why.

Extra idea

Tell SS that if they don't agree with any of the e-mails, to make their own suggestions.

• Get feedback, and find out whose advice the majority of the class thinks is best, or if they have any other suggestions. You could also tell them what you think.

2 GRAMMAR *should / shouldn't*

a • SS will probably have guessed the meaning of *should/shouldn't*. Get them to highlight examples in the e-mails, and check answers.

1 you should talk to your girlfriend
2 you should lock your clothes in a cupboard
3 You shouldn't be so sensitive.
4 you should pay for him
5 you should talk to her
6 You definitely shouldn't pay for him.

b • Focus on the meanings and elicit that *you should* = I think it's a good idea. It is not an obligation, and is not as strong as *you have to* or *you must*.

c • Tell SS to go to **Grammar Bank 6D** on *p.136*. Go through the rules and model and drill the example sentences.

Grammar notes

- *Should* does not usually cause problems as it has a clearly defined use and the form is simple. Remind SS to use the infinitive without *to* after *should.*
- You may want to point out to SS the alternative form *ought to*, but *should* is more common, especially in spoken English.
- The main problem with *should* is the pronunciation, i.e. the silent *l* (see **Pronunciation notes** below).

• Focus on the exercises for **6D** on *p.137*. SS do them individually or in pairs. Check answers.

a 1 shouldn't **2** shouldn't **3** should **4** should **5** shouldn't **6** shouldn't **7** should
b 1 should wear **2** should study **3** shouldn't walk **4** should relax **5** shouldn't drive **6** should go

• Tell SS to go back to the main lesson on *p.71*.

3 PRONUNCIATION & SPEAKING /ʊ/

a 6.12

• Focus on the phonetics and get SS to listen and repeat them. Then focus on the example (*should*) and tell SS to compare the word and the phonetics. Ask SS *Which consonant is not pronounced?* and elicit that it is the *l*. Then ask *How do you pronounce the* ou*?* and elicit /ʊ/.

• Play the tape/CD again and get SS to write the words. Check answers.

6.12	CD2 Track 49
1 should	**4** wouldn't
2 shouldn't	**5** could
3 would	**6** couldn't

Pronunciation notes

- *Should, would,* and *could* are often mispronounced partly because of the silent *l* but also because *ou* is not normally pronounced /ʊ/. Focussing on the phonetics should help SS to get the sounds right.
- If you don't want to focus on phonetics, you could just tell SS that in these three verbs the *l* is silent and the *ou* is pronounced like *bull.*

Extra challenge

Remind SS to get into the habit of looking at the phonetics when they look up a word in the dictionary, as it will show them if there is a silent letter and what the sounds are. You might also like to point out here that /wʊd/ could also be written *wood*, as the pronunciation is exactly the same.

b 6.13

• Now focus on the sentences and highlight that *shouldn't* is always stressed, but that *should* is only stressed in *yes/no* questions.

• Play the tape/CD pausing after each sentence for SS to listen and repeat.

6.13	CD2 Track 50
1 You should talk to your friend.	
2 You shouldn't be so sensitive.	
3 You should lock your clothes in a cupboard.	
4 You definitely shouldn't pay for your friend.	
5 What should I do?	
6 Should I write to him?	

4 WRITING & SPEAKING

a • Put SS into pairs. Focus on the problems, and tell SS to read them and choose one to give advice on. They should then write a note giving advice. Tell them:
- to use the e-mails from exercise **1** as a model.
- to use either *you should/shouldn't* or *If I were you I'd ...* to give advice and explain why.
- to begin their note with *Hi*, but not to put the number of the problem. They should end with their names.
- to write their note on a separate piece of paper (not in their notebooks).

• Allow SS at least five minutes to read and choose a problem, and write the note. Monitor and help with spelling, etc. Fast finishers could write another note for a different problem.

b • Now get each pair of SS to pass their note to the pair on their right (or take in the notes and redistribute them). Each pair then reads the new note and decides which problem it is answering and if they think it's good advice or not. They could make a record of the names of the SS who wrote it, write the number of the problem they're answering, and a put tick for good advice or a cross for bad advice.

• Either let SS carry on passing the notes round until they've read them all, or in a large class stop after they've read three or four. Get feedback by going through the five problems and asking SS what advice was given, and which advice they think is best.

5 VOCABULARY *get*

a • Tell SS that *get* is one of the most common verbs in English, and remind them that it can mean several different things. Focus on the instructions, sentences, and words/phrases in the box. Get SS to match and then compare their answers with a partner's. Then check answers.

1 A 2 D 3 C 4 B

b • Tell SS to go to **Vocabulary Bank *get*** on *p.152*. SS do the exercises individually or in pairs. Check answers.

1 get angry	13 get on (well) with
2 get lost	14 get up
3 get married	15 get into
4 get divorced	16 get on
5 get fit	17 get home
6 get better	18 get to work
7 get worse	19 get to school
8 get older	20 get a letter
9 get a newspaper	21 get an e-mail
10 get a ticket	22 get a present
11 get a job	23 get a salary
12 get a flat	

• Get SS to test themselves or each other.
• Tell SS to go back to the main lesson on *p.71*.

c • Focus on the questionnaire and go through the questions. Get SS to ask you one or two of the questions. SS then ask and answer in pairs. Monitor and help, making sure they are using *get* correctly.
• Get feedback from a few pairs.

Extra support

You could do 6 and 7 as open class questions.

Extra photocopiable activities

Grammar
should or *shouldn't? p.162*
Communicative
What should I do? *p.206* (instructions *p.180*)

HOMEWORK

Study Link **Workbook** *pp.55–56*

6 PRACTICAL ENGLISH AT THE PHARMACY

Revision Asking for help
Function Asking for medicine
Language *I have a headache and a cough; I'm allergic to penicillin.*

Lesson plan

In this lesson SS learn to talk about basic illness symptoms and ask for medicine at a chemist's or pharmacy. In the story in **Social English**, Mark apologizes to Allie for his behaviour the previous evening and they plan how to spend Allie's last day.

Study Link These lessons are on the *New English File Pre-intermediate* Video, which can be used instead of the Class Cassette/CD (see introduction *p.9*). The main functional section of each episode (the second section) is also on the MultiROM with additional activities.

Optional lead-in (books closed)

Revise what happened in the previous episode by eliciting the story from SS, e.g *What did Allie buy?* (a sweater) *What was wrong with it?* (It was too big.) *What did she do?* (She got her money back.) *What happened that evening?* (They went to the cocktail party.), etc.

ASKING FOR HELP

6.14

- Books open. Focus on the photo and elicit/explain that Allie doesn't feel well and has gone to reception for help.
- Then focus on the questions. Explain/translate *painkillers, headache,* and *backache.* Highlight the pronunciation of *ache* /eɪk/ and that we say *I have (a headache,* etc.).
- Play the tape/CD once the whole way through and tell SS just to listen. Then play it again, pausing if necessary to give SS time to underline the right phrases. Get them to compare their answers with a partner's before checking answers.

1 painkillers 2 headache 3 doesn't give
4 doesn't want 5 is

Extra support

Let SS listen again with the tapescript on *p.123.* Deal with any problematic vocabulary.

- Highlight that both *chemist's* and *pharmacy* are used in the UK, but only *pharmacy* in the US. Focus on the information box.

6.14 CD2 Track 51
(tapescript in Student's Book on *p.123*)
R = Receptionist, A = Allie
R Hi. How can I help you?
A Do you have any painkillers? I have a headache.
R I'm sorry. We can't give our guests medicine. But we can call a doctor for you if you like.
A No, it's OK. I don't need a doctor. It's just a cold. But is there a chemist's near the hotel?
R Do you mean a pharmacy?
A Sorry, that's right, a pharmacy.
R Sure. There's one right across the street.
A Thank you.
R You're welcome.

ASKING FOR MEDICINE

a 6.15

- Tell SS to cover the dialogue with their hand or a piece of paper. Focus on the picture. Ask *Where's Allie?* (At the pharmacy.)

⚠ If you think that SS won't cover their books properly, you could get them to close their books at this stage and write the first task on the board.

- Play the tape/CD once. Check answers.

The pharmacist gives her aspirin.
She has to take two every four hours.
They cost $4.75.

b
- Now tell SS to uncover the dialogue (or open their books). Explain that the **YOU HEAR** part is what they need to understand, and the **YOU SAY** part contains the phrases they need to be able to say.
- Give SS a minute to read through the dialogue and guess the missing words. Then play the tape/CD again, for them to complete the dialogue.

6.15 6.16 CD2 Tracks 52+53
P = Pharmacist, A = Allie
P Good morning. Can I help you?
A I have a bad cold. Do you have something I can take? (*repeat*)
P What **symptoms** do you have?
A I have a headache and a cough. (*repeat*)
P Do you have a **temperature**?
A No, I don't think so. (*repeat*)
P Does your back **hurt**?
A No.
P Are you allergic to any drugs?
A I'm allergic to penicillin. (*repeat*)
P No problem. These are **aspirin**. These will make you feel **better**.
A How many do I have to take? (*repeat*)
P Two every four hours.
A Sorry? How often? (*repeat*)
P Every four hours. If you don't feel better in **24** hours, you should see a doctor.
A OK, thanks. How much are they? (*repeat*)
P $4.75, please.
A Thank you.
P You're welcome.

- Go through the dialogue line by line with SS. Highlight that the word *ache* /eɪk/ can be used with *head, back, tooth, ear,* and *stomach*, and we use these words with *I have*. Alternatively (and with other parts of the body) we say *my* (*head*, etc.) *hurts*. Also highlight the irregular pronunciation of *cough* /kɒf/ and *temperature* /ˈtemprɪtʃə/.

c 6.16

- Now focus on the **YOU SAY** phrases. Tell SS they're going to hear the dialogue again. They repeat the **YOU SAY** phrases when they hear the beep. Encourage them to copy the rhythm.
- Play the tape/CD, pausing if necessary for SS to repeat the phrases.

d • Put SS into pairs, **A** and **B**. **A** is the pharmacist, **B** is Allie. Tell **B** to close his/her book and try to remember the phrases. Then **A** and **B** swap roles.

Extra support

Let SS practise the dialogue first in pairs, both with books open.

Extra challenge

Let SS roleplay with other symptoms, and say if they are really allergic to anything, etc.

SOCIAL ENGLISH talking about the party

a 6.17

- Elicit/remind SS what happened at the party in the previous episode, and that Mark got angry with Brad.
- Focus on the instructions. Go through the sentences with SS and make sure they understand *apologizes* and *annoying*.
- Play the tape/CD at least twice. Let SS compare their answers with a partner's and then check answers. Get SS to correct the false ones.

1 T
2 F She thinks he's very nice.
3 T
4 F Tomorrow is her last day
5 F They're going to go on a boat trip and later have dinner.

6.17 CD2 Track 54

(tapescript in Student's Book on *p.123*)
M = Mark, A = Allie
M **Bless** you! Are you OK?
A It's just a cold. I had a bad headache this morning, but I feel better now.
M Listen. I'm really sorry **about** last night.
A What do you mean?
M At the party. I got kind of angry at Brad. He was really annoying me.
A Oh, I think he's very nice.
M Yeah, women always think so.
A Don't worry, Mark. Brad's not my type.
M So what is your type, Allie?
A You know what my type is. Dark hair, 34 years old, lives in San Francisco ...
M Listen, tomorrow's your last day. I want to do something special. What would you like to do?
A I don't **mind**. You choose.
M **How** about a boat trip around the bay? We could do that in the morning, and then have a nice dinner in the evening.
A That **sounds** fantastic.
M It's too bad you can't stay longer.
A Yes, it's a **pity** – this week has gone so quickly. I feel I've just arrived and now I'm going home.
M Well, I'm going to make sure tomorrow is a really special day.

- Check comprehension by asking a few more questions, e.g. *How does Allie feel now?* (Better.) *Why did Mark get angry at the party?* (Because Brad was annoying him.) *What does Allie say about Brad?* (He's very nice.) *What is Allie's type of man?* (Dark hair, 34 years old, lives in San Francisco, i.e. Mark.) *What does Allie want to do on her last day?* (She doesn't mind.) *How does Allie feel?* (As if she's just arrived.)
- Get SS to speculate a bit about the story, and what will happen next. Ask *What do you think is going to happen on Allie's last day?*, etc.

b • Focus on the **USEFUL PHRASES**. Get SS to see if they can remember any of the missing words. Play the tape/CD again and check answers.

c 6.18

- Play the tape/CD pausing for SS to repeat each phrase. Encourage them to copy the rhythm.
- In a monolingual class get SS to decide together what the equivalent phrase would be in their language.
- Highlight that we say *Bless you!* when somebody sneezes, and *How about* + noun or verb + *-ing* to make a suggestion.

6.18 CD2 Track 55

M = Mark, A = Allie
M Bless you!
M I'm really sorry about last night.
A I don't mind. You choose.
M How about a boat trip around the bay?
A That sounds fantastic.
A It's a pity.

Extra challenge

Get SS to roleplay the conversation between Mark and Allie in pairs using the tapescript on *p.123*. Let SS read their parts first and then try to act it from memory.

HOMEWORK

Study Link **Workbook** *p.57*

6 Writing
Writing to a friend

Lesson plan

In this sixth writing lesson SS practise writing another informal e-mail, in answer to an imaginary one from Daniel in Argentina (see **Writing File 1**). This e-mail consolidates the expressions for giving advice that SS have studied in **File 6**, e.g *I think you should …, If I were you I'd …*, etc.

a
- Focus on the photos, and ask SS where they think it is (Argentina). Ask SS if anyone has been there, and what they know about it, e.g the capital is Buenos Aires, etc.
- Now focus on the e-mail. Ask *Who's it to?* (Alessandra) *Who's it from?* (Daniel). SS may remember that Alessandra wrote her first e-mail to Daniel in **Writing File 1** on *p.13*.
- Focus on the instructions and the words in the box. Give SS, in pairs, a few minutes to read the e-mail and complete the gaps.
- Check answers.

2 want	3 think	4 visit	5 hire
6 spend	7 meet	8 recommend	

- Ask a few more questions to check comprehension, e.g.:
  What is Daniel's exciting news?
  When is he going to go to Argentina?
  How long is he going to stay?

b
- Focus on the instructions. Stress that in the third paragraph, they must imagine that instead of Mendoza, he is asking about their town or city. Get SS to highlight Daniel's four questions, and then get SS to discuss the answers in pairs. Get feedback.

In a multilingual class, get SS to tell each other the answers about their countries/towns.

c
- Focus on the **USEFUL PHRASES**. SS complete them in pairs. Check answers.

1 for 2 from 3 to 4 in 5 by 6 to

Write an e-mail to Daniel

Either give SS at least fifteen minutes to write the e-mail in class, following the instructions, or set it for homework. If SS do the writing in class, get them to swap their e-mail with another S's to read and check for mistakes before you collect them all in.

6 Revise & Check

For instructions on how to use these pages, see *p.27*.

GRAMMAR

1 c 2 a 3 a 4 a 5 b 6 a 7 a 8 c 9 b 10 a

VOCABULARY

a 1 ~~know~~ 2 ~~making~~ 3 ~~win~~ 4 ~~wearing~~ 5 ~~look~~
b 1 lion 2 spider 3 horse 4 whale 5 bull
c 1 communication 2 organization 3 discussion 4 translation 5 decision

PRONUNCIATION

a 1 lose 2 lion 3 wasp 4 fall 5 mouse
b advice crocodile decision happen translation

CAN YOU UNDERSTAND THIS TEXT?

a A 3 B 2 C 5 D 1 E 4
b **telling lies:** saying something which is not true
offend: say something which makes another person feel sad
together: with another person
bald: no hair at all on your head
goldfish: an orange fish that children often keep as a pet
put on weight: to get fatter

CAN YOU UNDERSTAND THESE PEOPLE?

6.19 CD2 Track 56

1
A It's cold. Why don't we get a taxi?
B No, the bus will come in a minute.
A I'm freezing. Let's start walking.
B If we walk, the bus will come.
A Yeah, you're right. Let's wait another five minutes.

2
A Jim and his wife came to dinner last night. We had a great time.
B What's his wife's name?
A Deborah. Don't you know her?
B No, I've heard Jim talk about her but I've never met her.
A She's really nice.
B Well, I hope I'll meet her soon.

3
A What would you do if you saw a mouse in the kitchen?
B I'd stand on a chair and scream.
A But a mouse can't hurt you! It's just a little animal.
B I don't care.

4

A What are you going to do tonight?
B I don't know. I might see a film or I might just go home and stay in. What about you?
A I'm meeting Nicola in the pub. Do you want to come?
B OK.

5

A I want to buy a pet for my daughter but I don't know what to get.
B What about a cat or a dog? You told me she loves dogs.
A Yeah, but we don't have a garden. I don't think people should keep dogs in flats.
B What about a hamster?
A No, they smell. And they can bite.
B A goldfish then?
A That's a good idea.

a 1 b 2 b 3 a 4 b 5 a

6.20 CD2 Track 57

A Who's our next caller, please?
B Hi, my name's Dave.
A Hello Dave, where are you from?
B I'm from Southampton.
A And what's your problem, Dave?
B Well, I'm married. I've been married for five years now. And my wife Maureen and I were always very happy until last year.
A And what happened then?
B Well, seven months ago my wife had a baby – a little boy – and he's wonderful and all that, but now everything has changed.
A In what way?
B Well, my wife doesn't have time for me now. She's only interested in the baby. And at night when the baby goes to bed she's too tired to talk to me. She's like a different person now and I don't know what to do.
A Well Dave, first I think that maybe you should talk to her and explain how you're feeling. And if I were you, I'd help her with the baby. Then she wouldn't be so tired, and she'd have more time and energy …

1 T 2 F 3 T 4 F 5 T

CAN YOU SAY THIS IN ENGLISH?

b 1 What would you do if you lost your wallet?
2 What would you do if you won the lottery?
3 What would you do if you found some money in the street?
4 What would you do if you had more free time?
5 What would you do if you could speak perfect English?

Extra photocopiable activities

Quicktest 6 *p.236*

7 A

G present perfect + *for* and *since*
V words related to fear: *afraid*, *frightened*, etc.
P /ɪ/ or /aɪ/, sentence stress

Famous fears and phobias

File 7 overview

The main focus of File 7 is on SS learning to talk about their lives using the present perfect with *for* and *since* (**7A**), describing important events in your life, e.g. *be born*, *get married*, etc. in **7B**, and describing past habits with *used to* in **7C**. The final lesson in the file (**7D**) moves away from SS own lives and presents the present and past passive through the context of female inventors.

Lesson plan

In this lesson SS study the present perfect with *for* and *since* to talk about unfinished actions or states. The context is a magazine article about famous people and their phobias, and the vocabulary focus is on different ways of expressing fear, e.g. *afraid*, *frightened*, etc. This use of the present perfect is hard for most SS to use correctly, as their languages will probably use a different tense (often the present simple) in this context. In the following lesson the present perfect for unfinished actions/periods of time will be contrasted with the past simple for finished actions/periods.

Optional lead-in (books closed)

Write PHOBIA on the board. Ask SS *How do you feel if you have a phobia of something?* and elicit *afraid* (or *frightened/scared*).

Elicit from SS some examples of common phobias and write them on the board, e.g. *flying*, *spiders*, *high places*, etc. SS may come up with some more unusual phobias, e.g. *the number 13*, etc. They may also know the medical name for certain phobias, e.g. *agoraphobia* = fear of going outside. If they use one of these words, elicit what the phobia means. When you have elicited six phobias ask SS if they have any of these phobias and get a show of hands for each one. Then do exercise **1a**.

1 READING & VOCABULARY

a • Books open. Focus on the pictures and give SS a minute to match the words and pictures. Check answers by asking *What's picture 1?*, etc. Model and drill pronunciation as necessary, especially *heights* /haɪts/.

> **1** closed spaces **2** flying **3** wasps **4** open spaces **5** snakes **6** heights **7** spiders **8** water

b • Focus on the questions and the example speech bubbles. Go through the pictures again one by one finding out if anybody in the class is afraid of each thing or knows anybody who is. Encourage SS to briefly say why they or the person they know is afraid.

Extra support

Demonstrate the activity yourself and talk briefly about people you know.

c • Now focus on the photos of famous people and tell SS that they are going to read about these people, all of whom have one of the phobias from the list in **a**.

• Give SS three minutes to read the article and complete the gaps with one of the phobias in **a**. Tell SS to try to guess the meaning of new words from context and that vocabulary will be dealt with later.

• Get SS to compare their answers with a partner's and then check answers. Elicit the whole phrase (see key below). SS should be able to guess the meaning of the phrases but don't give a detailed grammatical explanation at this point as this is focused on below.

• Highlight the pronunciation of *since* /sɪns/and *ages* /ˈeɪdʒɪz/ and elicit that *ages* = a long time.

> **Winona Ryder** has been afraid of **water** since 1983.
> **Rupert Grint** has been been afraid of **spiders** since he was a child.
> **Dennis Bergkamp** has been afraid of **flying** since 1994.

d • In pairs SS underline the words in the text. Check answers.

> terrified, frightened, panic, fear

• Elicit/explain that *frightened* = afraid, *terrified* = very afraid, *panic* = lose control, and *fear* = the noun from *afraid*. Practise pronouncing the words.

Extra idea

Ask SS to choose five words or phrases from the text that they want to learn and to write them with their translation in their notebooks or vocabulary books. Get some feedback on which words SS have chosen.

2 GRAMMAR present perfect + *for* and *since*

a • Focus on the text about Winona Ryder. You could read the text aloud to the class or get a student to read it.

• Now focus on the two questions and give SS a few moments to answer them. Check answers.

> In 1983.
> YES

b • Focus on the task and the question (*How long has she been afraid of water?*) and elicit/remind SS that *How long?* = How much time? Give SS a few moments to complete the gaps and compare their answers with a partner's. Check answers.

> **since** 1983
> **for** ( ) years. (This will depend on the date when you are doing the lesson.)

c • Tell SS to look at the two examples in **b** and then to complete the rule. Check answers.

Use *for* with a period of time.
Use *since* with a point in time.

• Highlight that:
– we tend to use *since* when we want to be exact, e.g. *I've lived here since October 2003.*
– we tend to use *for* when we are approximating, e.g. *for about four years.* In this respect it is very common to use the expressions *for a long time* or *for ages* (= slightly more colloquial).

d • Tell SS to go to **Grammar Bank 7A** on *p.138*. Go through the rules with the class. Model and drill the example sentences.

Grammar notes

- The present perfect with *for* and *since* can be a tricky tense for SS as they may use a different tense in their language to express this concept, e.g. the present tense. Typical mistake:
I live here since three years/since three years ago.
- The important thing to highlight is that the present perfect with *for* and *since* is used to say how long a situation has continued until now, i.e. we use it for situations which are still true, e.g. *I've been in this class for two years* (= and I am still in this class).

• Focus on the exercises for **7A** on *p.139*. SS do the exercises individually or in pairs. Check answers.

a 1 How long has he had his car?
2 How long have your parents lived in this house?
3 How long have you been a teacher?
4 How long has she known her boyfriend?
5 How long has Poland been in the EU?
6 How long have you had your dog?
7 How long has Tim been frightened of water?

b 1 He's had his car for three years.
2 They've lived in this house for a long time.
3 I've been a teacher since 1990.
4 She's known her boyfriend since May.
5 It's been in the EU since 2004.
6 We've had our dog for about two years.
7 He's been frightened of water since he was a child.

• Tell SS to go back to the main lesson on *p.77*.

3 LISTENING

a 7.1

• Focus on the picture and ask SS *Do you like cats? Are you afraid of cats? Do you know anybody who is?* and elicit responses. Focus on the instructions and the question. Play the tape/CD once for SS to listen. Check answers.

He starts to feel very nervous, his heart beats quickly. And he has to go away very quickly from where the cat is.

b • Focus on questions 1–6. Play the tape/CD again for SS to answer the questions. Pause the tape as necessary to give SS time to write their answers.
• Get SS to compare their answers in pairs and play the tape a third time if SS need it. Check answers.

1 Felinophobia or Gatophobia.
2 Since he was five or six years old.
3 A friend's cat bit him.
4 Yes, sometimes. (He can't be in the same room as a cat. He has to ask people to take the cat out of the room.)
5 He's going to a therapist. (After three sessions he can look at a photo of a cat and touch a toy cat.)
6 Yes, he's optimistic. (He thinks one day he might have a cat as a pet.)

7.1 CD3 Track 2

(tapescript in Student's Book on *p.124*)
I= interviewer, S= Scott

I What exactly is your phobia, Scott?
S Well, the medical name is Felinophobia or Gatophobia.
I And what does that mean exactly?
S It means I'm afraid of cats.
I Cats?
S Yes.
I How long have you had this phobia?
S Since I was a child.
I And how did it start?
S When I was five or six years old, I remember going to a friend's house and I saw a cat on the stairs. And the cat was looking at me, well staring at me. I went to touch it, and it bit me. And since then I've always been afraid of cats.
I What happens if you see a cat?
S Well, I start to feel very nervous, my hearts beats quickly. And I have to go away very quickly from where the cat is. For example, if I see a cat in the street, I always cross to the other side.
I What do you do?
S I'm a doctor.
I Is your phobia a problem for you in your work?
S Yes, sometimes. For example, if I go to a house and there is a cat, I have to ask the people to put the cat in another room. I can't be in the same room as a cat.
I Have you ever had any treatment for your phobia?
S Yes, I've just started going to a therapist. I've had three sessions.
I How's it going?
S Well, now I can look at a photo of a cat without feeling nervous or afraid. And I can touch a toy cat. The next step will be to be in a room with a real cat.
I Do you think you will ever lose your phobia of cats?
S I hope so. I'm optimistic. Who knows, maybe one day I'll have a cat as a pet.

Extra support

If you have time you could get SS to listen to the tape/CD with the tapescript on *p.124* so they can see exactly what they understood. Translate/explain any new words or phrases.

4 PRONUNCIATION /ɪ/ and /aɪ/, sentence stress

- Here SS learn a useful pronunciation rule and practise pronouncing the /ɪ/ and /aɪ/ sounds.

Pronunciation notes

- There are two clear spelling/pronunciation rules for words with *i* but there are a few common exceptions like *live* (v) which trip SS up sometimes. By this time SS will instinctively pronounce most of these words correctly and it is just a question of making an effort to remember the tricky ones like *child/children* and *since* which they may mispronounce.
- *i* between consonants is usually pronounced /ɪ/, e.g. *win*.
  i + one consonant + *e* is usually pronounced /aɪ/, e.g. *wine*. SS should try to learn the exceptions, e.g. *give*.

a • Focus on the activity and give SS, in pairs, two minutes to put the words in the right column.

b 7.2

- Play the tape/CD for SS to listen and check. Check answers.

7.2 CD3 Track 3

fish /ɪ/	bike /aɪ/
children	child
in	I've
live	like
minute	life
since	line
win	mine

- Play the tape/CD again for SS to listen and repeat. Give more practise if these sounds are a problem for your SS.

Study Link SS can find more practice of these sounds on the MultiROM or on the *New English File Pre-intermediate* website.

c • Elicit how to say the two sentences. Drill the pronunciation and then get SS to practise saying them in pairs.

d 7.3

- Here SS practise sentence rhythm in *How long have you . . .?* questions, to prepare for the speaking activity in 5.
- Play the tape/CD. Pause after each section of the question for SS to repeat, building up to the whole question. Encourage them to copy the rhythm. Then get them to practise for a couple of minutes in pairs.

7.3 CD3 Track 4

1 lived here
have you lived here
How long have you lived here?
2 known him
have you known him
How long have you known him?
3 been married
have they been married
How long have they been married?
4 had his dog
has he had his dog
How long has he had his dog?

5 SPEAKING

- Focus on the chart, and instructions. Elicit the past participles of the four verbs (*known, lived, been, had*). Focus on the example in the speech bubbles.

Extra support

Check SS can make the questions correctly by getting them to ask you some of the questions first. Give short, natural answers with *for* and *since* and some more information if you can as a model for how SS should answer.

- Give SS a minute to choose their six questions.
- Focus on the speech bubbles. Get SS to ask and answer in pairs. Monitor, making sure they are using *for* and *since* correctly and are not mispronouncing *since*. Get feedback from different pairs.

Extra photocopiable activities

Grammar

present perfect + *for* and *since* *p.163*

Communicative

Class survey *p.207* (instructions on *p.180*)

Homework

Study Link **Workbook** *pp.58–59*

7B Born to direct

G present perfect or past simple?
V biographies
P word stress

Lesson plan

The lives of famous film directors, Quentin Tarantino, Alfred Hitchcock, and Sofia Coppola, provide the context for reading, talking, and listening about people's lives. The grammatical focus is the contrast between the past and present perfect and students learn common verb phrases for giving biographical information, e.g. *be born, leave school,* etc. In pronunciation SS get more practice of word stress.

Optional lead-in (books closed)

Write IMPORTANT MOMENTS IN OUR LIFE on the board and write *be born, go to school* underneath. Give SS, in pairs, two minutes to write down other important moments using verb phrases, e.g. *leave school, go to university, get a job, fall in love, get married,* etc. (See verbs in exercise **1** below.) Elicit the phrases onto the board. Then do **1a**.

1 VOCABULARY & PRONUNCIATION

a • Books open. Focus on the list of verbs. Elicit/teach the meaning of *events* (things which happen to you). Go through the verbs, making sure SS understand them all.

• Give SS time to mark the stress on the highlighted words.

b 7.4

• Play the tape/CD for SS to listen and check their answers. Play the tape/CD again for SS to repeat.

7.4 CD3 Track 5

go to uni<u>ver</u>sity
go to <u>pri</u>mary school
re<u>tire</u>
get di<u>vor</u>ced
have <u>chil</u>dren
get <u>ma</u>rried
go to <u>se</u>condary school
<u>se</u>parate

c • Tell SS to work individually and to number the expressions in **a** in a logical order. Elicit that the first expression is *be born*.

• Put SS into pairs and get them to compare their order with a partner's. Do they agree?

• Finally elicit from the class the usual order of the expressions.

A possible order

1 be born
2 go to primary school
3 go to secondary school
4 leave school
5 go to university
6 start work
7 fall in love
8 get married
9 have children
10 separate
11 get divorced
12 retire
13 die

Extra idea

You could get SS to mark the expressions: E = everybody does it, S = some people do it, M = most people do it.

2 READING & SPEAKING

a • Write *Alfred Hitchcock* and *Quentin Tarantino* on the board and ask SS *What do these two men have in common?* Elicit that they are both film directors. You could also try to elicit more information about them, e.g. their nationality (Hitchcock was British, Tarantino is American), their most famous films (Hitchcock: *Psycho, Rear Window,* etc. Tarantino: *Pulp Fiction, Reservoir Dogs,* etc.)

• Focus on the film stills and on the two questions. In pairs SS quickly answer the questions.

1 **The Birds**: Hitchcock
Kill Bill: Tarantino
2 The films are 'thrillers', i.e. exciting films often involving a crime and usually with violent scenes.

b • Focus on the information about the lives of the two film directors. Put SS into pairs and set a time limit for SS to read the facts and to mark them **H** or **T**. Check answers.

H:1, 3, 5, 6, 7, 10, 11, 13
T: 2, 4, 8, 9, 12, 14, 15

• Get SS to underline any words or phrases they don't understand and to try and guess the meaning with their partner. Deal with any vocabulary problems.

c • Put SS into pairs. Give them a couple of minutes for **A** to re-read the biographical information about Hitchcock, and **B** about Tarantino. They should try to remember as much as they can.

d • Now **A** (book closed) tells **B** everything he/she can remember about Hitchcock. **B** (book open) listens and helps, e.g. by jogging **A**'s memory with a word or phrase. SS swap roles.

Extra support

Write the following prompts on the board to help SS to remember their information:

Where/when born?
School?
Married? Children?
Muse?
Actor?
Oscar for best director?
Died?

3 GRAMMAR present perfect or past simple?

a • Give SS a minute or so to answer question **1**. Check answers and elicit a few examples.

All the verbs are in the **past tense** because he is dead (*he was born, he went to school, he died*, etc.).

• Now focus on question **2** and give SS a minute or so to answer it. Check answers and elicit a few examples. Highlight that if you are talking about the life of a person who is dead, you only use the past simple. If you are talking about the life of someone who is still alive, you will probably use the present, the past, and the present perfect.

Past tense *he was born, he went to work, he began his career*
This tense refers to past events in his life, e.g. his childhood and early life.
Present tense *his muse is Uma Thurman, he says he hates drugs and violence*
This refers to a situation which is true now in the present.
Present perfect *he has directed Uma Thurman in several of his most successful films. He has been nominated for an Oscar. He hasn't won one yet.*
This tense refers to past actions but which are still connected to the present, i.e. he might direct Uma Thurman in another film/he might win an Oscar in the future.

b • Tell SS to go to **Grammar Bank 7B** on *p.138*. Go through the rules with the class. Model and drill the example sentences.

Grammar notes

- The contrast between the past simple and the present perfect was first focused on in lesson **4A** (See **Grammar Bank 4A** *p.132*).
  Highlight that the present perfect is used in the two examples about Tarantino because his career as a film director hasn't finished. He is still a film director and will probably make more films.
- The past tense is used for Alfred Hitchcock because the sentences refer to a finished period of time. Hitchcock won't make any more films.
- Focus on the ⚠ box and explain that *since* can only be used with the present perfect. *For* can be used with both the present perfect and past simple (see examples about Tarantino and Hitchcock.)

• Focus on the exercises for **7B** on *p.139*. SS do the exercises individually or in pairs. Check answers.

a 1 ✗ He left school last year.
2 ✓
3 ✗ She has lived in Hollywood since 2004.
4 ✗ My sister had her baby yesterday!
5 ✗ I've worked there for twenty years.
6 ✓
7 ✗ They were married for a year.
b 1 has she lived, moved
2 did Picasso die, did he live, left
3 have they been

• Tell SS to go back to the main lesson on *p.79*.

4 SPEAKING

a • In this activity SS put into practice the contrast between the past simple and the present perfect through talking about a member of their family.
• Focus on the activity and give SS five minutes to think about who they are going to talk about and to prepare their answers to the questions. Stress that it should be an older relative, not a younger one.
• Focus on the question prompts and quickly elicit the questions. You could demonstrate the activity by getting the class to ask you about one of your grandparents or elderly relatives.

Extra support

Get SS to write the questions in their notebooks before they ask them. When they ask the questions, get them to ask them from the prompts and not just read them.

b • Sit SS in pairs, ideally face to face. Set a time limit for **A** to interview **B**. Encourage **B** to give as much information as possible and **A** to ask extra questions where possible. SS swap roles.

5 LISTENING

a • Focus on the photo and the question and elicit the answer that they are both film directors.

b • Explain the task and focus on the chart and the speech bubble. In pairs, SS quickly try to guess what connection there might be between the things in the chart and Sofia Coppola.
• Listen to their ideas but don't tell them if they are right or not.

c 7.5
• Play the tape/CD once and tell SS not to write anything, just to listen, to see whether they guessed the connection correctly. Play the tape again. SS make notes on the chart.

Extra support

Tell SS they can make notes in English or their own language. Pause the tape as necessary to give SS time to write their answers.

• Get SS to compare their answers with a partner's and play the tape again if SS need it. Then elicit answers. Don't expect SS to have all the information given.

New York 1971: She was born.
***The Godfather*:** Her father was making this film when she was born. She appeared in the film as a little baby.
***The Godfather Part III* (Mary Corleone):** She played the part of the Godfather's daughter in this film. The film was a disaster. People said bad things about her. She stopped being an actress.
California Institute of Art: She studied fine arts and photography there.
1999 *The Virgin Suicides*: The first film she directed.
Spike Jonze: She married him in 1999 (now separated).
***Lost in Translation*:** made in 2003, made her famous, she became the first American woman to be nominated for an Oscar for best director.

7.5 CD3 Track 6

(tapescript in Student's Book on *p.124*)

P = Presenter, A = Anthony

P Good evening and welcome to *Film of the week.* Tonight we are going to see Sofia Coppola's film *Lost in Translation.* This film came out in 2003, and it gave the young film director her first Oscar nomination. Before it starts, Anthony, can you tell us a bit about her.

A Well, of course as you know, Sofia Coppola is the daughter of Francis Ford Coppola, so you could say that she was born with a camera in her hand. She was born in New York in 1971 while her father was making the film *The Godfather,* and in fact she actually appeared in the film – she was the little baby in the baptism scene.
After she left school she decided to become an actress, but her career as an actress didn't last long. When her father made *The Godfather part III* he gave his daughter a part in the film. She played Mary Corleone, the Godfather's daughter. But it was a disaster and the film critics wrote terrible things about her. So she stopped being an actress and she went to the California Institute of Art where she studied fine arts and photography. Then she decided to become a film director.
1999 was a really big year for her. She directed her first film, *The Virgin Suicides,* and this time the critics thought she was great. She also got married to the film director Spike Jonze – but they separated after a few years.
And then in 2003 she made her next film which is the one we're going to see now, called *Lost in Translation. Lost in Translation* was the film which made Sofia Coppola famous. For this film she became the first American woman to be nominated for an Oscar for best director, although she didn't win it.

P Thank you very much, Anthony. And now, let's watch *Lost in Translation.*

Extra support

If you have time, you could get SS to listen to the tape/CD with the tapescript on *p.124* so they can see exactly what they understood. Translate/explain any new words or phrases.

d • SS ask and answer the questions in pairs. Get feedback from the class.

Extra photocopiable activities

Grammar

present perfect or past simple? *p.164*

Communicative

Two British stars *p.208* (instructions *p.180*)

HOMEWORK

Study Link **Workbook** *pp.60–61*

7C

G *used to*
V school subjects: *history, geography*, etc.
P sentence stress: *used to / didn't used to*

I used to be a rebel

Lesson plan

This lesson is about what people were like when they were at school and how they have changed now they are adults. A news story about the 'famous rebel' Mick Jagger of the Rolling Stones, and an interview with a school teacher provide the context for SS to learn *used to* for talking about things you did for a period of time in the past, (e.g. *I used to go to a secondary school in my town*) or for a past situation or state that has changed (e.g. *I used to have very long hair when I was a teenager*). The form of this structure is quite simple but an exact equivalent may not exist in your SS' language. *Used to* is also the focus for pronunciation and in vocabulary SS learn the names of school subjects. The lesson finishes with SS talking about their own school experiences.

Optional lead-in (books closed)

Write SECONDARY SCHOOL on the board and ask SS to tell you about a typical school in their country, e.g. *How old are pupils when they start/finish school? How many pupils are there in class? Are classes mixed or just boys or just girls? Do pupils behave well or badly?*

1 READING

a • Books open. Focus on the picture and get SS, in pairs, to talk about how it is similar or different from the school they went/go to, e.g. *My school is/was different because there are/were boys and girls, and we don't/didn't wear a uniform.* Get some feedback.

b • Focus on the photo of Mick Jagger and ask where he is (in a school). Get SS to read the article quickly and answer the question.

> Maybe. Mick says he used to argue with teachers and break the rules, but his friend says that he was a 'good boy'. The author of the article seems to believe the friend more, as Mick Jagger left school with good academic qualifications.

c • Get SS to read the article again and try to guess from context what the highlighted words mean. Check answers.

> **drama**: theatre and acting
> **honoured**: felt very proud and happy
> **at war**: fighting, in conflict
> **a mass protest**: a lot of people protesting/complaining together
> **appalling**: awful, terrible
> **deteriorated**: got worse
> **bright**: intelligent
> **qualifications**: diplomas or certificates which show you have passed exams

2 GRAMMAR *used to*

a • Give SS a few minutes to find the six sentences in the article. Elicit the sentences from the class and write them on the board.

> He used to be a rebel.
> He didn't use to do the homework.
> He used to break the rules.
> Mick didn't use to be a rebel.
> He used to work hard.
> He used to do a lot of sport.

• Now give SS a minute to answer the two questions.

> The past.
> Things that happened (or were true) for a long time.

• Focus on the six sentences on the board and model and drill the pronunciation.

b • Tell SS to go to **Grammar Bank 7C** on *p.138*. Go through the rules with the class. Model and drill the example sentences.

Grammar notes

• *Used to* only exists in the past, and is used for past habits or states. SS may not have an equivalent form in their language. If they do have an equivalent verb, it may also exist in the present (for present habits), which means SS may try to say *I use to* for present habits rather than using the present simple and an adverb of frequency. (*I usually* ...) Typical error: *I use to go to the gym every Friday.*

⚠ SS might confuse *used to* + infinitive with the past of the verb *use*, e.g. I *used my dictionary when I did my English homework.* As well as having a completely different meaning the two verbs are pronounced differently (*used to* is pronounced /juːs tə/ and *used* (past of *use*) is /juːzd/.

• Focus on the exercises for **7C** on *p.139*. SS do the exercises individually or in pairs. Check answers.

> **a** 1 He used to have short hair.
> 2 He used to be quite fat.
> 3 He didn't use to wear glasses.
> 4 He used to wear a uniform.
> 5 He didn't use to drink wine.
> **b** 1 Where did you use to go to school?
> 2 I didn't use to like vegetables when I was a child.
> 3 My sister used to hate maths at school.
> 4 What did you use to do in the summer?
> 5 They didn't use to live near here.
> 6 This building used to be a cinema.
> 7 Did your brother use to study here?

• Tell SS to go back to the main lesson on *p.81*.

3 LISTENING

a • Focus on the two photos of Melissa and get SS to say how she has changed (She used to have shorter hair. Now she has long hair. She used to look untidy. Now she looks smart.). Encourage SS to use *used to* in their answers.

b 7.6

• Tell SS that they are now going to hear Melissa talking. Focus on the two questions. Play the tape/CD. Check answers.

Extra idea

Pause the tape/CD at the point marked * in the tapescript and get SS to guess what they think her job is.

She was a bit of rebel. Now she is a primary school teacher.

c • Focus on sentences 1–8 and quickly run through them, dealing with any vocabulary problems.

• Play the tape/CD again, pausing and re-playing as necessary. SS mark the sentences true or false.

• Check answers. Elicit why the F sentences are false.

1 T
2 F She didn't use to write graffiti or anything like that.
3 F She liked English.
4 T
5 T
6 T
7 F She wanted to be a lawyer.
8 F They said, 'Don't be a teacher'.

7.6 CD3 Track 7

(tapescript in Student's Book on *p.124*.)

I = interviewer, M = Melissa

I How old are you in the photograph, Melissa?
M Twelve or thirteen, I think.
I Did you like school?
M Not really.
I Why not?
M Because I didn't like any of the subjects. Well, that's not quite true, I liked English, but that was the only lesson I used to look forward to. I didn't like maths, didn't like science at all, and I *hated* PE. I used to argue with the PE teacher all the time. She used to make us do impossible things, things we couldn't do, like climbing ropes and jumping over the 'horse'. I think she just wanted to humiliate us.
I Were you a 'good girl' at school?
M It depends what you mean by 'good'. I didn't smoke, I didn't use to write graffiti on the walls or anything like that. But I was a bit of a rebel. I used to break rules all the time, and of course the teachers didn't like that.
I What sort of rules did you break?
M Well, for example the school was very strict about the school uniform – we had to wear a blue skirt, and the skirt had to cover our knees. I used to make the skirt shorter. And then I sometimes used to wear blue socks and a black sweater like in the photograph, instead of a grey sweater, and grey socks. The teachers used to get really angry. I just thought it was silly.
I What did you want to be when you were at school?
M I wanted to be a lawyer.
I Why?
M Well, there were a lot of American TV programmes and films about lawyers at the time, and I used to think it would be fun to argue with people all day.*
I So why did you become a primary school teacher?
M Lots of reasons. But I think the main reason is that both my parents were teachers and they both used to tell me, when you grow up and get a job *don't* be a teacher. So as I was a rebel, I did exactly the opposite.

Extra support

If you have time, you could get SS to listen to the tape/CD with the tapescript on *p.124* so they can see exactly what they understood. Translate/explain any new words or phrases.

4 PRONUNCIATION sentence stress

a 7.7

• Focus on the warning box and point out that the affirmative form (*used to*) and the negative and interrogative form (*use to*) are pronounced the same.

• Focus on the task. Play the tape/CD for SS to underline the stressed words. Check answers.

7.7 CD3 Track 8

1 I <u>used</u> to go <u>out</u> a <u>lot</u>.
2 He <u>used</u> to <u>hate</u> <u>school</u>.
3 They <u>didn</u>'t <u>use</u> to be <u>friends</u>.
4 She <u>didn't</u> <u>use</u> to <u>like</u> him.
5 Did you <u>use</u> to wear <u>glasses</u>?

Extra challenge

You could ask SS to guess and underline the stressed words before they listen to the tape. Elicit again the kind of words that are usually stressed/unstressed (see **Pronunciation notes** in **3D**).

• Play the tape/CD again for SS to listen and repeat.

b 7.8

• Focus on the task and play the tape/CD. SS write the six *used to* sentences they hear. Pause and re-play as necessary.

• Elicit the sentences onto the board.

7.8 CD3 Track 9

1 Where did you use to live?
2 I didn't use to like exams.
3 I used to have long hair.
4 Did you use to work hard?
5 I used to be very shy.
6 I didn't use to do any sport.

5 VOCABULARY school subjects

a • Give SS time to match the photos and school subjects and then compare their answers with a partner's.

1 maths **2** history **3** geography **4** science
5 PE **6** literature **7** foreign languages
8 technology

b 7.9

- Play the tape/CD for SS to listen and repeat. Model and drill the pronunciation of *subjects* /sʌbdʒekts/.
- Tell SS, individually or in pairs, to cover the words in **a**, look at the pictures and try to remember the words.

> 7.9 CD3 Track 10
> maths
> history
> geography
> science
> physics
> chemistry
> biology
> PE
> literature
> foreign languages
> technology

c
- Focus on the task and the speech bubble. Demonstrate the activity by talking about the subjects yourself using *used to/didn't use to*.
- Put SS into pairs and give them a few minutes to talk to each other. Encourage them to use the pictures instead of just reading the list of subjects.

⚠ Remind SS to use *at* after *good/bad*, e.g. *I was/wasn't very good at maths*.

6 SPEAKING

a
- Focus on the activity. Tell SS to remember when they were 11 or 12 and to go through the list and decide if these things were true or false about them at that time and why. Give them at least two minutes to do this and tell them that later they will be talking to other SS about this.

Extra support

Demonstrate the activity by talking about a few of the things yourself.

b
- Put SS into groups of three **A**, **B**, and **C** (or pairs if this is not feasible). Tell **A** to go through the list in **a** and to tell **B** and **C** about how they used to be. **B** and **C** ask for more information when they can. Then they change roles and **B** talks to **A** and **C** about how they used to be, etc. Encourage **B** and **C** to talk about the things in a different order.
- Get quick feedback from the groups and find out if SS had anything in common.

7 SONG ♫ *It's all over now*

7.10

- Here SS listen to a song which was recorded by the Rolling Stones.
- If you want to do this song in class, use the photocopiable activity on *p.226*.

> 7.10 CD3 Track 11
> ***It's all over now***
> Well, baby used to stay out all night long
> She made me cry, she done me wrong
> She hurt my eyes open, that's no lie
> Tables turn and now her turn to cry
> Because I used to love her, but it's all over now
> Because I used to love her, but it's all over now
>
> Well, she used to run around with every man in town
> She spent all my money, playing her high class game
> She put me out, it was a pity how I cried
> Tables turn and now her turn to cry
> Because I used to love her …
>
> Well, I used to wake in the morning, get my breakfast in bed
> When I'd gotten worried she'd ease my aching head
> But now she's here and there, with every man in town
> Still trying to take me for that same old clown
>
> Because I used to love her …

Extra photocopiable activities

Grammar
used to p.165
Communicative
How have you changed? *p.209* (instructions on *p.181*)
Song
It's all over now p.226 (instructions *p.219*)

HOMEWORK

Study Link **Workbook** *pp.62–63*

7D

G passive
V verbs: *invent, discover*, etc.
P *-ed*, sentence stress

The mothers of invention

Lesson plan

We often assume that most inventors are men. This lesson challenges this assumption and shows that women were responsible for several significant inventions of the last century. These inventions provide the context for the introduction of the present and past forms of the passive. In Vocabulary the focus is on verbs which are frequently used in the passive, e.g. *designed, discovered, based (on)*. The lesson also focuses on the pronunciation of *-ed* endings and sentence stress in passive sentences. The title of the lesson is a pun on the famous saying of the Greek philosopher, Plato, 'Necessity is the mother of invention.'

Optional lead-in (books closed)

Write the following phrase on the board:
THE MOST USEFUL INVENTION OF THE LAST CENTURY WAS ...

Give SS, in pairs, two or three minutes to complete the sentence by deciding what they think was the most useful invention of the 20th century.

Get feedback and write SS ideas on the board. Then get SS to vote, with a show of hands, for the most useful invention. Now do exercise **1a**.

1 LISTENING

a • Books open. Focus on the photos. Give SS, in pairs, a couple of minutes to guess which five things were invented by women. Don't check answers at this point.

b 7.11

• Focus on the task and play the tape/CD for SS to complete 1–5 with the names of the inventions. Check answers. Get feedback to find out if SS had guessed correctly.

• Model and drill pronunciation and make sure SS understand what all the words mean, e.g. *disposable* = you throw it away after you have used it once, *bullet-proof* = bullets from a gun can't go through it.

1 The dishwasher
2 Windscreen wipers
3 Disposable nappies
4 Tipp-Ex
5 The bullet-proof vest

c • Focus on the questions. Play the tape/CD again for SS to listen for more detail. Pause the tape after each invention to give SS time to write their answers. Get SS to compare what they understood with a partner then play the tape/CD a third time if necessary. Check answers.

1 Her servants used to break plates and glasses when they were doing the washing up.
2 It was impossible for drivers to see where they were going.
3 More than 55 million.
4 She was a secretary.
5 It was very light but incredibly strong (stronger than metal).

Extra idea

Ask a few more questions to check comprehension, e.g. *Who was Josephine Cochrane?* (A rich American woman.) *Was the car invented by a woman?* (No, by a man.) *Why has the invention of disposable nappies helped many women?* (Because they used to spend many hours a day washing nappies.) etc.

7.11 CD3 Track 12

(tapescript in Student's Book on *p.124*)

P = presenter, S = Sally

P Good afternoon, and welcome to another edition of *Science Today*. In today's programme we are going to hear about women inventors. When we think of famous inventors we usually think of men, people like Alexander Graham Bell, Guglielmo Marconi, Thomas Edison. But, as Sally will tell us, many of the things which make our lives easier today were invented by women.

S That's absolutely right. Let's take the dishwasher for example. This was invented by a woman called Josephine Cochrane in 1886. She was a rich American who gave a lot of dinner parties. But she was annoyed that her servants used to break plates and glasses when they were washing them after the party. So, Josephine decided to try and invent a machine which could wash a lot of plates and glasses safely. Today the dishwasher is used by millions of people all over the world.

The car was invented by a man, but it was a woman, Mary Anderson, who in 1903 solved one of the biggest problems of driving. Until her invention it was impossible for drivers to see where they were going when it was raining or snowing. The name of her invention? Windscreen wipers.

A fantastic invention that definitely improved the lives of millions of people was disposable nappies. They were invented by a woman called Marion Donovan in 1950. Anybody who has a small baby will know what a big difference disposable nappies make to our lives. Today more than 55 million nappies are used every day in the world.

A few years later in 1956, Bette Nesmith Graham was working as a secretary. She used to get very frustrated and angry when she made typing mistakes. In those days if you made a mistake, you had to get a new sheet of paper and start again from the beginning. She had a brilliant idea, which was to use a white liquid to paint over mistakes. Her invention is called Tipp-Ex today. Mrs Graham was a divorced mother and her invention made her a very rich woman.

And finally ... policemen, soldiers, and politicians all over the world are protected by something which was invented by a woman. In 1966 Stephanie Kwolek invented kevlar, a special material which was very light but incredibly strong, much stronger than metal. This material is used to make the bullet-proof vest. Her invention has probably saved thousands of lives.

P Thanks very much, Sally. So ... if you thought that everything was invented by men, think again.

Extra support

If you have time, you could get SS to listen to the tape/CD with the tapescript on *p.124* so they can see exactly what they understood. Translate/explain any new words or phrases.

d • Focus on the question and get feedback from the whole class.

2 GRAMMAR passive

a • Focus on the task and give SS time to make five true sentences. Check answers.

1 The dishwasher was invented by an American woman.
2 Disposable nappies were invented by Marion Donovan.
3 More than 55 million nappies are used every day.
4 Mrs Graham's invention is called Tipp-Ex today.
5 Policemen all over the world are protected by the bullet-proof vest.

b • Focus on the two sentences, **a** and **b**, and read the three questions aloud to the class. Elicit answers from the whole class, getting a majority opinion on each one and confirming if it is right or wrong.

⚠ Depending on your SS' previous knowledge of English and their L1 they may or may not be familiar with the grammatical term *the passive*.

1 Yes.
2 No. In **a** the emphasis is more on the American woman, in **b** the emphasis is more on the dishwasher.
3 **b**

c • Tell SS to go to **Grammar Bank 7D** on *p.138*. Go through the rules with the class. Model and drill the example sentences.

Grammar notes

- This lesson provides an introduction to the passive and SS are taught present and past forms only.
- The formation of the passive is not difficult for SS as it is composed of known items: the verb *be* and a past participle.
- The passive is often used in English where other languages use an impersonal subject.

Extra challenge

You may want to point out to SS that all other tenses of the passive are made simply by changing the tense of *be*, e.g. *will be made, has been made*, etc.

• Focus on the exercises for **7D** on *p.139*. SS do the exercises individually or in pairs. Check answers.

a 1 are (were) made
2 is (was) cut
3 was discovered
4 was woken
5 is played
6 were recorded
7 are educated

b 1 Last night we were stopped by the police.
2 A lot of fast food is eaten by American teenagers.
3 *At the Moulin Rouge* was painted by Toulouse-Lautrec.
4 Weekly meetings are organized by the marketing manager.
5 Fiat cars are made by the Italians.

• Tell SS to go back to the main lesson on *p.83*.

3 READING & VOCABULARY

a • This exercise teaches/revises verbs which are often used in the passive and which SS will later use in **SPEAKING**.

• Focus on the text and the verbs in the box. Give SS three minutes to complete the text using the past participle of the correct verb from the box.

2 designed **3** named **4** designed **5** written
6 discovered **7** used **8** created **9** based

b • Give SS a minute or so to re-read the text and decide, in pairs, which one is most surprising. Get feedback, asking SS to say why they were surprised. Deal with any vocabulary problems. Explain/translate words and phrases which SS don't know.

Extra idea

Ask SS to choose five words or phrases from the text that they want to learn and to write them with their translation in their notebooks or vocabulary books. Get some feedback on which words SS have chosen.

Extra challenge

Get SS to read the text again and to try to remember the information. Then tell SS to cover the text. Write on the board:

The bikini
Light bulbs
Harry Potter
Penicillin
Spiders
Sherlock Holmes

SS, in pairs, try to remember as much as they can from the text for each thing. Then get feedback from the whole class to see how much they can collectively remember.

4 PRONUNCIATION *-ed*, sentence stress

- This activity revises the pronunciation of *-ed* endings.

Pronunciation notes

- *-ed* can be pronounced in three different ways:
  1. *-ed* is pronounced /t/ after verbs ending in these unvoiced sounds: /k/, /p/, /f/, /s/, /ʃ/ and /tʃ/, e.g. *looked, hoped, laughed, passed, washed, watched.*
  2. After voiced endings *-ed* is pronounced /d/, e.g. *arrived, changed, showed.*
  3. After verbs ending in /t/ or /d/ the pronunciation of *-ed* is /ɪd/, e.g. *hated, decided.*
- The difference between 1 and 2 is very small and only occasionally causes communication problems. The most important thing is for SS to be clear about rule 3, i.e. when they should pronounce *-ed* /ɪd/.

a
- Focus on the chart and remind SS that the *-ed* ending can be pronounced in these three different ways.
- Give SS, in pairs, a couple of minutes to try and put the verbs in the right place. They will find the /t/ and /d/ ones the most difficult to distinguish between.

b 7.12
- Play the tape/CD for SS to check their answers.
- Then play the tape again for SS to underline the stressed syllable in each multi-syllable verb.

7.12 CD3 Track 13

based
designed
directed
discovered
invented
named
painted
produced
used

/d/	/t/	/ɪd/
designed	based	directed
discovered	produced	invented
named		painted
used		

c 7.13
- In this exercise SS practise pronouncing the participles in context.
- Play the tape/CD and get SS to repeat the sentences, trying to copy the rhythm. Elicit from SS which words are stressed (the 'information' words).
- Give further practice as necessary.

7.13 CD3 Track 14

1 The film was based on a true story.
2 These clothes were designed by Armani.
3 This wine is produced near here.
4 My sister was named after our grandmother.
5 These pictures were painted by my aunt.
6 Garlic is used a lot in French cooking.

5 SPEAKING

- Put SS into pairs, **A** and **B**. Tell them to go to **Communication *Passives quiz*, A** on *p.111* and **B** on *p. 115*. Give SS time to complete their sentences and choose the correct answers.
- Get SS to sit opposite each other. **B** listens to **A**'s sentences and checks the answers. SS then swap roles.
- Monitor and help as SS do the task, making sure they are forming the passive and pronouncing the past participle correctly.
- Finish the activity when the majority of pairs have finished.

Extra photocopiable activities

Grammar
passive *p.166*
Communicative
What's it famous for? *p.210* (instructions *p.181*)

HOMEWORK

Study Link **Workbook** *pp.64–65*

7 PRACTICAL ENGLISH
A BOAT TRIP

Revision How to get there
Function Buying tickets
Language *What time does the next boat leave? How long does it take?*

Lesson plan

In this lesson SS learn to buy tickets for travel and ask about the journey. In **Social English**, Allie and Mark enjoy their boat trip and begin to talk about the future.

Study Link These lessons are on the *New English File Pre-intermediate* Video, which can be used instead of the Class Cassette/CD (see introduction *p.9*). The main functional section of each episode (the second section) is also on the MultiROM with additional activities.

Optional lead-in (books closed)

Revise what happened in the previous episode by eliciting the story from SS, e.g *What was the matter with Allie?* (She had a headache and a cough.) *What did she do?* (She went to the pharmacy and bought some aspirin.) *What did she and Mark plan for her last day?* (A boat trip and dinner in the evening.)

HOW TO GET THERE

7.14

- Focus on the photo and ask *What's Allie wearing? What do you think they're going to do?*
- Focus on the questions. Play the tape/CD once the whole way through and tell SS just to listen. Then play it again, pausing if necessary to give SS time to mark the sentences T or F.
- Get them to compare their answers with a partner's before checking answers. Get SS to correct the false ones.

1 F She's feeling better.
2 T
3 T
4 T
5 F An important phone call.

Extra support

Let SS listen again with the tapescript on *p.125*. Deal with any problematic vocabulary.

- Highlight that both *cab* and *taxi* are used in the UK and US (*taxi* is an abbreviation of *taxi cab*).

7.14 CD3 Track 15

(tapescript in Student's Book on *p.125*)
M = Mark, A = Allie
M Hi, Allie. How are you feeling today?
A Much better.
M Good. Are you going to be warm enough with just that sweater? It might be a little cold on the boat.
A I'll be fine. Are we going to walk to the bay?
M No, it's too far. It's better if we get a cab.
A How long does it take by cab?
M About ten minutes.
A And how long's the boat trip?
M I'm not sure. I think it's an hour. Why?
A Well, I have to be back here by 1.00 – I'm expecting an important phone call.
M Not from Brad, I hope?
A Well, actually … No, of course not! From the New York office.
M OK. Let's go.

- Ask a few more questions to check comprehension, e.g. *How long does it take to get to the bay by cab?* (Ten minutes.) *How long is the boat trip?* (About an hour.) *Who is Allie expecting a phone call from?* (The New York office.)

BUYING TICKETS

a 7.15

- Tell SS to cover the dialogue with their hand or a piece of paper. Focus on the picture. Ask *Where are Mark and Allie?* (At the boat.)

⚠ If you think that SS won't cover their books properly, you could get them to close their books at this stage and write the first task on the board.

- Play the tape/CD once. Check answers.

The next boat leaves at 10.00 a.m. The trip takes an hour, and costs $40.

b
- Now tell SS to uncover the dialogue (or open their books). Explain that the **YOU HEAR** part is what they need to understand, and the **YOU SAY** part contains the phrases they need to be able to say.
- Give SS a minute to read through the dialogue and guess the missing words. Then play the tape/CD again, for them to complete the dialogue.

7.15 7.16 CD3 Tracks 16+17

M = Mark, T = ticket seller, A = Allie
M Good morning. (*repeat*)
T Good morning, sir.
M What time does the next boat leave? (*repeat*)
T At 10.00.
A How long does it take? (*repeat*)
T **About** an hour.
M Where exactly does the boat go? (*repeat*)
T It goes **under** the bridge, **round** Angel Island and **past** Alcatraz, and then **back** here.
A Can we get anything to eat or drink on the boat? (*repeat*)
T Yes, ma'am, there's a **snack** bar.
M Can I have two tickets, please? (*repeat*)
T Sure. Two **adults**.
M How much is that? (*repeat*)
T That's $40.
M Here you are. (*repeat*)
T Thank you, sir.
M Thank you.

- Go through the dialogue line by line and check answers.

c 7.16

- Now focus on the **YOU SAY** phrases. Tell SS they're going to hear the dialogue again. They repeat the **YOU SAY** phrases when they hear the beep. Encourage them to copy the rhythm.
- Play the tape/CD, pausing if necessary for SS to repeat the phrases.

d • Put SS into pairs, **A** and **B**. **A** is the ticket seller, **B** is Mark/Allie. Tell **B** to close his/her book and try to remember the phrases. Then **A** and **B** swap roles.

Extra support

Let SS practise the dialogue first in pairs, both with books open.

SOCIAL ENGLISH on the boat

a 7.17

- Focus on the questions and the photo. Ask *Where are they?* and elicit that they're on the boat.
- Go through the questions with SS and make sure they understand them.
- Play the tape/CD at least twice. Let SS compare their answers with a partner's and then check answers.

1 No.
2 No. Because it's a long way from London and she would miss her family and friends.
3 A prison.
4 It's cold.
5 To take a photo of the two of them.

7.17 CD3 Track 18

(tapescript in Student's Book on *p.125*)
M = Mark, A = Allie, B = Boatman
M So, what do you **think** of San Francisco?
A It's beautiful, Mark. I love it.
M Better than London?
A Not better. Different.
M Do you think you could live here?
A No, I don't think so.
M Oh. Why?
A Well, it's a long way from London. I think I'd miss all my family and friends.
M Could you live somewhere else – but in *Europe*?
A Maybe. Why do you **ask**?
M Oh, no reason. I **just** wondered.
Tannoy On your left you can see the island of Alcatraz.
M Look, can you see that building? That used to be the prison, but it was closed in 1963. It's a museum now.
A Where are we going for dinner tonight?
M It's a surprise.
A I'm really **looking** forward to it.
M Me too.
A I'm cold.
M Do you want to borrow my coat?
A No. It's OK. I'm going to miss you, Mark.
M Hey, excuse me! **Could** you take a photo of us, please?
B Sure. Are you **ready**?
A Ready.
B Say cheese!

- Check comprehension by asking a few more questions, e.g. *What does Allie think about San Francisco?* (She loves it.) *What does Mark ask Allie when she says she couldn't live in San Francisco?* (Could you live somewhere else but in Europe?) *When was the prison closed?* (1963) *What is the prison now?* (A museum.) *Where are they going for dinner tonight?* (It's a surprise.)
- Ask SS what the boatman says just before he takes the photo (*Say cheese!*) and tell them this is the typical thing people in the UK say when they want someone to smile for a photo.

Extra support

If there's time, you could get SS to listen again with tapescript on *p.125* so they can see exactly what Mark and Allie said, and see how much they understood. Translate/explain any new words/phrases.

- Get SS to speculate a bit about the story, and what will happen next. Ask *Why do you you think Mark says 'Could you live somewhere else – but in Europe?'?* But don't tell them what's going to happen.

b • Focus on the **USEFUL PHRASES**. Get SS to see if they can remember any of the missing words. Play the tape/CD again and check answers.

c 7.18

- Play the tape/CD pausing for SS to repeat each phrase. Encourage them to copy the rhythm.
- In a monolingual class get SS to decide together what the equivalent phrase would be in their language. Highlight that *Could you take a photo ...?* is a bit more polite than *Can you ...?* and that *wonder* = ask yourself.
- In a monolingual class get SS to decide together what the equivalent phrase would be in their language.

7.18 CD3 Track 19

M = Mark, A = Allie, B = boatman
M What do you think of San Francisco?
A Why do you ask?
M Oh, no reason. I just wondered.
A I'm really looking forward to it.
M Could you take a photo of us, please?
B Are you ready?

Extra challenge

Get SS to roleplay the conversation between Mark and Allie in pairs using the tapescript on *p.125*. Let SS read their parts first and then try to act it from memory.

HOMEWORK

Study Link **Workbook** *p.66*

7 WRITING DESCRIBING A BUILDING

Lesson plan

In this seventh writing lesson SS write a description of a building in their town, and consolidate the use of the passive from lesson **7D**. The writing skills focus is on organizing a description and correcting spelling mistakes. SS may need to do some research, on the Internet or in a library, to find information for this writing, so it may be best to set it for homework or you could make it a class project.

a • Focus on the photos and ask SS if they know where it is (Milan), and if anyone has ever been there.
• Focus on the instructions. Go through the words in the box and check SS remember their meaning.
• Set a time limit for SS to read the description and complete the gaps. Get SS to compare their answers with a partner's and then check answers.

2 designed **3** completed **4** statue **5** windows **6** roof **7** view **8** steps

• Give SS a few minutes, in pairs, to underline any words or phrases they don't know. Go through them, e.g. spire (= a tower which ends in a point)

b • Focus on the questions and instructions. Give SS a few minutes, in pairs, to match the questions and paragraphs. Check answers.

Is there a view from the building?	5
Describe the building outside.	3
Describe the building inside.	4
How much does it cost to go in?	6
What's the most beautiful building in your town? Where is it?	1
Who was it designed by? When was it built?	2

Extra idea

Get SS to cover the description and try to remember five things about the Duomo.

c • Focus on the instructions and ask *Where's the spelling mistake in paragraph 1?* Elicit that it is *beatiful*, and that the correct spelling is *beautiful*. Get SS to continue in pairs. Check answers.

paragraph **2** peopel – people
paragraph **3** allthought – although
paragraph **4** intresting – interesting
paragraph **5** cleer – clear
paragraph **6** apropriately – appropriately

Write a description of a building in your town

SS will probably not have all the information they need, so tell them to first research it on the Internet or in a library. Then give SS at least fifteen minutes to write the description in class, following the instructions, or set it for homework. Ask SS to attach a photo of the building or scan one in if they write on a computer.

If SS do the writing in class, get them to swap their descriptions with another S's to read and check for mistakes before you collect them all in.

7 REVISE & CHECK

For instructions on how to use these pages, see *p.27*.

GRAMMAR

1 c **2** a **3** b **4** c **5** a **6** a **7** b **8** c **9** c **10** a

VOCABULARY

a **1** since **2** since **3** for **4** for **5** since
b **1** fall **2** leave **3** get **4** retire **5** be
c **1** history **2** geography **3** maths **4** science **5** biology

PRONUNCIATION

a **1** since **2** book **3** ugly **4** scarf **5** school
b a<u>fraid</u> <u>fa</u>vourite di<u>rec</u>ted dis<u>co</u>vered in<u>ven</u>ted

CAN YOU UNDERSTAND THIS TEXT?

a She is 100 and she still drives a car. She has only ever had one accident.
b 4, 6, 7
c **1** people who are 100 or more
2 received
3 stupid
4 broken
5 Although the accident happened/Although she had an accident
6 It makes me angry
7 most important/biggest
8 terrible

CAN YOU UNDERSTAND THESE PEOPLE?

7.19 CD3 Track 20

1
A How long have you lived in Glasgow, Matt?
B Not very long. After university I lived in Newcastle for six months, and I moved to Glasgow two years ago.
A Do you like it?
B Yes, it's great. I love it.

2
A Is your sister married, John?
B Well, she was married for fifteen years, but she's just got divorced.
A Do you think she'll get married again?
B I don't think so.

3
A Have you always liked sport?
B No, I used to hate PE when I was at school.
A So when did you start running?

B A few years ago. A friend asked me to come with him, and I really enjoyed it.
A Do you run every day?
B Yes, every morning before work. Except when it's raining.

4
A What's your favourite subject?
B Well, I quite like history and geography, but I think I like literature best.
A What about maths and science?
B They're definitely not my favourites. I'm awful at them.

5
And on your right you can see the White Tower. It was built by William the Conqueror in about 1068. The rest of the castle was completed by Edward I in 1285. The castle was used as a palace and prison until the 17th century, when …

a 1 c **2** c **3** a **4** b **5** b

7.20 CD3 Track 21

Good afternoon everyone, and welcome to the Market Square Museum. Before you go round, I'd like to tell you a bit about the museum. It was opened in 1952 by Queen Elizabeth – well, she was Princess Elizabeth then. Here on the ground floor there's a collection of pictures painted by our local artist, Graham Richmond – they show the town as it used to be in the last century.
If you go upstairs, you can see our famous collection of old children's toys – there are some from the 16th century, and the oldest is over 500 years old.
Here in the entrance hall you can see there is a museum shop, where you can buy postcards and other souvenirs. There is also an excellent guidebook, which costs just £2.50.

The museum is open until half past five today, so you have plenty of time, and I hope you enjoy your visit.

b 1 pictures **2** toys **3** shop **4** £2.50 **5** 5.30

CAN YOU SAY THIS IN ENGLISH?

b 1 have **2** were **3** did **4** was

Extra photocopiable activities

Quicktest 7 *p.237*

G *something, anything, nothing*, etc.
V adjectives ending *-ed* and *-ing*: bored, boring, etc.
P /e/, /əʊ/, /ʌ/

8A I hate weekends!

File 8 overview

In this file the general topic area is lifestyle and daily routine, and the present simple is revised throughout. In the first lesson SS learn compounds with *some, any,* etc. in the context of people who hate weekends. In **8B** quantifiers *a lot of, how much,* etc. are revised and extended: *too much/too many, not enough,* etc. through a text and questionnaire about body age. **8C** brings together phrasal verbs which have come up throughout the course and some new ones, and focuses on their word order. It looks at why some people are better than others first thing in the morning. Finally in **8D** two identical twins who were separated at birth, but are remarkably similar, provide a context for *So am I, Neither do* I.

Lesson plan

In this lesson SS learn how to use *something, anything, nothing,* etc. These words will be familiar to SS by this stage but here they are focused on in detail. The context is an article about three people who hate weekends, mainly due to the obligations of their jobs, which leads to SS talking about their own weekends. The vocabulary focus is on the contrast between *-ed* and *-ing* adjectives, and SS also look at the pronunciation of the letter *o* in *nobody, nothing,* and *somebody* and the irregular pronunciation of *a* in *anybody,* etc. The lesson ends with the listening activity where SS hear about a man who spent the weekend trapped in a lift.

Optional lead-in (books closed)

Write the following sentence on the board, completing the start and finish times for you.

My _____ starts on Friday at (time) and finishes on Sunday at (time).

Elicit the missing word *(weekend)* and explain why it starts and finishes at these times for you, e.g. *because you finish work on Friday evening and start again on Monday morning.*

Then put SS into pairs to tell each other when their weekends start and finish and why. Get feedback to see who has the longest/shortest weekend.

1 READING

a • Books open. Do this as an open class question and elicit the reason (*Because I don't have to go to work/school etc.*). If there is anybody who says *no*, ask them to explain why.

b • Focus on the article and tell SS to read it quickly once and say what they think the three people do. Get feedback, but don't tell them if they're right or wrong.

c 8.1

• Tell SS they are going to hear sounds from the places the people spend time in at the weekend. Play the tape/CD for SS to check. Check answers.

Marco is a waiter.
Kirsten is a housewife.
Steve is a footballer.

8.1 CD3 Track 22

Sound effects:
1 busy restaurant
2 washing up, children crying
3 football match

d • Focus on the instructions and give SS a few minutes to complete the sentences. Get them to compare their answers with a partner's before you check answers.

1 Marco 2 Steve 3 Kirsten 4 Steve 5 Kirsten
6 Marco

Extra challenge

Get SS to complete the sentences in pairs from memory and say why the people feel as they do.

e • Now focus on the gaps in the text. Show how number 1 has been completed with **any***where*, and elicit the completion for 2 (**any***thing*). Make sure they realize that they have to look carefully at the whole sentence to know how to complete the words.

• Let SS complete the rest individually or in pairs. Check answers.

2 any**thing** 3 any**body** 4 any**thing** 5 some**body**
6 no**body** 7 no**where** 8 no**thing** 9 no**body**
10 some**thing** 11 any**where** 12 some**where**

• Finally go through the three texts and explain/translate any words or expressions that SS didn't understand, e.g. *be on my feet* (= stand up), *day off* (free day), etc.

2 GRAMMAR *something, anything, nothing,* etc.

a • Focus on the instructions and give SS a few moments to complete the rules in pairs. Check answers.

1 things 2 people 3 places

Extra challenge

Ask SS *What's the difference between something, anything, and nothing?* and see if they can explain some of the rules to you before going to the **Grammar Bank**.

b • Tell SS to go to **Grammar Bank 8A** on *p.140.* Go through the rules and model and drill the example sentences.

Grammar notes

- SS may have problems with the negative form. The typical mistakes are:
  1 using *nobody/nothing/nowhere* with a negative verb, e.g. *I didn't see nobody*. Highlight that you cannot use a 'double negative' in English.
  2 using *anybody/anything/anywhere* in one word answers to convey a negative meaning, e.g. *Who did you see? Anybody.*
- To talk about people there are two alternative forms: *-body* and *-one*, e.g. *somebody/someone*. They are identical in meaning although it may be easier for SS to get used to using one form.

⚠ *something* (like *some*) is also used in question form to make an offer or request, e.g. *Would you like something to drink? Could you go somewhere for me this afternoon?* To avoid overloading SS it may be best to focus on this rule only if SS bring it up.

- Focus on the exercises for **8A** on *p.141*. SS do them individually or in pairs. Check answers.

a **1** anything **2** Somebody **3** somewhere **4** anybody **5** anywhere **6** something **7** nobody **8** anything
b **1** Nothing. **2** Nowhere. **3** Nobody.
c **1** I didn't do anything.
2 I didn't go anywhere.
3 I didn't see anybody.

- Tell SS to go back to the main lesson on *p. 89*.

3 PRONUNCIATION /e/, /əʊ/, /ʌ/

a • Focus on the three sound pictures and elicit the words and sounds: *egg* /e/, *phone* /əʊ/, *up* /ʌ/.

b • Focus on the sentences and the pink letters. Give SS, in pairs, a few minutes to say them out loud and decide which sound they are.

c 8.2
- Play the tape/CD once for SS to listen and check. Check answers. Play the tape/CD again for SS to listen and repeat.

8.2 CD3 Track 23
1 Nobody knows where he goes.
2 Somebody's coming to lunch.
3 I never said anything.
4 I've done nothing since Sunday.
5 Don't tell anybody about the message.
6 There's nowhere to go except home.

1 2 2 3 3 1 4 3 5 1 6 2

4 VOCABULARY adjectives ending *-ed* and *-ing*

a • Several common adjectives in English have two forms which have different meanings, e.g. *tired* and *tiring*.
- Focus on the two sentences and elicit that *tired* = how you feel, *tiring* = It makes you feel tired.

b • Focus on the adjectives and highlight that we use the *-ed* adjectives mainly for people, because they refer to feelings, e.g. *I'm bored.* We use the *-ing* adjectives for things (and sometimes people) which produce the feeling, e.g. *This book is boring.*

⚠ Not all adjectives that end in *-ed* also exist ending in *-ing*, e.g. *I'm feeling stressed. My job is very stressful.* NOT ~~*My job is very stressing*~~.

- Check that SS understand the meaning of all the adjectives.

⚠ Be careful with *excited/exciting*. It is a false friend in some languages.

- Drill the pronunciation of the adjectives. Remind SS that the *-ed* is pronounced in the same way as regular past verbs, i.e. /t/, /d/ or /ɪd/, and get them to underline the stress.

Extra challenge

You could elicit/teach some more *-ed/-ing* adjectives, e.g *surprised/surprising, frightened/frightening* etc.

c • Focus on the exercise and give SS a few minutes to do it in pairs. Check answers.

1 bored **2** boring **3** depressing **4** depressed
5 relaxed **6** relaxing **7** interested **8** interesting
9 exciting **10** excited

5 SPEAKING

- Focus on the questionnaire. Elicit that the first group of questions are all with *Do you ...?*, the second with *Did you ...?* and the third with *Are you going to ...?*
- Get SS to choose a few questions to ask you. Encourage them to ask follow-up questions to demonstrate the activity.

Extra support

Write *Where? When? What? Why (not)?*, etc. on the board to remind SS to ask more questions.

- SS interview each other in pairs. Get **A** to interview **B** with the first section, then **B** interviews **A** with the second, etc. until both SS have answered all of the questions. Monitor and help, encouraging SS to keep the conversation going. Get feedback from the class.

6 LISTENING

a 8.3
- Here SS listen to a true story about a man who was stuck in a lift for a whole weekend. The story recycles some of the words from the new grammar.
- Focus on the pictures and instructions. Ask SS *What do you think the story is about?* and elicit some vocabulary to help SS understand the story, e.g. *lift, press the button, alarm*, etc.
- Now play the tape/CD once the whole way through. Let SS compare their answers with a partner's. Then play it again before you check answers.

1 Sven in the office looking at his watch.
2 Sven going into the lift.
3 Sven in the lift shouting.
4 Sven phoning.
5 Sven sleeping on the floor.
6 Sven's wife Silvia phoning the police.
7 A police car looking for Sven.
8 Sven coming out of the lift.

Extra support

Pause the tape after each picture to give SS time to number the pictures.

8.3 CD3 Track 24

(tapescript in Student's Book on *p.125*)

N = newsreader, Sv = Sven, Si = Silvia

N Last Friday Sven, a company lawyer from Stockholm, was looking forward to a relaxing two days in the mountains. He and his wife had booked a skiing weekend in a luxury hotel. But the weekend didn't work out exactly as they had planned.

Sven worked until late on Friday evening. His office was on the 12th floor. When he finished, at 8 o'clock, he locked his office and got into the lift ... and he didn't get out again until Monday morning!

Sv I pressed the button for the ground floor and the lift started going down but then stopped. I pressed the button again but nothing happened. I pressed the alarm and shouted but nobody heard me. Most people had already gone home. I tried to phone my wife but my mobile didn't work in the lift ... I couldn't do anything. I just sat on the floor and hoped maybe somebody would realize what had happened. But on Saturday and Sunday I knew nobody would be there. I slept most of the time to forget how hungry I was.

N Meanwhile Sven's wife, Silvia, was waiting for her husband to come home.

Si I was very worried when he didn't come home on Friday evening and I couldn't understand why his mobile wasn't going. I phoned the police and they looked for him but they couldn't find him anywhere. I thought maybe he was with another woman.

N So Sven was in the lift the whole weekend from Friday evening until Monday morning. At eight o'clock, when the office workers arrived, they phoned the emergency number and somebody came and repaired the lift.

Sv I was very happy to get out. I hadn't eaten since Friday afternoon and I was very hungry. It's lucky that I am not claustrophobic because the lift was very small. The first thing I did was to phone my wife to say that I was OK.

N Sven will soon be the fittest man in his office – from now on he's going to take the stairs every day – even though it's 12 floors.

Extra support

Get SS to listen again and answer these questions:

1 What does Sven do? (He's a company lawyer.)
2 What was he planning to do that weekend? (Go skiing with his wife.)
3 Which floor is Sven's office on? (The 12th.)
4 What did he do when the lift stopped? (He pressed the button again shouted, and tried to phone his wife.)
5 Why couldn't he phone his wife? (His phone didn't work.)
6 What did he do on Saturday and Sunday? (He slept.)
7 What did Silvia do when Sven didn't come home? (She phoned the police.)
8 What did the police do? (They looked for him but couldn't find him.)
9 When did Sven get out of the lift? (On Monday morning.)
10 What's Sven going to do in the future? (He's going to walk up the stairs to his office.)

b • Focus on the instructions. Tell **A** to use the first four pictures. Tell **B** to use the tapescript on *p.125* to help correct **A. B** then uses the second four pictures and **A** corrects.

• Finally ask SS *Have you ever been stuck in a lift? What happened?*

Extra photocopiable activities

Grammar

something, anything, nothing p.167

Communicative

Is it true? *p.211* (instructions on *p.181*)

HOMEWORK

Study Link **Workbook** *pp.67–68*

8B

G quantifiers, *too, not enough*
V health and lifestyle: *wear sunscreen*, etc.
P /ʌ/, /uː/, /aɪ/, /e/; linking

How old is your body?

Lesson plan

In this lesson SS revise quantifiers and learn new ones: *a little/few, too much/many, not enough.* The presentation is a magazine article about how people's calendar age (their real age) is not necessarily the same as their body age. The pronunciation focuses on pronouncing the new words correctly, e.g. *enough,* and on understanding linked speech. The lesson ends with a questionnaire where SS find out their own body age. Depending on the level of your class, you may want to do more or less revision of countability and basic quantifiers (see *Optional lead-in* and *Extra support*).

Optional lead-in (books closed)

Revise countability. Write on the board in two columns:

1	*2*
coffee	*vegetables*
bread	*biscuits*
meat	*sweets*

Ask SS *What's the difference between the words in columns 1 and 2?* and elicit that the words in column 1 are uncountable, and normally used in the singular, but the words in column 2 are countable and can be used in singular and plural. Elicit a few more words for each column, e.g. *water, rice, apples,* etc. and remind SS that not only food words are countable and uncountable, e.g. *cigarettes* are countable, *free time* is uncountable.

Ask SS *When do we use a, some, and any?* and elicit that you use *a* with singular countable nouns and *some/any* with plural countable nouns and uncountable nouns, *some* in positive sentences and *any* in negatives and questions, e.g. *I ate a biscuit and some bread. I didn't eat any vegetables or any fruit.*

1 READING

a • Books open. Focus on the instructions. Give SS a minute to read the introduction and answer the questions together. Check answers.

> 1 No. Our calendar age is the number of years we have lived. Our body age depends on our lifestyle, genes etc.
> 2 By answering questions about our lifestyle.
> 3 Change our lifestyle.

b • Focus on the photo, and ask SS if they think Tariq looks his calendar age (32). Then focus on the article and give SS three minutes to read it to find the good and bad things. Get SS to compare their answers with a partner's, and then check answers. Make sure SS use the third person singular when they tell you about Tariq's good and bad habits.

> **Possible answers**
> **Good:** plays squash, eats a lot of fresh food and fruit, drinks a little alcohol
> **Bad:** doesn't do enough exercise, eats too much meat, doesn't drink enough water, drinks a lot of coffee, too busy, works too much, smokes, only wears sunscreen on the beach, pessimistic

c • Focus on the instructions. Get SS, in pairs, to discuss their advice. Get feedback and write their ideas on the board.

d • SS read the doctor's verdict. Did any of them give the same advice?
• Ask SS what they think his body age is. Encourage SS to say why they think his body age is older (or younger) than his calendar age.
• Tell SS that after he had answered the questionnaire and done some tests, his body age was established as 37.

Extra idea

Write the headings from the article on the board. **A** (book closed) says as much as he/she can remember about the first three. **B** (book open) prompts and corrects. They swap roles for the last three headings.

• Finally check any new vocabulary, e.g. *tense, skin, give up smoking,* etc.

2 GRAMMAR quantifiers, *too, not enough*

Extra support

If you didn't do the optional lead-in, do it here.

a • This exercise revises what SS should already know. Focus on the instructions. Stress that SS must say why one is right and the other wrong while they are doing the exercise. Check answers, and elicit the rules from them.

1 much	Use *much* with uncountable nouns.
2 many	Use *many* with plural countable nouns.
3 a lot of	Use *a lot of* + uncountable or countable nouns.
4 a lot	Use *a lot* without a noun.
5 None	In short answers *none* = zero quantity. It can refer to countable or uncountable nouns.

b • Here the new language of the lesson is introduced. Focus on the instructions and get SS to match in pairs. Check answers.

> 1 F 2 E 3 D 4 B 5 A 6 C

c • Now tell SS to go to **Grammar Bank 8B** on *p.140.* Go through the rules and model and drill the example sentences.

Grammar notes

- ***Too, too much / many***
  SS often use *too much* + adjective. Typical mistake: *It's too much big.*
  It is also important to highlight the difference between *too* and *very*:
  It's very big. (= a statement of fact, neither good nor bad)
  It's too big. (= more than it should be/than you want)
- ***(Not) enough***
  The main problem here is the pronunciation of *enough* /ɪˈnʌf/and the different position: *before* nouns but *after* adjectives. Some SS may confuse *quite* and *enough* because of L1 interference.
- ***A little / a few***
  These words are used more often in short answers than in full sentences. They are often avoided by using *much* and *many*, e.g. *I don't eat much meat* is more common than *I only eat a little meat.*

- Focus on the exercises for **8B** on *p.141*. SS do them individually or in pairs. Check answers.

a	1 ~~too~~		5 ~~too many~~
	2 ~~too much~~		6 ~~a few~~
	3 ~~water enough~~		7 ~~time enough~~
	4 ~~too much~~		8 ~~a little~~
b	1 enough		4 enough
	2 too		5 too
	3 too many		6 too many

- Tell SS to go back to the main lesson on *p.91*.

3 PRONUNCIATION /ʌ/, /uː/, /aɪ/, /e/; linking

a • This exercise helps SS with the pronunciation of some of the more irregular words from the lesson.
- Focus on the sound pictures and elicit the words and sounds: *up* /ʌ/, *boot* /uː/, *bike* /aɪ/, *egg* /e/.
- Get SS, in pairs, to say the words out loud to identify the one with a different sound.

b 8.4
- Play the tape/CD once for SS to check answers.

8.4 CD3 Track 25

up /ʌ/	enough	much	none	busy
boot /uː/	few	should	too	food
bike /aɪ/	quite	diet	little	like
egg /e/	many	any	healthy	water

1 busy 2 should 3 little 4 water

- Play it again pausing after each word for SS to repeat.

c 8.5
- Here SS practise deciphering connected speech. Write on the board as an example *It's an old house* and remind SS that when a word ends with a consonant sound and the next word begins with a vowel sound they are linked together and sound like one word, especially when people speak quickly. Draw linking marks on the sentence between *It's* and *an*, and between *an* and *old* to show them.
- Play the tape/CD once for SS to hear the six sentences. Tell them just to listen, not to write. Then play the tape/CD again, pausing after each sentence to give SS time to write.
- Check answers, eliciting the sentences onto the board.

8.5 CD3 Track 26

1 I don't have enough time for exercise.
2 I eat a lot of vegetables.
3 I only have a few friends.
4 I'm too busy to help you.
5 You drink too much coffee.
6 I have a little free time this afternoon.

d • Play the tape/CD again pausing for SS to repeat the sentences and copy the rhythm.

4 SPEAKING

a • Focus on the questionnaire. Go through the questions making sure SS understand them all. Give SS three or four minutes to circle their answers.

⚠ Stress that they should circle, not underline.

b • Focus on the instructions and speech bubbles. Allow at least five minutes for SS to interview each other.

Extra challenge

Get the person who is answering the questions to close his/her book. The person asking the questions should read out the alternatives and then ask for more information.

c • Tell SS to go to **Communication *Body age?*** on *p.111*. They work out their own body age.

⚠ If you think some of your SS will be sensitive about their calendar age or possible body age, stress that the results are secret – they don't have to tell anybody.

Extra idea

You could get SS to interview you and work out your body age if you feel relaxed about the possible results!

- Tell SS to go back to the main lesson on *p.91*.

d • Focus on the instructions and speech bubble. Tell SS they should make at least three recommendations for their partner based on their answers to the questionnaire. Remind them to use *should/shouldn't* for advice.
- Get feedback, and ask a few SS if their partner has given them good advice.

Extra photocopiable activities

Grammar
too, too much / many, enough, etc. *p.168*
Communicative
But on the other hand . . . *p.212* (instructions on *p.181*)

HOMEWORK

Study Link **Workbook** *pp.69–70*

G word order of phrasal verbs
V phrasal verbs: *look up, look after, find out,* etc.
P /g/ and /dʒ/

8C Waking up is hard to do

Lesson plan

This lesson provides a gentle introduction to phrasal verbs and how they work. Phrasal verbs are an important feature of English, and are very frequently used by native speakers. SS need to be able to understand them, and to use very common ones like *turn on/off, get on with, look for*. In Vocabulary, common phrasal verbs which SS already know are revised and some new ones are introduced. The grammar of phrasal verbs is analyzed focusing mainly on the position of object pronouns, e.g. *turn it off.* In Pronunciation SS are given practise in pronouncing the letter *g* correctly. The topic of the lesson is how SS feel in the morning, and whether they are 'morning' or 'evening' people. SS read about some new research done at a British university which suggests that our 'body clock' is determined by our genes.

Optional lead-in (books closed)

Draw a clock on the board and quickly revise telling the time. Ask SS *What time do you usually get up?* and do a class survey to find out who gets up earliest/latest in the class (during the week).

1 VOCABULARY phrasal verbs

a • Books open. Focus on the instructions and give SS a few minutes to match the questions and pictures. Make sure SS remember the meaning of all the verbs, e.g. the difference between *wake up* (= stop sleeping) and *get up* (= leave your bed). Check answers.

1 D 2 G 3 B 4 A 5 C 6 E 7 F

b • Get SS to cover the questions and look at the pictures. Elicit the seven questions from the whole class. Then get SS to remember them in pairs.

Extra support

Get SS to write the number of the question next to the picture, and then ask the questions in this order. This will help them to remember the questions..

c • Still with the questions covered, SS ask and answer the questions using the pictures as prompts. Get feedback from a few pairs.

d • Tell SS to go to **Vocabulary Bank *Phrasal verbs*** on *p.153*. Explain that *phrasal verbs* are verbs + *off, on,* etc. like *get up, turn on,* where the meaning of the two words together is usually not the same as the two words individually.

⚠ Technically a phrasal verb is a verb + particle. The particle can be a preposition or an adverb. However at this level it is not a problem if you call them 'prepositions', which many of them are anyway, rather than confusing SS with a new term.

• Focus on **a.** SS match the verbs and pictures individually or in pairs. Check answers and meaning.

1 looked up (found in a reference book or on the Internet)
2 get on with (have a good relationship with)
3 stay up (not go to bed)
4 fill in (complete)
5 turn up (make the volume, or temperature, higher)
6 put away (put in cupboards, drawers, etc.)
7 pick up (take from the floor)
8 be over (finish)
9 throw away (put in the rubbish bin)
10 find out (get information about)
11 give up (stop doing something)
12 turn down (make the volume, or temperature, lower)

• Focus on **b**. Give SS a few minutes to test themselves or each other. Encourage them to say the whole sentence, as learning phrasal verbs in context makes it easier to remember their meaning.
• Focus on **c** and the list of phrasal verbs SS already know. Go through them and make sure SS remember what they mean, either explaining or translating them.
• Tell SS to look at the colour coding. Go through the explanations. Tell SS that they will be looking at the difference between the groups in the **Grammar Bank**.

Study Link SS can find more practice of these phrases on the MultiROM and on the *New English File Pre-intermediate* website.

• Tell SS to go back to the main lesson on *p.92*.

2 GRAMMAR word order of phrasal verbs

a • Here SS focus on the grammar of phrasal verbs. Focus on the pictures and instructions. Get SS to compare which words they have underlined and check answers.

the alarm clock in the first two sentences, *it* in the third.

b • Get SS to read and complete the rules in pairs. Check answers.

1 noun 2 pronoun

c • Tell SS to go to **Grammar Bank 8C** on *p.140*. Go through the rules, and remind SS that the green phrasal verbs in the **Vocabulary Bank** are type 1, the red are type 2, and the blue are type 3.

Grammar notes

• SS will probably ask *How do we know if a phrasal verb which takes an object is type 2 or type 3?* There is no easy rule. Tell them:

1 To always put phrasal verbs into an example sentence, and if they are type 2, to write the object in the middle, e.g. *turn (the radio) down.*

2 In a dictionary, a type 2 phrasal verb will always be given with *sth/sb* between the verb and the particle, e.g *turn sth down*.

- Now focus on the exercises for **8C** on *p.141*. SS do them individually or in pairs. Check answers.

a 1 down **2** up **3** back **4** for **5** away **6** on **7** after **8** down
b 1, 5, 6, and 8
c 1 it up **2** them up **3** it on **4** it up **5** them off **6** them away **7** it off

- Tell SS to go back to the main lesson on *p.92*.

d • The easiest way to remember the rule about putting pronouns between the verb and particle is to learn set phrases, like *Turn it off, Pick it up*, etc.

- Focus on the sentences and give SS a minute to match them.

1 E 2 G 3 C 4 H 5 F 6 A 7 B 8 D

- Tell SS to cover A–H and try to remember them.
- Then tell SS to close their books. Read out sentences 1–8 and elicit A–H from the whole class. You could repeat this a couple of times to get them to respond faster.

3 READING

a • Here SS read an article about some research done at the University of Surrey which explains why some people are good in the morning and others aren't.

- Focus on the words in the box, and ask SS if they can translate them. If they can't, let them look them up in a dictionary. Model and drill the pronunciation.

b • Focus on the instructions. Check that SS understand that *researchers* in **2** are people who are doing research. Give SS three minutes to read the article, and choose a, b, or c.

- Get SS to compare their choices, and then check answers.

1 a 2 a 3 c 4 b

Extra support

Get SS to read the article individually and then choose the correct option in pairs.

4 LISTENING & SPEAKING

a 8.6

- Here SS listen to a person answering the kind of questions that were in the University of Surrey questionnaire.
- Focus on the instructions. Play the tape/CD once. Check answers.

He's a morning person.

b • Focus on the questions. Give SS time to read them and see if they can remember any of the answers. Tell SS just to write numbers or a few words, not whole sentences. Play the tape/CD again. Let SS compare answers, and then play it once more if necessary. Check answers.

1 magazine editor
2 Monday to Friday 8 till 4
3 5.45
4 morning
5 morning
6 He doesn't mind them.
7 Because he finishes work early, so he can be with his daughter in the afternoon.
8 Yes, he'd like to work four days a week.

Extra support

Pause the tape/CD after each answer to give SS time to write. Allow SS to write their answers in L1 if they like. The objective is to understand what he says.

8.6 CD3 Track 27

I = interviewer, D = David

I Hello. Could I ask you a few questions? We're doing some research.
D Sure. What's it about?
I Well, we want to find out if you are a morning or an evening person.
D OK, fine.
I OK and what's your name?
D David Cope.
I And what do you do, David?
D I'm a magazine editor.
I OK, and when do you work?
D Monday to Friday, eight till four.
I What time do you get up in the morning?
D 5.45. I have to get up early because I start work at 8 and it takes me an hour to get to work.
I And what time do you go to bed?
D Probably around 10 o'clock.
I If you have an exam, do you study best in the morning, afternoon, or at night?
D Let me think. I haven't done an exam for a long time, but when I was a student I used to study better in the morning.
I And if you do exercise, when do you prefer to do it?
D In the morning, definitely. I love going for a long walk or cycling. It's great early in the morning because you feel that you're the only person in the world who's awake at that time.
I Do you like your working hours?
D I don't mind them. Finishing work early means I can pick up my daughter from school, and look after her in the afternoons. It's true that I can't really have a social life during the week, because I go to bed at ten, but that's OK.
I Right, and the last question. Would you like to change your working hours?
D Yes, I would. I'd like to work four days a week, maybe working more hours in the day and have a three-day weekend. Then I could spend three full days a week with my family.
I That's great. Thank you very much for your time.

c • Focus on the instructions. Put SS into pairs. **A** (book open) interviews **B** (book closed) and takes notes. Encourage SS to ask for more information where appropriate. SS swap roles.

Extra idea

Get SS to interview you first. If you are neither a morning nor evening person, explain that you are 'in the middle'.

- Get feedback and find out if the majority of the class are morning, evening, or 'middle' people.

5 PRONUNCIATION /g/ and /dʒ/

a
- Here the focus is on the pronunciation of the letter *g*. Focus on the sound pictures and elicit the words and sounds: *girl* /g/ and *jazz* /dʒ/.
- Focus on the first word in the box and ask SS *Is it* /g/ *or* /dʒ/? Elicit that it's /dʒ/, and get SS to write it in the second column.
- SS continue in pairs with the other words. Tell them that if they're not sure about a word, to say it out loud both ways, and decide which sounds best.

b 8.7
- Play the tape/CD once for SS to check. Then play it again pausing after each word or group of words for SS to repeat.

8.7 CD3 Track 28

girl /g/
get go good give hungry
jazz /dʒ/
gene change energetic gym age

Pronunciation notes

- *g* is always pronounced /g/ before *a, o,* and *u.*
- Before *e, i,* and *y* it can be /g/ or /dʒ/.
- You may also want to remind them that *j* is always /dʒ/, and that *gh* and *gu* as in *ghost, guest* are pronounced /g/.

c
- Focus on the sentences. Model and drill them with the whole class. Then get SS to practise saying them in pairs.

6 SONG ♫ *I say a little prayer*

8.8
- Here SS listen to a song made famous by Aretha Franklin in the 1960s.
- If you want to do this song in class, use the photocopiable activity on *p.227*.

8.8 CD3 Track 29

I say a little prayer

The moment I wake up
Before I put on my make-up
I say a little prayer for you
And while combing my hair, now,
And wondering what dress to wear, now,
I say a little prayer for you

Forever, forever, you'll stay in my heart
And I will love you
Forever, forever, we never will part
Oh, how I'll love you
Together, together, that's how it must be
To live without you
Would only mean heartbreak for me.

I run for the bus, dear,
While riding I think of us, dear,
I say a little prayer for you.
At work I just take time
And all through my coffee break-time,
I say a little prayer for you.

Forever, forever, etc.
My darling, believe me,
For me there is no one
But you.

Please love me true
This is my prayer
Answer my prayer, baby

Extra photocopiable activities

Grammar
phrasal verbs *p.169*
Communicative
Phrasal verb questions *p.213* (instructions on *p.181*)
Song
I say a little prayer p.227 (instructions *p.219*)

HOMEWORK

Study Link **Workbook** *pp.71–72*

8 D

G *so, neither* + auxiliaries
V similarities
P vowel and consonant sounds, sentence stress

'I'm Jim.' 'So am I.'

Lesson plan

This lesson is based on the true case of identical twins who were separated at birth, but re-united 40 years later. The twins provide the context for presenting the structure *So am I, Neither am I.* At this level SS will find it hard to manipulate this structure with any fluency. For this reason, in Speaking SS just practise using the present forms *So am/do I, Neither am/do I.* The vocabulary focus is on different words/phrases used to express similarity, and in Pronunciation SS look at vowel and consonant combinations that can be pronounced in different ways.

Optional lead-in (books closed)

Get SS to ask each other how many brothers and sisters they have, and how old they are. Get feedback. Elicit the word *twin* and find out if anyone has a twin. You could also teach *identical* and *non-identical twin.*

1 LISTENING

a • Books open. Focus on the photo, and elicit descriptions from SS, e.g. *The man on the left has dark hair*, etc.

• Ask SS if the two men look similar and elicit that they are twins.

b • Focus on the instructions. Give SS a minute to read the introduction and answer the questions in pairs. Check answers.

> 1 Identical twins.
> 2 Because they were adopted by two different families when they were babies.
> 3 When they were 40 years old.

c 8.9

• Make sure SS cover the dialogue or get them to close their books. Play the tape/CD once. Get SS, in pairs, to try to remember three things the brothers have in common. Elicit ideas, e.g. *They've been married twice.*

d • Focus on the dialogue. Play the tape/CD again for SS to fill the gaps. Let SS compare answers. Play the tape/CD again if necessary. Go through the dialogue line by line and check answers (see tapescript 8.9).

> **8.9** CD3 Track 30
>
> A Hi! I'm Jim.
> B So **am** I. Great to meet you. Are you married, Jim?
> A Yes ... well, I've been married twice.
> B Yeah? So **have** I. Do you have any children?
> A I have one son.
> B So **do** I. What's his name?
> A James.
> B That's amazing! My son's name is James too.
> A Did you go to university, Jim?
> B No, I didn't.
> A Neither **did** I. I was a terrible student.
> B So **was** I. What do you like doing in your free time, Jim?
> A I like making things, especially with wood.
> B That's incredible! So **do** I.
> A But I don't do any exercise at all. Look at me.
> B Don't worry. Neither **do** I.
> A Do you smoke?
> B Yes. I smoke Salem cigarettes.
> A So **do** I! What car do you have?
> B A Chevrolet.
> A Me too! Let's go and have a drink. What beer do you drink?
> B Miller Lite.
> A So **do** I!

2 GRAMMAR *so, neither* + auxiliaries

a • Focus on the instructions and get SS to complete the rules in pairs. Check answers.

> 1 So (am, have, etc.) I. 2 Neither (did, do, etc.) I.

b • Tell SS to go to **Grammar Bank 8D** on *p.140.* Go through the rules and model and drill the examples.

Grammar notes

• The main problem SS may have is thinking that *So (do) I* is used to agree with a statement and *Neither (do) I* to disagree. It is important to stress that both are used to say that two people have the same opinion or do the same thing, but we use *So*, etc. when it is a [+] thing and *Neither*, etc. when it is a [–] thing.

• SS will probably already know the expression *Me too*, which is a 'short cut' way to express *So do I*, etc. You may want to teach SS the negative version, *Me neither.*

⚠ *Neither* can be pronounced /ˈnaɪðə/ or /ˈniːðə/. In the UK it is always /ˈniːðə/.

• Focus on the exercises for **8D** on *p.141.* SS do them individually or in pairs. Check answers.

> **a** 1 am 2 did 3 was 4 do 5 have 6 can 7 would 8 did
> **b** 1 So do I. 2 Neither am I. 3 So did I. 4 Neither have I. 5 Neither do I. 6 So can I. 7 So do I.

• Tell SS to go back to the main lesson on *p.95.*

3 READING & VOCABULARY

a • Focus on the instructions, and check that SS understand the questions. Give them a few minutes to read and answer the questions in pairs. Check answers.

1 Dr (Thomas) Bouchard. 2 How much of our personality depends on our genes. 3 The enormous similarities in the two Jims' personalities, lifestyle, etc. 4 James Allen and James Alan, Toy. 5 They leave romantic love letters around the house. 6 That genes are more important in determining our personality that people used to think.

b • Focus on the sentences and get SS to complete them in pairs. Check answers.

1 like 2 as 3 both 4 so 5 neither 6 similar

• Highlight that the *So… Neither…* structure can be used with all persons, e.g. *I live in London and so do my parents/they*, etc.

Extra challenge

You may also want to teach the rules for the position of *both*, i.e. before the main verb but after *be*.

c • Say the first two sentences about yourself. Encourage SS to ask for more information.

• Then give SS a few moments to complete the sentences with a family word.

⚠ For 4, 5, and 6 they need to add other words too. They can use the same family member more than once.

• SS discuss their answers with a partner. Get feedback by eliciting different sentences from several pairs.

4 PRONUNCIATION sounds, sentence stress

a • Highlight that in English certain letters or combinations can be pronounced in different ways.

• SS in pairs choose the odd word out.

b 8.10

• Play the tape/CD once for SS to check. Check answers.

8.10 CD3 Track 31

1 so	no	do
2 they	neither	both
3 two	twice	twins
4 identical	incredible	immediately
5 food	good	wood
6 now	know	how
7 speak	great	each
8 beer	free	weekend

1 do 2 both 3 two 4 identical 5 food 6 know 7 great 8 beer

Pronunciation notes

Do is unusual, *o* at the end of a word is usually pronounced /aʊ/.
Two is unusual, *tw* is usually pronounced /tw/.
Great is unusual. There are very few words where *ea* is pronounced /eɪ/, the most common being *great, break* and *steak*. The most typical pronunciation of *ea* is /iː/ as in *each*.
Beer is unusual, *ee* is usually pronounced /iː/ as in *free*.

• Let SS practise in pairs, or play the tape/CD again pausing after each group for SS to repeat.

c 8.11

• Play the tape/CD once and pause for SS to repeat each line. Then tell them to underline the stressed words. Play the tape/CD again for them to check.

8.11 CD3 Track 32

1 A <u>I</u> <u>like</u> <u>tea</u>.
B <u>So</u> do <u>I</u>.
2 A <u>I'm</u> <u>tired</u>.
B <u>So</u> am <u>I</u>.
3 A <u>I</u> <u>don't</u> <u>smoke</u>.
B <u>Neither</u> do <u>I</u>.
4 A <u>I'm</u> <u>not</u> <u>hungry</u>.
B <u>Neither</u> am <u>I</u>.

• Highlight the stress pattern with *So/Neither do I*.

d 8.12

• Focus on the instructions. Explain that SS are going to hear a sentence on the tape/CD, and they have to say that they are the same.

• Play the tape/CD, and pause after the first sentence, to elicit *So do I* from the whole class. Continue, eliciting the **bold** sentences in the tapescript below.

8.12 CD3 Track 33

I like chocolate.	(**So do I.**)
I'm tired.	(**So am I.**)
I'm not hungry.	(**Neither am I.**)
I don't like football.	(**Neither do I.**)
I'm going out tonight.	(**So am I.**)
I have a big family.	(**So do I.**)
I'm not English.	(**Neither am I.**)
I live in a flat.	(**So do I.**)

• Play the tape/CD again, eliciting the sentences from individual SS by pointing to a student before each sentence. Repeat the exercise until SS are responding quickly and accurately.

5 SPEAKING

a • Focus on the instructions. Make sure SS understand all the categories, and give them a few minutes to complete the sentences.

⚠ You may need to teach star signs in English.

b • Go through the instructions and focus on the speech bubbles. Demonstrate by going to different students and saying *I love* (whatever kind of music you like) to individual SS until somebody says *So do I*. If they don't like it, encourage them to say a whole sentence, e.g. *I don't like it/I hate it*.

• Tell SS to stand up and start saying their sentences from **a** to each other to find someone who is the same. Stop the activity when one student has a name for all his/her sentences.

Extra photocopiable activities

Grammar
So do I / Neither do I p.170
Communicative
So do I! *p.214* (instructions on *p.182*)

HOMEWORK

Study Link **Workbook** *pp.73–74*

8 Practical English
On the phone

Revision Checking out
Function Making phone calls
Language *Can I speak to …? Can I leave a message?*

Lesson plan

In this final Practical English lesson SS revise expressions for checking out of a hotel, and learn language for making phone calls. Allie and Mark have their last dinner together. They both have something important they want to say to each other.

Study Link These lessons are on the *New English File Pre-intermediate* Video, which can be used instead of the Class Cassette/CD (see introduction *p.9*). The main functional section of each episode (the second section) is also on the MultiROM with additional activities.

Optional lead-in (books closed)

Revise what happened in the previous episode by eliciting the story from SS, e.g *What happened on Allie's last morning?* (They went on a boat trip.) *Why did she want to be back early?* (Because she was expecting an important phone call.) *What do they have planned for the evening?* (Dinner.)

CHECKING OUT

8.13

- Books open. Focus on the photo and ask *Where's Allie?* (In reception.) *Where has she just been?* (On a boat trip with Mark.)
- Focus on the questions. Play the tape/CD once the whole way through and tell SS just to listen. Then play it again, pausing if necessary to give SS time to answer the questions.
- Get them to compare their answers with a partner's before checking answers.

1 tomorrow morning
2 this evening
3 at 9.15
4 at 7.15
5 to call New York

Extra support

If you have time, you could get SS to listen to the tape/CD with the tapescript on *p.125* so they can see exactly what they understood. Translate/explain any new words or phrases.

- Elicit the key phrases Allie uses, e.g *Could you prepare my bill? Could you order me a cab?* And write them on the board if necessary.

8.13 CD3 Track 34

(tapescript in Student's Book on *p.125*)
R = Receptionist, A = Allie
R Good afternoon. How can I help you?
A Hi. I'm leaving tomorrow morning very early. Could you prepare my bill so I can pay this evening?
R Of course.
A And could you order me a cab?
R For what time?
A My flight's at 9.15, so I have to be at the airport at 7.15.
R Then you'll need a cab at six o'clock. I'll order one for you.
A Thanks. Oh, and has there been a phone call for me?
R Oh yes. There's a message for you. Can you call this number in New York?
A Right. Thanks.
R You're welcome.

- Ask a few more questions to check comprehension, e.g. *What is the receptionist going to do?* (Book her a cab) *For what time?* (6 o'clock).

MAKING PHONE CALLS

a 8.14

- Tell SS to cover the dialogue with their hand or a piece of paper. Focus on the picture and ask SS *Who is she phoning?* (The New York office).

⚠ If you think that SS won't cover their books properly, you could get them to close their books at this stage and write the first task on the board.

- Play the tape/CD once or twice. Check answers.

1 Lisa Formosa
2 She gets the wrong number.
3 Good.
4 She got the job in Paris.

b
- Now tell SS to uncover the dialogue (or open their books). Explain that the **YOU HEAR** part is what they need to understand, and the **YOU SAY** part contains the phrases they need to be able to say.
- Give SS a minute to read through the dialogue and guess the missing words. Then play the tape/CD again, for them to complete the dialogue.

8.14 8.15 CD3 Tracks 35+36

A = Allie, L = Lisa
B Hello.
A Hello. Is that MTC? (*repeat*)
B Sorry, you've got the **wrong** number.
A Oh sorry. (*repeat*)

C MTC New York. How can I help you?
A Hello. Can I speak to Lisa Formosa, please? (*repeat*)
C Just a moment. I'll **put** you **through**.
D Hello.
A Hi, is that Lisa? (*repeat*)
D No, I'm sorry. She's not at her desk right now.
A Can I leave a message, please? (*repeat*)
D Sure.
A Tell her Allie Gray called. I'll call back in five minutes. (*repeat*)

C MTC New York. How can I help you?
A Hello. Can I speak to Lisa Formosa, please? (*repeat*)
C Just a moment. I'm sorry, the line's **busy**. Do you want to **hold**?
A OK, I'll hold. (*repeat*)
L Hello.
A Hi Lisa. It's Allie Gray. (*repeat*)
L Allie, hi. How's California?
A Great, great. Well? Is it good news or bad news?
L It's good. You got the job in Paris!
A Oh wonderful! That's fantastic!

- Go through the dialogue line by line with SS and check answers. Highlight:
  put through = connect
  Is that (Lisa)? NOT ~~*Are you Lisa?*~~
  Hi Lisa. ***It's*** *Allie* NOT ~~*I'm Allie*~~.
  hold = *wait* and is very typical on the phone, as is *Hold on (a minute/ moment).*

c 8.15

- Now focus on the **YOU SAY** phrases. Tell SS they're going to hear the dialogue again. They repeat the **YOU SAY** phrases when they hear the beep. Encourage them to copy the rhythm.
- Play the tape/CD, pausing if necessary for SS to repeat the phrases.

d • Put SS into pairs, **A** and **B**. **A** is Allie (book closed), **B** is all the other people (book open). Tell **A** to close his/her book and try to remember the phrases. Then **A** and **B** swap roles.

Extra support

Let SS practise the dialogue first in pairs, both with books open.

SOCIAL ENGLISH saying goodbye?

a 8.16

- Focus on the photo. Ask *Where are they?* and elicit that they're in a restaurant. Ask *What do you think they're saying?* And see if anyone comes up with *Cheers.*
- In this last episode it would be a good idea to just let SS listen the first time to see how the story ends. Play the tape/CD. Build up as much suspense as possible by pausing after Mark says *I have something to tell you*, and after Allie says *I have something to tell you too* and get SS to predict what they're going to say. Give them time to react to the ending before doing the T/F sentences.
- Focus on the sentences and make sure SS understand everything, e.g. *relationship*. Play the tape/CD again.
- Let SS compare their answers with a partner's and then check answers. Get SS to correct the false ones.

1 T
2 F She thinks it's a problem that they live so far apart.
3 F To another office but with the same company.
4 T
5 F She's going to be Mark's boss!

8.16 CD3 Track 37

A = Allie, M = Mark
A Thanks for **everything**. I've had a great time here.
M **Cheers.** To us. Allie – we need to talk – about the future. I mean, about *our* future.
A Yes.
M Allie, I really think we have a future together. I'm serious.
A So am I, Mark. But the problem is you live here and I live in London. We're 6,000 miles apart.
M Maybe that's not going to be a problem – I have something to tell you. We're not going to be 6,000 miles apart. We're only going to be 300 miles apart.
A What do you **mean?**
M You know the new MTC office that's opening in Paris next month?
A Yes?
M Well, I'm going there. I'm going to be the marketing manager. **Isn't** that amazing? I'll only be an hour away from you!
A You're joking.
M No, I'm serious. What's the **matter?** Aren't you pleased? You don't look very happy.
A Yes, I *am* happy. It's amazing. But I have something to tell you too.
M Oh?
A I'm going to the Paris office too! I've just heard. That was the phone call I was waiting for.
M I don't **believe** it. That's wonderful! We'll be together!
A Yes. But there's just one little thing, Mark.
M What's that?
A I'm going to be the director in Paris. I'm going to be your boss!

- Check comprehension by asking a few more questions. e.g.:
  1 *What does Mark say they need to talk about?* (The future.)
  2 *How far apart do they live at the moment?* (6,000 miles = approx 9,600 kms.)
  3 *How far apart are they going to be soon?* (300 miles = approx 480 kms.)
  4 *What is Mark's new job?* (Marketing manager in the new office in Paris.)
  5 *What is Allie's new job?* (Director in the new office in Paris.)
- Ask SS if they think their relationship will work in Paris or not, and elicit all their ideas.

b • Focus on the **USEFUL PHRASES**. Get SS to see if they can remember any of the missing words. Play the tape/CD again and check answers (see tapescript above).

c 8.17

- Play the tape/CD pausing for SS to repeat each phrase. Encourage them to copy the rhythm.
- In a monolingual class get SS to decide together what the equivalent phrase would be in their language.

8.17 CD3 Track 38

A = Allie, M = Mark
A Thanks for everything.
M Cheers! To us.
A What do you mean?
M Isn't that amazing?
M What's the matter?
M I don't believe it.

HOMEWORK

Study Link **Workbook** *p.75*

8 Writing
Giving your opinion

In this final writing lesson SS write an article giving their opinion about the weekend. The writing skills focus is on using connectors, and the article recycles language from **File 8.** This lesson introduces SS to the idea of a very simple discursive composition.

a • Focus on the article and the instructions. Go through the words in the box and check SS remember their meaning.

• Set a time limit for SS to read the article and complete the gaps. Get SS to compare their answers with a partner's and then check answers.

> **2** who
> **3** Another
> **4** above all
> **5** However
> **6** Secondly
> **7** Although
> **8** which
> **9** general

• Highlight:

– the way *Firstly, secondly* are used to introduce different points.

– the use of *However* to begin a paragraph which contrasts with the previous one.

– the use of *in general* to sum up.

b • Focus on the instructions and sentences. Give SS a few minutes to re-read the article and mark the sentences T or F. Check answers, asking why the F sentences are false.

> **1** F She works in an office.
> **2** T
> **3** F She doesn't like it because the supermarket is always crowded.
> **4** F Her mother-in-law makes the lunch.
> **5** T

• Ask a few more questions to check comprehension, e.g *What time does she get up during the week? Why does she hate it in the winter? What does she like doing in her free time?*

Extra idea

Get SS to cover the article. Put SS into pairs, **A** and **B**. **A** remembers as much as possible about the good side, **B** about the bad side.

Write about what you think of the weekend

Either give SS at least fifteen minutes to write the text in class, following the instructions, or set it for homework.

Extra support

To help SS plan the content, get them to discuss orally first what they think is the good side and the bad side of their weekends.

If SS do the writing in class, get them to swap their texts with another S's to read and check for mistakes before you collect them all in.

8 Revise & Check

For instructions on how to use these pages, see *p.27*.

GRAMMAR

> **1** a **2** b **3** b **4** c **5** b **6** b **7** b **8** b **9** c **10** b

VOCABULARY

> **a 1** relaxing **2** tired **3** interesting **4** depressed **5** boring
> **b 1** do **2** wear (put on) **3** eats **4** see/meet **5** give up (stop)
> **c 1** turn **2** look **3** Wake **4** Put **5** look

PRONUNCIATION

> **a 1** nobody **2** not **3** energetic **4** both **5** great
> **b** <u>some</u>body re<u>lax</u> <u>di</u>et e<u>nough</u> i<u>den</u>tical

CAN YOU UNDERSTAND THIS TEXT?

> **a 1** T **2** T **3** F **4** DS **5** T **6** F
> **b 1** a nap **2** brought up **3** share **4** freezing **5** shout

CAN YOU UNDERSTAND THESE PEOPLE?

8.18 CD3 Track 39

1
A Did you have a good weekend?
B Yeah, fine, thanks.
A Did you go anywhere nice?
B Well, we wanted to go to the beach but the weather was awful, so we didn't.
A Did you go out on Saturday night?
B No, we stayed at home and watched a film.

2
A Do you eat a lot of fast food?
B No, almost none. I think my diet is quite healthy. I eat lots of fruit and vegetables, although I should probably eat more fish.

3
A How often do you go to the gym?
B Not as often as I'd like to.
A I thought you went every day!
B No, only Mondays and Fridays now. I'm too busy.

4
A What time do you get up?
B I wake up at 7.00 but I always go back to sleep for fifteen minutes. Then I get up.

5
A Do you want a coffee?
B No, I don't drink coffee, thanks.
A What do you do?
B I'm a teacher. What about you?

A I work in computers.
B Are you married?
A Divorced.
B So am I.

a 1 b 2 b 3 b 4 b 5 b

8.19 CD3 Track 40

A Morning.
B Good morning.
A I'm really tired. I didn't get enough sleep last night.
B Why not?
A I went out for dinner with an old friend from university and I went to bed late.
B What time?
A 1.00, and then I had to get up at 7.00. I'm terrible in the mornings, too.
B Are you? I'm the opposite. I'm at my best in the mornings. What university did you go to?
A Liverpool.
B Yeah? So did I! When did you finish?
A In 1999. What about you?
B I finished in '97.
A What did you study?
B French and German.
A I studied Economics.
B Economics? I used to know a girl who studied Economics at Liverpool.
A What was her name?
B Fiona … Fiona Kennedy. Don't tell me you know her?
A Know her? I married her.
B You're joking! I don't believe it. What a coincidence!

b 1 M 2 W 3 B 4 M 5 B

CAN YOU SAY THIS IN ENGLISH?

SS own answers.

Extra photocopiable activities

Quicktest 8 *p.238*

9 A What a week!

G past perfect
V adverbs: *suddenly, immediately*, etc.
P revision of vowel sounds, sentence stress

File 9 overview

File 9 only has two lessons which present new language, **9A** and **9B**. **9A** presents the past perfect, which is then recycled in reported speech in **9B**. If these two structures are not in your syllabus, you may want to go straight to File 9 **Revise & Check** which revise the grammar, vocabulary, and pronunciation of the whole book.

Lesson plan

In this lesson the past perfect is presented through the context of a Sunday newspaper feature where six strange-but-true stories are collected from around the world every week. The pronunciation section revises several of the vowel sounds focused on during the course, and the vocabulary highlights some of the adverbs from the stories, e.g. *suddenly, immediately*, etc. The lesson ends with a communication game.

Optional lead-in (books closed)

Revise irregular past participles, by saying a verb from the Irregular Verb list on *p.155* and eliciting the past simple and past participle.

Then ask SS *When do you use past participles?* and elicit in the present perfect (with *have*) and the passive (with *be*). Now they're going to learn another tense where you use the past participle of the verb.

1 SPEAKING & READING

a • Books open. Focus on the pictures and phrases. Tell SS in pairs to find the correct picture for each detail and try to work out what the bold words mean. Check answers, and if necessary explain/translate the words.

> screaming (crying loudly in a high voice) 2
> a fine (money you have to pay for breaking a law) 3
> a raffle (where tickets are sold and the winner gets a prize) 1
> snoring (breathing noisily when you are asleep) 4
> arrested (taken by the police to be questioned) 5
> amazed (very surprised) 6

b • Focus on the stories and instructions. Give SS a few minutes to read the stories. Then in pairs they match them with their endings. Check answers.

> 1 E 2 F 3 A 4 D 5 C 6 B

Extra support

Read the first story out loud with the class. Then ask SS to find the ending and elicit that it is **E**. Get SS to continue in pairs.

c • Write the six headings on the board. Then get SS, in pairs, to read the stories again, and then cover the text and try to retell the stories using the pictures to help them.

2 GRAMMAR past perfect

a • Focus on the sentences and get SS to answer the questions in pairs, or answer them as a whole class. Check answers.

> 1 b happened first 2 *had* + the past participle (= the past perfect)

b • Check that SS have highlighted the right verbs (*had discovered, had stolen, had robbed, had seen, had given, had worked, had lost, had gone, had left*). Elicit that all these actions happened before the main part of the story.

c • Tell SS to go to **Grammar Bank 9A** on *p.142*. Go through the rules and chart. Model and drill the examples.

Grammar notes

- The form and use of this tense is not normally problematic for most SS.
- The past perfect is very common after verbs like *realized, remembered, saw*, etc.

• Focus on the exercises for **9A** on *p.143*. SS do them individually or in pairs. Check answers.

> **a** 1 G 2 F 3 A 4 H 5 C 6 B 7 E
> **b** 1 didn't recognize, had cut
> 2 phoned, had left
> 3 turned on, had finished
> 4 didn't lend, hadn't finished
> 5 failed, hadn't studied
> 6 got, had broken

• Tell SS to go back to the main lesson on *p.101*.

3 PRONUNCIATION vowel sounds, sentence stress

a • This exercises revises vowels sounds in sentences which practise the past perfect. Focus on the sound pictures and elicit the example words and sounds: *horse* /ɔː/, *fish* /ɪ/, *up* /ʌ/, *train* /eɪ/, *bird* /ɜː/, *tree* /iː/).

• Now focus on the pink letters in each sentence. Elicit that the sound in the first sentence is /ʌ/, and the sound picture is C, *up*.

• In pairs, SS match the sentences and sound pictures. Monitor and encourage them to say the words/sentences out loud. Check answers.

> 1 C 2 B 3 F 4 A 5 E 6 D

b 9.1

• Play the tape/CD once the whole way through for SS to hear the sentence rhythm. Elicit that *had* is not stressed in (+) sentences.

• Play it again, pausing after each sentence for SS to repeat and copy the rhythm.

9.1 CD3 Track 41

1 He suddenly understood why his brother hadn't come.
2 I didn't know Linda hadn't written since the spring.
3 The police had seen me in the street.
4 Paul thought the train had left at four-forty.
5 We hadn't heard a word about the third murder.
6 We'd waited for ages to see the famous painting.

4 VOCABULARY adverbs

a • Here SS learn some high frequency adverbs that came up in the reading text. Focus on the sentences and instructions. Check answers.

1 acci<u>den</u>tally 2 un<u>for</u>tunately 3 <u>su</u>ddenly
4 <u>lu</u>ckily 5 im<u>me</u>diately
2 and 4 are opposites

• Highlight that adverbs usually describe a verb, but can also describe a whole sentence or phrase, e.g. *unfortunately, luckily.*

Extra challenge

You might also like to point out that:

– *fortunately* also exists and is a synonym for *luckily.*

– the expression *by mistake* is often used instead of *accidentally.*

b • Focus on the instructions and give SS a minute to complete the sentences, in pairs or individually. Check answers.

1 accidentally 2 suddenly 3 immediately
4 Unfortunately 5 Luckily

c • Give SS a few minutes to complete the sentences. Get feedback, accepting all endings that fit the meaning of the adverbs.

Possible completions
1 nobody saw her.
2 the phone rang.
3 hadn't brought an umbrella.
4 started making dinner.
5 lost it.

5 SPEAKING

• Put SS into pairs **A** and **B**, sitting face to face if possible. Tell them to go to **Communication *What had happened?***, **A** on *p.111* and **B** on *p.115*. Go through the instructions and make sure SS understand what they have to do.

• Give SS time to think of verbs that could go into the sentences.

Extra support

Demonstrate the activity. Write this sentence on a piece of paper.

When Jason had finished his homework, he turned on the TV.

Then write on the board:

When Jason ________ his homework, he turned on the TV (+).

Tell SS that you have written the complete sentence on a piece of paper, and that you want them to guess the missing words. Tell them what's missing is a past perfect verb, and that the (+) sign means that it is positive. Ask a student to say the whole sentence with the missing verb. If he/she says it with *had done,* say that it is possible, but not what you have on your piece of paper, and say *Try again.* Carry on until the student (or another one) says *had finished.*

• Monitor while SS are doing the activity, and encourage them to say the sentences with the right rhythm.

• Fast finishers could write their own sentences and read them to their partner with the verb missed out. Their partner guesses the missing verb.

Extra photocopiable activities

Grammar
past perfect *p.171*
Communicative
Match the sentences *p.215* (instructions *p.182*)

HOMEWORK

Study Link **Workbook** *pp.76–77*

9B Then he kissed me

G reported speech
V *say, tell* or *ask?*
P rhyming verbs

Lesson plan

This lesson provides a clear and simple introduction to reported (or indirect) speech which will be focused on in more detail in *New English File Intermediate*. The context for the presentation is a classic song *Then he kissed me* which has some clear examples of the target language. In vocabulary SS practise distinguishing between *say, tell,* and *ask* and Pronunciation revises the pronunciation of some common past participles.

Optional lead-in (books closed)

Draw a picture of a boy and a girl on the board and tell SS that they are at a disco or club. Establish that they don't know each other. Draw a speech bubble by the boy's face and elicit ideas for what the boy says to try to start a conversation with the girl, e.g. *What's your name? Do you want to dance?*, etc. Try to elicit five or six ideas and write them on the board. Get the girls/women in the class to vote which is the most unusual one/the best one/the worst one. Now do exercise **1a**.

1 SPEAKING & LISTENING

a • Focus on the pictures and give SS a couple of minutes, in pairs, to order them 1–8. You could elicit the first one from the whole class (C). **Don't check answers yet.**

> **Suggested story**
> Dean met Millie at a disco. They danced together. He walked her home.
> (The stars were shining). He kissed her. She said 'I love you.' He said 'I love you too.'
> He took her home to meet his parents (mum and dad). Then he said 'Will you marry me?'
> Millie said 'Yes.' They got married (in a church.)

b • Now focus SS' attention on the song and the verbs in the three boxes. Elicit the past simple of each verb, e.g. *ask–asked*, etc. Give them time, in pairs, to complete it with the verbs from the box in the past simple.

• Now give SS time, in pairs, to complete the song with the verbs in the past simple, using the glossary to help them.

c 9.2

• Play the tape/CD for SS to check their answers.

> 9.2 CD3 Track 42
> ***Then he kissed me***
> Well, he [1]**walked** up to me and he [2]**asked** me if I [3]**wanted** to dance.
> He looked kind of nice and so I [4]**said** I might take a chance.
> When he [5]**danced** he held me tight
> And when he [6]**walked** me home that night
> All the stars were shining bright
> And then he kissed me.
>
> Each time I [7]**saw** him I [8]**couldn't** wait to see him again.
> I wanted to let him know that he [9]**was** more than a friend.
> I [10]**didn't know** just what to do
> So I whispered 'I love you'
> And he [11]**said** that he loved me too
> And then he kissed me.
>
> He kissed me in a way that I've never been kissed before,
> He kissed me in a way that I wanna be kissed forever more.
>
> I [12]**knew** that he was mine so I [13]**gave** him all the love that I had
> And one day he [14]**took** me home to meet his mum and his dad.
> Then he [15]**asked** me to be his bride
> And always be right by his side.
> I [16]**felt** so happy I almost cried
> And then he kissed me.

• Go through the song line by line, and deal with any vocabulary SS don't understand. Then play the song again for SS just to listen and follow the lyrics.
• Now tell SS to check if they have the pictures in the right order.

> 1 C 2 E 3 A 4 F 5 H 6 B 7 D 8 G

Extra challenge

Get SS to tell the story in pairs using the pictures. Then elicit it picture by picture from the whole class.

Extra idea

If your SS like singing, you could play the tape/CD again for them to sing along with it.

2 GRAMMAR reported speech

a • Focus on the sentences and get SS, in pairs, to answer the questions. Check answers.

> 1 sentences A and B
> 2 sentences C and D
> 3 present simple
> 4 past simple

b • Tell SS to go to **Grammar Bank 9B** on *p.142*. Go through the rules with the class. Model and drill the example sentences.

Grammar notes

• This is an introduction to reported (or indirect) speech. The reporting of sentences and questions is covered here but not reported commands, e.g. *He told me to open the window.*
• SS tend to confuse the verbs *say* and *tell*. Typical mistake:
He said me that he was tired.

- Focus on the exercises for **9B** on *p.143*. SS do the exercises individually or in pairs. Check answers.

a 1 was tired
2 didn't like rock music
3 he'd/would book a table
4 he'd/had bought a new car
5 lived in the city centre
6 they could do it
7 she had seen the film on TV

b 1 liked football
2 she liked
3 if I was tired
4 if they had been to New York
5 where I had lived before
6 if he could swim
7 where he was from

- Tell SS to go back to the main lesson on *p.103*.

c • This exercise gives SS extra practise converting direct speech to reported speech. Focus on the task and tell SS that the sentences in the speech marks are more of the conversation between Dean and Millie. Give SS, in pairs, a couple of minutes to complete the sentences. Check answers.

2 He asked her if she wanted a drink.
3 She said (that) she wasn't thirsty.
4 He asked her if she would go out with him.
5 He asked her if he could walk her home.
6 He asked her where she lived.
7 She said (that) she lived quite near.
8 He told Millie (that) he had fallen in love at first sight.

Extra challenge

Get SS to cover their answers in the right-hand column with a piece of paper so they are covering what they wrote but can see the beginning of the sentences *He said that*, etc. SS look at the direct speech on the left and try to remember the reported speech, uncovering the sentences one by one to see if they were right.

3 VOCABULARY *say, tell,* or *ask?*

- Focus on the task and give SS time to complete the sentences. Get them to compare their answers with a partner's before you check answers.

Extra support

If SS are having problems with *say/tell*, get them to look back at the note in **Grammar Bank 9B** on *p.142*.

1 asked **2** told **3** said **4** asked **5** said **6** told
7 told **8** told

4 PRONUNCIATION rhyming verbs

a • This revision exercise focuses on the pronunciation of past participles. Focus on the two columns and demonstrate the activity. Give SS, in pairs, three minutes to match the rhyming verbs.

b 9.3

- Play the tape/CD for SS to check their answers.

9.3 CD3 Track 43

said – read
paid – played
caught – bought
lost – crossed
spent – meant
told – sold
saw – wore
heard – preferred
could – stood

- Play the tape/CD again for SS to listen and repeat.

Extra idea

Get SS to cover the past participles in **B** and just look at the ones in **A.** They try to remember the rhyming verbs.

5 SPEAKING

a • Focus on the task and the example in the speech bubble. Give SS a minute or so to choose their five questions. Put SS into pairs and give them time to ask each other their five questions and write down the answers.

b • Get SS to change partners and explain that they must now tell their new partner what questions they asked their first partner and what that person answered. To do this they must change both the question and answer into reported speech. Focus on the example in the speech bubble and if necessary demonstrate the activity.

- Give SS time to report their conversations to their new partners.
- Get feedback by asking individual SS to report one exchange.

Extra photocopiable activities

Grammar
reported speech *p.172*
Communicative
Who said what? *p.216* (instructions *p.182*)

HOMEWORK

Study Link **Workbook** *pp.78–79*

9 Revise & Check

The last two sections in File 9, **Revise and Check Grammar** and **Revise and Check Vocabulary** and **Pronunciation** are intended to help SS revise for a final end-of-course test.

GRAMMAR

The grammar is divided up by files and gives the **Grammar Bank** page reference. SS should read through the rules again, and then test themselves with the exercises. They can either do this File by File or all at once. We suggest doing them in pairs or small groups in a final class, where SS can talk together about which is the right answer and why, but they can also be done individually or at home.

File 1
1 c 2 a 3 c 4 a 5 b

File 2
1 c 2 c 3 a 4 b 5 c

File 3
1 b 2 b 3 a 4 c 5 c

File 4
1 c 2 a 3 c 4 a 5 a

File 5
1 c 2 a 3 c 4 b 5 c

File 6
1 b 2 a 3 b 4 b 5 c

File 7
1 b 2 c 3 b 4 b 5 c

File 8
1 a 2 b 3 c 4 b 5 b

File 9
1 a 2 b 3 b 4 c 5 c

VOCABULARY

This section provides exercises to test SS on all the **Vocabulary Banks** of *New English File Pre-intermediate.* If possible, give SS time to revise the **Vocabulary Banks** before doing the exercises. If this is not feasible, the exercises should highlight which ones SS need to look back at. We suggest doing them in pairs or small groups in a final class, where SS can talk together about which is the right answer and why, but they can also be done individually or at home.

a 1 lazy (the others are positive)
2 toe (the others are part of your face)
3 fingers (you have ten, not two)
4 ear (the others are verbs)
5 sunny (the others are bad weather)
6 cap (it's not only for women)
7 pyjamas (you don't wear them on your feet)
8 get home (*get* = arrive. In the others, *get* = receive)
9 butterfly (it's not a bird)
10 eagle (it can't swim)

b 1 sunbathe
2 wear
3 carry
4 make
5 do
6 know
7 meet
8 go
9 get
10 spend

c 1 on
2 at
3 in
4 with
5 for
6 away
7 on
8 up
9 after
10 back

d 1 unfriendly
2 quiet
3 empty
4 polite
5 impatient
6 borrow money
7 fail an exam
8 pull the door
9 lose your keys
10 sell clothes

e 1 tongue
2 over
3 jacket
4 through
5 bear
6 T-shirt
7 bee
8 teeth
9 past
10 heart

PRONUNCIATION

This section provides exercises to test sounds and word stress.

a 1 mouse
2 trousers
3 since
4 secret
5 come
6 won't
7 worn
8 slowly
9 work
10 walk
11 hour
12 glasses
13 gym
14 eyes
15 two

b 1 biography
2 exercise
3 university
4 divorced
5 borrow
6 decision
7 always
8 promise
9 dangerous
10 polite
11 towards
12 afraid
13 education
14 interesting
15 along
16 important
17 anything
18 depressing
19 language
20 unfortunately

c 1 should
2 quite
3 lose
4 although
5 teacher
6 nothing
7 really
8 housework
9 enjoy
10 laugh

Extra photocopiable activities

Grammar
revise and check *p.173*
Communicative
Revision questions *p.217*
End-of-course test *p.239* (tapescript *p.230*)

PHOTOCOPIABLE ACTIVITIES

CONTENTS

Photocopiable material

- There is a **Grammar activity** for each main (A, B, C and D) lesson of the Student's Book.
- There is a **Communicative activity** for each main (A, B, C and D) lesson of the Student's Book.
- There are eight **Song activities.** These can be used as part of the main lesson in the Student's Book or in a later lesson. The recording of the song can be found in the main lesson on the Class Cassette / CD.
- There is a **Quicktest** for Files 1–8. These are short tests of the main Grammar, Vocabulary, and Pronunciation to be used at the end of each file.
- There is an **End-of-course test** which tests Grammar, Vocabulary, and Pronunciation from the course as well as Reading, Listening, and Writing.

Using extra activities in mixed-ability classes

Some teachers have classes with a very wide range of levels, and where some SS finish SB activities much more quickly than others. You could give these fast-finishers a photocopiable activity (either Communicative or Grammar) while you help the slower students. Alternatively some teachers might want to give faster students extra oral practice with a communicative activity while slower students consolidate their knowledge with an extra grammar activity.

Tips for using Grammar activities

The Grammar activities are designed to give students extra practice in the main grammar point from each lesson. How you use these activities depends on the needs of your students and the time you have available. They can be used in the lesson if you think all of your class would benefit from the extra practice or you could set them as homework for some or all of your students.

- All of the activities start with a writing stage. If you use the activities in class, get students to work individually or in pairs. Allow students to compare before checking the answers.
- Some of the activities have a final section that gets students to cover the sentences and to test their memory. If you are using the activities in class, students can work in pairs and test their partner. If you set them for homework, encourage SS to use this stage to test themselves.
- If SS are having trouble with any of the activities, make sure they refer to the relevant Grammar Bank in the Student's Book.
- Make sure that SS keep their copies of the activities and that they review any difficult areas regularly. Encourage them to go back to activities and cover and test themselves. This will help with their revision.

1A questions

a 2 How are you today?
3 Where are you from?
4 Where do you live?
5 Do you live in a flat or a house?
6 Where are your parents from?
7 Where are you living in London?
8 What do you do in your free time?
9 Why are you studying English?
10 What was your favourite subject at school?
11 What kind of films do you watch?
12 What did you have for breakfast?
13 What are you going to do this weekend?
14 Are you going to have a holiday this year?
15 Did you watch television last night?

1B present simple

2 don't work **3** do you have **4** don't eat **5** do you want **6** watches **7** get on **8** Do they go **9** do you live **10** has **11** do you drink **12** don't smoke **13** doesn't travel **14** does Linda get up **15** get **16** finishes **17** do you listen to **18** don't go **19** doesn't see **20** doesn't your father like

1C present simple or present continuous?

a **2** 'm watching **3** don't like **4** hate **5** Do you want **6** 're studying **7** have **8** Are you using **9** is waiting **10** need **11** 's not working **12** want **13** 's he studying **14** 's doing **15** 's working **16** wants **17** needs

1D relative clauses

a **2** where, borrow **3** who cuts **4** where, keep **5** which, light **6** which, wear **7** who answers **8** where, live **9** who writes **10** which, listen to **11** who writes **12** where, buy **13** which, cut **14** which, put **15** where, relax

2A past simple regular and irregular

2 Did … have **3** was **4** stayed **5** thought **6** didn't go **7** did … do **8** Did … go **9** saw **10** spent **11** bought **12** didn't buy **13** had **14** did … stay **15** stayed **16** were **17** went **18** did … study **19** didn't like **20** didn't … like **21** was **22** left **23** took **24** was **25** did … happen **26** arrived **27** went **28** Did … see **29** came **30** wasn't **31** Did … have

2B past simple or past continuous?

a **2** rang, was driving **3** heard, were sunbathing **4** was looking, took **5** was having, saw **6** saw, was walking

b **2** looked **3** didn't see **4** were holding **5** weren't waiting **6** didn't know **7** was **8** decided **9** went **10** looked **11** were waiting **12** caught **13** stopped **14** got **15** walked **16** gave **17** was talking **18** ran **19** was carrying **20** said **21** was waiting **22** thought **23** were **24** said

2C questions with and without auxiliaries

a 2 Where do Manga comics come from? **Japan**
3 Where did John Lennon die? **New York**
4 Which country won the 2002 World Cup? **Brazil**
5 When did the Vietnam war end? **1975**
6 Who invented the electric light bulb? **Thomas Edison**
7 Who directed the *Star Wars* films? **George Lucas**
8 When did the first man walk on the moon? **1969**
9 Where do polar bears live? **The North Pole**
10 Which actor played Spiderman? **Tobey Maguire**
11 How many countries belong to the United Nations? **191**
12 Which machine did Marconi invent in 1895? **The radio**
13 Who married Tom Cruise/Who did Tom cruise marry in 1990? **Nicole Kidman**
14 When did Nelson Mandela become president of South Africa? **1994**
15 Which country has a red, white, and blue flag? **Russia**

2D *so, because, but, although*

a **2** d because **3** j so **4** a so **5** i but **6** h because **7** e although **8** b although **9** f but **10** c so

b **2** Although **3** but **4** so **5** because **6** but **7** but **8** So **9** but **10** because **11** Although

3A *going to*, present continuous

Suggested answers

a **2** 's going to rain **3** 's going to buy a car **4** 's going to catch a bus **5** 's going to watch television **6** isn't going to swim **7** 're going to go to Paris **8** 're going to go to the cinema / watch a film

b 3 What's he doing on Sunday? He's meeting his mum at the airport.
4 What's he doing on Friday morning? He's doing his final exam.
5 Is he having dinner with Anna on Monday? Yes, he is.
6 When's he going to the dentist? On Tuesday.
7 What's he doing on Friday night? He's going to Frank's party.
8 What's he doing on Saturday? He's going shopping.
9 When's he working? He's working on Wednesday.
10 Is he meeting Chris on Thursday? Yes, he is.

3B *will / won't* (predictions)

2 d she'll come back **3** h she'll be **4** a they'll be **5** l won't have **6** j he'll get **7** g you'll feel **8** c she'll … lose **9** i he'll get **10** k it'll rain **11** b you'll pass **12** e won't like

3C *will* or *going to*?

2 he's going to stay **3** he's going to travel **4** I'll call **5** I'll take **6** are you going to do **7** I'm going to stay **8** we're going to have **9** I'll make **10** I'm going to have **11** I'll bring **12** I'll have **13** Are you going to stay **14** I'm going to catch **15** I'll pay **16** I'll pay **17** I'm going to paint **18** I'll help

3D tense revision

2 Does … have 3 isn't playing 4 wrote 5 is giving/is going to give 6 are … doing 7 did … get, took 8 were arguing 9 were … doing 10 does … get 11 was driving 12 do … do 13 won't hurt 14 'm not working 15 are … doing/going to do, Do … want 16 are … going to study 17 'll meet 18 went 19 did … go 20 was walking

4A present perfect or past simple?

a eat, ate, eaten
fly, flew, flown
hear, heard, heard
lose, lost, lost
read, read, read
see, saw, seen
win, won, won
work, worked, worked
write, wrote, written

b 2 She's never eaten octopus.
3 Have they ever been late for work?
4 We've never seen a Tarantino film.
5 She's written more than ten mystery novels.
6 I haven't read *The Lord of the Rings.*
7 Have you ever worked in a clothes shop?
8 He's won won three gold medals.
9 They haven't lost a match this year.
10 I've heard three of their albums.

c 2 haven't 3 saw 4 Was 5 liked 6 Have … ever lost 7 have 8 did … happen 9 was 10 did … do 11 phoned 12 made

4B present perfect + *yet, just, already*

a 3 Has he eaten the sandwich yet? No, he hasn't.
4 Has he turned off the computer yet? Yes, he has.
5 Has he drunk his coffee yet? Yes, he has.
6 Has he tidied his desk yet? No, he hasn't.
7 Has he put away his CDs yet? Yes, he has.
8 Has he made his bed yet? No, he hasn't.
9 Has he put away his clothes yet? No, he hasn't.
10 Has he finished talking on the phone yet? No, he hasn't.

b 2 He's just been on holiday. 3 She's just failed an exam. 4 She's just missed her train. 5 We've just had lunch. 6 He's just woken up.

4C comparative adjectives and adverbs

a 2 She's happier than her husband.
3 Men drive faster than women.
4 Spain is hotter than France.
5 The sandwiches are more expensive than the cakes.
6 Tom works more slowly than Greg.
7 Laura speaks better Italian than Jake.
8 Football is more popular than tennis.
9 Singapore is further than Tokyo.

b 2 isn't as happy has her 3 don't drive as fast as men 4 isn't as hot as Spain 5 aren't as expensive as the sandwiches 6 doesn't work as fast as Greg 7 doesn't speak Italian as well as Laura 8 isn't as popular as football 9 isn't as far as Singapore

4D superlatives

a 2 Who's the most generous person you've ever met?
3 What's the best restaurant you've ever been to?
4 What's the cheapest hotel you've ever stayed in?
5 What's the coldest place you've ever visited?
6 What's the longest journey you've ever made?
7 What's the most delicious food you've ever eaten?
8 Where's the most dangerous place you've ever been to?
9 What's the most exciting book you've ever read?
10 Where's the furthest you've ever been on holiday?

c 2 ✔ 3 worst 4 ✔ 5 ✔ 6 best 7 the most 8 in the most 9 the most expensive 10 ✔

5A the infinitive with *to*

a 2 not to tell 3 to see 4 to sell 5 to shut 6 not to lose 7 to do 8 to build 9 to be to take photos

b 2 She went to the travel agent to book tickets.
3 She went to the bakers to buy some bread.
4 She went to *Zara* to buy some new clothes.
5 She went to the Internet café to send some e-mails.
6 She went to the gym to do some exercise.
7 She went to the park to go for a walk.
8 She went to the bank to get some money.
9 She went to the garage to get some petrol.

5B infinitive or verb + *-ing*?

3 to come 4 not talking 5 to see 6 to earn 7 relaxing, not doing 8 to give 9 to learn 10 winning 11 not to hit 12 drinking 13 to go 14 stopping 15 going 16 to be 17 to go 18 Eating 19 not to understand 20 remembering

5C *have to, don't have to, mustn't*

a 2 don't have to pay 3 mustn't smoke 4 have to drive 5 have to wear 6 don't have to come 7 don't have to pay 8 have to wear 9 mustn't park 10 have to be 11 have to turn off 12 mustn't play

5D verbs and prepositions

a 2 out of 3 under 4 round 5 towards 6 along 7 through 8 up 9 into 10 down 11 across

6A first conditional

2 'll miss 3 miss 4 I'll be 5 I'm 6 will be 7 is 8 I'll lose 9 lend 10 you'll buy 11 buy 12 you'll start 13 start 14 you'll never get 15 don't get 16 you'll never pay 17 help 18 won't do 19 don't do 20 won't learn 21 don't learn 22 won't pass 23 don't pass 24 won't go

6B second conditional

a 2 I wouldn't do that if I were you.
3 Would you tidy my room if I gave you a pound?
4 If I could remember her name, I'd talk to her.
5 You'd feel better if you did more exercise.
6 If she wasn't ill, she'd go to class.
7 I'd ask somebody if I spoke Japanese.
8 What would you do if you won the lottery?

b 2 wouldn't go 3 would you do 4 'll see 5 rains 6 studied 7 'd lend 8 don't hurry up

6C *may* or *might*?

2 may/might fall **3** may/might like **4** may/might be **5** may/might buy **6** may/might go **7** may/might not come **8** may/might meet **9** may/might phone **10** may/might take **11** may/might be **12** may/might sell

6D *should* or *shouldn't*?

a **2** shouldn't spend **3** should turn down **4** should go **5** shouldn't wear **6** shouldn't leave **7** should get up **8** should practise **9** shouldn't play **10** should learn **11** should see **12** should be

7A present perfect + *for* and *since*

a **2** have … known, 've known, for ages **3** hasn't eaten since **4** 've been married since 1972 **5** have … had, 've had, since **6** hasn't worked for **7** 've been, since **8** has … worked, 's worked, for **9** have … been, 've played, since **10** hasn't rained for

7B present perfect or past simple?

a **1** was, 've seen, saw
2 Have … ever been, did, did … last, learnt
3 have … known, 've been, Did … meet, worked
4 've lived, lived, did … leave, retired
5 have … been, Didn't … go, didn't have **6** 's been, got

7C *used to*

2 He used to have **3** He didn't use to eat **4** He didn't use to wear **5** He used to smoke **6** He didn't use to play **7** She didn't use to have **8** She used to wear **9** She didn't use to play **10** She used to wear **11** She used to play **12** She didn't use to ride

7D passive

2 was made **3** are checked **4** was painted **5** are written **6** isn't locked **7** was bitten **8** was … sold **9** was worn **10** were built **11** was given **12** were stopped

8A *something, anything, nothing,* etc.

1 somewhere **2** somebody, nobody
3 anything, nowhere **4** nobody **5** something
6 anywhere **7** Somebody, anybody
8 anything, nothing, anything

8B *too, too much / many, enough,* etc.

2 a lot of **3** None **4** enough money **5** any **6** too **7** a little **8** too much **9** too many **10** too **11** safe enough **12** too much **13** too much **14** enough experience **15** too many **16** a few **17** too **18** very little **19** too much **20** too many

8C phrasal verbs

a **2** picking up **3** looking for **4** putting away **5** turning up **6** trying on **7** taking off **8** looking up **9** writing down **10** going back

c **2** ✔ **3** pay them back **4** take it back **5** ✔ **6** looking after them **7** call me back **8** ✔ **9** looking for it **10** ✔

8D *So do I / Neither do I*

3 Neither can **4** Neither am **5** So did **6** Neither did **7** So have **8** So was **9** Neither would **10** So am **11** So do **12** Neither am **13** So was **14** So did **15** Neither have **16** So do **17** So am **18** Neither will **19** So did **20** Neither can

9A past perfect

a **2** was, hadn't taken **3** wasn't working, hadn't turned it on
4 arrive, had gone out **5** 'd never flown, were
6 couldn't take, had disappeared **7** 'd just had, wasn't
8 ran, hadn't paid **9** arrived, hadn't brought
10 had to, 'd lost **11** could, 'd studied
12 was, 'd been

9B reported speech

a **2** that they had lost the match **3** that he had found the key **4** we spoke English **5** why she was angry **6** it was too crowded **7** the police were coming **8** when he would be home

b **2** It's my mother's car. **3** I'm staying in that hotel. **4** I've never been in love before. **5** I'll be back. **6** Do you smoke? **7** Did you see/Have you seen anything strange? **8** I can't swim!

9 revise and check

1 have you known
2 haven't finished
3 did you leave
4 didn't like
5 rain
6 Shall I help
7 does your brother work
8 painted
9 'll lend
10 Have you eaten
11 are you going
12 would you do
13 've ever seen
14 were you doing
15 remember
16 was built
17 flying
18 won't get
19 's already written
20 're going to visit / 're visiting

a Put the words in the right order to make questions.

1 name / your / is / what
What is your name ? Andrea.

2 how / you / are / today
___ ? Fine, thank you.

3 from / you / where / are
___ ? From Hungary.

4 live / you / where / do
___ ? In Budapest.

5 in / a / flat / you / do / live / or / a / house
___ ? In a flat.

6 parents / are / from / where / your
___ ? My mother's Hungarian and my father's French.

7 London / living / are / in / where / you
___ ? In a student residence near Oxford Street.

8 do / do / free / what / time / you / in / your
___ ? I read a lot and play volleyball.

9 studying / English / are / why / you
___ ? Because I want to travel and English helps.

10 school / subject / what / your / was / at / favourite
___ ? I really liked history.

11 watch / of / do / what / kind / films / you
___ ? I love science fictions films.

12 breakfast / have / did / what / you / for
___ ? Coffee and cereal.

13 you / do / what / are / this / weekend / going / to
___ ? I'm going to have dinner with some friends.

14 a / holiday / year / are / you / this / to / going / have
___ ? No, I have too much work!

15 last / you / did / television / watch / night
___ ? Yes, I watched the news and a film.

b **Test your memory.** Cover the questions. Look at the answers. Can you remember the questions?

c Ask a partner the questions.

● Complete the sentences with the present simple of the verbs in brackets.

1 I *do yoga* every morning. (do yoga)
2 My parents ______________. (not work)
3 What time ______________ lunch? (you / have)
4 I ______________ meat. (not eat)
5 When ______________ to go shopping? (you / want)
6 Jim ______________ television every morning. (watch)
7 My mother and I ______________ very well. (get on)
8 ______________ to the gym every day? (they / go)
9 Excuse me, ______________ here? (you / live)
10 She always ______________ a shower before breakfast. (have)
11 How much coffee ______________? (you / drink)
12 We ______________ at work. (not smoke)
13 He ______________ by plane very often. (not travel)
14 Why ______________ at 6.00? (Linda / get up)
15 They sometimes ______________ a taxi home. (get)
16 He ______________ work at 5.00. (finish)
17 What kind of music ______________? (you / listen to)
18 They ______________ away at the weekend. (not go)
19 She ______________ him very often. (not see)
20 Why ______________ me? (your father / not like)

20

16–20 Excellent. You can use the present simple very well.

11–15 Quite good, but check the rules in the Grammar Bank (Student's Book *p.126*) and look at the exercise again.

1–10 This is difficult for you. Read the rules in the Grammar Bank (Student's Book *p.126*). Then ask your teacher for another photocopy and do the exercise again at home.

a Complete the sentences with the present simple or present continuous of the verbs in brackets.

A What [1] *are* you *doing* (do)?
B I [2] ______________ (watch) this film. It's a musical.
A But you [3] ______________ (not like) musicals!
B I know, I usually [4] ______________ (hate) them. But this one is really good. [5] ______________ you ______________ (want) to watch it?
A Not right now, Susie's here and we [6] ______________ (study) for our English test.
B A test?
A Yes, we [7] ______________ (have) a test every Friday.

A [8] ______________ you ______________ (use) this computer now?
B No, the boss [9] ______________ (wait) for me in the other office. Why?
A Because I [10] ______________ (need) to use it.
B What's wrong with your computer?
A It [11] ______________ (not work) at the moment and I [12] ______________ (want) to send an e-mail.
B OK.

A How's your son?
B He's fine. He's at university now.
A Really? What [13] ______________ he ______________ (study)?
B Medicine. He's going to be a doctor. He [14] ______________ (do) his final exams at the moment. How's your daughter?
A She's fine too. She [15] ______________ (work) in a shop at the moment. She [16] ______________ (want) to go travelling this summer so she [17] ______________ (need) to earn some money.

b Practise reading the dialogues with a partner.

a Complete the definitions with *who*, *which*, or *where* and the correct form of a verb in the box.

keep	buy	put	light	borrow	wear	write	
live	~~build~~	write	answer	cut	cut	listen to	relax

1 A **builder** is a person *who* *builds* houses.
2 A **library** is a place ______ you ______ books.
3 A **hairdresser** is somebody ______ ______ your hair.
4 A **bank** is a place ______ you ______ your money.
5 **Matches** are things ______ you use to ______ a fire.
6 A **cap** is something ______ you ______ on your head.
7 A **receptionist** is a person ______ ______ the phone.
8 A **zoo** is a place ______ animals ______ .
9 A **composer** is somebody ______ ______ music.
10 An **iPod** is something ______ you ______ music with.
11 A **journalist** is a person ______ ______ for a newspaper or magazine.
12 A **bookshop** is a place ______ you ______ books.
13 **Scissors** are things ______ you use to ______ paper with.
14 **Lipstick** is something ______ you ______ on your lips.
15 A **health spa** is a place ______ you ______ and feel good.

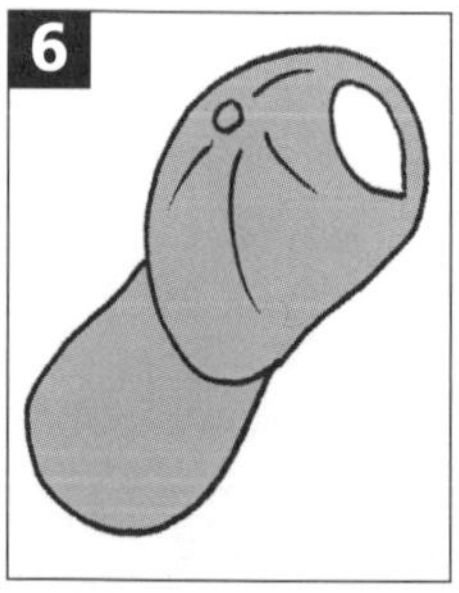

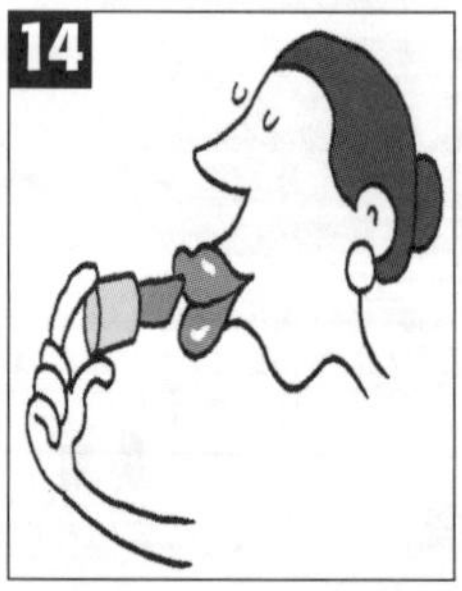

b **Test your memory.** Cover the definitions. Look at the pictures. Can you remember the definitions?

Complete the dialogues with the past simple of the verbs in brackets.

1 **A** Susan! You're back! How [1] _was_ (be) it? [2] ________ you ________ (have) a good time?
B No. It [3] ________ (be) awful.
A Why? What happened?
B We [4] ________ (stay) in a really boring hotel, and James [5] ________ (think) the city was dangerous at night so we [6] ________ (not go) out much in the evening.
A What [7] ________ you ________ (do) during the day? [8] ________ you ________ (go) sightseeing?
B Yes, we [9] ________ (see) all the famous things, but we [10] ________ (spend) a lot of money in restaurants. And James [11] ________ (buy) very expensive souvenirs for all his family! I [12] ________ (not buy) anything.

2 **A** Is this your first time in England?
B No, I [13] ________ (have) a holiday in Liverpool two years ago.
A Really? I know Liverpool! Where [14] ________ you ________ (stay)?
B We [15] ________ (stay) at a hotel near the train station. I can't remember the name. When [16] ________ (be) you in Liverpool?
A I [17] ________ (go) to university there.
B Really? What [18] ________ you ________ (study)?
A Hotel Management. But I [19] ________ ________ (not like) it much.
B Why [20] ________ you ________ (not like) it?
A It [21] ________ (be) boring. I [22] ________ (leave) after the first year.

3 **A** What's the problem?
B Somebody [23] ________ (take) my clothes and my bag when I [24] ________ (be) in the sea!
A When [25] ________ this ________ (happen)?
B Well, I [26] ________ (arrive) at the beach at nine o'clock this morning and I [27] ________ (go) for a swim at about ten.
A [28] ________ you ________ (see) the person take your bag?
B No. When I [29] ________ (come) out of the sea my bag [30] ________ (not be) there.
A [31] ________ you ________ (have) anything valuable in your bag?
B Yes! My mobile phone, my credit cards …
A Well, come with me to the police station, sir.

a Look at the pictures and write the sentences. Use the past simple and past continuous.

1 They *were playing* golf when it *started* to rain. (play, start)

2 His mobile ______________ when he ______________ . (ring, drive)

3 We ______________ the news when we ______________ in Corsica. (hear, sunbathe)

4 He ______________ at the tower when someone ______________ his bag. (look, take)

5 I ______________ a coffee when I ______________ her. (have, see)

6 She ______________ an accident when she ______________ to the shops. (see, walk)

b Complete the story with the past simple or past continuous of the verbs in brackets.

When Alex Jones [1] *arrived* at JFK International airport she [2] __________ (look) around but she [3] __________ (not see) anybody there to meet her. A lot of people [4] __________ (hold) cards with names on them, but they [5] __________ (not wait) for her. She [6] __________ (not know) what to do, but it [7] __________ (be) a beautiful, sunny day so she [8] __________ (decide) to go to the hotel on her own.

She [9] __________ (go) outside and [10] __________ (look) for a taxi. A lot of people [11] __________ (wait) so she [12] __________ (catch) the airport bus into New York. The bus [13] __________ (stop) in Manhattan, quite near her hotel, and she [14] __________ (get) off.

She [15] __________ (walk) into the hotel and [16] __________ (give) her name, Alexandra Jones. She [17] __________ (talk) to the hotel receptionist when suddenly a man [18] __________ (run) up to her. He [19] __________ (carry) a card which [20] __________ (say) 'Mr Jones'.

'Ms Jones? I'm terribly sorry! I [21] __________ (wait) for you at the airport but I [22] __________ (think) you [23] __________ (be) a man!'

'That's OK,' [24] __________ (say) Alex. 'It happens to me all the time!'

a Make questions using the present simple or past simple. Then circle the correct answer.

1 Who / write / *Pride and Prejudice*
Who wrote Pride and Prejudice ? Jane Austen / Charles Dickens

2 Where / come from / Manga comics
Where do Manga comics come from ? Japan / China

3 Where / die / John Lennon
_______________ ? Los Angeles / New York

4 Which country / win / the 2002 World Cup
_______________ ? Germany / Brazil

5 When / end / the Vietnam War
_______________ ? 1963 / 1975

6 Who / invent / the electric light bulb
_______________ ? Thomas Edison / Alexander Bell

7 Who / direct / the *Star Wars* films
_______________ ? Steven Spielberg / George Lucas

8 When / walk on the moon / the first man
_______________ ? 1969 / 1970

9 Where / live / polar bears
_______________ ? the North Pole / the South Pole

10 Which actor / play / Spiderman
_______________ ? Toby Maguire / Orlando Bloom

11 How many countries / belong to / the United Nations
_______________ ? 127 / 191

12 Which machine / invent / Marconi / in 1895
_______________ ? the television / the radio

13 Who / marry / Tom Cruise in 1990
_______________ ? Penelope Cruz / Nicole Kidman

14 When / Nelson Mandela / become president of South Africa
_______________ ? 1964 / 1994

15 Which country / have / a red, white, and blue flag
_______________ ? Russia / Germany

b **Test your memory.** Cover the questions. Look at the answers. Can you remember the questions?

a Match the sentence halves and underline the correct word, *so*, *because*, *but*, or *although*.

1 We wanted to visit the museum	*g*	**a** **so / but** I failed the exam.
2 I took off my jacket	☐	**b** **because / although** the water is very dirty.
3 They didn't have much money	☐	**c** **but / so** we didn't go to the park.
4 I didn't study	☐	**d** **because / although** it was very hot inside.
5 He's an intelligent student	☐	**e** **because / although** she was very tired.
6 They couldn't get on the bus	☐	**f** **so / but** the food wasn't very nice.
7 She didn't go to bed	☐	**g** **<u>but</u> / so** we couldn't find it on the map.
8 The beach looks beautiful	☐	**h** **although / because** it was too crowded.
9 It was a very expensive restaurant	☐	**i** **because / but** he's very lazy.
10 It was raining	☐	**j** **so / because** they didn't buy any souvenirs.

b Complete the story with *so*, *because*, *but*, or *although*.

One night in Rio

★ ★

Julian Black was a very famous singer, [1] *but* he was also very lonely. In the evenings, if he wasn't playing a concert, he was usually at home alone, watching television and reading. [2] __________ he knew a lot of people, he didn't have any friends. Everybody knew Julian Black the singer, [3] __________ nobody knew the real man.

It was November and Julian was on a world tour with his band. They were in Rio de Janeiro. After the concert, Julian felt very tired, [4] __________ he went back to his hotel. He was wearing his sunglasses and hat [5] __________ he didn't want people to recognize him. He got into the lift with a young woman. She looked at him [6] __________ she didn't say anything. The lift started going up.

A moment later the lift stopped. Julian and the woman waited, [7] __________ nothing happened. [8] __________ Julian pressed the emergency button [9] __________ it didn't work. Julian looked at the woman. 'What do we do now?' he asked. They were both very worried.

Julian took off his hat and sunglasses. They began to talk together while they were waiting. 'What's your name?' asked the woman. 'Julian,' answered Julian. He was surprised, [10] __________ she didn't know who he was. It was a nice feeling. They talked about books and television shows.

An hour later, the lift started working again. Julian got off at his floor. 'Maybe I can see you again?' he asked. 'That would be nice,' said the woman. Julian went back to his room. [11] __________ he was very tired, he couldn't sleep. He felt very happy. His life was about to change.

a What's going to happen? Write a [+] or [−] sentence with *be* + *going to* for pictures 1–8.

1 They *'re going to play tennis*.
2 It ______.
3 He ______.
4 He ______.
5 She ______.
6 He ______.
7 They ______.
8 They ______.

b Look at Luke's diary. Write the questions and the answers. Use the present continuous.

MONDAY
Dinner with Anna

TUESDAY
Dentist ☹ 11.30 a.m.

WEDNESDAY
Work 4.00–8.00 p.m.

THURSDAY
Meet Chris to study

FRIDAY
Final exam 10.00 a.m.
Party at Frank's! 8.00 p.m.

SATURDAY
Go shopping – buy Mum's present!!!

SUNDAY
Meet Mum at airport

1 When / go to the airport?
'When's he going to the airport?' 'He's going to the airport on Sunday.'

2 / meet Chris on Wednesday?
'Is he meeting Chris on Wednesday?' 'No, he isn't.'

3 What / do on Sunday?
______

4 What / do on Friday morning?
______

5 / have dinner with Anna on Monday?
______

6 When / go to the dentist?
______

7 What do / on Friday night?
______

8 What / do on Saturday?
______

9 When / work?
______

10 / meet Chris on Thursday?
______

Read sentences 1–12 and match them to predictions a–l. Complete the predictions with *will* / *won't*. Use the verbs in brackets.

1 'There's a new drinks machine in the office.' [*f*]
2 'She's going to live in France for a year.' [ ]
3 'I broke one of my mum's best glasses.' [ ]
4 'We're going to get tickets for the concert tonight.' [ ]
5 'The teacher isn't going to be here tomorrow.' [ ]
6 'My brother's going to sell his flat in London.' [ ]
7 'I'm going to stop smoking.' [ ]
8 'She's going to buy another mobile phone.' [ ]
9 'My son has a degree in Computer Science.' [ ]
10 'I'm going on a walking holiday in Scotland.' [ ]
11 'I'm taking my driving test tomorrow.' [ ]
12 'I'm going to see *Terminator 3* tonight.' [ ]

a 'They ______________ very expensive.' (be)
b 'Don't worry. You ______________.' (pass)
c 'She ______________ probably ______________ it, just like the other two.' (lose)
d 'She ______________ speaking French fluently.' (come back)
e 'You __________ it. It's very violent.' (not like)
f 'The coffee *won't be* very good.' (not be)
g 'You ______________ much healthier.' (feel)
h 'She ______________ furious.' (be)
i 'I'm sure he ______________ a good job.' (get)
j 'He ______________ a lot of money for it.' (get)
k 'It ______________ every day.' (rain)
l 'Great! So we ______________ the exam!' (not have)

● Complete the dialogues with *will* or *going to*. Use the infinitive of the verbs in brackets.

1 A Remember to turn off the lights when you leave.
B Don't worry, I [1]*won't forget* (not forget).

2 A What are Mike's plans for the summer?
B Well, first he [2]__________ (stay) with a friend in Italy, and then he [3]__________ (travel) round France and Spain.

3 A Here's my phone number.
B Thanks. I [4]__________ (call) you tomorrow morning.

4 A How much is this sweater?
B 24.99.
A Fine. I [5]__________ (take) it.

5 A What [6]__________ you __________ (do) tonight?
B I [7]__________ (stay) at home. I have to study.

6 A Have you decided what to do on Saturday night?
B Yes, we have tickets for the theatre and after that we [8]__________ (have) dinner at that new Italian restaurant.

7 A I've had a terrible day today.
B Sit down, I [9]__________ (make) you a cup of tea.

8 A My parents are away this weekend, so I [10]__________ (have) a party.
B Great! I [11]__________ (bring) some food.

9 A Would you like fruit juice or mineral water?
B I [12]________ (have) an orange juice please.

10 A [13]__________ you __________ (stay) here tonight?
B No, I [14]__________ (catch) the last train home. I have a return ticket.

11 A I [15]__________ (pay) for the coffees.
B No, please. I [16]__________ (pay) this time. It's my turn.

12 A I [17]__________ (paint) my flat at the weekend.
B I [18]__________ (help) you if you like.

● Complete the dialogues with the correct form of the verbs in brackets: present simple, present continuous, past simple, past continuous, *going to* + infinitive, *will* / *won't* + infinitive.

1 A They *don't answer* (not answer) the phone after six o'clock. The office is closed.
B OK, I *'ll call* (call) them tomorrow.

2 A __________ your brother __________ (have) a girlfriend?
B Yes, he does. She's French.

3 A Our goalkeeper __________ (not play) very well at the moment.
B That's unusual. He's usually good.

4 A Who __________ (write) the music for the *Star Wars* films?
B I have no idea!

5 A The teacher __________ (give) us an exam tomorrow.
B Are you sure? Isn't it next week?

6 A What __________ you __________ (do)?
B I'm finishing my homework.

7 A How __________ they __________ (get) home last night?
B They __________ (take) a taxi.

8 A Why couldn't you sleep?
B Because the neighbours __________ (argue) again.

9 A What __________ you __________ (do) when I phoned you?
B I was in the shower.

10 A What time __________ he usually __________ (get) to work?
B About 9.30.

11 A Did you hear about the elections?
B Yes, I heard it on the news when I __________ (drive) home.

12 A What __________ you __________ (do)?
B I work for a German software company.

13 A Doctor, I'm a bit nervous.
B Don't worry, this __________ (not hurt).

14 A Hi, can you talk now?
B Yes, I __________ (not work) at the moment.

15 A What __________ you __________ (do) this afternoon?
B Nothing. Why?
A __________ you __________ (want) to go to the swimming pool?

16 A When __________ we __________ (study) the present perfect?
B It's the next lesson in the book.

17 A My plane is arriving at one o'clock in the afternoon.
B Fine, we __________ (meet) you at the airport.

18 A Last October we __________ (go) to Italy.
B Really, did you like it?

19 A What time __________ you __________ (go) to bed last night?
B Not until 2.00!

20 A How was your weekend?
B It was great. This time yesterday I __________ (walk) on the beach.

☐ **20**

16–20 Excellent. You can use the past, present, and future very well.

11–15 Quite good, but check the rules in the Grammar Bank (Student's Book *p.130*) and look at the exercise again.

1–10 This is difficult for you. Read the rules in the Grammar Bank (Student's Book *p.130*). Then ask your teacher for another photocopy and do the exercise again at home.

Grammar **present perfect or past simple?**

a Complete the chart.

verb	past	past participle
be	*was / were*	*been*
eat	________	________
fly	________	________
hear	________	________
lose	________	________
read	________	________
see	________	________
win	________	________
work	________	________
write	________	________

b Write sentences in the present perfect.

1 you / ever **fly** / in a helicopter
Have you ever flown in a helicopter?

2 she / never **eat** / octopus
________________________________.

3 they / ever **be** / late for work
________________________________?

4 we / never **see** / a Tarantino film
________________________________.

5 she / **write** / more than ten mystery novels
________________________________.

6 I / not **read** / *The Lord of the Rings*
________________________________.

7 you / ever **work** / in a clothes shop
________________________________?

8 he / **win** / three gold medals
________________________________.

9 They / not **lose** / a match this year
________________________________.

10 I / **hear** / three of their albums
________________________________.

c Complete the dialogues with the correct form of the verb: present perfect or past simple.

1

A 1 *Have* you *ever heard* (ever / hear) the group The Darkness?

B No, I 2 ________ . What kind of music do they play?

A Rock music. I 3 ________ (see) them in concert last night.

B 4 ________ (be) it a good concert?

A Yes, I really 5 ________ (like) it.

2

A 6 ________ you ________ (ever / lose) your car keys?

B Yes, I 7 ________ .

A When 8 ________ that ________ (happen)?

B In Portugal. I 9 ________ (be) there on holiday.

A What 10 ________ you ________ (do)?

B I 11 ________ (phone) the car hire company. But they 12 ________ (make) me pay €100 for the new keys.

a Write questions and answers for the picture. Use present perfect + *yet* / *already*.

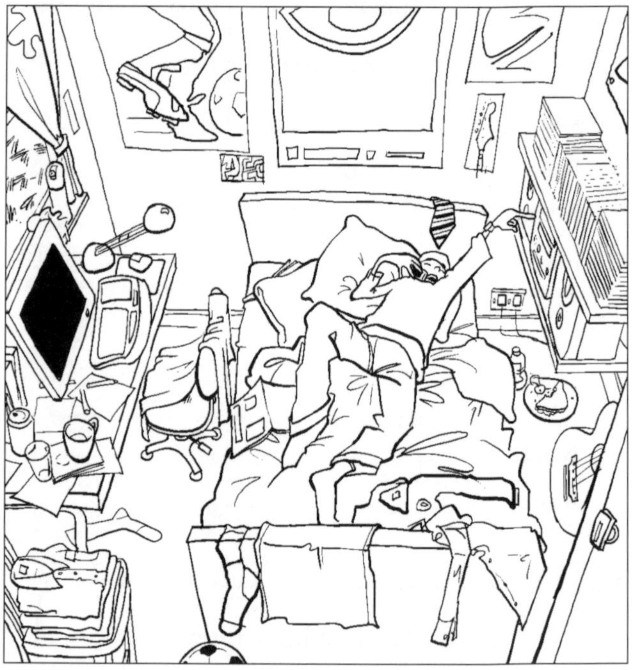

1 tidy / his room
Has he tidied his room yet?
No, he hasn't.

2 wash / his clothes
Has he washed his clothes yet?
Yes, he's already done it.

3 eat / the sandwich
______________________________?
______________________________.

4 turn off / the computer
______________________________?
______________________________.

5 drink / his coffee
______________________________?
______________________________.

6 tidy / his desk
______________________________?
______________________________.

7 put away / his CDs
______________________________?
______________________________.

8 make / his bed
______________________________?
______________________________.

9 put away / his clothes
______________________________?
______________________________.

10 finish / talking on the phone
______________________________?
______________________________.

b Write sentences for the pictures. Use *just* + present perfect.

They / have / argument
They've just had an argument.

He / be on holiday
____
______________________________.

She / fail an exam
____
______________________________.

She / miss her train
____
______________________________.

No, thanks. We / have lunch
____
______________________________.

He / wake up
____
______________________________.

a Write comparative sentences for the pictures using adjectives and adverbs.

I'm / tall / my brother

I'm taller than my brother.

She's / happy / her husband

______________________________.

Men drive / fast / women

______________________________.

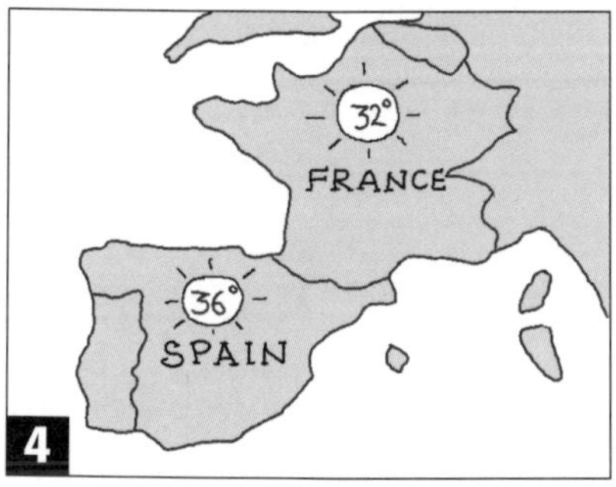

Spain is / hot / France

______________________________.

The sandwiches are / expensive / the cakes

______________________________.

Tom works / slowly / Greg

______________________________.

Laura speaks Italian / good / Jake

______________________________.

Football is / popular / tennis

______________________________.

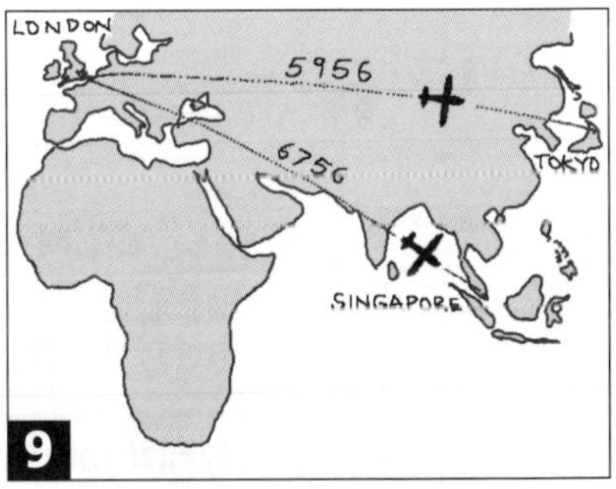

Singapore is / far / Tokyo

______________________________.

b Rewrite the sentences from **a** using *as … as*.

1 My brother *isn't as tall as me*.
2 Her husband ______________________.
3 Women ______________________.
4 France ______________________.
5 The cakes ______________________.
6 Tom ______________________.
7 Jake ______________________.
8 Tennis ______________________.
9 Tokyo ______________________.

a Write the questions with the superlative form of the adjective.

1 What / difficult / language you / learn
What's the most difficult language you've ever learnt?

2 Who / generous / person you / meet
____?

3 What / good / restaurant you / be to
____?

4 What / cheap / hotel you / stay in
____?

5 What / cold / place you / visit
____?

6 What / long / journey you / make
____?

7 What / delicious / food you / eat
____?

8 Where / dangerous / place you / be to
____?

9 What / exciting / book you / read
____?

10 Where / far / you / be on holiday
____?

b Work with a partner. Ask and answer the questions in **a**.

c Are these sentences right (✓) or wrong (✗)? Correct the wrong sentences.

1 She is the ~~older~~ *oldest* person I have ever met. ✗

2 This is the most beautiful place in the country.

3 My last job was the worse job I've ever had.

4 February is the shortest month of the year.

5 Cricket is the most boring sport I have ever seen.

6 The service in this restaurant is the better in the city.

7 My first English teacher was the more patient person I have ever met.

8 You're sitting in most comfortable chair.

9 We hired the expensivest car on our holiday.

10 He was the funniest actor in the play.

a Complete the sentences with *to* + a verb.

not lose	~~pass~~	be	see	take photos	shut	build	sell	do	not tell

1 It's difficult *to pass* your driving test.
2 Promise __________ our secret to anyone.
3 It was really nice __________ you again.
4 We've decided __________ our house.
5 Who forgot __________ the door?
6 It's important __________ your ticket. It has your seat number on it.
7 Did you remember __________ your homework?
8 They're planning __________ a garage next to their house.
9 Don't pretend __________ happy if you aren't.
10 Is it possible __________ in here?

b Why did she go there? Write sentences with *to* + a phrase from the box.

buy some bread	send some e-mails	go for a walk	do some exercise	book tickets
get some money	buy some new clothes	~~borrow a book~~	get some petrol	

1 *She went to the library to borrow a book*.
2 __________________________.
3 __________________________.
4 __________________________.
5 __________________________.
6 __________________________.
7 __________________________.
8 __________________________.
9 __________________________.

Grammar **infinitive or verb + *-ing*?**

Complete the sentences with the infinitive or verb + *-ing*.

1 I can't promise *to be* (be) on time.

2 *Swimming* (swim) is better exercise than running.

3 Would you like ______________ (come) to my party?

4 Do you mind ______________ (not talk) so loudly?

5 It was very interesting ______________ (see) my old school again.

6 He worked at weekends ______________ (earn) more money.

7 She likes ______________ and ______________ (relax, not do) anything on Sundays.

8 We were unhappy with the service so the restaurant offered ______________ (give) us a free dinner.

9 Is it difficult ______________ (learn) Japanese?

10 He's very competitive. He thinks ______________ (win) is the most important thing.

11 She tried ______________ (not hit) the man but she was driving too fast.

12 They spent all night ______________ (drink) coffee and studying.

13 Do you need ______________ (go) to the bathroom?

14 They drove without ______________ (stop) for fourteen hours.

15 We're thinking of ______________ (go) abroad for our holiday next year.

16 I'm very happy ______________ (be) here again.

17 I decided ______________ (go) camping because I didn't have much money.

18 ______________ (eat) cakes and junk food will make you fat.

19 He pretended ______________ (not understand) the police officer.

20 Are you good at ______________ (remember) people's names?

20

16–20 Excellent. You can use the infinitive and verb + *-ing* very well.

11–15 Quite good, but check the rules in the Grammar Bank (Student's Book *p.134*) and look at the exercise again.

1–10 This is difficult for you. Read the rules in the Grammar Bank (Student's Book *p.134*). Then ask your teacher for another photocopy and do the exercise again at home.

a Complete the sentences with *have to* / *mustn't* / *don't have to* + a verb from the box.

come pay smoke ~~touch~~ drive wear spend park play be turn off wear

1 You *mustn't touch* this door.

2 Children ______________________.

3 You ______________________ in here.

4 You ______________________ in one direction.

5 You ______________________ a jacket.

6 You ______________________ to class on Saturdays.

7 You ______________________ any money now.

8 You ______________________ sports shoes in here.

9 You ______________________ your car here.

10 You ______________________ over 18 to see this film.

11 You ______________________ your computer.

12 You ______________________ football here at night.

b **Test your memory.** Cover the sentences. Look at the signs and remember the sentences.

a Complete the sentences with a preposition of movement.

out of ~~over~~ along up down across through into under towards round

1

2

3

4

5

6

7

8
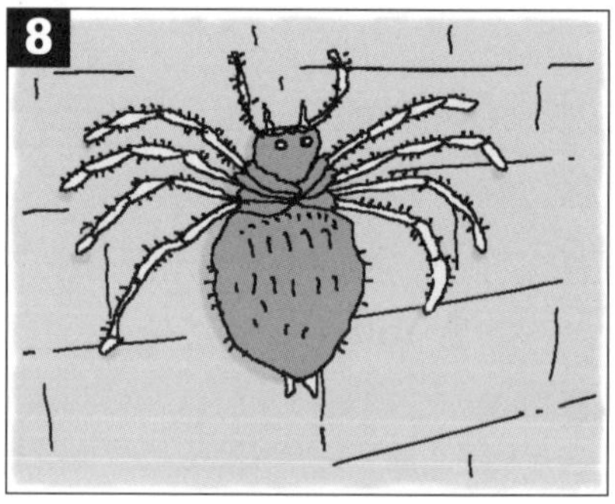

9

10

11

1 The police helicopter flew *over* the houses.
2 The rock star threw a television __________ the window.
3 A bird flew __________ the bridge.
4 They danced __________ the fire.
5 He walked __________ the saloon.
6 The cat ran __________ the wall.
7 The motorway goes __________ that village.
8 A spider is climbing __________ the wall.
9 He jumped __________ the swimming pool.
10 The policemen fell __________ the stairs.
11 The dog swam __________ the river.

b **Test your memory.** Cover the sentences. Look at the pictures and remember the sentences.

● Complete the stories with the correct form of the verbs in brackets.

If I [1] *talk* to you now, I [2] ________ the bus. (talk, miss)

If I [3] ________ the bus, I [4] ________ late for work. (miss, be)

If I [5] ________ late for work, my boss [6] ________ angry with me. (be, be)

If my boss [7] ________ angry with me, I [8] ________ my job. (be, lose)

If I [9] ________ you £1,000, you [10] ________ a new guitar. (lend, buy)

If you [11] ________ a new guitar, you [12] ________ a band. (buy, start)

If you [13] ________ a band, you [14] ________ a job. (start, never get)

If you [15] ________ a job, you [16] ________ me the money back. (not get, never pay)

If I [17] ________ you with your homework, you [18] ________ it yourself. (help, not do)

If you [19] ________ it yourself, you [20] ________ anything. (not do, not learn)

If you [21] ________ anything, you [22] ________ your exams. (not learn, not pass)

If you [23] ________ your exams, you [24] ________ to university. (not pass, not go)

a Write second conditional sentences for the pictures.

1 If I / have more money, I / buy that dress
If I had more money, I'd buy that dress.

2 I / not do that if I / be you
________________________________.

3 / you tidy my room if I / give you a pound
________________________________?

4 If I / can remember her name, I / talk to her
________________________________.

5 You / feel better if you / do more exercise
________________________________.

6 If she / not be ill, she / go to class
________________________________.

7 I / ask somebody if I / speak Japanese
________________________________.

8 What / you do if you / win the lottery
________________________________?

b First or second conditional? Complete the sentences with the correct form of the verb.

1 I'll be surprised if he *pays* (pay) you back tomorrow.
2 If I were you, I __________ (not go) to England in the winter.
3 What __________ (you / do) if you saw a snake in your bed?
4 If I don't see you this evening, I __________ (see) you on Friday.
5 Where will we go tomorrow if it __________ (rain)?
6 She'd pass her exams if she __________ (study) harder.
7 If you asked her nicely, she __________ (lend) you the money.
8 If you __________ (not hurry up), we'll miss the train.

● Complete the dialogues with *may* or *might* + a verb.

phone be (x2) sell go meet not come like ~~not have~~ take buy fall

1 A Where are you going for your holiday?
B I don't know. I'm really busy at work so I *might not have* a holiday this year.

2 A Look, Mummy, I can ride a bicycle without using my hands!
B Oh, be careful! You ________________!

3 A What's this? It looks very strange.
B It's a special dish from my country. Try it, you ________________ it.

4 A Can I speak to Jack Linden, please?
B I'm sorry, he's in a meeting until 4.00. He ________________ free after that. I'll just check with his diary.

5 A I think I ________________ this T-shirt.
B Don't be silly, it's too small for you.

6 A Do you have any plans for this weekend?
B We're not sure yet. We ________________ to the mountains.

7 A I ________________ to class tomorrow. I think I'll have to work late.
B OK, but don't forget to do the homework.

8 A Are you going to be in this evening?
B I'm not sure. I ________________ some friends for a drink.

9 A Are you going to send them an e-mail?
B No, I think I ________________ them.

10 A How are you getting home tonight?
B It depends. If it's raining we ________________ a taxi.

11 A Let's go to that nice new restaurant.
B Oh, no. My ex-girlfriend ________________ there! It's her favourite place to have dinner.

12 A What are you going to do with your old car?
B I don't know. I ________________ it, but I probably won't get much money for it.

a Write sentences giving advice for the people in the pictures. Use *should* / *shouldn't* + a verb.

play leave ~~buy~~ turn down see go wear spend be learn get up practise

1 He *should buy* a new car.
2 She ________________ so long on the telephone.
3 She ________________ the volume.
4 He ________________ to the hairdresser's.
5 He ________________ that shirt.
6 They ________________ their bags on the ground.
7 She ________________ earlier.
8 You ________________ your English more.
9 He ________________ games on his computer all day.
10 He ________________ to cook.
11 You ________________ this film. You'd love it!
12 She ________________ careful with her umbrella.

b **Test your memory.** Cover the sentences. Look at the pictures and remember the sentences.

a Complete the sentences with the present perfect + *for* or *since* if necessary.

1 A How long *have* you *lived* here? (live)
B We *'ve lived* here *since* 2001. (live)

2 A How long __________ they __________ each other? (know)
B They __________ each other __________ ages. (know)

3 She ________________ three o'clock. (not eat)

4 They ________________ 1972. (be married)

5 A How long __________ you __________ your kitten? (have)
B I __________ it __________ April 4th. It was a birthday present. (have)

6 He ________________ three months. (not work)

7 They __________ at school eight o'clock. (be)

8 A How long __________ she __________ in Paris? (work)
B She __________ there __________ two years. (work)

9 A How long __________ you __________ in this team? (be)
B I __________ for Arsenal __________ I was a teenager. (play)

10 It ________________ a long time. (not rain)

b **Test your memory.** Cover the sentences. Look at the pictures. Can you remember the sentences?

a Complete the dialogues with the present perfect or past simple.

1 A How long _have_ you _been_ (be) a *Star Wars* fan?
B Since I ______________ (be) five. I ______________ (see) all the films many times. In fact I ______________ (see) *Phantom Menace* on DVD last week.

2 A ______________ you ______________ (ever be) to the UK?
B Yes, I ______________ (do) a language course in Oxford two years ago.
A Really? How long ______________ the course ______________ (last)?
B A month. I ______________ (learn) a lot of English there.

3 A How long ______________ you ______________ (know) Bill?
B We ______________ (be) friends for a long time. For more than twenty years.
A ______________ you ______________ (meet) at school?
B No, we ______________ (work) at the same restaurant in 1985.

4 A Where do your parents live?
B They ______________ (live) in Cheltenham since last year. But before that they ______________ (live) in London.
A Why ______________ they ______________ (leave) London?
B Because my dad ______________ (retire).

5 A You look tired. How long ______________ you ______________ (be) at work today?
B Since eight o'clock this morning.
A ______________ you ______________ (not go) for lunch with the others?
B No, I ______________(not have) time.

6 A Is your sister married?
B Yes, she ______________ (be) married for ages. About ten years. She ______________ (get) married when she was only 18.

b Practise reading the dialogues with a partner.

● Look at how Katie and Tony have changed. Write six sentences for each person about what they were like in the past.

1 *He used to wear* jeans.

2 ______________________ long hair.

3 ______________________ meat.

4 ______________________ a tie.

5 ______________________ ten cigarettes a day.

6 ______________________ tennis.

7 ______________________ a tattoo.

8 ______________________ glasses.

9 ______________________ the guitar.

10 ______________________ dresses.

11 ______________________ the piano.

12 ______________________ a motorbike.

a Look at the pictures. Complete the sentences with present or past passive.

1 How _is_ it _pronounced_? (pronounce)

2 It's a very old film. It __________ __________ in 1942. (made)

3 Nowadays all bags ____________________ at airports. (check)

4 This ____________________ by Picasso. (paint)

5 All the instructions ____________________ in Japanese! (write)

6 This door ____________________ at night. It's the emergency exit. (not lock)

7 A man ____________________ by a shark yesterday. (bite)

8 When __________ the house __________? (sell)

9 This dress ____________________ by Marilyn Monroe. (wear)

10 The Pyramids ____________________ nearly 5,000 years ago. (build)

11 I ____________________ it for my birthday. (give)

12 I forgot to turn my lights on and we ____________________ by the police. (stop)

b **Test your memory.** Cover the sentences. Look at the pictures. Can you remember the sentences?

● Complete the dialogues with a word from the box.

somewhere	nowhere	somebody	anybody	nobody	something	anything
~~anywhere~~	nobody	anything	somebody	anywhere	nothing	anything

1 **A** Are you going *anywhere* this summer?
B We haven't decided yet. But my wife wants to go ______________ nice and hot.

2 **A** Why are you looking out of the window?
B I think there's ______________ in the house opposite.
A But ______________ has lived there for years!
B I know, that's why I'm looking.

3 **A** I'm so bored. There isn't ______________ to do in this town!
B That's not true. There are lots of things to do.
A But there's ______________ for young people to go.

4 **A** I phoned your office at 2.00 today but ______________ answered.
B Sorry. We were all at lunch.

5 **A** I'm hungry, I need ______________ to eat.
B Well, there's food in the fridge.

6 **A** Where did you go last night?
B I didn't go ______________. I was too tired. I stayed in.

7 **A** ______________ told me that their new album is very good.
B Really? I don't know ______________ who likes it.

8 **A** Did you buy ______________ this afternoon?
B No, ______________. I didn't see ______________ I liked.

● Choose the correct word or phrase for each sentence. ~~Cross out~~ the wrong form.

1 How **much** / ~~**many**~~ milk do you drink?

2 He knows **a lot of** / **lot of** important people in the company.

3 'How much exercise do you do?' '**None** / **Any**.'

4 I think I have **enough money** / **money enough** to pay for this.

5 I don't drink **no** / **any** alcohol.

6 You should be friendly, but not **too** / **too much** friendly.

7 Could I have **a little** / **a few** water, please?

8 She spends **too many** / **too much** on shoes.

9 There were **too many** / **too much** mosquitoes outside.

10 I didn't like my last teacher. She was **too much** / **too** impatient with me.

11 It isn't **safe enough** / **enough safe** to walk here at night.

12 I can't hear you. The children are making **too many** / **too much** noise.

13 Try not to spend **too many** / **too much** time on the homework.

14 You would get the job if you had **enough experience** / **experience enough**.

15 I have **too many** / **too much** clothes. I can't decide what to wear.

16 We're buying **a few** / **a little** things for our new flat.

17 We stopped driving because it was **too** / **enough** foggy.

18 I'm going to have **very little** / **very few** free time this weekend.

19 There's **too many** / **too much** pollution in this city.

20 He buys **too many** / **too much** books. He'll never read them all.

a What are the people doing? Complete the sentences with phrasal verbs.

~~fill~~	go	look	write	try	look	put	turn	take	pick
off	down	~~in~~	up	up	up	back	for	on	away

1 She's *filling in* a form.
2 He's ________________ her books.
3 He's ________________ his pen.
4 She's ________________ the glasses.
5 She's ________________ the volume.
6 He's ________________ his new suit.
7 They're ________________ their boots.
8 She's ________________ a new word.
9 They're ________________ the questions.
10 She's ________________ to Italy.

b **Test your memory.** Cover the sentences. Look at the pictures and remember the sentences.

c Are the highlighted phrases right ✓ or wrong ✗? Correct the wrong phrases.

1 Here's the form. Please fill in it. ✗
2 I'm waiting for an important call on my mobile, so I can't turn it off.
3 When are you going to pay back them?
4 This mobile doesn't work. I'm going to take back it to the shop.
5 I know these are the right translations because I looked them up.
6 They're my sister's children. I'm looking them after while she's on holiday.
7 I'm in class at the moment, can you call back me?
8 He never throws anything away.
9 She lost her purse and she spent hours looking it for.
10 He gets on with her very well.

● Complete the dialogues.

1 A I don't like our new boss much.
B *Neither do* I. She's very unfriendly.

2 A I'd like a drink.
B *So would* I. I'm really thirsty.

3 A I can't swim.
B ______________ I. Perhaps we should learn.

4 A I'm not sure where we are.
B ______________ I. Let's ask someone.

5 A I passed the test!
B ______________ I! I got 92%.

6 A She didn't send any postcards.
B ______________ I, but I sent a few e-mails.

7 A Mark has finished university.
B ______________ I. We'll have to start looking for a job now!

8 A She was born in 1975.
B Really? ______________ I.

9 A That shirt's too expensive. I wouldn't buy it.
B ______________ I. It's a horrible colour, too.

10 A I'm going to catch the last bus.
B ______________ I.

11 A I have to go to work tomorrow.
B ______________ I. I hate working on Saturdays.

12 A He's not a very hard-working student.
B ______________ I! I prefer seeing my friends.

13 A I was hoping to go the party.
B ______________ I, but I was ill and I couldn't go.

14 A They got married in 1998.
B ______________ I. But I got divorced a year later.

15 A We haven't seen the Eiffel Tower yet.
B ______________ I. I only arrived in Paris yesterday.

16 A I want to go to the beach.
B ______________ I. It's a beautiful day.

17 A He's going to study in England.
B ______________ I. Which city is he going to?

18 A I won't lend him any money.
B ______________ I. He never pays it back.

19 A I threw away my notes.
B ______________ I. I didn't think we needed them.

20 A I can't give up coffee.
B ______________ I. I have to have a cup to wake me up in the morning.

a Look at the pictures and complete the sentences. Use the past simple and the past perfect.

1 When they *got* (get) to the station the train *had already left* (already leave).

2 She __________ (be) very cold because she __________ (not take) her coat.

3 The printer __________ (not work) because he __________ (not turn it on).

4 The fire engine __________ (arrive) after the fire __________ (go out).

5 They __________ (never fly) before and they __________ (be) very nervous.

6 I __________ (not can) take a photo of the crocodile because it __________ (disappear) into the water.

7 She __________ (just have) dinner so she __________ (not be) hungry.

8 The waiter __________ (run) after her because she __________ (not pay) the bill.

9 When he __________ (arrive) at the pool he realized he __________ (not bring) his swimsuit.

10 She __________ (have to) pay again because she __________ (lose) her ticket.

11 They __________ (can) speak French because they __________ (study) it at school.

12 She __________ (be) tired because she __________ (be) in the queue all night.

b **Test your memory.** Cover the sentences. Look at the pictures and remember the sentences.

a Change the direct speech to reported speech.

1 She asked if *she was at the right party* .
2 He told me ________________________ .
3 He said ________________________ .
4 He asked us if ________________________ .
5 He asked her ________________________ .
6 She said ________________________ .
7 He told him ________________________ .
8 She asked him ________________________ .

b Change the reported speech to direct speech.

1 He asked him if he could turn off his mobile.
' *Can you turn off your mobile?* '

2 He told them it was his mother's car.
' ________________________ '

3 She said that she was staying in that hotel.
' ________________________ '

4 He told her he had never been in love before.
' ________________________ '

5 He said that he would be back.
' ________________________ '

6 He asked her if she smoked.
' ________________________ '

7 They asked me if I had seen anything strange.
' ________________________ '

8 He said that he couldn't swim.
' ________________________ '

Complete the sentences with the correct form of the verb in brackets.

1 A How long __________ you __________ each other? (**know**)
B Since 2001. We met at university.

2 A Can I read your newspaper?
B Sorry. I __________ it yet. (**not finish**)

3 A When __________ you __________ university? (**leave**)
B Last year.

4 A I __________ the film. (**not like**)
B Neither did I.

5 A Do you think the weather will be good tomorrow?
B I'm not sure. I think it might __________. (**rain**)

6 A I have some English homework to do.
B __________ I__________ you? (**help**)

7 A Who __________ your brother __________ for? (**work**)
B For a computer software company. He's a sales manager.

8 A That's a beautiful picture. Who __________ it? (**paint**)
B I did.

9 A My mobile isn't working. I don't know why.
B Here! I __________ you mine. (**lend**)

10 A __________ you __________ in that restaurant? (**eat**)
B Only once but I wouldn't recommend it.

11 A Where __________ you __________ tonight? (**go**)
B I'm not sure. I might see a film.

12 A What __________ you __________ if you lost your job? (**do**)
B I don't know. I hope it doesn't happen!

13 A What's the best film you __________ ever __________? (**see**)
B I can't think of just one - there are five or six.

14 A What __________ you __________ when the boss came into your office? (**do**)
B Talking to my girlfriend on the phone.

15 A Don't forget it's Mum's birthday tomorrow.
B Thanks. I must __________ to phone her in the morning. (**remember**)

16 A That's a beautiful building over there.
B Yes, it __________ in the eighteenth century. (**build**)

17 A Why don't your parents travel more often?
B Because my father is very afraid of __________. (**fly**)

18 A There's no need to run. We're not late. The concert starts at 8.00.
B But if we don't get there early, we __________ a good seat. (**not get**)

19 A What does your wife do?
B She's a writer. She __________ already __________ three novels and she's writing a book of short stories. (**write**)

20 A Have you got any plans for next summer?
B Yes, we __________ my cousin in the Czech Republic. (**visit**)

☐ **20**

18–20 Excellent. You understand the verb tenses presented in *New English File Pre-intermediate* very well.

13–17 Quite good, but check the rules in the Grammar Bank (Student's Book *p.122*) for any questions that you got wrong.

0–12 This is difficult for you. Read the rules in the Grammar Bank (Student's Book *p.122*). Then ask your teacher for another photocopy and do the exercise again at home.

Tips for using Communicative activities

- We have suggested the ideal number of copies for each activity. However, you can often manage with fewer, e.g. one copy per pair instead of one per student.
- When SS are working in pairs, if possible get them to sit face to face. This will encourage them to really talk to each other and also means they can't see each other's sheet.
- If your class doesn't divide into pairs or groups, take part yourself, get two SS to share one role, or get one SS to monitor, help and correct.
- If some SS finish early, they can swap roles and do the activity again, or you could get them to write some of the sentences from the activity.

1A Student profile

A pairwork activity

SS interview each other and complete a form for their partner. The forms revise question forms and provide the teacher with useful information about SS. Copy one sheet per person.

LANGUAGE	*What's your first name? What do you do? Why are you learning English?*

- Give each student one copy. Focus on the questions. Give SS in pairs a few minutes to decide what each question should be. Check answers. Model and drill the questions for SS to copy the rhythm.

 1 What's your first name?
 2 What's your surname?
 3 Where are you from?
 4 Where do you live?
 5 What do you do?
 6 Where were you born?
 7 When were you born?
 8 What languages do you speak?
 9 What do you do (like doing) in your free time?
 10 Why are you learning English?

- Demonstrate the activity by getting SS to ask you the first two questions. Encourage them to ask you to spell your name and surname. Put SS in pairs to interview each other and write the information in the forms. Make sure they cover the questions and ask them from memory.
- You could collect in the forms for your own reference.

1B Who's their ideal partner?

A pairwork speaking activity

SS describe people to each other and try to match them to their 'ideal partners'. Copy one sheet per pair and cut into **A** and **B**.

LANGUAGE	*He's thirty and he's a writer. He's tall and dark.*

- Put SS into pairs and give out the sheets. Sit **A** and **B** so they can't see each other's sheet. Explain to SS that the **A**s have information about five men, and the **B**s about five women. They must try to find an ideal partner for each man/woman. Give SS a few minutes to read their information.
- Demonstrate the activity by talking about **A**s first man (Richard) and tell the **B**s to decide which woman would suit him best. Stop after his name, age, and job, and tell the **B**s to eliminate any women they think are not suitable. Continue, encouraging **B**s to ask questions if necessary. SS should say *He likes … He doesn't like …* according to the face symbols.
- **B**s should decide that his 'ideal partner' is Gill. Get **A**s to write *Gill* on Richard's card, and **B**s write *Richard* on Gill's.
- SS continue in their pairs. Monitor, encouraging SS to check information. When SS have finished, let them compare their sheets, and check answers.

Ideal couples Richard and Gill; Mark and Maria; David and Rebecca; Andy and Sara; Ian and Martina

1C At an art gallery

A pairwork information gap activity.

SS describe their pictures to each other to find ten differences between them. Copy one sheet per pair and cut into A and B.

LANGUAGE	*On the left there's a painting of a woman. She's smiling.* *In my picture she isn't smiling. She looks sad.* prepositions of place parts of the body

- Pre-teach/revise any words you think SS don't know or may have forgotten, e.g. *statue, attendant, sculpture, audioguide.* Also pre-teach expressions they will need, e.g. *on the left etc.*
- Put SS into pairs and give out the sheets. Sit **A** and **B** so they can't see each other's sheet. Focus on the instructions and explain that they both have a picture of the same art gallery but there are ten differences between the two pictures.
- SS describe their pictures to each other and find and circle the differences. Demonstrate being both **A** and **B**, e.g.:

 A *In my picture, there's a painting of a chair.*
 B *In my picture, there's a chair and a cat is sitting on the chair.*

- SS continue in pairs to find nine more differences. Check the differences orally with the class, writing up any difficult sentences for SS to copy.

1 In **A** there's a painting of a woman looking sad. In **B** the woman is smiling.
2 In **A** a man and a woman with a child are looking at a picture. In **B** the child is sitting on the floor crying.
3 In **A** there's a painting of a chair. In **B** a cat is sitting on the chair.
4 In **A** a man and woman are sitting down and talking. In **B** they're looking at a guidebook.
5 In **A** a student is listening to an audioguide. In **B** the student doesn't have an audioguide.
6 In **A** a man is sitting on a seat reading a paper. In **B** a man is sitting on a seat sending a text.
7 In **A** the girl in jeans has short hair. In **B** the girl in jeans has long hair.
8 In **A** a man is holding a camera. In **B** the man is taking a photo.
9 In **A** there's a statue with no right arm. In **B** there's a statue with no left arm.
10 In **A** a woman is touching a sculpture. In **B** the woman is looking at the sculpture.

1 D What's the word?

A group card game

SS practise giving definitions using relative pronouns. Copy and cut up one set of cards per four SS.

LANGUAGE *It's a thing which/person who…, etc.*
It's a kind of… It's like …
You do it when …

- If necessary, revise language for giving definitions before you start. Put SS in small groups. Give each group a set of cards face down or in an envelope.
- Demonstrate the activity. Pick up a card and describe the word/phrase until SS guess it. Insist they say the exact word/phrase on the card with correct pronunciation before showing them the card.
- SS play the game, taking turns to take a card and define the word. Tell SS they **must not use the word on the card**. The first student in the group who says the word correctly gets the card. The winner is the student with the most cards.

Non-cut alternative Copy one sheet per pair of SS, and cut in half. Put SS into pairs and give them one half each. **A** begins by defining one of the words on his/her sheet. If **B** can say the word, then it's **B**'s turn to give a definition.

2 A Irregular past simple bingo

A grammar and pronunciation game

SS revise irregular past tense forms. Copy and cut up one sheet per 20 SS. If you have more than twenty students, copy another sheet and give out the necessary number of extra cards. It doesn't matter if more than one pair have the same card.

LANGUAGE Irregular past tenses

- Put SS into pairs and give each pair a card. Give them time to remember the past tense of each verb.
- Tell SS they are going to play 'past tense bingo'. Explain that you will say the past tense of different verbs. If they have the infinitive of the verb on their card, they cross it through. When they have crossed through all nine verbs, they shout *Bingo!*
- Go to the **Irregular verb list** (**SB** ***p. 155***) and start saying the past tense verbs in random order. Use a pencil to tick the verbs you have read out.
- When a student shouts *Bingo*, get him/her to read out the nine verbs saying the infinitive and the past tense. Check they are all verbs that you have ticked. If the verbs are correct the SS is the winner. If they have made a mistake, the game continues.

Extra idea Play the game with new cards, or get SS to play in groups when one student reads out the past tenses.

2 B It was a cold, dark night

A reading and predicting activity

SS read a story paragraph by paragraph and predict what happened next. Copy one sheet per person (or per pair), or make a transparency (see Extra idea).

LANGUAGE Past simple and continuous: *She was driving past some trees when she hit something in the road.*

- Give out one sheet per student or pair, face down. Make sure they have a piece of paper ready to cover the story before they start.
- Tell SS to turn over the sheet and cover everything except the pictures and the first paragraph. Tell SS to read it, or ask a student to read it aloud.
- Now tell SS to uncover the first question and elicit ideas. Encourage SS to give reasons for their suggestions. Don't tell SS who is right.
- Get SS to uncover the next paragraph. They will find the answer to the first question then come to the next question. Again elicit ideas. Continue this process, getting SS to read and predict the whole story.

Extra idea Make a transparency of the story and project it on the board. Use a sheet of paper to uncover the paragraphs and ask the questions to the whole class.

2 C Make your own quiz

A general knowledge quiz

SS revise question formation by writing their own quizzes. Copy one sheet per pair or group.

LANGUAGE Questions without auxiliaries:
Who painted ...? Who discovered ...? Who said ...?

- If necessary, revise the difference between questions with and without auxiliaries.
- Put SS into pairs or groups of 3 or 4. Give out one sheet per pair or group. SS put their names at the top or choose a team name.

- Explain that they are going to write their own quizzes. Go through the question stems, checking that they understand them. For questions 10–12 they invent their own questions (either with or without auxiliaries). Explain that SS can only write questions to which they know the answers.
- Set a time limit. Monitor and help, making sure that SS are writing sensible questions which other SS will have a chance of answering.
- Get each pair/group to sit with another pair/group, and ask each other their questions. If it's difficult for SS to move around, you could just get them to swap quizzes and write the answers.

Extra idea Stick the completed quizzes up round the room, and get SS to go round reading the questions and writing down the answers. Then have a feedback session checking answers to see who got the most right.

2D Finish the sentences

A group activity

SS race to complete sentences. Copy and cut up one sheet per 4 or 5 SS.

LANGUAGE	Connectors: *so, because, but, although*

- Put SS in small groups (four or five). Give each group a set of strips in an envelope.
- Each group picks a strip and tries to complete the sentence in a logical and correct way. They should then write their sentence. As soon as they've written it, one SS comes to you with their sentence. If it's correct, the group gets a point. Keep the score on the board. If the sentence is not correct, the group rewrites it.
- Set a time limit, e.g. eight minutes. When the time is up, the group with the most correct sentences wins.

Non-cut alternative Put SS into pairs and give out one sheet per pair. SS work in pairs to complete the sentences. Set a time limit. When the time is up, get the pair who has completed the most to read out their sentences. The pair with the most correct sentences is the winner.

Extra challenge Give students **A** and **B** time to memorize the main facts of the story. Then, students **A** (text covered) try to re-tell the story, using the pictures to help. Students **B** (looking at the text) help and correct. Then they change roles. Emphasize that SS don't have to re-tell the story word for word.

3A Find someone who ...

A class mingle

SS ask each other questions to complete a survey. Copy one sheet per student.

LANGUAGE	
Going to and present continuous:	
Are you going to study tonight?	*What are you going to study?*
Are you going away next weekend?	*Where are you going?*

- Elicit the questions SS will need to ask. Make sure SS don't try and ask negative questions for 4 and 8.
- Focus on **More information**. Elicit follow-up questions for 1 and 2 (see LANGUAGE).
- Demonstrate the activity. Ask a student the first question. Elicit *Yes, I am* or *No, I'm not*. If the student answers *Yes*, write their name in the column on your sheet, then ask a follow-up question and write the answer under **More information**. If the student answers *No*, then say *Thank you* and ask other students until somebody answers *Yes*.
- Tell SS to write the name of a different student for each question. SS mingle, asking and answering questions. Feedback to find out who is going to do what.

3B The optimist's phrase book

A pairwork activity

SS practise making positive predictions. Copy one sheet per pair or per student.

LANGUAGE	*I'm sure you'll pass.*
You won't lose next time.	*Good luck, Cheer up,* etc.

- Give out one sheet per pair or per student. Go through sentences 1–10 in **You say** and the responses.
- Focus on instruction **a**. Tell SS to imagine that they are all optimists. Focus on sentence 1 and elicit a prediction, e.g. *I'm sure you'll pass* or *You won't fail*.
- SS continue in pairs, writing positive predictions. Monitor and help/correct. Encourage SS to use *I'm sure* before the prediction where you think it sounds more natural.
- When SS have finished, get them to compare with another pair to see which sounds most positive.
- Focus on instructions **b** and **c**. Get **A** to read out the **You say** sentences. **B** responds from memory. Then they swap roles. Encourage SS to use positive intonation in their responses.

3C *I'll / I won't / Shall I?*

A pairwork activity

SS revise offers and promises. Copy one sheet per pair and cut into A and B.

LANGUAGE	*I'll (help you)!* *Shall I (turn on the light)?*
I won't (forget)	*I won't ...*

- Put SS into pairs and give out the sheets. Sit **A** and **B** so they can't see each other's sheets.
- Focus on instructions **a** and **b**. Demonstrate the activity. Take the part of Student **A** and read out the first sentence from **You say**. Tell the **B**s to respond using ***I'll/Shall I ...?*** etc. + a verb from the box and a pronoun if necessary.
- If the **B**s' response is not quite right, say *Try again* and give them help if necessary. When **B**s say *I'll answer it* say *That's right!* and tell **B**s to write it in.
- SS continue in pairs. When **A** has read all his/her sentences, SS swap roles.

Extra challenge Get SS to repeat the activity responding from memory.

3D Talk about it

A group board game

SS revise past, present and future tenses. Make one copy of the board game for every four SS. You also need one dice per group and one counter per SS.

LANGUAGE Question formation in past, present and future tenses.

- Put SS into small groups of 3 or 4. Give each group a copy of the board game and a dice.

⚠ If you don't have dice, give each group a coin. SS toss the coin for their go and move 1 for heads and 3 for tails.

- Explain the rules of the game. SS throw a dice and move the corresponding number of squares on the board. When they land on a square, they must talk for 30 seconds about the topic. Then each of the other SS in the group must ask them a question about the topic.
- SS play the game in their groups. The game finishes when someone reaches the finish square.

4A Are you telling the truth?

A pairwork speaking activity

SS ask each other questions about experiences and try to find out if their partner is telling the truth or not. Copy and cut up one sheet per pair and cut into A and B.

LANGUAGE Present perfect (experience): *Have you ever won a cup or a medal? Yes, I have.* *When did you win it? What did you win it for?*

- Put SS into pairs and give out the sheets. Sit **A** and **B** so they can't see each other's sheet.
- Focus on instruction **a.** Give SS time to complete the questions with the past participle and check answers.

A	had, studied, been, spoken, met, left
B	won, failed, sent, sung, had, seen

- Focus on instructions **b** and **c**. Demonstrate the activity. Get one student to ask you one of their questions. Answer *Yes, I have* (even if you haven't). Get SS to continue asking more questions, and answer with the truth or with invented details. Finally, tell SS to guess if your story was true or not.
- SS take turns to ask and answer. They should write **T** (true) or **F** (false) after each answer. When SS have finished, they compare their sheets and see whether they guessed right. Get feedback from some of the pairs.

Extra support Let **A** read **B**'s questions and vice versa before they start to give SS time to prepare their true and 'invented' answers.

4B I haven't done it yet

A pairwork activity

SS practise using the present perfect with *yet* and *already*. Copy one sheet per pair and cut into A and B.

LANGUAGE Present perfect: *Have you finished your homework?* *No, I haven't started it yet.*

- Put SS into pairs and give out the sheets. Sit **A** and **B** so they can't see each other's sheets. Tell SS to read instructions **a** and **b**.
- Demonstrate the activity. Ask the **A**s what their first question is (*Have you finished your homework?*) and elicit the correct response from **B** (*No, I haven't started it yet*).
- **A**s ask all their questions. **B**s choose a response. SS swap roles.

Extra challenge Get **A** to repeat the questions for **B** to answer from memory.

4C Which do you prefer? Why?

A pair/groupwork speaking activity

SS say which of two things/activities they prefer and why. Copy and cut up one sheet per pair or per 4 or 5 SS. You can personalize the activity by writing two more cards.

LANGUAGE Comparative forms: *I prefer swimming in the sea because it's healthier.*

- Put SS into pairs or groups of 4 or 5 and give out a set of cards face down.
- Demonstrate the activity by asking a student to pick a card and ask you. SS take turns to pick a card and ask the other student(s) *Which do you prefer, … or …? Why?*
- Monitor while SS are talking, correcting any mistakes with comparative forms. When SS have finished, get feedback from a few pairs or groups.

Non-cut alternative Give out one uncut sheet to each pair or group. Get them to discuss the topics on each card saying which they prefer and why.

4D The best in town

A group role play

SS take turns to play the role of a tourist in their town. Copy and cut up one sheet per 3 SS.

LANGUAGE Superlatives: *What the most famous place in the town? What's the best souvenir to buy?*

- Put SS into groups of 3: **A**, **B** and **C**. Tell them that they are going to be tourists. When **A** is the tourist, **B** and **C** are local residents; when **B** is the tourist **A** and **C** are local residents, etc. Each tourist has different questions.
- Give out the role cards and remind SS that they have to make the adjective in brackets superlative.
- Demonstrate the activity. You are the tourist. Say *Excuse me, can you help me? I'm a tourist. What are the most interesting monuments in this town?* Elicit ideas.
- Remind the 'local residents' that, as they are speaking to a tourist who doesn't speak their language, they must explain everything in English. Remind the 'tourists' that if a local resident uses a L1 word or expression to say *I'm sorry, I don't understand. What is(…)?*

- When SS have finished, get some feedback.

⚠ In a multilingual class get SS to talk about the town where they are studying.

5A Language school party

A mingle roleplay activity

SS practise making 'small talk' at a party. Copy and cut up enough sheets for SS to have one card each.

LANGUAGE *Hello I'm .... Nice to meet you. What do you do? Really? Why are you learning English?*

- Give each student one card. Tell SS to imagine that they are studying English at a language school in the UK/USA. On the first night there is a party at the school for all the new SS to get to know each other.
- Tell SS to complete the gaps in their role card. Explain that they must invent a job, a reason for studying English, and a first name. Quickly check that SS have completed their role cards properly.
- Go through the information on the card highlighting that *Really? That's interesting* is a response to hearing what other people's jobs are; *I love your.... Where did you get it/them?* is a comment on what other people are wearing; and *Excuse me. I need to ...* is where they have to make an excuse to talk to someone else. Elicit ideas, e.g. *I need to get a drink/go to the bathroom, go home now,* etc.
- Get everybody to stand up as if they were at a party. Demonstrate the activity by holding a role card and talking to a student, inventing your name, job, etc. Encourage the other student to ask you the questions too. Then one of you makes an excuse to 'escape'.
- Set a time limit, e.g. five minutes, and tell SS to mingle and to try to talk to as many SS at the party as they can.

Extra idea Put on some background music while SS talk to each other.

5B Find someone who ...

A class mingle

SS find someone in the class for each sentence and ask follow-up questions. Copy one survey per student. Before photocopying you can personalize the activity by adding two more sentences.

LANGUAGE The *-ing* form: enjoy *cooking*, stop *smoking*, good at *dancing* etc.

- Elicit the questions SS need to ask, e.g. *Do you enjoy cooking? Do you like shopping for clothes?* Make sure SS don't use a negative question for questions 2, 5 and 9.
- Demonstrate the activity. Ask a student the first question. If he/she answers *Yes* write his/her name on your sheet and ask a follow-up question(s), e.g. *What do you cook? What's your favourite dish?* and write his/her answer in **More information**. If he/she answers *No*, say *Thank you* and ask other SS until you get a *Yes* answer.
- Tell SS to write the name of a different student for each question. SS mingle, asking and answering questions. Get some feedback.

5C UK rules, OK?

A pairwork speaking activity

SS decide if sentences about laws in the UK are true or false, and then talk about the situation in their own country(ies). Copy one sheet per student.

LANGUAGE Modal verbs: *You have to wear a helmet.* *You don't have to have a dog licence.* *You must be over 18 to ride a motorbike.* *Pubs mustn't serve beer to anyone under 18.*

- Give out one sheet per student and focus on the instructions for **a**. Go through sentences 1–15 and make sure SS understand them.
- Put SS into pairs and set a time limit. Tell SS to decide if the sentences are true or false and to tick the box.
- Focus on the instructions for **b** and elicit their answers.

1 F **2** F (it's until 16) **3** T **4** F **5** F **6** F
7 T **8** F **9** T **10** T **11** F **12** F
13 T (You can educate your child at home) **14** T **15** T

- Get SS to tell you if these sentences are true or false in their country. You could get SS to do this in pairs first and then get feedback from the class. In a multilingual class try to mix the nationalities in pairs or small groups.

5D Prepositions race

A brainstorm activity

SS race to think of two answers for questions using a preposition of movement. Copy one sheet per pair or group of 3 or 4 SS.

LANGUAGE verbs + prepositions of movement: *swim across, walk through, go up,* etc.

- Put SS into pairs or groups of three or four and give out the sheets. Don't go through all the questions but demonstrate the activity, eliciting answers to the first question, e.g. *You can swim across a swimming pool/river/lake,* etc.
- Explain that the activity is a race. Each pair or group should have a 'secretary' who writes down their answers, clearly. The winner is the pair/group which can find the most correct answers in the time limit.
- Set a time limit, e.g. 5 minutes, and tell SS to start. Give more time if you can see that SS need it.
- When the time limit is up, check answers and find out which team has the most correct answers.

⚠ Encourage SS to use full sentences when you elicit answers, e.g. *You hit a ball over the net in tennis and badminton.*

Suggested answers (but others are possible):
You can...
swim across a river, lake, swimming pool, etc.
walk through a door, park, forest, etc.
hit something **over** a net in tennis, badminton, volleyball, etc.
go up and down a mountain, a hill, stairs, in a lift, etc.
You can't **go into** a cinema, theatre without a ticket.

You **move** pieces **across** the board in chess, draughts (accept names of games in SS's own language here).
You can **drive into** a garage, a car park.
You **go round and round** a track in athletics and cycling.
A lorry driver, a messenger, a waiter, etc **take things from one place to another**.
To get to Japan from the UK you have to **fly over** Sweden and Russia (SS answers will depend on where they live).
You can **put** keys, money, a mobile, etc **into** your pocket/bag every day (and take them out).
On our way to this school we **go past**, e.g. a park and a petrol station. (SS answers will depend on where they live).
When it's raining you can **stand under** an umbrella, a tree, etc.
A cat can **walk along** a roof, branch, (narrow) wall, etc.

6 A Guess my sentence

A pairwork activity

SS practise first conditional sentences by trying to guess the missing half of their partner's sentences. Copy one sheet per pair and cut into A and B.

LANGUAGE First conditional: *If we don't hurry up, we'll be late. You won't pass the exam if you don't study.*

- Put SS into pairs and give out the sheets. Sit **A** and **B** so they can't see each other's sheet.
- Demonstrate the activity by writing on the board:
  If you live in Britain for a year, ______ .
- On a separate piece of paper write the complete sentence but don't show it to the class, e.g. *If you live in Britain for a year, you'll speak English perfectly.*
- Tell the class that they have to guess the missing words in the sentence on the board. Elicit several possible completions until someone says what you have written on the paper, and then show the class the piece of paper.
- Focus on the sheets and explain that half of their sentences have gaps, and their partner has the complete sentences. SS take turns trying to guess the missing words in their incomplete sentences. They should continue guessing until they say the exact sentence their partner has. Their partner should help and prompt if necessary.
- Give SS a minute or so to read their sentences and think of possible completions, but not to write them.
- Student **A** begins by trying to guess his/her first sentence. Stress that SS should say the whole sentence each time, not just the missing words. When **A** correctly guesses the sentence he/she writes in the missing words.
- Now **B** tries to guess his/her first sentence, etc.

6 B I think you'd ...

A pairwork activity

SS complete sentences by guessing real information about their partner. Copy one sheet per pair and cut into **A** and **B**.

LANGUAGE Second conditional: *If you won a lot of money, I think the first thing you'd buy is a car.*

- Demonstrate the activity by writing on the board:
  If you could go on holiday anywhere in the world, I think you'd go to ______ .
- Tell SS to think about *you* and complete the sentence, i.e. guessing where you would go. Elicit answers and then tell the class where you would, in fact, go.
- Put SS into pairs and give out the sheets. Sit **A** and **B** so they can't see each other's sheets. Tell them to complete the sentences trying to guess what their partner would do in each situation.
- SS take turns to read their completed sentences to their partner, who tells them if they have guessed correctly or not. Encourage them to say *No I wouldn't. I'd ...* if the guess is wrong.
- Get feedback from several pairs and find out who, in the pair, had more correct guesses.

6 C It might rain

A group card game

SS practise making *may/might* sentences. Copy and cut up one set of cards for each group of 3 or 4.

LANGUAGE *I'm going to take an umbrella because it may/might rain.*

- Put SS into small groups of 3 or 4. Put a set of cards face down in the middle.
- Tell SS to imagine that they are in London on holiday. They are going to go out for the day and must say what they are going to take and why.
- Demonstrate the activity by picking up a card, e.g. sunglasses, and say *I'm going to take some sunglasses because it might (or may) be sunny.* Pick up another card, e.g. a mobile phone, and say *I'm going to take a mobile because I might want to phone my friends.*
- Tell SS that if they make a correct sentence then they keep the card. The winner is the student with the most cards at the end. If a student makes an incorrect sentence, the card is put back at the bottom of the pile.
- SS now take turns to take a card and try to make a correct sentence using *I'm going to ... because + might or may ...* . The game ends when all the cards have been won.
- Get feedback for each card by saying *I'm going to take (my passport) because ...* and eliciting a *might/may* sentence from the class.

Non-cut alternative Do this as a pairwork activity without cutting up the cards. Give one sheet to each pair and they take turns to make sentences.

Suggested sentences (but others are possible):
umbrella – It may/might rain.
chocolate – I may/might be hungry.
a sweater – It may/might be cold.
a map – I may/might get lost.
a phrase book – I may/might speak to someone in English.
a mobile phone – I may/might need to phone someone.

my passport – I may/might want to change money.
a bottle of water – I may/might be thirsty.
a credit card – I may/might want to buy something.
a pair of sunglasses – it may/might be sunny.
a pen and some paper – I may/might write some postcards.
a camera – I may/might take some photos.
an address book – I may/might make a new friend.
an MP3 player – I may/might want to listen to music.
the name and address of my hotel – I may/might forget it.
a guidebook – I may/might want to read about a place.

6 D What should I do?

A group speaking activity

SS practise giving advice to each other. Copy and cut up one sheet per group of 3 or 4.

LANGUAGE *What should I do? (I think) you should … You shouldn't … If I were you, I'd …*

- Demonstrate the activity by inventing a problem, e.g. *I want to buy a pet but I live in a flat.* Quickly elicit/revise the phrases from **LANGUAGE** by asking the class to give you advice.
- Put SS into groups of 3 or 4. Give each group a set of cards face down or in an envelope.
- One SS picks up a card and reads out his/her situation. Each SS in the group has to try to give a different piece of advice. The SS should say which piece of advice he/she thinks is the best, and give the card to that person. Now another SS takes a card and the others offer advice. The student who is given the most cards is the winner.

Non-cut alternative Copy one sheet per pair and cut it in half (six problems each). **A** explains a problem to **B** and **B** gives advice. Then swap roles.

7 A Class survey

A class mingle activity

SS practise asking and answering present perfect questions. Copy and cut up one set of cards. If you have more than twelve SS, you can give the extra SS a repeated card or invent some more questions and write them on pieces of paper.

⚠ If you have only teenage SS, you may want to omit numbers 8 and 11.

LANGUAGE Present perfect + *for/since*: *How long have you lived in this town? For ten years./Since last August.*

- Tell the class that they are going to do a survey. Explain that each SS will ask a present perfect question to as many SS as they can. Give one card to each student and tell them to think what question they need to ask to find the answer, e.g. for card 1 the question will be: *How long have you lived in your house?*
- Check that SS know what question they are going to ask. Point out that the object is for each student to find the answer to the question on their card, e.g. *Who has been in this school the longest?*
- Demonstrate the activity by asking some students the first question and eliciting answers, e.g.:

T *How long have you lived in your house or flat?*
S1 *(I've lived there) for eight years.*
S2 *(I've lived there) since 2004, etc.*

- Set a time limit, e.g. 7–8 minutes. SS mingle and ask their question to as many SS as they can. Tell them to remember or write down the name of the student. Monitor and help. When the time limit is up, get the result of the survey from each student.

7 B Two British stars

A pairwork information gap activity

SS question each other to discover missing biographical information about a young British actor and actress using the present perfect and past simple. Copy one sheet per pair and cut into A and B.

LANGUAGE Past simple and Present perfect:
When was she born? How old was he when he left school?
How many films has she made?
How long has he lived in London?

- Put SS into pairs and give out the sheets. Sit **A** and **B** so they can't see each other's sheet. Explain that they have one complete biography and one with missing information.
- Give SS time to read both the biographies and deal with any vocabulary problems that come up.
- Focus on the questions in **a**. Tell **A** and **B** to read the first biography they have again and to complete questions 1–7. Set a time limit, e.g. 7–8 minutes. Monitor and check that SS are writing correct questions.
- Quickly check all the questions before starting the activity. Elicit the questions and write them on the board.

Keira Knightley
1 When was she/Keira Knightley born?
2 Why did she have a lot of problems at school?
3 How old was she when she made her first film?
4 When did she become famous?
5 When did she leave school?
6 How many films has she made since 1998?
7 How long has she lived in London?

Orlando Bloom
1 When was he born?
2 Who was his father?
3 How old was he when he left school?
4 What was his first film?
5 When did he become really famous?
6 How many films has he made since 2001?
7 How long has he lived in London?

- Focus on **b**. Students **A** and **B** take turns to ask their questions and complete their biographies with the missing information.

Extra challenge You could get SS to cover the complete biography and answer their partner's questions from memory.

- When SS have completed their biographies, they discuss and write down what the actors have in common.

- Feedback SS's ideas. You may want to teach both.

They're both actors, they were both born in England, they both have one brother or sister, they were both dyslexic when they were young, they both left school when they were young (15 and 16) They both live in London.

Note*: All the information correct at the date of publication.*

7 C How have you changed?

A pairwork speaking activity

SS complete a grid and then use the information talk about past habits using *used to* and *didn't use to*. Copy one sheet per student.

LANGUAGE *I used to play football but I don't now.* *I didn't use to like vegetables but now I love them.*

- Put SS into pairs and give out the sheets. Sit **A** and **B** so they can't see each other's sheets. Focus on instruction **a**. Go through sentences 1–10 and make sure SS know what they have to do. Demonstrate by giving some personal examples for sentences 1–3. Make it clear that SS only have to write words, e.g. *football, the Rolling Stones, coffee* and not complete sentences.
- Give SS time to write something in as many circles as they can (sometimes they may not be able to think of anything). Monitor and help.
- Now focus on instruction **b**. SS use what they have written in the circles to tell their partner about their past habits using *I used to/I didn't use to*. Again, demonstrate the activity yourself and give more information, e.g. *I used to play rugby at school. I hated it because I was very bad at it* etc. If necessary, remind SS of the pronunciation of *used to/didn't use to*.
- SS work together, talking about their past habits. When they have finished, get some feedback from the class.

7 D What's it famous for?

A quiz about the students' country

SS practise using present and past passives by discussing and compiling a list of famous buildings, films etc. which have been built, produced etc. by people in their country. Copy one sheet per student/pair/group.

LANGUAGE Present and past passive: *It was built by ...* *The film was directed by ...* *This dish is eaten a lot in my region.* *I think this animal is only found in my country.*

- Put SS into pairs or small groups. Give out the sheets. Focus on sentences 1–15 and go through them quickly making sure SS understand everything.
- Set a time limit, e.g. 5 minutes, and tell SS to discuss each sentence and try to write the name of a building, person, book, dish etc.
- When the time limit is up, join pairs/groups together to discuss what they have written. Encourage them to ask for extra information, e.g. *When was (...) built? Who was the film directed by?*

⚠ In a multinational class this activity will work better if SS work separately to complete the sheet and then discuss what they have written with a student or students from a different country.

8 A Is it true?

A pairwork activity

SS practise *something/anything/nothing* etc. by agreeing with or contradicting a series of statements. Copy one sheet per student.

LANGUAGE *Something, anything etc.* *No one in my family has long hair.* *Somebody in my family speaks English very well.* *I didn't go anywhere last night.*

- Put SS into pairs and give out the sheets. Focus on the instructions and give SS time to tick the sentences which are true for them.
- Demonstrate the activity by talking to the class about some of the statements, e.g. *Sentence 1 isn't true for me. My brother has very long hair.* Encourage the class to ask for more information, e.g. *How old is your brother?*
- SS take it in turns to talk about each statement. Stop the activity when most pairs seem to have finished.

8 B But on the other hand ...

A pairwork activity

SS compare information about their diet, lifestyle etc. and practise using quantifiers. Copy one sheet per student.

LANGUAGE Quantifiers: *I eat too much.* *I don't relax enough.* *But on the other hand, I play squash twice a week.*

- Put SS into pairs and give out the sheets. Focus on instruction **a**. Demonstrate the activity by completing the sentences yourself for **My lifestyle,** e.g. *I think I worry too much. I don't see my friends enough. I'm too busy. But on the other hand, I enjoy life.*
- Make sure SS understand that they should say something negative in all the sentences except the last one. Check that they understand the meaning of *But on the other hand, ...* which is always used to introduce an opposite idea to the one previously mentioned.
- Give SS enough time to complete their sheets. Monitor to check that they are making correct sentences.
- Focus on instruction **b**. SS compare with a partner and decide how similar or different their answers are. Feedback some answers from the class.

8 C Phrasal verb questions

A pairwork speaking activity

SS ask each other a series of questions using phrasal verbs. Copy one sheet per student.

LANGUAGE Phrasal verbs: *Do you enjoy* ***trying on*** *clothes?* *Have you ever forgotten to* ***turn off*** *your mobile phone in the cinema?* *What's the best way to* ***give up*** *smoking?*

- Put SS into pairs and give out the sheets. Give SS time to read all the questions and revise the verbs.
- Focus on the instructions. Tell SS they can ask the questions in any order and that they should try to ask for more information.
- Demonstrate the activity by getting SS to ask you two of the questions. Give as much information as you can.
- Set a time limit, e.g. 6–8 minutes and tell SS to take turns asking questions. Monitor and help as necessary. Feedback answers from the class.

8 D So do I!

A speaking activity

SS discuss different topics using *So do I/Neither do I* when they find points in common with their partner(s). Copy and cut up one set of cards per pair. You can write two more topics on the blank cards.

> **LANGUAGE**
> **A** *I have two brothers and sisters.*
> **B** *So do I.*
> **A** *I never have breakfast.*
> **B** *Neither do I.*

- Sit SS in pairs and give each pair a set of cards face down. Explain the activity:

  A picks a card and makes a few sentences about the topic. **B** listens and says if he/she is the same or different. If **B** finds something in common with **A**, he/she should try to use *So (do) I/ Neither (do) I*, changing the auxiliary according to the tense used, e.g.:

  (Family)

  A *I have a brother and a sister.*

  B *So do I.*

  A *My father is retired.*

  B *My father works. He's a civil servant.*
- Demonstrate the activity with a student. Pick a card and start the conversation to find something in common.
- Set a time limit. SS take turns to pick a card and start talking. Monitor but don't over-correct.
- Stop the activity when you think SS have had enough practice or seem to be running out of steam.

Non-cut alternative Give each student an uncut sheet. They take turns to choose a topic and start a conversation.

9 A Match the sentences

A mingle activity

SS mingle and try to match their sentence half to another to make a past perfect sentence. Copy and cut up enough cards for one card per SS. If you have more than 24 SS but still an even number, you can give the extra SS repeated cards. If you have a very small class, give two cards (a beginning and a different ending) to each SS.

⚠ If you have an odd number of SS take one card yourself to make sure each SS has a match.

> **LANGUAGE** Past perfect: *I couldn't go in the sea because I hadn't brought my swimsuit.*

- Give each student one card. Explain or demonstrate the activity. SS must move around the class saying their half sentences to each other until they think they have found the half that matches theirs.

⚠ Elicit that the sentence half containing the past perfect will always be the second half of the sentence.

- When two SS think their cards match, they show them to you. If it's correct, they write it on the board. They then help other SS find their matching sentence halves.
- The activity finishes when everyone has found their matching half and all the sentences are on the board.
- For further practice, shuffle the cards and begin again.

9 B Who said what?

A pairwork memory test

SS practise reported speech by remembering what people said in a picture of a classroom. Copy one sheet per student/pair and fold on the dotted line so only the picture with speech bubbles is visible.

> **LANGUAGE** Reported speech: *Halma said she couldn't see the board. The teacher asked if they had done the homework.*

- Put SS into pairs and give out the sheets folded on the dotted line.
- Focus on the instructions. Give SS time to match the sentences to the speech bubbles and to write in the sentences. Check answers.

> A 2 B 5 C 4 D 6 E 1 F 3

- Tell SS to turn over the sheets so that only the second picture is visible (the one without speech bubbles). Tell them not to look back at the first picture.
- Focus on instruction **b**. Elicit the answer to the first sentence. Tell SS that they must use reported speech because they are remembering and saying what somebody said. When somebody gets the right answer, tell SS to complete sentence A.
- Give SS time to complete sentences B–F. Check answers.

> **A** Ana said (that) she had missed the bus.
> **B** Susana asked what page it was.
> **C** David said (that) he had left his book at home.
> **D** The teacher asked if they had done the homework.
> **E** Halma said (that) she couldn't see the board.
> **F** Miriam asked if she could open the window.

9 Revision questions

Questions to revise vocabulary and verb tenses

SS ask questions about key vocabulary areas using a range of verb tenses from Files 1–9. This could be used as final 'pre-test' revision. Alternatively, it could be used as an oral exam. Copy and cut up one set of cards per pair.

> **LANGUAGE** Questions and answers using a variety of vocabulary, structures, and verb tenses.

- SS work in pairs. Give each pair a set of cards. Set a time limit, e.g. ten minutes. SS take turns to take a card and ask their partner questions. **Encourage SS to ask follow-up questions**. Monitor, help, and correct.

STUDENT PROFILE

1	First name	
2	Surname	
3	Nationality	
4	Address	
5	Occupation	
6	Place of birth	
7	Date of birth	
8	Languages	
9	Interests	
10	Reasons for learning English	

a Complete the questions you need to ask to fill in thc form.

1 What ______________________________?
2 What ______________________________?
3 Where ______________________________?
4 Where ______________________________?
5 What ______________________________?
6 Where ______________________________?
7 When ______________________________?
8 What languages ______________________________?
9 What ______________________ in your free time?
10 Why ______________________________?

b Cover the questions. Interview a partner and complete the form.
Ask him / her to spell names and places if necessary.

Richard

Age 30
Job writer
Appearance very tall, dark
Personality intelligent, generous, very talkative
☺ women with a sense of humour
☹ women who talk a lot, women with very short hair
Ideal partner ____________

Sara

Age 20
Job computer technician
Appearance short, with very short dark hair
Personality generous and funny, not very good at listening
☺ men who are open and friendly
☹ men who talk all the time
Ideal partner ____________

Mark

Age 32
Job vet
Appearance short, quite fat
Personality very kind, a bit mean
☺ extrovert women, women with long hair
☹ shy women, women who spend money all the time
Ideal partner ____________

Rebecca

Age 21
Job model
Appearance tall, slim
Personality not very intelligent, not very careful with money, always on a diet
☺ sporty men with a sense of humour
☹ men who are shorter than her, men who aren't generous
Ideal partner ____________

David

Age 25
Job footballer
Appearance tall, fair hair, good-looking
Personality funny, quite lazy
☺ attractive women who don't talk much
☹ very intelligent women
Ideal partner ____________

Gill

Age 31
Job journalist
Appearance quite tall, long blond hair
Personality good at listening, funny, quite shy
☺ intelligent men who are taller than her
☹ men who are mean, men with long hair
Ideal partner ____________

Andy

Age 21
Job student
Appearance long hair, quite thin, not very tall
Personality extrovert, not very hardworking
☺ women who make him laugh, women with short hair
☹ women who are mean
Ideal partner ____________

Martina

Age 19
Job hairdresser
Appearance not very tall, long fair hair
Personality funny, very talkative
☺ men who work hard
☹ men with long hair, very tall men
Ideal partner ____________

Ian

Age 18
Job mechanic
Appearance short, thin, with dark hair
Personality very hard-working, quite funny, a bit mean
☺ women with long hair and a sense of humour
☹ quiet, shy women
Ideal partner ____________

Maria

Age 24
Job nurse
Appearance long dark hair, not very tall
Personality open and friendly, very talkative
☺ men who are good with animals
☹ very talkative, thin men
Ideal partner ____________

A Describe your picture to **B**. Find ten differences. Mark the differences on your pictures.
My picture is of an art gallery. There are four paintings …

B Describe your picture to **A**. Find ten differences. Mark the differences on your pictures.
My picture is of an art gallery. There are four paintings …

tired

lazy

happy

have a shower

go on holiday

go shopping

university

living room

station

travel agent's

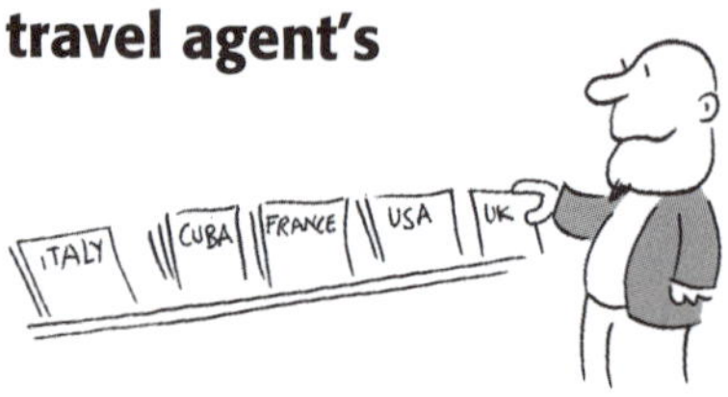

museum

supermarket

cat

credit card

sunglasses

foot

hair

ticket

pilot

actor

aunt

sister-in-law

chess

horse

New English File Teacher's Book Pre-intermediate

forget	learn	write	understand	fly	know
think	go	sleep	get	leave	lose
run	come	speak	write	eat	break
wear	do	buy	cost	bring	know
think	steal	learn	win	shut	catch
become	say	throw	drink	steal	begin
tell	ring	grow	drive	win	have
buy	give	send	make	stand	put
swim	can	fall	lend	teach	catch
earn	meet	feel	fall	say	think
wake up	spend	read	grow	find	hit
take	sell	buy	lose	send	write
lend	choose	put	keep	become	make
bring	hear	fall	sing	break	ring
win	see	find	think	come	let

It was a cold, dark night

It was a cold dark evening in November. It was six o'clock and people were going home from work. Vanessa was driving out of the town. She was in a hurry, but she wasn't going home. She stopped to buy a bottle of wine, and then got back into the car and continued driving.

Where do you think she was going?

She was driving to her friend's house to have dinner. Her friend's name was Martin. He was a farmer and he lived in the country. Vanessa was listening to the radio. She began to relax after a hard day at work. She was driving past some trees when suddenly she hit something in the road. She stopped and got out of the car.

What do you think she saw?

There was a dog lying in the road. It was dead. Vanessa moved the dog to the side of the road and then continued her journey. Suddenly she saw in the mirror that there was a black car behind her. When she turned right the car turned right and when she turned left the car turned left too. It was following her!

Why was the car following her?

Vanessa was sure that the driver of the car was following her because the dead dog was his, and he was angry. Now he was flashing his lights.

What do you think Vanessa did?

Vanessa drove faster but the car drove faster too. Suddenly the seven o'clock news started on the radio. It said: 'The police are looking for a murderer who escaped from prison last night. Be careful! He is very dangerous.'

How do you think Vanessa felt now? Why?

Vanessa felt very afraid. Now she was sure that the man in the car was the murderer! She drove faster. Martin's farm was very near now but the black car was right behind her! At last she arrived at Martin's farm. She got out of the car and ran up to the door. She rang the doorbell. 'Martin! Help, help!' she shouted.

Where do you think Martin was?

Martin was in the kitchen making the dinner when the doorbell rang. He heard Vanessa shouting, so he ran to get his shotgun. He opened the door. At that moment the black car stopped next to Vanessa's car. A tall man got out.

Who do you think the man was?

'That man is the murderer who escaped from prison last night,' Vanessa shouted. 'He's going to kill us.' 'No, no!' said the tall man. '*I'm* not the murderer. The murderer is in there, in the back of your car!'

When did the murderer get into Vanessa's car?

'I was driving behind you,' the tall man said, 'and I saw you stop when you hit the dog. There was a man behind a tree. I saw him get in your car. I recognized him from the newspaper. He's the murderer who escaped from prison last night. That's why I was following you.' Martin ran to the car with his shotgun. He opened the back door. There was a man on the floor. 'OK,' said Martin, 'come out, with your hands up.'

____________________ 's quiz

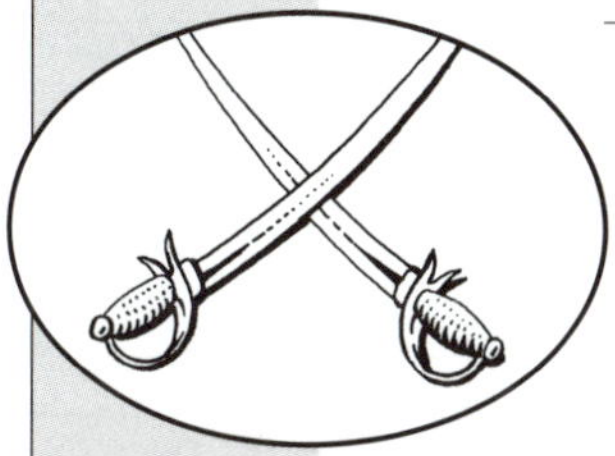

1. Who won the battle of ____________________?
2. Who discovered ____________________?

3. Who wrote ____________________?

4. Which team won ____________ in ________?

5. Who invented ____________________?
6. Which country has ____________________ flag?

7. Who played the part of ____________________ in the film ____________________?

8. Who painted ____________________?
9. Who said ____________________?
10. ____________________?
11. ____________________?
12. ____________________?

a In pairs, complete quiz questions 1–9. Then add three questions of your own. Remember, you must know the answers!

b Ask another pair the questions and answer theirs. Who got the most right answers?

I was really tired **so** …

I didn't phone you **because** …

It was quite a good film **but** …

Although my job isn't very well paid …

My father is French and my mother is Spanish **so** …

He was driving fast **because** …

I wanted to buy some bread **but** …

Although my boss is very friendly …

She wasn't feeling well **so** …

I couldn't come to class last week **because** …

She likes him a lot **but** …

We really like that restaurant **although** …

I wanted to improve my English **so** …

I woke up in the middle of the night **because** …

We took our umbrella **but** …

Although we played very well …

The weather was very cold **so** …

We couldn't understand the man **because** …

They're poor **but** …

Although it was a five-star hotel …

Find someone who …	Student's name	More information
1 is going out tonight.		
2 is going to look after children at the weekend.		
3 is meeting a friend after class.		
4 isn't coming to the next class.		
5 is going abroad soon.		
6 is going away next weekend.		
7 is going to go to a gym tomorrow.		
8 isn't going to study tonight.		
9 is going to buy a new mobile soon.		
10 is having dinner at home tonight.		
11 is going to the cinema at the weekend.		

YOU SAY	THE OPTIMIST SAYS
1 I'm taking my driving test tomorrow.	Good luck. ______
2 I lost at tennis again.	Cheer up! ______
3 I have a bad cold.	Don't worry! ______
4 I'm going to cut my hair very short.	That's a good idea. ______
5 I'm going to see that new film tonight.	Oh, ______
6 I'm making a cake for dessert.	Mmm. I'm sure ______
7 I'm going to be the new boss!	Congratulations. I'm sure ______
8 I'm going to Anna's party tonight.	Great! ______
9 I have a job interview tomorrow.	Don't worry. ______
10 I'm going to a language school in London this summer.	Fantastic! ______

a In pairs, complete **THE OPTIMIST SAYS** with positive predictions.

b **A** read sentences 1–10. **B** cover the optimist's sentences. Respond from memory.

c Swap roles.

A **a** Read **B** sentences 1–8. If he / she says your **RESPONSE** sentences correctly, say 'That's right'. If not, say 'Try again'.

YOU SAY ... →	RESPONSE
1 The phone's ringing.	**I'll answer it.**
2 I can't do my homework.	**I'll help you.**
3 It's very hot in here.	**Shall I open the window?**
4 It's a secret.	**I won't tell anybody.**
5 It's Paul's birthday tomorrow.	**I'll buy him a card.**
6 You left the door open.	**I'll close it.**
7 I don't have any money.	**I'll lend you some.**
8 It's very dark in here.	**Shall I turn on the light?**

b Now respond to **B**'s sentences. Use a verb / phrase from the box. Begin with *I'll*, *I won't*, or *Shall I?* If **B** says 'Try again', make another sentence until **B** says 'That's right'. Then write it down.

teach   lend / mine   turn on / TV   not forget   carry?   call / doctor   clean   get / glass of water?

1 ______________________ 5 ______________________
2 ______________________ 6 ______________________
3 ______________________ 7 ______________________
4 ______________________ 8 ______________________

B **a** Respond to **A**'s sentences. Use a verb / phrase from the box. Begin with *I'll*, *I won't*, or *Shall I?* If **A** says 'Try again', make another sentence until **A** says 'That's right'. Then write it down.

buy / card   turn on / light?   answer   lend   open / window?   not tell anybody   help   close

1 ______________________ 5 ______________________
2 ______________________ 6 ______________________
3 ______________________ 7 ______________________
4 ______________________ 8 ______________________

b Now read **A** sentences 1–8. If he / she says your **RESPONSE** sentences correctly, say 'That's right'. If not, say 'Try again'.

YOU SAY ... →	RESPONSE
1 My bag's very heavy.	**Shall I carry it?**
2 The floor's very dirty.	**I'll clean it.**
3 I left my book at home.	**I'll lend you mine.**
4 Please remember to phone.	**I won't forget.**
5 I don't feel very well.	**I'll call a doctor.**
6 I'm thirsty.	**Shall I get you a glass of water?**
7 I don't know how to play chess.	**I'll teach you.**
8 The programme's starting in a minute.	**I'll turn on the TV.**

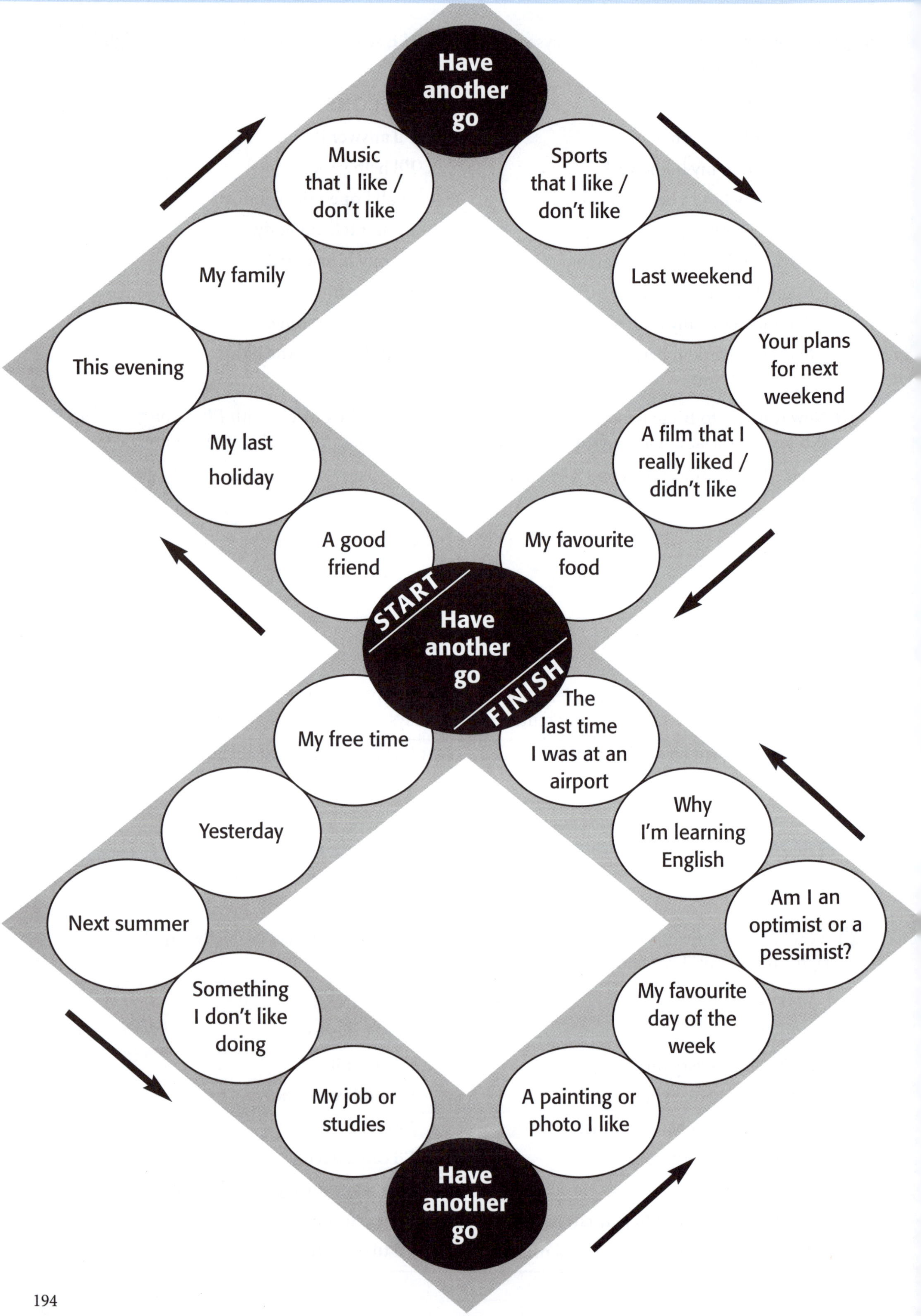
START
Have another go
A good friend
My last holiday
This evening
My family
Music that I like / don't like
Have another go
Sports that I like / don't like
Last weekend
Your plans for next weekend
A film that I really liked / didn't like
My favourite food
My free time
Yesterday
Next summer
Something I don't like doing
My job or studies
Have another go
A painting or photo I like
My favourite day of the week
Am I an optimist or a pessimist?
Why I'm learning English
The last time I was at an airport
FINISH

A **a** Complete the questions with the verb in brackets.

b Ask **B** questions 1–6. After each question ask **B** for more information (use the past simple). Decide if **B** is telling the truth. Write **T** (true) or **F** (false).

c Answer **B**'s questions. Say 'Yes, I have', and give more information. If you have really done it, tell the truth. If you haven't, invent the details.

Are you telling the truth?

True or false?

1 Have you ever ________ a dream which came true? (have) ____

2 Have you ever ________ all night? (study) ____

3 Have you ever ________ in the newspaper or on TV? (be) ____

4 Have you ever ________ in front of a lot of people? (speak) ____

5 Have you ever ________ a famous person? (meet) ____

6 Have you ever ________ something in a bus or taxi? (leave) ____

B **a** Complete the questions with the verb in brackets.

b Answer **A**'s questions. Say 'Yes, I have', and give more information. If you have really done it, tell the truth. If you haven't, invent the details.

c Ask **A** questions 1–6. After each question ask **A** for more information (use the past simple). Decide if **A** is telling the truth. Write **T** (true) or **F** (false).

Are you telling the truth?

True or false?

1 Have you ever ________ a cup or a medal? (win) ____

2 Have you ever ________ a very important exam? (fail) ____

3 Have you ever ________ an e-mail or text message to the wrong person? (send) ____

4 Have you ever ________ in public? (sing) ____

5 Have you ever ________ an argument with your neighbours? (have) ____

6 Have you ever ________ a film at the cinema twice? (see) ____

A

a Ask **B** your questions.

Have you finished your  ?

Did you buy the 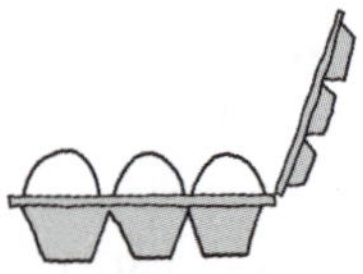 ?

Don't forget to get the 

.

Do you want a  ?

You look  .

Would you like to see 

?

b Answer **B**'s questions with a phrase from the box.

Sorry, I can't. I haven't been to the bank yet.	I haven't read it yet.
Yes, I've already done it.	No, thanks. I've already had three.
Yes, I am. I've just had some good news!	Thanks! I've just bought them.

c Cover the box. Answer **B**'s questions from memory.

B

a Answer **A**'s questions with a phrase from the box.

No, I haven't been to the supermarket yet.	No, I haven't started it yet.
No, I've already seen it. It's terrible!	It's OK, I've already got them.
No, thanks. I've just had one.	I am. I've just got up.

b Ask **A** your questions.

Can I borrow your 

?

I like your  .

Can you lend me some 

?

Have you booked a 

?

Would you like another  ?

You look  .

c Cover the box. Answer **A**'s questions from memory.

swimming in the sea **OR** swimming in a swimming pool	travelling by car **OR** travelling by train
studying in the evening **OR** studying at weekends	the summer **OR** the winter
sending e-mails **OR** sending text messages	watching a film at the cinema **OR** watching a film on video or DVD
working at home **OR** working in an office	speaking in English **OR** writing in English
a holiday with your family **OR** a holiday with your friends	eating at home **OR** eating in a bar or restaurant
staying at a campsite **OR** staying in a hotel	
eating fish **OR** eating meat	

Tourist A

What (interesting) thing to do?

What's (beautiful) park?

What's (dangerous) area?

Where's (good) place to take a photo of the town?

What's (easy) way to get around?

What's (interesting) local festival?

Tourist B

What's (famous) place in the town?

What's (typical) thing to eat?

What's (old) building?

What's (popular) area to go out at night?

What's (good) hotel here?

What's (beautiful) place near here to go for an excursion?

Tourist C

What's (typical) thing to drink?

Where's (exciting) nightlife?

What's (good) souvenir to buy?

What's (easy) way to meet some local people?

Where's (good) shopping area?

What's (famous) sports team?

You are a/an ________________________.

You are learning English because __________

____.

Hello, I'm __________.

Nice to meet you.

What do you do?

Really?

That's interesting.

Do you like your job?

Why are you learning English?

I love your …

Where did you get it / them?

Excuse me. I need to …

You are a/an ________________________.

You are learning English because __________

____.

Hello, I'm __________.

Nice to meet you.

What do you do?

Really?

That's interesting.

Do you like your job?

Why are you learning English?

I love your …

Where did you get it / them?

Excuse me. I need to …

You are a/an ________________________.

You are learning English because __________

____.

Hello, I'm __________.

Nice to meet you.

What do you do?

Really?

That's interesting.

Do you like your job?

Why are you learning English?

I love your …

Where did you get it / them?

Excuse me. I need to …

You are a/an ________________________.

You are learning English because __________

____.

Hello, I'm __________.

Nice to meet you.

What do you do?

Really?

That's interesting.

Do you like your job?

Why are you learning English?

I love your …

Where did you get it / them?

Excuse me. I need to …

You are a/an ________________________.

You are learning English because __________

____.

Hello, I'm __________.

Nice to meet you.

What do you do?

Really?

That's interesting.

Do you like your job?

Why are you learning English?

I love your …

Where did you get it / them?

Excuse me. I need to …

You are a/an ________________________.

You are learning English because __________

____.

Hello, I'm __________.

Nice to meet you.

What do you do?

Really?

That's interesting.

Do you like your job?

Why are you learning English?

I love your …

Where did you get it / them?

Excuse me. I need to …

You are a/an ________________________.

You are learning English because __________

____.

Hello, I'm __________.

Nice to meet you.

What do you do?

Really?

That's interesting.

Do you like your job?

Why are you learning English?

I love your …

Where did you get it / them?

Excuse me. I need to …

You are a/an ________________________.

You are learning English because __________

____.

Hello, I'm __________.

Nice to meet you.

What do you do?

Really?

That's interesting.

Do you like your job?

Why are you learning English?

I love your …

Where did you get it / them?

Excuse me. I need to …

Find someone who …	Student's name	More information
1 enjoys cooking.		
2 doesn't like shopping for clothes.		
3 has stopped smoking recently.		
4 thinks watching football is boring.		
5 doesn't mind doing housework.		
6 is good at dancing.		
7 likes getting up early.		
8 spends a lot of time driving.		
9 can't study / work without listening to music.		
10 thinks eating meat is wrong.		
11 has started doing more exercise recently.		
12 is afraid of flying.		

a In pairs, read the sentences about the UK and decide if you think they are true or false.

	True	False
1 You mustn't play loud music in your house after 9.00 p.m.	☐	☐
2 Children have to stay at school until they are 18.	☐	☐
3 If you have a dog, you must have a dog licence.	☐	☐
4 If you have a cat, you must have a cat licence.	☐	☐
5 All cyclists have to wear a helmet.	☐	☐
6 You must be over 12 years old to have a mobile phone.	☐	☐
7 TV programmes before 9.00 p.m. mustn't include bad language.	☐	☐
8 All shops except newsagents must close on Sundays.	☐	☐
9 Pubs mustn't serve beer to anyone under 18.	☐	☐
10 You don't have to study a foreign language at school.	☐	☐
11 You don't have to wear seatbelts in the back of a car.	☐	☐
12 Female Members of Parliament have to wear skirts or dresses.	☐	☐
13 Parents don't have to send their children to school.	☐	☐
14 You have to be 18 to drive a 49 cc motorbike.	☐	☐
15 Parents mustn't leave children under 12 alone in the house.	☐	☐

b Check with your teacher. Are they true or false in your country?

Can you think of ...?

- 2 places you can **swim across**
- 2 places you can **walk through**
- 2 sports where you **hit** something **over** a net
- 2 places where you can **go up** and **down**
- 2 places you can't **go into** without a ticket
- 2 games where you **move** pieces **across** a board
- 2 places you can **drive into**
- 2 sports where you **go round and round** a track
- 2 jobs where people **take** things **from** one place **to** another
- 2 countries you have to **fly over** to get from your country to Japan
- 2 things you **put into** (and **take out of**) your pocket / bag every day
- 2 places you **go past** on your way to this school
- 2 things you can **stand under** when it's raining
- 2 things a cat can **walk along** but a person can't

A

1 **If we don't hurry up, ______________________________.**

2 You won't pass the exam if you don't study.

3 **If I don't have time to do it today, ______________________.**

4 If you don't take a jacket, you'll be cold.

5 **If you don't drive more slowly, __________________________.**

6 If you give me your e-mail address, I'll write to you.

7 **I'll do the washing up if ______________________________.**

8 If you don't do your homework, the teacher will be angry.

9 **We'll have the party inside if ___________________________.**

10 Will you pay me back tomorrow if I lend you some money?

B

1 If we don't hurry up, we'll be late.

2 **You won't pass the exam if ____________________________.**

3 If I don't have time to do it today, I'll do it tomorrow.

4 **If you don't take a jacket, ______________________________.**

5 If you don't drive more slowly, you'll have an accident.

6 **If you give me your e-mail address, ______________________.**

7 I'll do the washing up if you cook.

8 **If you don't do your homework, ________________________.**

9 We'll have the party inside if it rains.

10 **Will you pay me back tomorrow if ______________________?**

A **a** Complete the sentences about **B**.

1 If you could go on holiday anywhere in the world, I think you'd go to ______________.
2 If you won a trip to London for two people, I think you'd take ______________.
3 If you decided to learn another language, I think you'd learn ______________.
4 If someone invited you to a very expensive restaurant, I think you'd order ______________.
5 If you could meet a famous person, I think you'd choose ______________.
6 If you went to a karaoke evening, I think you'd sing '______________'.
7 If you could play any musical instrument, I think you'd choose ______________.
8 If someone offered to buy you a new car, I think you'd choose ______________.

b Read the sentences to **B**. Were you right?

c Listen to **B**'s sentences about you. Tell him / her if they are right or wrong, and why.

B **a** Complete the sentences about **A**.

1 If you won a lot of money, I think the first thing you'd buy would be ______________.
2 If you could live anywhere in the world, I think you'd choose ______________.
3 If somebody offered to teach you a new sport, I think you'd choose ______________.
4 If you could appear on a TV programme, I think you'd like to be on '______________'.
5 If a friend wanted to buy you a pet, I think you'd ask for a ______________.
6 If you could choose your ideal job, I think you'd be a ______________.
7 If you could have something to eat or drink right now, I think you'd have ______________.
8 If you decided to go to an English-speaking country on holiday, I think you'd go to ______________.

b Listen to **A**'s sentences about you. Tell him / her if they are right or wrong, and why.

c Read your sentences to **A**. Were you right?

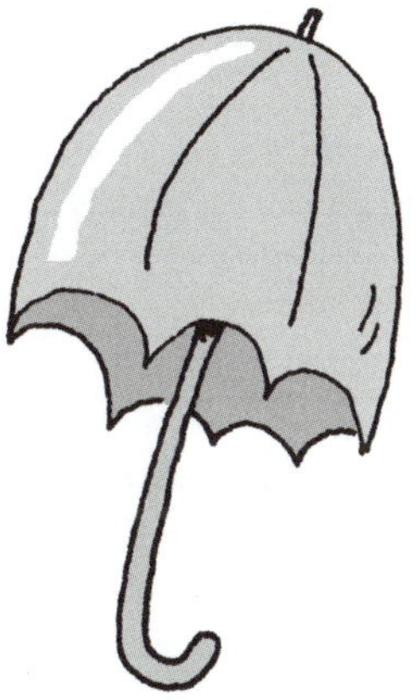

Chocolate
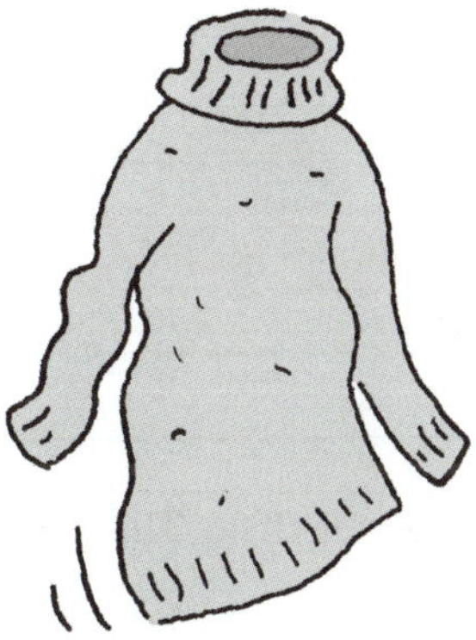
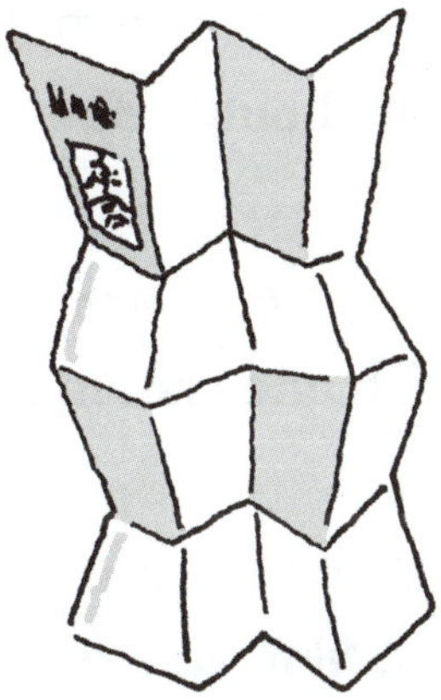

Phrasebook

PASSPORT
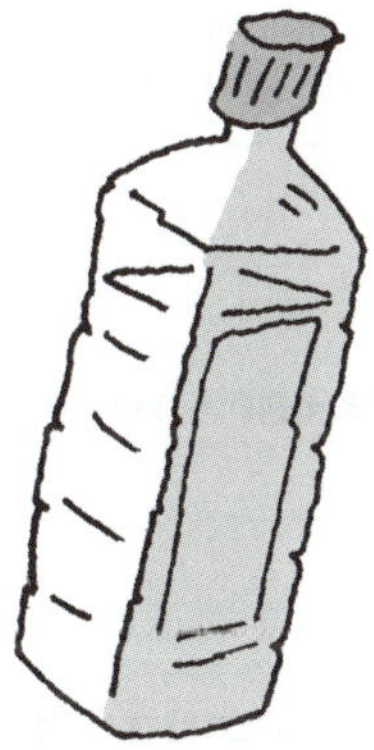

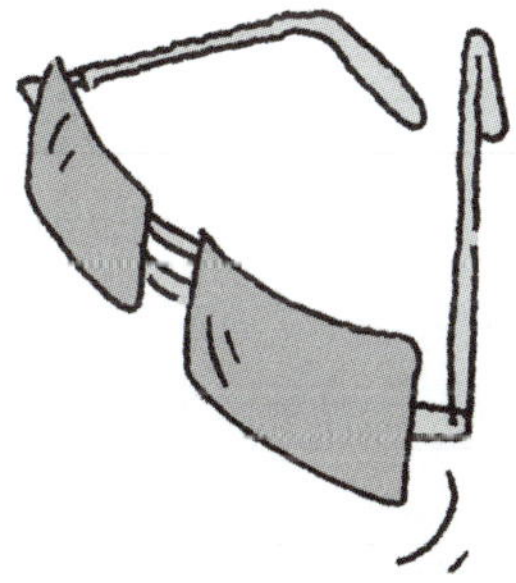
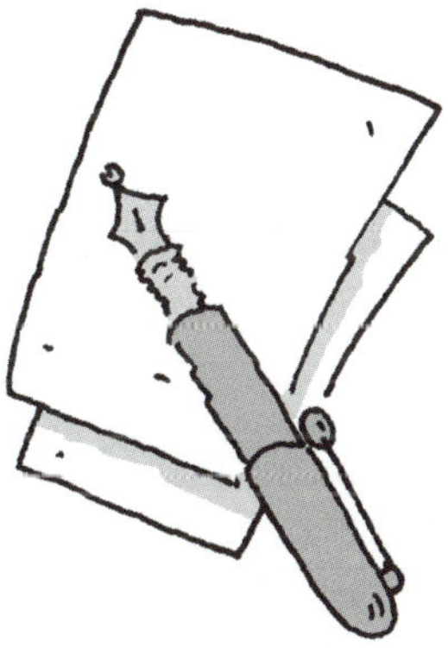

Addresses

MP3-PLAYER

Hotel address
222 Sunny Boulevard Cityville

Guide book

I want to improve my English pronunciation.
What should I do?

I'd like to learn another language.
Which one should I learn?

I want to see a good film at the cinema this weekend.
What film should I see?

I'd like to go on holiday somewhere relaxing this year.
Where should I go?

I want to buy a new car.
What car should I buy?

I need to buy my father a birthday present.
What should I buy?

I can't sleep at night.
What should I do?

I want to take some foreign visitors for a fantastic meal.
Where should I take them?

I want to buy my teacher a present.
What should I buy him / her?

I want to get fit quickly.
What sport or exercise should I do?

I want to feel more relaxed.
What should I do?

I'd like to go to a new show or exhibition.
Where should I go?

1. **Who has lived in their house / flat the longest?**

2. **Who has had their car / motorbike the longest?**

3. **Who has had their computer the longest?**

4. **Who has lived in this town / city the longest?**

5. **Who has had their bag the longest?**

6. **Who has been in this school the longest?**

7. **Who has been awake today the longest?**

8. **Who has been married the longest?**

9. **Who has worn glasses the longest?**

10. **Who has had their mobile the longest?**

11. **Who has been a parent the longest?**

12. **Who has known their best friend the longest?**

KEIRA KNIGHTLEY

Keira Knightley was born in [1] ____________, England, in 1983. She has an older brother, Caleb. At school she had a lot of problems because [2] ____________. Keira made her first film when she was only [3] ____________ years old. She became famous in [4] ____________, when she was chosen for the *Star Wars* films. She played the part of the double of the heroine, Queen Amidala (Natalie Portman). The two girls looked so similar that after make-up their mothers couldn't tell which was their daughter. She left school in [5] ____________ when she was only15, to concentrate on acting. She has made [6] ____________ films since then. One of the most famous is *Pirates of the Caribbean*. Keira has lived in London [7] ____________.

ORLANDO BLOOM

Orlando Bloom was born in Canterbury, England, in 1977. He has a sister who is two years younger than him. When he was a child, Orlando thought his father was Harry Bloom, his mother's husband, who died when he was only four. But the truth was that his father was a family friend. He went to school in Canterbury but he left when he was 16 years old (he was dyslexic). He then moved to London where he trained with the British American Drama Academy. His first film was *Wilde*, about the Irish writer Oscar Wilde. He became really famous in 2001 when he played Legolas Greenleaf in *The Lord of the Rings* films. He has made 11 films since then. He has lived in London since 1993.

A **a** Read the biographies. Complete questions 1–7 to find the missing information about Keira Knightley.

1 ______________________________ born?

2 ______________ a lot of problems at school?

3 ____________ when she made her first film?

4 When ______________________________?

5 ______________________________ school?

6 How many ______________________ since 1998?

7 How long ______________________________?

b Ask **B** the questions and write the answers in the gaps in the biography. Answer **B**'s questions about Orlando Bloom. What do the actors have in common?

ORLANDO BLOOM

Orlando Bloom was born in [1] ____________, England, in 1977. He has a sister who is two years younger than him. When he was a child, Orlando thought his father was Harry Bloom, his mother's husband, who died when he was only four. But the truth was that his father was [2] ____________. He went to school in Canterbury but he left when he was [3] ____________ years old (he was dyslexic). He then moved to London where he trained with the British American Drama Academy. His first film was [4] ____________, about the Irish writer Oscar Wilde. He became really famous in [5] ____________ when he played Legolas Greenleaf in *The Lord of the Rings* films. He has made [6] ____________ films since then. He has lived in London since [7] ____________.

KEIRA KNIGHTLEY

Keira Knightley was born in Teddington, England, in 1983. She has an older brother, Caleb. At school she had a lot of problems because she was dyslexic. Keira made her first film when she was only nine years old. She became famous in 1999, when she was chosen for the *Star Wars* films. She played the part of the double of the heroine, Queen Amidala (Natalie Portman). The two girls looked so similar that after make-up their mothers couldn't tell which was their daughter. She left school in 1998 when she was only 15 to concentrate on acting. She has made 11 films since then. One of the most famous is *Pirates of the Caribbean*. Keira has lived in London all her life.

B **a** Read the biographies. Complete questions 1–7 to find the missing information about Orlando Bloom.

1 ______________________________ born ?

2 ______________________________ father?

3 ____________________ when he left school ?

4 ______________________________ first film?

5 When ______________________________?

6 How many ______________________ since 2001?

7 How long ______________________________?

b Ask **A** the questions and write the answers in the gaps in the biography. Answer **A**'s questions about Keira Knightley. What do the actors have in common?

a Write a name or phrase in as many circles as you can.

1 A sport you used to play but don't now.

2 A singer or band you used to listen to but don't now.

3 A kind of food or drink you didn't use to like but like now.

4 A game you used to play a lot but don't now.

5 A pet you used to have but don't have now.

6 Something you used to wear but don't now.

7 A TV programme you used to watch a lot but don't now.

8 Something you didn't use to do at weekends but do now.

9 An actor / actress you used to like but don't now.

10 A bad habit you used to have but don't now.

b Compare your circles with a partner's. Ask for / give more information about how and why you've changed.

What's it famous for?

1 A building in your town which was built more than 200 years ago. ____________________

2 A film which was directed by somebody from your country. ____________________

3 A competition which was won by a person or team from your country. ____________________

4 Something which was invented by a person from your country. ____________________

5 Something which is made in your town / region. ____________________

6 A famous picture which was painted by somebody from your country. ____________________

7 A famous dish which is eaten a lot in your town / region. ____________________

8 A building which was designed by someone from your country. ____________________

9 A well-known film which was filmed in your country. ____________________

10 A famous book which was written by someone from your country. ____________________

11 A place which was discovered by somebody from your country. ____________________

12 A wild animal or plant which is only found in your country. ____________________

13 A piece of music which was composed by somebody from your country. ____________________

14 A fictional character who was created by somebody from your country. ____________________

15 A well-known song which was written by someone from your country. ____________________

a Read the sentences. Tick (✓) the ones which are true for you.

b Talk to your partner. Read the true sentences and give more information. Correct the wrong sentences.

Sentence 1 is true. No one in my family has long hair.
OR *Sentence 1 isn't true. My sister has very long hair.*

c Listen to your partner. Ask for more information.

1 **No one** in my family has very long hair. ☐
2 **Somebody** in my family speaks English very well. ☐
3 I didn't go **anywhere** last night. ☐
4 I didn't come to school with **anybody** today. ☐
5 I saw **something** good on TV last night. ☐
6 I bought **something** for **somebody** yesterday. ☐
7 **Nobody** in my family smokes. ☐
8 I went **somewhere** nice last weekend. ☐
9 I didn't speak to **anybody** before the class started. ☐
10 I didn't have **anything** for breakfast today. ☐
11 I didn't read **anything** in English yesterday. ☐
12 There's **nothing** I really want to buy at the moment. ☐
13 I'm not planning to go **anywhere** this summer. ☐
14 I like relaxing and doing **nothing** at the weekend. ☐
15 If I need information about **something**, I always look on the Internet first. ☐

a Complete the sentences. Try to write something positive after *'But on the other hand, … '.*

b Compare what you've written with a partner. How similar are you?

My lifestyle

☹ I think I ______________________ too much.

☹ I don't ______________________ enough.

☹ I'm too ______________________.

☺ *But on the other hand,* ______________________.

My diet

☹ I don't eat enough ______________________.

☹ I eat too much ______________________.

☹ I eat too many ______________________.

☺ *But on the other hand,* ______________________.

My town / city

☹ There are too many ______________________.

☹ There's too much ______________________.

☹ There aren't enough ______________________.

☹ My town is too ______________________.

☺ *But on the other hand,* ______________________.

On TV / the radio

☹ There aren't enough programmes about

______________________.

☹ There's too much ______________________.

☹ There are too many ______________________.

☺ *But on the other hand,* ______________________.

● Ask and answer with a partner. Ask for more information.

What do you think is the best way to **give up** smoking?

Have you ever forgotten to **turn** your mobile **off** in the cinema?

Do you always **call** people **back** when they phone and leave you a message?

Do you **throw** old clothes **away** or do you give them to other people?

Do you ever **look after** other people's children?

How often do you **put** sunscreen **on**?

How many things in your house do you **turn on** with a remote control?

Do you usually **write down** what you have to do next day (or what you need to buy)?

Do you enjoy **trying on** clothes when you go shopping?

When was the last time you **filled in** a form?

Do you often **go away** at the weekend?

Do you normally **look up** new words when you read something in English?

Do you usually **stay up** late the night before an exam?

Do you **get on** badly with anybody in your family?

How many nights do you **go out** in a typical week?

Have you **taken** anything **back** to a shop recently?

my family

languages

tomorrow

food and drink

daily routine

TV

films and cinema

my house / flat

clothes

last night

breakfast

free time

music

sport

animals

school / university

I couldn't go in the sea because …	… I hadn't studied enough.
I couldn't find the restaurant because …	… I'd drunk too much coffee.
I didn't recognize my friend because …	… I hadn't charged the battery.
I couldn't sleep because …	… the chef had put too much salt on it.
I couldn't use my mobile phone because …	… she had changed the colour of her hair.
I turned on the TV to watch the football, but …	… I hadn't looked at the map.
I couldn't read the menu because …	… I hadn't set the alarm.
I argued with my husband because …	… I hadn't brought my swimsuit.
I couldn't eat the fish because …	… I'd forgotten where I parked it.
I failed the exam because …	… I'd left my glasses at home.
I couldn't find my car because …	… the match had finished.
I didn't wake up because …	… he hadn't done the washing up.

a Match sentences 1–6 with the people in the picture. Write the sentence in the speech bubble.

1 I can't see the board.
2 I missed the bus.
3 Can I open the window?
4 I left my book at home.
5 What page is it?
6 Have you done the homework?

FOLD

b Who said what? Can you remember? Complete the sentences in reported speech.

A Ana said that ______________________.
B Susana asked ______________________.
C David said ______________________.
D The teacher asked ______________________.
E Halma said ______________________.
F Miriam asked ______________________.

1 Family

- Do you have any brothers and sisters? What do they do?
- Who do you get on with best in your family?
- Have you ever had a big argument with someone in your family?
- Describe a person in your family.

2 Personality

- Are you an optimist or a pessimist?
- Do you know anyone who's very mean? Describe him/her.
- Who are you most similar to in your family?
- What kind of personality would your 'perfect partner' have?

3 Sport

- Do you do any sport or exercise?
- What sport do you like watching on TV?
- What's the most exciting sports event you've ever seen?
- What sport would you like to be good at?

4 Music

- What kind of music do you like to dance to?
- What's the best concert you've ever been to?
- Do you like listening to music when you're studying?
- If you had to do karaoke, what song would you sing?

5 Clothes

- Where do you usually buy clothes?
- What would you wear if you had an important interview?
- Do you ever borrow clothes from friends or family?
- Have you ever bought something but never worn it?

6 Animals

- Do you have any pets?
- Did you use to have any pets when you were a child?
- Would you like to go on a safari?
- If you could be an animal, which animal would you be?

7 School

- Where did you go to primary school?
- Did you like it? Why (not)?
- Describe the best teacher you've ever had.
- What's (or was) your favourite subject at school?

8 Holidays

- When did you last go on holiday? Where?
- Did you have a good time? Why (not)?
- What do you like doing when you're on holiday?
- What's the best holiday you've ever had?

9 Health and diet

- How much do you walk every day?
- What do you eat too much of?
- What don't you eat enough of?
- Do you think you're very stressed? Why (not)?

10 Time

- Do you have more or less free time than two years ago?
- How long does it take you to get to this school?
- How much time a week do you spend doing homework?
- What would you like to have more time for?

11 Towns and cities

- What are the best and worst things about your town?
- Do you like it, or would you like to live somewhere else?
- What town would you most like to visit? Why?
- What's the most beautiful town you've ever been to?

12 Cinema

- How often do you go to the cinema?
- What's the next film you're going to see?
- What's the best film you've ever seen?
- Who's your favourite director?

1 C Ain't got no / I got life 1.9 — CD1 Track 10

Listening for specific words

LANGUAGE Parts of the body, common nouns

- Give each student a sheet. Focus on **a** and ask SS if songs in their language also use slang or incorrect grammar. Elicit that *I ain't = I'm not.* Then give SS in pairs a few minutes to complete the rest. Check answers.

1 d	2 a	3 e	4 b	5 f	6 c

- Remind SS that *I've got* is grammatical and is an alternative form of *I have.*
- Focus on **b**. Give SS, in pairs, a few minutes to say what they can see in the pictures. **Check answers.**

Picture 1: money, sweater, name, perfume, home, mother, ticket, friends.
Picture 2: head, arms, mouth, lips, ears, tongue, nose, legs, toes

- Now play the tape/CD once, pausing as necessary for SS to write the words in. Get SS to compare answers with a partner and play the song again for SS to fill in the gaps.
- Repeat if necessary and then check answers.

1 home	6 friends	11 nose	16 legs
2 money	7 name	12 mouth	17 toes
3 sweater	8 ticket	13 tongue	
4 perfume	9 head	14 lips	
5 mother	10 ears	15 arms	

- Now get SS to read the lyrics with the glossary and ask them if they think it's an optimistic or pessimistic song (optimistic).
- You may want to play the song for the class to sing along.
- Finally, get SS to read the **Song facts**.

2 C Imagine 2.10 — CD1 Track 31

Abstract nouns

LANGUAGE Abstract nouns: *brotherhood, hunger,* etc.

- Give each student a sheet. Focus on **a** and give SS time to match the words and definitions. Check answers.

A 10	B 2	C 6	D8	E 9
F 1	G 3	H 5	I 4	J 7

- Focus on **b**. Play the tape/CD once for SS to fill in the gaps.

EXTRA support Tell SS they can just write the letter of the words if they don't have time to write the whole word.

- Get SS to compare with a partner. Play the song again for SS to check. Check answers.

1 heaven	4 religion	7 possessions	10 brotherhood
2 hell	5 peace	8 greed	11 dreamer
3 sky	6 dreamer	9 hunger	

- You may want to play the song for the class to sing along.
- Finally, get SS to read the **Song facts**.

3 C White flag 3.11 — CD1 Track 54

Listening for verbs

LANGUAGE Common verbs, *will/won't*

- Give each student a sheet. Focus on **a** and give SS a few minutes in pairs to guess the missing verbs. **Don't check answers at this point.**
- Now play the tape/CD once for SS to fill the gaps. Get SS to compare with a partner, and then play the song again for them to check. Check answers.

2 tell	7 be	12 meet
3 promise	8 know	13 pass
4 return	9 come	14 think
5 go	10 understand	
6 put	11 live	

- Now focus on **c**. Play the song again while SS read the lyrics with the glossary. Then give them a few minutes to answer the questions in pairs. Check answers.

1 She's broken up with her partner.
2 Yes.
3 The captain of the ship.
4 Soldiers.
5 When they want to surrender.
6 Her partner left her.
7 She won't say anything. He'll think she's OK, but she will still feel the same as before.

- If you think students would like to hear the song again, play it one more time.
- Finally, get SS to read the **Song facts**.

4 A True blue 4.3 — CD2 Track 4

Listening for past simple and past participles

LANGUAGE Present perfect and past simple

- Give each SS a sheet. Focus on **a** and give SS a few moments to decide what the past simple / past participles are. Check answers and make sure SS know the meaning of the verbs (*search* and *whisper* are in the glossary).

irregular: have, had, had; know, knew, known; hear, heard, heard
regular: look, walk, sail, cry, whisper, search

- Focus on **b**. Give SS a few moments to read the lyrics and see if they can guess where some of the verbs go, **but don't check answers yet**.
- Now play the tape/CD once for SS to fill the gaps. Repeat if necessary. Check answers.

2 looked	5 had	8 cried
3 knew	6 sailed	9 whispered
4 walked	7 heard	10 searched

- Focus on **c**, and give SS in pairs a few moments to find the lines. Check answers.

2 I've sailed a thousand ships
3 Your heart fits me like a glove
4 Those teardrops they won't fall again
5 So if you should ever doubt
6 The sun is bursting right out of the sky

- You may want to play the song for the class to sing along.
- Finally, get SS to read the **Song facts**.

5 D We are the champions 5.11 CD2 Track 30

Listening for phrases

LANGUAGE	Present perfect (experience) Phrases: *time after time*, etc.

- Give each student a sheet. Focus on **a** and give SS, in pairs, time to match the phrases A–J with their meanings 1–10. Check answers, clarifying meaning where necessary.

A 5	D 2	G 3	J 1
B 9	E 8	H 6	
C 7	F 4	I 10	

- Play the tape/CD once and SS try to write the letter of each phrase in **a** in the column. Get them to compare their answers in pairs. Then play the song again so that they can write the missing phrases into the song.

2 E	3 B	4 G	5 I	6 H
7 A	8 C	9 D	10 J	

- Give SS a few minutes to read through the song with the glossary and look at the pictures. Elicit the gist of the meaning from the whole class. The singer has had a lot of 'ups and downs' in his life but has survived. The singer (and us) will keep fighting all our lives. *We* are (figuratively speaking) the world champions.
- You may want to play the song for the class to sing along.
- Finally get SS to read the **Song facts**.

6 B Wouldn't it be nice 6.7 CD2 Track 44

Listening for detail

LANGUAGE	2nd conditional

- Give each student a sheet. Focus on the song and the task in **a**. Explain that an extra word has been added to every line of the song. The extra word makes sense but is not sung. SS have to listen carefully and cross out this word.
- Demonstrate by playing the first two lines. Then play the rest of the song. You could play lines 1–6, then replay, then lines 7–13, then lines 14–22. SS can compare answers with their partner after they listen, then listen a second time. Check answers.

1 much	9 whole	17 really
2 for	10 long	18 so
3 both	11 that	19 together
4 really	12 little	20 much
5 all	13 very	21 now
6 darling	14 all	22 really
7 always	15 little	
8 early	16 maybe	

- Now get SS to read the song with the glossary and in pairs decide the answer to the question (they're optimistic).
- You may want to play the song for the class to sing along.
- Finally get SS to read the **Song facts**.

7 C It's all over now 7.10 CD3 Track 11

Correcting words

LANGUAGE	*used to*

- Give each student a sheet and focus on **a**. Go through the words in **bold** and explain that SS have to listen and decide if these words are right (what the singer sings) or wrong (different). On the first listen, SS just have to put a tick or cross. They shouldn't try to correct the wrong words at this stage. Elicit which words are right and wrong, but tell SS not to call out the right words.
- Now play the song again and this time SS have to try and correct the wrong words.

  Let SS compare their answers with their partner. Check answers, going through the song line by line.

1 ✗ stay	4 ✓	7 ✓	10 ✗ head
2 ✗ cry	5 ✗ run	8 ✓	11 ✓
3 ✗ open	6 ✗ spent	9 ✗ wake	12 ✗ same

- Give SS a few minutes to read the song with the glossary. Ask them what the title means (= our relationship is finished now).
- You may want to play the song for the class to sing along.
- Finally, get SS to read the **Song facts**.

8 C I say a little prayer 8.8 CD3 Track 29

Listening for specific words

LANGUAGE	Phrasal verbs and routines

- Focus on the task and give SS in pairs time to read the song and look at the pictures.

  Set a time limit, e.g. 5 minutes, for them to guess the missing words and write them in **Our guess**. Tell SS **NOT** to write the words in the song at this stage.
- Now play the song for SS to listen and check their answers. Replay lines and verses as necessary.
- Check answers. Tell SS to write the verbs in the song.

1 wake	4 be	7 live	10 take
2 put	5 love	8 run	11 believe
3 wear	6 be	9 think	

- You may want to play the song for the class to sing along.
- Finally, get SS to read the **Song facts**.

Ain't got no / I've got life

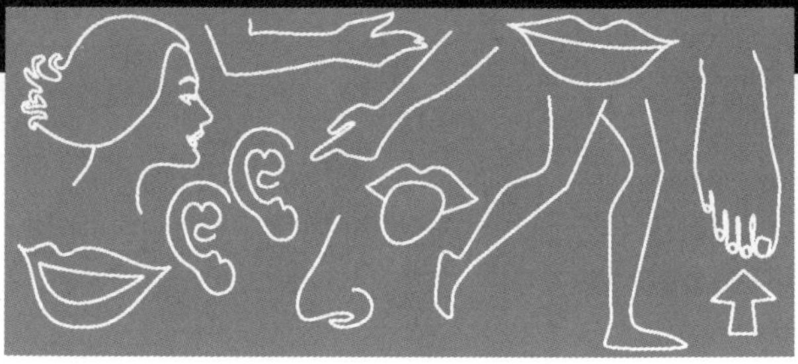

I ain't got no [1] *home*, ain't got no shoes
Ain't got no [2] ________, ain't got no class
Ain't got no skirts, ain't got no [3] ________
Ain't got no [4] ________, ain't got no beer
Ain't got no man
Ain't got no [5] ________, ain't got no culture
Ain't got no [6] ________, ain't got no schooling
Ain't got no love, ain't got no [7] ________
Ain't got no [8] ________, ain't got no token
Ain't got no god

What have I got?
Why am I alive anyway?
Yeah, what have I got
Nobody can take away?

I've got my hair, got my [9] ________
I've got my brains, got my [10] ________,
I've got my eyes, got my [11] ________
I've got my [12] ________, I've got my smile
I've got my [13] ________, got my chin
I've got my neck, got my [14] ________
I've got my heart, got my soul
I've got my back, I got my self
I've got my [15] ________, got my hands,
I've got my fingers, got my [16] ________
I've got my feet, got my [17] ________
I've got my liver, got my blood

I've got life, I've got my freedom
I've got life
I've got life
And I'm gonna keep it
I've got life
And nobody's gonna take it away

⚠ Pop songs often use words and phrases which are slang or are not grammatically correct.

a Match the words and phrases.

In songs		Grammatically correct
1 I ain't (rich)	☐	a I don't have
2 I ain't got no (money)	☐	b I'm going to ...
3 I wanna (be free)	☐	c because
4 I'm gonna (leave you)	☐	d I'm not ...
5 Yeah	☐	e I want to ...
6 'cos / 'cause	☐	f Yes

b Look at the pictures in the song which show the missing words. What can you see?

c Listen and complete the song.

Glossary

class = (in this context) style
culture = (in this context) knowledge about art and literature, etc.
schooling = education
token = a piece of paper or plastic that you can use to buy things
soul = the spiritual part of a person
liver = the part of your body that cleans your blood
blood = the red liquid that flows through your body
freedom = the noun from *free*

Song facts

Ain't got no / I got life was originally recorded by Nina Simone in 1968. It was an adaptation of two songs from the 1960s musical *Hair* and it became one of her most popular songs.

a Match the words with the definitions.

A religion	☐	1 Things that are yours, which belong to you.
B heaven	☐	2 The place where some religions believe that good people go when they die.
C hell	☐	3 A feeling of community and great friendship between people.
D hunger	☐	4 A person who dreams.
E peace	☐	5 Wanting more than you need.
F possessions	☐	6 The place where some religions believe that bad people go when they die.
G brotherhood	☐	7 The place where you can see the sun, moon and stars.
H greed	☐	8 The noun from *hungry*.
I dreamer	☐	9 The opposite of *war*.
J sky	☐	10 For example, Christianity, Hinduism, Islam, etc.

b Listen and complete the song with the words from **a**.

Imagine

Imagine there's no [1] _________,
It's easy if you try,
No [2] _________ below us,
Above us only [3] _________,
Imagine all the people
living for today ...

Imagine there's no countries,
It isn't hard to do,
Nothing to kill or die for,
And no [4] _________ too,
Imagine all the people
living life in [5] _________ ...

You may say I'm a [6] _________,
but I'm not the only one,
I hope some day you'll join us,
And the world will be as one.

Imagine no [7] _________,
I wonder if you can,
No need for [8] _________ or [9] _________,
A [10] _________ of man,
Imagine all the people
sharing all the world ...

You may say I'm a [11] _________,
but I'm not the only one,
I hope some day you'll join us,
And the world will live as one.

Glossary

there's no countries = there aren't any ...
wonder = ask yourself
share = divide between two or more people
join = become a member e.g. of a club or organization

Song facts

Imagine was originally recorded by the ex-Beatle John Lennon in 1975 and it became his most famous and popular song. It became a big hit again after Lennon's death in 1980 and again after the attacks on the World Trade Centre in 2001. It was recently voted the UK's most popular song of all time.

a Read the song lyrics and guess the missing verbs. Don't write them in yet.

b Listen to the song and fill the gaps with a verb.

White flag

I know you **1 t***hink*_____ that I shouldn't still love you,
or **2 t**_________ you that.
But if I didn't say it, well I'd still have felt it
where's the sense in that?
I **3 p**_________ I'm not trying to make your life harder
or **4 r**_________ to where we were

I will **5 g**_________ down with this ship
And I won't **6 p**_________ my hands up and surrender
There will be no white flag above my door
I'm in love and always will **7 b**_________

I **8 k**_________ I left too much mess and
destruction to **9 c**_________ back again.
And I caused nothing but trouble
I **10 u**_________ if you can't talk to me again.
And if you **11 l**_________ by the rules of 'it's over'
then I'm sure that that makes sense

I will, etc.

And when we **12 m**_________ , which I'm sure we will,
all that was there, will be there still .
I'll let it **13 p**_________and hold my tongue
and you will **14 t**_________ that I've moved on ... .

Well I will, etc.

c Read your song with the glossary. In pairs, answer the questions.

1 What has happened to the singer?
2 Does she still love her ex-partner?
3 Who usually 'goes down with their ship'?
4 Who usually 'puts their hands up to surrender'?
5 When does somebody hold up a white flag?
6 Do you think the singer left her partner, or her partner left the singer?
7 What does she think will happen when they meet again?

Glossary

I shouldn't still love you = It's bad for me to continue to love you.
surrender = stop fighting and say you have lost
mess = a lot of problems
destruction (noun from *destroy*) = when everything is broken
trouble = problems
that makes sense = It's the right thing to do.
I'll let it pass and hold my tongue = I won't say anything
I've moved on = I am not in love with you now

Song facts

White flag was originally recorded by the British singer Dido in 2003. It became her biggest UK hit. The song was written about breaking up from her boyfriend in 2002 when they were engaged to be married.

a Look at the verbs. Are they regular or irregular? What's the past simple and the past participle of the irregular ones? How do you pronounce them?

~~have~~	know	look	walk	sail
hear	cry	have	whisper	search

b Listen and complete the song with the past simple or past participle of the verbs from **a**.

True blue

I've [1] *had* other guys
I've [2] ________ into their eyes
But I never [3] ________ love before
Till you [4] ________ through my door
I've [5] ________ other lips
I've [6] ________ a thousand ships
But no matter where I go
You're the one for me baby this I know, 'cause it's...

True love
You're the one I'm dreaming of
Your heart fits me like a glove
And I'm gonna be true blue baby I love you

I've [7] ________ all the lines
I've [8] ________ oh so many times
Those teardrops they won't fall again
I'm so excited 'cause you're my best friend
So if you should ever doubt
Wonder what love is all about
Just think back and remember dear
Those words [9] ________ in your ear, I said

True love
You're the one I'm dreaming of, etc.

No more sadness, I kiss it good-bye
The sun is bursting right out of the sky
I [10] ________ the whole world for someone like you
Don't you know, don't you know that

True love
You're the one I'm dreaming of, etc.

c Read the song with the glossary. Which line means ...?

1 Until I met you the first time
'til you walked through my door
2 I've travelled a lot
3 You are exactly right for me
4 I won't cry again
5 If one day you're not sure
6 It's a wonderful day

Glossary

guys (informal) = men, boyfriends
till = until
no matter where = It doesn't matter where
I'm gonna be true = I'm going to be faithful
gloves = things you wear on your hands
search = look for
'cause = because
doubt = not be sure
wonder = ask yourself
whisper = speak very quietly
burst = break open

Song facts

True blue was written and recorded by Madonna on her third album, *True blue* in 1986. The single was a big hit in the UK and the USA.

We are the champions

Missing phrase

I've paid my dues, ______ — 1 *F*
I've done my sentence, but ______ — 2 ______
And bad mistakes, I've made ______ — 3 ______
I've had ______ of sand kicked in my face — 4 ______
But I've ______ — 5 ______
And we mean to go on and on and on

We are the champions, my friends
And we'll ______ fighting till the end — 6 ______
We are the champions, we are the champions
No time for losers 'cos we are the champions of the world

I've taken my bows, and my ______ — 7 ______
You brought me ______ — 8 ______
And everything that goes with it, I thank you all
But it's been ______, no pleasure cruise — 9 ______
I consider it a challenge before ______ — 10 ______
And I ain't gonna lose
And we mean to go on and on and on
We are the champions, my friends, etc.

a Match the phrases with their meanings.

A curtain calls	☐	1 all the people in the world
B a few	☐	2 not easy
C fame and fortune	☐	3 the part that belongs to me
D no bed of roses	☐	4 again and again
E committed no crime	☐	5 when actors come out at the end of a show
F time after time	☐	6 continue
G my share	☐	7 success and money
H keep on	☐	8 not done anything wrong
I come through	☐	9 not many
J the whole human race	☐	10 survive

b Now listen to the song. Write the letter of the missing phrase in the column.

c Listen again and check. Write in the phrases.

Glossary

paid my dues = paid what I owed
we mean to = we intend to, are going to
go on = continue
'cos = because
pleasure cruise = (literally) a trip in a boat, (in this context) something easy and fun
I consider = in my opinion
challenge = something new and difficult that you want to do
I ain't going to = I'm not going to

Song facts

We are the champions was first recorded by Queen in 1977, and was written by their lead singer Freddie Mercury. It was a number one hit, and soon became the anthem of successful sport teams around the world, though most people only know the chorus!

In 2001, Queen members Brian May and Roger Taylor recorded a new version of this song with British singer Robbie Williams.

a Listen to the song. There is one extra word in each line. Cross it out.

Wouldn't it be nice

Wouldn't it be nice if we were ~~much~~ older
Then we wouldn't have to wait for so long
And wouldn't it be nice to both live together
In the kind of world where we really belong
You know it's going to make it all that much better
When we can say goodnight darling and stay together

Wouldn't it be nice if we could always wake up
In the early morning when the day is new
And after having spent the whole day together
Hold each other close the whole long night through
Happy times together that we've been spending
I wish that every little kiss was never-ending
Wouldn't it be very nice

Maybe if we think and wish and hope and pray it might all come true
Baby then there wouldn't be a single little thing we couldn't do
Maybe we could be married
And then we'd be really happy
Wouldn't it be so nice

You know it seems the more we talk about it together
It only makes it much worse to live without it
But let's talk about it now
Wouldn't it be really nice

b Listen again and read the song with the glossary. Do you think the singers are optimistic, pessimistic, or realistic about the future?

Glossary

belong = to be part of
the whole day = all the day
hold = have something in your hand(s) / arms
wish = to want something that can't happen now
pray = ask God for something
a single thing = one thing

Song facts

Wouldn't it be nice was written by Brian Wilson of the American group The Beach Boys, who recorded the song in 1966 on their album *Pet Sounds*. This song, and others on the album, had an important influence on other pop artists, including the Beatles and Pink Floyd. In a UK music magazine, *Pet Sounds* was recently voted the greatest album of all time.

a Listen to the song. Are the words in **bold** right or wrong? Put a tick or cross in column **A**.

b Listen again and correct the wrong words in column **B**.

It's all over now

Lyrics		A	B
Well, baby used to **play** out all night long	1	☐	________
She made me **laugh**, she done me wrong	2	☐	________
She hurt my eyes **closed**, that's no lie	3	☐	________
Tables turn and now her turn to **cry**	4	☐	________
Because I used to love her, but it's all over now			
Because I used to love her, but it's all over now			
Well, she used to **walk** around with every man in town	5	☐	________
She **took** all my money, playing her high class game	6	☐	________
She put me out, it was a **pity** how I cried	7	☐	________
Tables turn and now her turn to **cry**	8	☐	________
Because I used to love her, but it's all over now			
Because I used to love her, but it's all over now			
Well, I used to **work** in the morning, get my breakfast in bed	9	☐	________
When I'd gotten worried she'd ease my aching **heart**	10	☐	________
But now she's here and **there**, with every man in town	11	☐	________
Still trying to take me for that **stupid** old clown	12	☐	________

Because I used to love her, but it's all over now
Because I used to love her, but it's all over now
Because I used to love her, but it's all over now

Glossary

lie = something which isn't true
she done me wrong (US slang) = she was bad to me
tables turn = the situation has changed
it's over = it's finished
gotten (US English) = got
ease = make something feel better
aching = hurting
(She's) still trying to take me for = (She) still thinks I am

Song facts

I used to love her was written by Bobby Womack and was originally recorded by an American Rhythm and Blues band called the Valentinos. The British rock band, the Rolling Stones recorded the song as *It's all over now* in 1964, and it was their first number one hit. Bobby Womack hated the Stones' version, but when he got his first royalty cheque he tried to get them to record more of his songs! This was the first song that Bruce Springsteen learnt to play on the guitar.

a In pairs, read the song and look at the pictures. Guess the missing verbs. Write your guess in the column on the right.

b Listen and check. Write the words in the song.

Song facts

I say a little prayer was originally written for Dionne Warwick by Burt Bacharach and Hal David, in 1967. A year later the song was recorded by 'the Queen of Soul', American singer Aretha Franklin, and it became a very big hit.

I say a little prayer

	Our guess
The moment I ________ up	1 ________
Before I ________ on my make-up	2 ________
I say a little prayer for you	
And while combing my hair, now,	
And wondering what dress to ________, now,	3 ________
I say a little prayer for you	
Forever, forever, you'll ________ in my heart	4 ________
And I will ________ you	5 ________
Forever, forever, we never will part	
Oh, how I'll love you	
Together, together, that's how it must ________	6 ________
To ________ without you	7 ________
Would only mean heartbreak for me.	
I ________ for the bus, dear,	8 ________
While riding I ________ of us, dear,	9 ________
I say a little prayer for you.	
At work I just ________ time	10 ________
And all through my coffee break-time,	
I say a little prayer for you.	
Forever, forever, etc.	
My darling, ________ me,	11 ________
For me there is no one	
But you.	
Please love me true.	
This is my prayer	
Answer my prayer, baby	

Quicktests

Instructions

There are eight photocopiable Quicktests, one for each File 1–8. These test the Grammar, Vocabulary, and Pronunciation from the A, B, C, and D lessons.

There is one mark for each answer so SS will get a total mark out of 50 for each test.

Each test should take between 20 and 30 minutes.

Answers

1 Quicktest

GRAMMAR

a 1 c 2 b 3 a 4 c 5 b 6 a 7 c 8 a 9 c 10 b

b 11 did 12 about 13 a 14 don't 15 does 16 wearing 17 isn't 18 which 19 where 20 who

VOCABULARY

a 1 mean 2 lazy 3 Sit down. 4 Answer a question. 5 on the left

b 6 eyes 7 hands 8 toes 9 lips 10 teeth

c 11 spell 12 Have 13 See 14 Thursday 15 date 16 next 17 aunt 18 off/on 19 kind/type 20 opposite

PRONUNCIATION

a 1 toes 2 cooks 3 has 4 head 5 serious

b 6 nephew 7 behind 8 unfriendly 9 similar 10 example

2 Quicktest

GRAMMAR

a 1 c 2 a 3 b 4 c 5 a 6 b 7 b 8 a 9 b 10 a

b 11 didn't 12 was 13 Did 14 went 15 was 16 weren't 17 Which 18 won 19 so 20 Although

VOCABULARY

a 1 broke 2 bought 3 told 4 took 5 chose

b 6 knock 7 hire 8 rent 9 go 10 stay

c 11 windy 12 sunny 13 foggy 14 cloudy 15 raining

d 16 on 17 at 18 at 19 in 20 on

PRONUNCIATION

a 1 abroad 2 who 3 which 4 sunbathe 5 although

b 6 because 7 together 8 sightseeing 9 evening 10 accident

3 Quicktest

GRAMMAR

a 1 c 2 a 3 c 4 b 5 a 6 c 7 a 8 b 9 a 10 b

b 11 to 12 Are 13 won't 14 don't 15 do 16 Shall/Can 17 does 18 doesn't 19 were 20 did

VOCABULARY

a 1 learn 2 arrive 3 miss 4 remember 5 lose 6 turn on 7 lend 8 push 9 lose 10 send

b 11 for 12 back 13 with 14 to 15 at 16 to 17 of 18 to 19 to 20 about

PRONUNCIATION

a 1 find 2 miss 3 turn 4 leave 5 push

b 6 arrive 7 pessimist 8 secret 9 probably 10 argue

4 Quicktest

GRAMMAR

a 1 b 2 c 3 b 4 a 5 c 6 b 7 a 8 b 9 b 10 c

b 11 been 12 has 13 yet 14 just 15 seen 16 than 17 as 18 more 19 most 20 ever

VOCABULARY

a 1 skirt 2 cap 3 scarf 4 dress 5 trainers 6 try 7 on 8 Take 9 pyjamas 10 dressed

b 11 empty 12 quiet 13 uncomfortable 14 dangerous 15 untidy

c 16 make 17 take 18 time 19 spend 20 on

PRONUNCIATION

a 1 skirt 2 already 3 yet 4 crowded 5 just

b 6 comfortable 7 relaxed 8 dangerous 9 exciting 10 impossible

5 Quicktest

GRAMMAR

a 1 c 2 c 3 a 4 b 5 b 6 a 7 c 8 b 9 a 10 b

b 11 to 12 speak/write 13 see 14 Reading 15 waiting 16 cooking 17 has 18 mustn't 19 have 20 over

VOCABULARY

a 1 trying 2 planning 3 forget 4 mind 5 offers 6 need 7 decided 8 hoping 9 promised 10 hate

b 11 across 12 into 13 round 14 down 15 to

c 16 do 17 hit 18 go 19 kick 20 play

PRONUNCIATION

a 1 think 2 enjoy 3 offer 4 mind 5 along

b 6 decide 7 remember 8 interested 9 across 10 towards

6 Quicktest

GRAMMAR

a 1 b 2 c 3 a 4 b 5 b 6 c 7 a 8 b 9 a 10 a

b 11 If 12 invite 13 don't 14 Would 15 were 16 have 17 may/might 18 not 19 drink 20 should

VOCABULARY

a 1 miss 2 meet 3 do 4 looks like 5 looked at

b 6 Giraffes 7 bee 8 Mouse 9 lion 10 shark

c 11 education 12 election 13 information 14 decision 15 invitation

d 16 married/engaged 17 better 18 off 19 on 20 home

PRONUNCIATION

a 1 swan 2 bear 3 would 4 eagle 5 if

b 6 newspaper 7 survive 8 elephant 9 indecisive 10 advice

7 Quicktest

GRAMMAR

a 1 c 2 a 3 b 4 a 5 b 6 a 7 b 8 b 9 a 10 b

b 11 long 12 since 13 been 14 has 15 did 16 used 17 wear 18 by 19 are 20 were

VOCABULARY

a 1 history 2 geography 3 literature 4 science 5 maths

b 6 primary 7 left 8 working 9 fell 10 married 11 had 12 separated 13 divorced 14 retired 15 died

c 16 discovered 17 invented 18 based 19 directed 20 designed

PRONUNCIATION

a 1 since 2 afraid 3 born 4 famous 5 science

b 6 frightened 7 university 8 literature 9 invent 10 design

8 Quicktest

GRAMMAR

a 1 c 2 a 3 b 4 a 5 b 6 a 7 a 8 c 9 a 10 a

b 11 something 12 didn't 13 too 14 many 15 enough 16 off 17 it 18 Neither 19 have 20 did

VOCABULARY

a 1 relaxing 2 excited 3 tired 4 depressing 5 bored

b 6 do 7 fill 8 give 9 Hurry 10 get

c 11 None 12 few 13 down 14 be 15 find 16 up 17 like 18 both 19 as 20 to

PRONUNCIATION

a 1 healthy 2 early 3 enough 4 allergic 5 again

b 6 exciting 7 anywhere 8 lifestyle 9 personality 10 exactly

END-OF-COURSE TEST

Instructions

The End-of-course test is a test of all of the Grammar, Vocabulary, and Pronunciation from the A, B, C, and D lessons. It also includes Reading, Listening, and Writing.

Grammar
25 marks one mark for each answer

Vocabulary
25 marks one mark for each answer

Pronunciation
10 marks one mark for each answer

Reading
10 marks one mark for each answer

Listening
10 marks one mark for each answer (tapescript *p.230*)

Writing
10 marks We suggest you allocate 6 marks for grammar, vocabulary, and spelling, and 4 marks for content, presentation, and layout.

Speaking
10 marks Either give a mark for their speaking during the course, or use Communicative activity *Revision questions* on *p.217* as an oral test. Give SS a mark out of 10.

ANSWERS

GRAMMAR

a 1c 2b 3a 4c 5b 6b 7c 8b 9b 10a 11b 12a 13c 14b 15c

b 16 which / that 17 won't 18 as 19 most 20 to 21 had 22 may / might 23 were 24 Neither 25 had

VOCABULARY

a 1 fingers 2 abroad 3 foggy 4 quiet 5 trainers 6 better 7 mind 8 spider 9 crowded 10 earns

b 11 lend 12 push 13 die 14 sell 15 uncomfortable 16 mean 17 impolite / rude

c 18 at 19 across 20 through 21 on 22 up 23 on 24 in 25 forward

PRONUNCIATION

a 1 round 2 since 3 must 4 just 5 begin

b 6 unfriendly 7 promise 8 remember 9 afraid 10 interested

READING

1 F 2 F 3 DS 4 DS 5 F 6 F 7 T 8 T 9 T 10 DS

LISTENING

a 1a 2b 3c 4c 5b

b 6a 7c 8b 9a 10c

Listening A CD3 Track 44

1

A Do you have this sweater in any other colours?
B Just a moment. Yes. In beige, green, and brown.
A Could I have a brown one, please?
B What size are you?
A Small.
B Let me have a look... No, sorry I've only got it in a medium.
A How about green? It's a bit bright. What about beige?
B Let me see. Yes, this one's a small.
A Yes, that one's fine. How much is it?
B It's 30 euros.
A That's great. I'll take it.

2

A How long are you going to stay here?
B Well, it depends. I have a return flight to London at the end of June, but if I can find a job, I want to stay until the middle of September. My university course starts in October so I have to be back in time for that.

3

A How old is your brother?
B Let me work it out. I'm 35 and he's three years older than me.
A That's amazing. He looks much younger than that. I thought he was about 30.
B Yeah, he looks after himself. Goes to the gym and all that.

4

A Are you happy with your new flat?
B Yeah. We're really happy with it. The rent is a bit more than I wanted to pay but you can see the mountains from our bedroom window. It's not enormous, but there are only two of us so it's big enough for the moment.

5

A The Travel Lodge. How can I help you?
B Good evening. I'd like to make a reservation.
A When for?
B For next Friday... the eighteenth. For three nights.
A Just one room?
A No. Two doubles and a single. A double room for me and my wife, a single room for my son…
B Yes.
A ....and then another double for my daughter and her husband. Oh yes, and a cot for their baby.
B How old is the baby?
A Sixteen months.
B OK, so that's two double rooms, one with a cot ...

Listening B CD3 Track 45

I = interviewer, E= Emma

I So where did you work before, Emma?
E At a big clothes store in London. I was a sales manager there.
I How long did you work there?
E Let's see, I started when I finished school, when I was 18, and I left when I was 30, so about 12 years altogether.
I Was it a well-paid job?
E Yes, very. I was earning a lot of money. But I had to work incredibly hard and my days were really long. I started work at 9 every morning and I often didn't finish till 7 or 8 in the evening. I travelled a lot too. I had to go to fashion shows and so on.
I Did you enjoy that?
E Yes, it was great. Milan, Paris, New York – all those glamorous places.
I So why did you decide to leave London?
E Well, it wasn't because I didn't like my job – in fact I loved it. It was just that I always felt stressed and I was always in a hurry. I didn't have enough time for myself – and I didn't spend enough time with my son, Sam. When I got home in the evening I was always too tired to play with him.
I So what did you do?
E I left my job and I bought a house in the south of France. I worked hard to do it up, and renovate it, and now I use it as a little hotel really, for six months of the year.
I How do you live now?
E Well, from April to September I work in the guesthouse. It's very small – there are only six rooms. And then from October to March I work in the garden, pick the olives, things like that.
I And are you happier?
E It's a very different life – I don't earn as much money – so no more designer clothes or expensive cars… I'm still quite busy but I'm not as stressed as I was before. And I can spend more time with my son. Life here is much slower than in London. I sleep better and I'm healthier, because I do more physical work. So yes, I'm much happier.

GRAMMAR

a Circle a, b, or c.

Example: My brother ____ Russian.
a speak ⓑ speaks c do speak

1 Where ____ work?
a you b you do c do you
2 What time ____ to come?
a she's going b is she going c going she
3 ____ away last weekend?
a Did you go b Did you went c Went you
4 He ____ a shower before breakfast.
a usually have b has usually c usually has
5 She ____ men who talk a lot.
a not likes b doesn't like c don't like
6 My brother ____ law at university.
a studies b studys c studyes
7 Be careful! You ____ a mistake.
a are makeing b making c are making
8 **A** Why ____ ?
B Because I'm happy.
a are you smiling b do you smile c you smile
9 How often ____ your grandparents?
a are you seeing b you see c do you see
10 That's the shop ____ I bought my computer.
a which b where c who

b Complete the sentences.

Example: She's waiting *for* the bus.

11 What ________ you do last weekend?
12 **A** What are you talking ________?
B It's a secret.
13 We have classes twice ________ week.
14 My parents ________ work. They're retired.
15 What time ________ the shop open?
16 **A** Why are you ________ a jacket?
B Because I'm cold!
17 My computer ________ working. It's broken.
18 I've bought a new machine ________ makes fantastic coffee.
19 Is this the restaurant ________ we had dinner last month?
20 They're the children ________ live next door to us.

20

VOCABULARY

a Write the opposites.

Example: shy *extrovert*

1 generous ________
2 hard-working ________
3 Stand up. ________
4 Ask a question. ________
5 on the right ________

b Write the words.

Example: You use these to hear. *ears*

6 You use these to see. ________
7 You have two of these at the end of your arms. ________
8 You have ten of these on your feet. ________
9 You use these to kiss. ________
10 You have 32 of these in your mouth. ________

c Complete with one word.

11 **A** How do you ________ your name?
B J-A-C-E-K.
12 ________ a good weekend!
13 Bye. ________ you on Monday.
14 Today's Wednesday so tomorrow's ________ .
15 **A** What's the ________ today?
B The 5th of September.
16 Maria is sitting ________ to Salvador.
17 Your mother's sister is your ________ .
18 Turn ________ your mobile phone.
19 **A** What's that?
B A guava. It's a ________ of fruit.
20 *Extrovert* is the ________ of *shy*.

20

PRONUNCIATION

a Write the words from the list in the chart.

cooks toes head has serious

nose	lips	friends
1 ________	2 ________	3 ________
smell	hear	
4 ________	5 ________	

b Underline the stressed syllable.

Example: after<u>noon</u>

6 nephew 8 unfriendly 10 example
7 behind 9 similar

10

Total 50

2 Quicktest

GRAMMAR

a Circle a, b, or c.

Example: My brother ____ Russian.
a speak ⓑ speaks c do speak

1 They ____ their holiday.
a didn't enjoyed b don't enjoyed c didn't enjoy

2 ____ to the bank this morning?
a Did you go b Did you went c Were you

3 When the bus ____ we got off.
a stoped b stopped c stop

4 When I woke up it ____ .
a was rain b were raining c was raining

5 What ____ when I phoned you?
a were you doing b was you doing
c you were doing

6 When I ____ her she was working in a cybercafé.
a meet b met c was meeting

7 Who ____ to?
a he wrote b did he write c he was writing

8 Who ____ the tickets?
a bought b did buy c did bought

9 It was really hot in Oslo, ____ it's normally cold there.
a because b although c so

10 I was really tired ____ I decided not to go to the gym.
a so b but c because

b Complete the sentences.

Example: She's waiting *for* the bus.

11 **A** Why ________ you come to the party?
B I wasn't invited!

12 What ________ the weather like when you were there?

13 ________ you buy the paper this morning?

14 I usually go by bus, but yesterday I ________ by train.

15 When I saw him he wasn't running, he ________ walking.

16 **A** Were the children watching TV?
B No, they ________ .

17 **A** ________ jacket do you prefer?
B I think I prefer the black one.

18 **A** Who ________ the match?
B Liverpool. It was 1–0.

19 We were very late, ________ we took a taxi.

20 ________ she isn't very tall, she's very good at basketball.

20

VOCABULARY

a Write the irregular past simple verbs.

Example: speak *spoke*

1 break ________
2 buy ________
3 tell ________
4 take ________
5 choose ________

b Complete with a verb from the list.

Example: *take* photos

rent hire go stay knock

6 ________ on the door
7 ________ a car
8 ________ a flat
9 ________ camping
10 ________ in a hotel

c What's the weather like?

It's snowing.

11 It's ________ .

12 It's ________ .

13 It's ________ .

14 It's ________ .

15 It's ________ .

d Complete with *in*, *at*, or *on*.

Example: I do aerobics *on* Tuesdays.

16 We always meet ________ Friday night.
17 What are you going to do ________ Christmas?
18 What did you study ________ university?
19 My aunt lives ________ Mexico.
20 Don't leave your books ________ the floor!

20

PRONUNCIATION

a Write the words from the list in the chart.

which who abroad sunbathe although

ago	holiday	weather
1 ________	2 ________	3 ________
take	horse	
4 ________	5 ________	

b Underline the stressed syllable.

Example: after*noon*

6 because
7 together
8 sightseeing
9 evening
10 accident

10

Total 50

GRAMMAR

a Circle a, b, or c.

Example: My brother ____ Russian
a speak ⓑ speaks c do speak

1 Where ____?
a you are going b you going c are you going
2 Do you think ____ tomorrow?
a it's going to rain b it's raining. c it rains
3 ____ some friends this evening.
a I meet b I'm going meet c I'm meeting
4 Don't worry. I'm sure you ____ your driving test.
a don't fail b won't fail c won't to fail
5 Do you think ____?
a they'll come b they come c they'll will come
6 ____ I phone the restaurant and book a table?
a Will b Won't c Shall
7 **A** It's very dark here.
B Yes. ____ the light.
a I'll turn on b I'm turning on c I turn on
8 I broke my leg last month when I ____ .
a skiied b was skiing c am skiing
9 I ____ in the evening. I'm too tired.
a never study b am never studying c study never
10 What ____ next Christmas?
a you will do b are you going to do c do you do

b Complete the sentences.

Example: She's waiting *for* the bus.

11 When are they going ________ leave?
12 ________ we going by car or by bus?
13 I haven't studied at all. I ________ pass the exam.
14 I ________ think she'll like him. He's not her type.
15 I'll ________ my homework after supper, I promise.
16 ________ I help you with the cooking?
17 He's very lazy. He never ________ any exercise.
18 My cat ________ like milk. It only drinks water.
19 What ________ they doing when he took the photograph?
20 What time ________ you get up this morning?

20

VOCABULARY

a Write the opposite verbs.

Example: pass (an exam) *fail*

1 teach (French) ________
2 leave (at 6.00) ________
3 catch (the bus) ________
4 forget (to pay) ________
5 find (your glasses) ________
6 turn off (the TV) ________
7 borrow (money) ________
8 pull (the door) ________
9 win (a match) ________
10 get (an e-mail) ________

b Write the missing prepositions.

Example: I went *to* Chicago two years ago.

11 I'm looking ________ my keys. I can't find them.
12 We're leaving on Friday and coming ________ on Sunday.
13 I'm sorry, but I don't agree ________ you.
14 I wrote ________ Mike but he didn't answer.
15 Would you like to look ________ my holiday photos?
16 That's my pen. Give it ________ me.
17 What do you think ________ his latest film?
18 Shh! I'm listening ________ the radio.
19 Did you speak ________ the boss yesterday?
20 We never talk ________ politics. It's boring.

20

PRONUNCIATION

a Write the words from the list in the chart.

find leave miss turn push

like	think	her
1 ________	2 ________	3 ________
see	good	
4 ________	5 ________	

b Underline the stressed syllable.

Example: after*noon*

6 arrive
7 pessimist
8 secret
9 probably
10 argue

10

Total 50

GRAMMAR

a Circle, a, b, or c.

Example: My brother _____ Russian.
a speak (b) speaks c do speak

1 _____ you ever bought anything in that shop?
a Did b Have c Has

2 He's never _____ a suit in his life.
a wear b wore c worn

3 _____ finished your homework yet?
a Are you b Have you c Did you

4 I've _____ had three meetings this week.
a already b just c yet

5 Jane isn't here. She has just _____ out.
a go b went c gone

6 I'm _____ in my new job than in my old job.
a busy b busier c more busy

7 You drive _____ than me.
a more slowly b more slow c more slower

8 My boss isn't _____ stressed as I am.
a more b as c the

9 It's the _____ city in the world.
a the crowded b most crowded c more crowded

10 This is the _____ summer we've ever had.
a worse b baddest c worst

b Complete the sentences.

Example: She's waiting *for* the bus.

11 Have you ever _________ to New York?
12 My mother _________ never flown.
13 I haven't finished _________. I need two more minutes.
14 Don't touch that wall. I've _________ painted it.
15 I've already _________ this film three times.
16 Your flat is bigger _________ mine.
17 I don't speak German as well _________ my wife.
18 This car is _________ expensive than that one.
19 Venice is the _________ beautiful city I know.
20 It was the best holiday I've _________ had.

[ ] 20

VOCABULARY

a Write the clothes words.

Example: Put your c*oat* on. It's cold.

1 My sister can't wear a short **sk**_____ to school.
2 He was wearing a baseball **c**_____ on his head.
3 I always wear a hat and **sc**_____ in the winter.
4 She's going to wear her black **d**_____ to the party.
5 I wear **tr**_____ on my feet when I go running.
6 I always **tr**_____ on new clothes in the shop.
7 Put **o**_____ a coat. It's very cold.
8 **T**_____ off your boots when you come in.
9 I always wear **p**_____ in bed.
10 I usually get **dr**_____ before I have breakfast.

b Write the opposite adjectives.

Example: boring *exciting*

11 crowded _________
12 noisy _________
13 comfortable _________
14 safe _________
15 tidy _________

c Complete with one word.

16 Don't forget to _________ your bed before you go to school.
17 I always _________ the dog for a walk in the evening.
18 We were late so we took a taxi to save _________ .
19 I _________ half an hour every day answering e-mails.
20 James is always late. He never arrives _________ time.

[ ] 20

PRONUNCIATION

a Write the words from the list in the chart.

yet just sk**ir**t cr**ow**ded alr**ea**dy

d**ir**ty	dr**e**ss	**u**niform
1 _________	2 _________	3 _________
tr**ou**sers	**j**acket	
4 _________	5 _________	

b Underline the stressed syllable.

Example: after*noon*

6 comfortable
7 relaxed
8 dangerous
9 exciting
10 impossible

[ ] 10

Total [ ] 50

GRAMMAR

a Circle a, b, or c.

Example: My brother ___ Russian.
a speak (b) speaks c do speak

1 I need ____ English quickly.
a learning b learn c to learn

2 I don't mind ____ up early in the morning.
a to get b get c getting

3 We stopped at a petrol station ____ some petrol.
a to get b get c for get

4 ____ is very bad for your health.
a Smoke b Smoking c The smoking

5 It's dangerous ____ here late at night.
a walk b to walk c for walk

6 He went to work without ____ breakfast.
a having b have c to have

7 You ____ pay to go into that art gallery. It's free.
a don't must b mustn't c don't have to

8 It's a secret, so you ____ tell anybody.
a mustn't to b mustn't c don't have to

9 We walked ____ the park.
a through b over c under

10 John ____ of the room and didn't come back.
a went b went out c went in

b Complete the sentences.

Example: I'm English. I'm *from* London.

11 I would like ________ go to China.
12 It's important to ________ good English in my job.
13 I opened the door to ________ who was there.
14 ________ books or magazines helps me to learn new words.
15 I hate ________ for buses when it's cold.
16 She's good at ________ . She makes fantastic pasta.
17 She ________ to go to work on Saturdays. She's a shop assistant.
18 You ________ touch that. It's very dangerous.
19 Do you ________ to wear a uniform at your school?
20 In tennis you hit the ball ________ a net.

20

VOCABULARY

a Complete with a verb in the right form.

Example: She **l***ikes* going to parties.

1 I'm **tr**____ to find a new job.
2 We're **pl**____ to go abroad next summer.
3 Don't **f**____ to turn off the light.
4 I don't **m**____ living with my parents.
5 He always **off**____ to help me with my homework.
6 I **n**____ to go to the bank today.
7 We've **d**____ to buy a new house.
8 We're **h**____ to buy a new flat soon.
9 She **pr**____ to phone me last night.
10 I **h**____ being late.

b Write the missing prepositions.

Example: The train went *through* the tunnel.

11 The cat ran ________ the road.
12 Our ball fell ________ the river.
13 In athletics you have to run ________ a track.
14 We walked up the hill and then ________ again.
15 Pass the ball ________ me!

c Complete with one word.

16 I ________ aerobics at my local gym.
17 In tennis you have to ________ the ball with a racket.
18 They always ________ skiing at Christmas.
19 In football you have to ________ the ball into the net.
20 We're learning to ________ golf.

20

PRONUNCIATION

a Write the words from the list in the chart.

mind enjoy think along offer

sitting	noise	stop
1 ________	2 ________	3 ________
try	arrive	
4 ________	5 ________	

b Underline the stressed syllable.

Example: *after<u>noon</u>*

6 decide
7 remember
8 interested
9 across
10 towards

10

Total 50

GRAMMAR

a Circle a, b, or c.

Example: My brother ____ Russian.
a speak (b) speaks c do speak

1 If the shop is open, ____ some fruit.
a I buy b I'll buy c I'd buy

2 She ____ speak to you again if you do that.
a doesn't b don't c won't

3 If you ____ time, will you help me?
a have b will have c had

4 What ____ she do if she lost her job?
a will b would c did

5 If I ____ English better I'd get a job in a hotel.
a speak b spoke c will speak

6 We aren't sure but we ____ go away this weekend.
a might to b will c might

7 She ____ at home. Her car isn't there.
a may not be b may not to be c might to be

8 You ____ walk home at night. It's dangerous.
a should b shouldn't c shouldn't to

9 I think they ____ buy a new car.
a should b should to c must

10 I ____ listen to him if I were you.
a wouldn't b won't c don't

b Complete the sentences.

Example: She's waiting *for* the bus.

11 ________ we change queues, the other queue will move quicker.

12 She'll be really happy if we ________ her to our party.

13 If they ________ arrive in five minutes, we'll go.

14 ________ you stop working if you won the lottery?

15 If I ________ you, I wouldn't go to London in the winter.

16 We would travel more if we didn't ________ children.

17 Take a map because you ________ get lost.

18 You might ________ like the film. It's very violent.

19 You shouldn't ________ a lot of coffee. It's bad for you.

20 I don't think you ________ go out tonight. You're very tired.

[ ] 20

VOCABULARY

a Complete with the right verb.

Example: I always *wear* a suit to work. (wear/carry)

1 We should hurry or we'll ________ the bus. (miss/lose)

2 A party is a good place to ________ people. (know/meet)

3 Don't forget to ________ your homework. (do/make)

4 My sister ________ my mother. (looks/looks like)

5 He ________ the photograph. (watched/looked at)

b Write the animal.

Example: A **m***osquito* bit me last night.

6 **G**____s have very long necks.

7 Be careful! There's a **b**____ on that flower.

8 Mickey **M**____ is a famous Disney character.

9 The **l**____ is the king of the jungle.

10 A **sh**____ is a very dangerous fish.

c Write the noun.

Example: imagine *imagination*

11 educate ________

12 elect ________

13 inform ________

14 decide ________

15 invite ________

d Complete with one word.

Example: Take a map. You might get *lost*.

16 My sister and her boyfriend are getting ________ next year.

17 He studies a lot and his English is getting ________.

18 She got ________ the bus and walked home.

19 I get ________ well with my brothers and sisters.

20 I left work at 6.00 and got ________ at 6.30.

[ ] 20

PRONUNCIATION

a Write the words from the list in the chart.

would swan if bear eagle

crocodile	there	look
1 ________	2 ________	3 ________
bee	will	
4 ________	5 ________	

b Underline the stressed syllable.

Example: after<u>noon</u>

6 newspaper 8 elephant 10 advice

7 survive 9 indecisive

[ ] 10

Total [ ] 50

GRAMMAR

a Circle a, b, or c.

Example: My brother ____ Russian.
a speak (b) speaks c do speak

1 How long ____ here?
a are you work b do you work c have you worked
2 I've studied English ____ .
a for two years b since two years c two years ago
3 She ____ in this house since she was five.
a lives b has lived c is living
4 When ____ university?
a did you leave b have you left c did you left
5 Alfred Hitchcock, who died in 1980, ____ a lot of great films.
a has made b made c makes
6 He ____ play football when he was young.
a used to b use to c used
7 I ____ like flying. Now I love it.
a don't use to b didn't use to c didn't used to
8 A lot of novels ____ into English.
a are translate b are translated c is translated
9 Disposable nappies ____ by a woman.
a were invented b was invented c invented
10 When was this church ____?
a build b built c be built

b Complete the sentences.

Example: She's waiting *for* the bus.

11 How ________ have you known David?
12 We've been in this house ________ October.
13 I have ________ afraid of water all my life.
14 How many films ________ George Lucas made?
15 When ________ your parents get married?
16 I ________ to smoke but I stopped last year.
17 Did you use to ________ glasses?
18 The film was directed ________ Sofia Coppola.
19 Fiat cars ________ made in Italy.
20 When ________ DVDs invented?

20

VOCABULARY

a Write the school subject.

Example: All insects have six legs. *biology*

1 Henry VIII had six wives. ________
2 The capital of Argentina is Buenos Aires. ________
3 'To be or not to be ...' ________
4 There is oxygen and nitrogen in the air. ________
5 4+2 = 6

b Complete the biography words.

Example: He was b*orn* in 1929.

6 He went to **pr**____ school when he was five.
7 He **l**____ secondary school when he was eighteen.
8 He started **w**____ in a bank.
9 He **f**____ in love when he was twenty-two.
10 He got **m**____ when he was twenty-seven.
11 They **h**____ their first child when he was thirty.
12 They **se**____ in 1989.
13 They got **d**____ two years later.
14 He **r**____ when he was sixty.
15 He **d**____ when he was eighty-five.

c Complete the past participles.

Example: *Harry Potter* was w*ritten* by JK Rowling.

16 Penicillin was first **d**____ by Alexander Fleming.
17 The dishwasher was **i**____ by a woman.
18 Sherlock Holmes was **b**____ on a real person.
19 *Pulp Fiction* was **d**____ by Quentin Tarantino.
20 This suit was **d**____ by Armani.

PRONUNCIATION

a Write the words from the list in the chart.

b**or**n s**i**nce af**ra**id sc**i**ence f**a**mous

l**i**ved	direct**or**	s**aw**
1 ________	2 ________	3 ________
m**a**de	ch**i**ld	
4 ________	5 ________	

20

b Underline the stressed syllable.

Example: after*noon*

6 frightened
7 university
8 literature
9 invent
10 design

10

Total 50

GRAMMAR

a Circle a, b, or c.

Example: My name ____ David.
a am (b) is c are

1 **A** Did Sam phone this afternoon?
B No, ____ phoned.
a anybody b somebody c nobody

2 We didn't go ____ this summer.
a anywhere b somewhere c nowhere

3 I've bought ____ really nice for your birthday.
a anything b something c nothing

4 **A** How much milk is there? **B** Only a ____ .
a little b few c none

5 This car isn't ____. We need a larger one.
a enough big b big enough c too big

6 I'm on a diet so I shouldn't eat ____ bread.
a too much b too many too

7 I can't find my wallet. Please help me ____ .
a look for it b look it for c look for them

8 Here are your boots. ____ .
a Put on them b Put on they c Put them on

9 **A** I love Italian food. **B** ____. It's delicious.
a So do I b So I do c Neither do I

10 **A** I can't drive. **B** Neither ____ I.
a can b can't c am

b Complete the sentences.

Example: I'm English. I'm *from* London.

11 Listen – I have ________ important to tell you!

12 I ________ do anything last night.

13 I can't drink this coffee. It's ________ hot.

14 There are too ________ people in my class. Forty!

15 I don't have ________ money for the bus. I need 30 cents more.

16 It's warm. Why don't you take your coat ________ ?

17 There's a towel on the floor in the bathroom. Pick ________ up, please.

18 **A** I don't like pop music.
B ________ do I. It's awful.

19 **A** I've seen that film.
B So ________ I. I saw it last week.

20 **A** I didn't go out last night.
B Neither ________ I. I was tired.

[ ] 20

VOCABULARY

a Complete the adjective with *-ing* or *-ed*.

Example: This book is very **bor***ing* .

1 Did you have a **relax**____ weekend?

2 We're going to India tomorrow! I'm really **excit**____.

3 You look **tir**____ . Why don't you sit down?

4 I don't want to see that film. It's very **depress**____.

5 I'm **bor**____ . Let's do something this afternoon.

b Complete with a verb.

Example: You're very fair. You should *wear* sunscreen.

6 I don't ________ enough exercise.

7 Could you ________ in this form, please?

8 You should ________ up smoking. It's not good for you.

9 ________ up! We're going to be late.

10 They don't ________ on very well. They always argue.

c Complete with one word.

11 **A** How much meat do you eat?
B ________. I'm a vegetarian.

12 I have a ________ close friends, five or six.

13 Turn the radio ________. It's too loud.

14 The class will ________ over in ten minutes.

15 Could you ________ out what time the match starts?

16 Can you look ________ these words in your dictionaries?

17 Carol looks ________ her mother. They're identical.

18 Martin and John ________ have red hair.

19 Your bag's exactly the same ________ mine.

20 His new film is quite similar ________ the last one.

PRONUNCIATION

a Write the words from the box in the chart.

allergic enough healthy again early

exercise	turn	photo
1 ________	2 ________	3 ________
just	begin	
4 ________	5 ________	

[ ] 20

b Underline the stressed syllable.

Example: after*noon*

6 exciting

7 anywhere

8 lifestyle

9 personality

10 exactly

[ ] 10

Total [ ] 50